THE SEVEN ARTS
PROSE: 1916-1917

THE SEVEN ARTS
PROSE: 1916-1917

A MODERN TIMES ANTHOLOGY

JAMES OPPENHEIM, WALDO FRANK,
VAN WYCK BROOKS (EDITORS)

MODERN
TIMES

TABLE OF CONTENTS

Editorial Preface vii

The Son • Katharine Baker 1
Night and The Madman (From "The Madman") • Khalil Gibran 4
Emerging Greatness • Waldo Frank. 6
Young America • Van Wyck Brooks 11
Aesthetic Form • Willard Huntington Wright. .18
The Strong Young Modern • James Oppenheim 24
David's Birthright • Edna Wahlert McCourt. 27
The Untold Lie • Sherwood Anderson 40
The Scar • Elizabeth Stead Taber. 46
Vicarious Fiction • Waldo Frank 58
Groping • Helen R. Hull 67
The Escape • J. D. Beresford 83
Life, Art, and America • Theodore Dreiser 89
The Thimble • D. H. Lawrence. 111
The Seven Arts and the Seven Confusions • Joel Elias Spingarn 123
A Poor Thing, But Our Own • Harold Stearns. 130
A Devil of a Fellow • Wilbur Daniel Steele. 136
A Modern Accident • Peter Minuit 151
Young Japan • Seichi Naruse 156
The Puritan's Will to Power • Randolph Bourne. 165
American Independence and the War • Editorial 171
In a Time of National Hesitation • John Dewey. 182
The Song of Ariel • S. N. Behrman. 186
Bread-Crumbs • Waldo Frank 197

American Optimism • Leo Stein. 211

The War and the Intellectuals • Randolph Bourne 229

Tomorrow • Eugene O'Neill 241

The Little Town • J. D. Beresford 261

Art, Religion, and Science • James Oppenheim. 268

Three Improbables • Benjamin De Casseres. 273

This Unpopular War • John Reed 278

Friday, June 22, 1917 • Hendrik Willem van Loon 288

Rudd • Waldo Frank 291

Young Spain • John Dos Passos 303

Black Magic • Margaret Widdemer. 317

Farmhands • Mabel Dodge. 329

Hours with a Revivalist • Theodore Schroeder 334

Twilight of Idols • Randolph Bourne 345

Is Nationalism Moribund? • Bertrand Russell. 357

Young India • Lajpat Rai 370

Editorial Postface • "The Story of *The Seven Arts*"
    by James Oppenheim. 383

EDITORIAL PREFACE

*T*he Seven Arts was a short-lived literary journal with grandiose ambitions. Conceived by writer and poet James Oppenheim, it was realized together with writer and activist Waldo Frank, music critic Paul Rosenfeld, poet Louis Untermeyer, and historian and critic Van Wyck Brooks. In all, the journal propagated a cultural vision that recognized the challenges of the moment—not least of which was the ongoing Great War in Europe—while looking ahead to a period of spiritual, intellectual, and social renewal in the United States. "It is our faith," wrote the editors in their call for contributions, "and the faith of many, that we are living in the first days of a renascent period, a time which means for America the coming of that national self-consciousness which is the beginning of greatness." *The Seven Arts* did not merely want to take part in this regeneration. It wanted to manifest its greatest potential.

Unlike *The Smart Set,* a literary magazine driven by both aesthetics and economics, *The Seven Arts* was founded with the intention of placing art above business. The editors knew, deep down, that it could not last—or earn them any serious income in the long term. The goal was to bring ideas into the American social, cultural, and political debates of the times. The mission was to make its mark on an emerging intellectual discourse about the direction of America as a nation focused not only on itself, but also on its place in the world.

Naming the journal *The Seven Arts,* the editors made it clear that they used language not only as its own creative medium, but also as a medium to critique and promote other creative arts. But with the United States increasing its military preparedness, and pressure on President Woodrow Wilson building to enter World War I, writers, poets, and artists were concerned not only with aesthetic matters, but also with the ideas and ideals that would lead the charge once the conflict ended. Alongside business and aesthetics, politics began to vie for its place in the social order. As these writers became aware of the unprecedented scale of killing in Europe, and began to internalize and process the realities of modern warfare, their focus shifted from the great feats of humankind to its potential for destruction.

The editors had ended their first call for contributions with the words, "*The Seven Arts* is not a magazine for artists, but an expression of artists for the community." And writers and artists responded in kind. In addition to the editors, whose writing was regularly featured, the journal's contributors included Sherwood Anderson, S. N. Behrman, John Dewey, Mabel Dodge, John Dos Passos, Theodore Dreiser, Robert Frost, Kahlil Gibran, Helen R. Hull, D. H. Lawrence, Amy Lowell, Paul Rosenfeld, Bertrand Russell, Elizabeth Stead Taber, Louis Untermeyer, and Margaret Widdemer. One of its notable contributors, Randolph Bourne, was a young intellectual and anti-war activist who published at least six pieces in almost as many months—"The Puritan's Will to Power" (April 1917), "The War and the Intellectuals" (June 1917), "Below the Battle" (July 1917), "The Collapse of American Strategy" (August 1917), "A War Diary" (September 1917), and "Twilight of Idols" (October 1917). Bourne, whose intellectual star rose with *The Seven Arts*, died of the 1918 flu epidemic at the age of thirty-two—just a year after the journal itself ended publication.

The journal's end was directly connected to Bourne's influence on its editorial direction. Though the editors did not directly express an unequivocal anti-war position, they were skeptical enough to give the anti-war camp a major platform. In the end, despite their statements about the significance of the arts, they continued their policy of political critique, which led their financial backer, Annette Rankine, to pull her support. On August 17, 1917, the New York *Tribune* ran an article headlined "Enemies Within," and with the Espionage Act having been passed two months earlier, this made the opinions expressed in the journal potentially criminal. A New York *Tribune* article from August 30, 1917, headlined "'Seven Arts' Loses a Financial Baker," quoted Rankine as saying, "I was opposed to its policy on the war," and noted that Oppenheim refused to change his editorial policy. The anti-intellectual trend in American life, which Richard Hofstadter wrote about in his seminal 1963 study, was rearing its head and stamping out a source of measured and serious opposition to war. The result led to increased division between political camps as many of the journal's writers, looking for outlets to express their ideas and concerns, turned to openly political journals to voice their fears, opinions, and hopes.

The Modern Times anthology of *The Seven Arts* focuses on prose—stories and essays—that exemplify the cultural complexities of this period. The pieces appear chronologically, as they did in the original publication, in unedited form. Still, a few minor notes should be made about the editorial process. First, one of the listed authors, Peter Minuit, is most likely not the historical figure—a Director of the Dutch North American colony of New Netherland from 1626 until 1631—but rather a pseudonym, perhaps for one of the journal's editors. Second, the anthology includes an unsigned supplement, "American Independence and the War," published with the April 1917 issue—the month when the United States entered World War I. The piece has been credited in turn to Oppenheim, Frank, or Bourne, and appears here as an "editorial." Finally, the anthology includes a reminiscence published by Oppenheim in *The American Mercury*, "The Story of *The Seven Arts*" (June 1930), telling the story of the journal's life and death from his perspective as its editor-in-chief.

The story of *The Seven Arts* is a perennial tale of ideals crashing into reality. In the social and cultural realms, there is an ever-present tension between art, business, and politics. The real danger appears when one threatens the open expression of one of the others. The notion of art-for-art's-sake can be as corrosive as purely commercial art or as dangerous as the idea of an art that is strictly political. At a time of extreme upheaval, *The Seven Arts* was a living experiment at balancing these tensions. It succeeded for twelve months, which may not seem like much from a historical perspective, but for those fighting in the trenches of the period's culture wars, probably felt like a lifetime.

—David Stromberg

THE SON

Katharine Baker

THE stout baker toiled up the stair, carrying an armful of bundles. He did not knock at his wife's door. He was not good at polite forms. But he beamed upon her as he set down his parcels and began to clear a table.

The wife got up to help him. She had been used to waiting on her man. He waved her back.

"You just sit still once," he commanded. "I'll tend to this. We're going to have a supper party together."

"You're real foolish about it," she complained. "I ain't so much as been downstairs for two weeks already. I bet you that girl wastes, something wonderful." But she was secretly pleased at her husband's care.

He set the table painstakingly, with a white cloth, and a large lamp that had no shade, and glared. There were all kinds of delicatessen in the parcels, only no cakes or bread. The baker's wife had seen enough cakes and bread in her time. They had no thrill left in them for her.

The baker was full of jokes, and laughed a great deal, but under his gayety he was keenly watching his wife. She was not beautiful nor young. She was on her way down to the gate where life comes in and goes out.

They did not know how near she had drawn to the gate. Two days later the baker, sitting in the next room waiting, with his head in his hands, heard a faint cry. Hardly could he believe that sound. Twenty years he had been married, and never a child till now. It was a great moment for the baker.

Soon came the nurse, and let him in. There was his middle-aged wife. There was the desired little face beside her. With a hot heart, he stooped to touch the child.

She sat up, and leaned over it.

"Well," she said, smiling, "you ought to be satisfied now. There's your son at last. A regular little Dutchman."

She fell back on her pillow.

"She feels bad," he suggested to the nurse.

But he was mistaken. She was dead.

You could not expect a man to realize that. He sat down in a kind of stupid amazement, while other people became very busy in his house.

The wife was gone. There was no doubt about it. They put him out of the room once more, but he would not be parted from the new-born son.

"What makes the child's hands and feet such a bright blue?" someone asked the nurse.

She said it was often so. The circulation would start up better presently. But it did not. In a few hours they took the baby back to its mother to stay.

After a while the baker could see his wife again. This did not seem to be the same woman at all. She had been rather fat and untidy. Now she wore a shroud of the finest white satin, and lay in a satin-lined coffin, which the undertaker called a casket. He was a pompous undertaker, and walked about in squeaking shoes.

It was a pity the baker's wife could not see that satin dress. She had not been married in anything half so splendid.

There was the baby's little face also, beside her in the coffin. He was not a pretty child. Lots of babies that nobody wants are much nicer to look at. But he was the baker's only son, and the father had longed for him these twenty years.

There they both were, in the coffin. He gazed at them through blind eyes. He fancied he heard the faint cry again that had made his heart so hot. He took the baby's hand in his with fearful hope. It was cold, like a little stone. Then he turned and went back to the room where he had waited, and sat with his head in his hands.

The wasteful girl came up to ask about the shop. What should she do, since nothing must be sold today?

"Send for the poor," he directed. "Tell them all to come. Give them the bread and cake and pies, everything. It will be closed. Who knows when it will open?"

There was a rusty revolver in the bureau drawer. He was thinking of that.

But the girl went down and did as she was told. So the poor had reason to be glad that the baker's little son was dead.

NIGHT AND THE MADMAN

From "The Madman"

Kahlil Gibran

"I AM like thee, O, Night, dark and naked; I walk on the flaming path which is above my day-dreams, and whenever my foot touches earth a giant oaktree comes forth."

"Nay, thou art not like me, O, Madman, for thou still lookest backward to see how large a foot-print thou leavest on the sand."

"I am like thee, O, Night, silent and deep; and in the heart of my loneliness lies a Goddess in child-bed; and in him who is being born Heaven touches Hell."

"Nay, thou art not like me, O, Madman, for thou shudderest yet before pain, and the song of the abyss terrifies thee."

"I am like thee, O, Night, wild and terrible; for my ears are crowded with cries of conquered nations and sighs of forgotten lands."

"Nay, thou art not like me, O, Madman, for thou still takest thy little-self for a comrade, and with thy monster-self thou canst not be friend."

"I am like thee, O, Night, cruel and awful; for my bosom is lit by burning ships at sea, and my lips are wet with blood of slain warriors."

"Nay, thou art not like me, O, Madman; for the desire for a sister-spirit is yet upon thee, and thou hast not become a law unto thyself."

"I am like thee, O, Night, joyous and glad; for he who dwells in my shadow is now drunk with virgin wine, and she who follows me is sinning mirthfully."

"Nay, thou art not like me, O, Madman, for thy soul is wrapped in the veil of seven folds and thou holdest not thy heart in thine hand."

"I am like thee, O, Night, patient and passionate; for in my breast a thousand dead lovers are buried in shrouds of withered kisses."

"Yea, Madman, art thou like me? Art thou like me? And canst thou ride the tempest as a steed, and grasp the lightning as a sword?"

"Like thee, O, Night, like thee, mighty and high, and my throne is built upon heaps of fallen Gods; and before me too pass the days to kiss the hem of my garment but never to gaze at my face."

"Art thou like me, child of my darkest heart? And dost thou think my untamed thoughts and speak my vast language?"

"Yea, we are twin brothers, O, Night; for thou revealest space and I reveal my soul."

EMERGING GREATNESS

Waldo Frank

W E do not expect an Apocalypse, here in America. Out of our terrifying welter of steel and scarlet, a design must come. But it will come haltingly, laboriously. It will be warped by the steel, clotted with the scarlet. There have been pure and delicate visions among us. In art, there has been Whistler; and Henry James took it into his head to write novels. But the clear subtlety of these men was achieved by a rigorous avoidance of native stuff and native issues. Literally, they escaped America; and their followers have done the same, though in a more figurative meaning. Artist-senses have gone out, felt the raw of us, been repulsed by it, and so withdrawn to a magnificent introversion. So, when we found vision in America, we have found mostly an abstract art—an art that remained pure by remaining neuter. What would have happened to these artists, had they grappled with their country, is an academic question. But I suspect that the true reason for their *ivory tower* was lack of strength to venture forth and not be overwhelmed. This much is sure, however—and true particularly of the novel—that our artists have been of two extremes: those who gained an almost unbelievable purity of expression by the very violence of their self-isolation, and those who, plunging into the American maelstrom, were submerged in it, lost their vision altogether, and gave forth a gross chronicle and a blind cult of the American Fact.

The significance of Sherwood Anderson whose first novel, "Windy McPherson's Son," has recently appeared (published by The John Lane Company), is simply that he has escaped these two extremes, that he suggests at last a presentation of life shot through with the searching color of truth, which is a signal for a native culture.

Mr. Anderson is no accident. The appearance of his book is a gesture of logic. Indeed, commentators of tomorrow might gauge the station at which America has arrived today by a study of the impulses—conscious and unconscious—which compose this novel. But it is not a prophetic work. Its author is simply a man who has felt the moving passions of his people, yet sustained himself against them just enough in a crude way to set them forth.

His story has its beginning in an Iowa town. His hero, with a naive unswervingness from type, is a newsboy. His passion is money and power. He goes to Chicago. He becomes rich. He marries the daughter of his employer. And then, he becomes powerful. There is nothing new in this; although the way of telling it is fresh and sensitive. This is the romance of inchoate America. Like the Greek fables, it is a generic wish-fulfillment to be garbed by each poet in his own dress. It has been done in a folk way by Horatio Alger; with a classic might by Theodore Dreiser. But so far, it has been the entire story. With Mr. Anderson, it is only the story's introduction.

When Sam McPherson, by a succession of clumsy assaults, charges to the control of the Arms Trust of America, he does not find there, like his novelistic brothers, a romantic and sentimental and overweening satisfaction. He finds a great disgust, a great emptiness. And he becomes interested in his soul! He learns that what he has done is spiritually nothing; that it has left him as helpless before the commands of life, as in the old days when he amassed pennies in Caxton, Iowa. It dawns on him, that if man is a measurer of truth, he has paralyzed competition, enslaved wealth, disposed of power without really growing at all. So Sam McPherson puts aside his gains; and pilgrimages forth, searching for truth.

This is the second part of the novel; and in it lies the book's importance. McPherson's quest of the grail is an awkward Odyssey indeed. It has the improbability of certain passages of Dostoëvski—the improbability of truth poorly or clumsily materialized. Moreover, in it we find an unleashed and unsophisticated power that we have all along awaited in the American novel. The resemblance to the Russian is, I am convinced, a consequence of a like quality in the two men. It is a temperamental, not a literary thing.

The abdicated millionaire works as a bartender in Ohio, as a builder in Illinois; he joins a threshing crew in the West and a mining camp in the South. He knows prostitutes and working-girls. He tries to help and seeks truth. He learns that labor-unions are more concerned over the use of scab machinery than by the prospect of losing a righteous strike; that the men are more interested in a raise of wages than in preventing a private band of grafters from stealing the town's water-works. He becomes very miserable over the lot of the street-walkers. He asks the drinkers in the saloon where he is employed why they get drunk, and is discharged with an oath. Puerile, fumbling stuff it is—its efficiency of presentment about on a level with McPherson's method of gaining the light. Yet through it all, is a radiant glow of the truth. Read the newspapers and the Congressional reports; read the platitudes of investigating commissions, of charity organizations, of revivalists and mushroom mysticisms—and you have the same helpless thing in extension. Sam McPherson, bewildered with his affluence and power, seeking the truth in the fair plains and the cancerous cities, ignorant and awkward and eager—is America today. And Sam McPherson, the boy, arrogant and keen and certain, hiding from himself his emptiness with the extent and occupation of the materials that his land floods upon him, is the America of our fathers.

For a feel of the America of tomorrow, do not look to this book. I am sure that Mr. Anderson will conduct himself better in subsequent works than he has in the conclusion of "Windy McPherson's Son." As we find the faint footprints of Horatio Alger at the book's beginning, so at the end is the smirch of Robert W. Chambers. (But after all, Balzac could not so wholeheartedly have swallowed France, had he not taken Pixérécourt and Madame de Scudéry along.) When Sam marries Sue Rainey, it is with the understanding that they are to have children and that they are to live gloriously for them. For a while, the magnate's money-madness slackens. But the pact fails, for the children can not come. Coolness between the two, with the goal of their creed denied them:—and at length, when Sam sacrifices his wife's father in his grapple toward dominion, she flees to New York. The man over whose fat body he has stepped to power shoots himself. And, sick of his tawdry, superficial kingdom, McPherson wanders off.

He gains nothing from his experiments, and this is well enough. He hunts in Africa, leisures in Paris, canoes in Canada and sentimentalizes in New York. All this we forgive him. But one day, he finds himself in St. Louis. He encounters a drunken mother, buys her three children, packs them into a train and drops them at the feet of his wife who, like some diluted Penelope, has been awaiting his return in a villa on the Hudson. "Not our children, but just *some* children is our need," he pronounces. And so, walks "across the lighted room to sit again with Sue at his own table, and to try to force himself back into the ranks of life." This is the last sentence of the book; the one episode that is *made* and insincere. I hope Mr. Anderson is ashamed of it. I hope he does not really believe that all man has to do, to find God, is to increase and multiply more helpless creatures like himself. This pretty surcease to trouble that comes from transferring the problems of life to the next generation is a biological fact. But it is not art. For with it is dimmed all the voluptuous speculation which flushes the novel as a sunrise transfigures a plain. Let life be happy, if it can. The sacred duty of art is to remain sorrowful, when it has challenged a consciousness of sorrow; to abide in the uncertain search of truth so long as the movement of mankind is hazardous. Let our heroes be joyous; but by conquering themselves, not by adopting children. The virtue of Mr. Anderson's book is that it is dynamic. His static ending is bad, because it breaks the rhythm. But it is worse since it slams the door on the vista of passionate inquiry which the book unfolds. Up to the end, we have a clear symbol of America's groping. At the end, we have nothing—in lieu of the suggested everything. But, of course, we may ignore the end. Or, in its fatuous simplicity, we may read still another symbol of America—a token of what might happen to us, if we sought at this stage to read our lives as a conclusion, rather than a commencement.

I was not certain that Theodore Dreiser was a classic, until I had read this novel of Mr. Anderson. Its first half is a portal from which emerges an American soul. This portal is the immediate past, and in the works of Mr. Dreiser we find its definite expression. Beside their magnificent mass-rhythms, the opening chapters of Mr. Anderson are paltry. One feels, indeed, that the uneasy spirit of Sam McPherson has come forth, not from his own youth, not from his own pages, but from the choking structures of Mr. Dreiser.

Mr. Dreiser may of course yet surprise us by the sudden discovery of a new spiritual light. He has not stopped writing. But I feel in his work the profound massiveness of a completed growth. Mr. Dreiser has caught the crass life of the American, armoring himself with luxury and wealth that he misunderstands, with power whose heritage of uses he ignores. The tragedy of his hero is that of a child suddenly in possession of a continent; too unknowing to know that he is ignorant; too dazzled to be amazed. His books are a dull, hard mosaic of materials beneath which one senses vaguely a grandiose movement—like the blind shifting of quicksands or the imperceptible breathing of a glacier. This is Mr. Dreiser, and this is enough. But with Mr. Anderson, the elemental movement begins to have form and direction; the force that causes it is being borne into the air.

Before Mr. Dreiser, there was "Huckleberry Finn"—there was, in other words, a formless delirium of color and of tangent. These are pre-cultural novels. And in the book of Mr. Anderson, I still find much of them. Indeed, the wandering of Sam McPherson has more than a super-ficial kinship with Huck Finn's passage down the Mississippi. The land that McPherson walks is still a land marred by men and women "who have not learned to be clean and noble like their forests and their plains." But Huck Finn is an animal boy, floating rudderless down a natural cur-rent, avid for food and play. And McPherson is a man, flung against his stream, avid for the Truth. . . .

In conclusion, let us not forget that this is Mr. Anderson's first book, and that a succession of them are already written and will appear in their turn. The fact that Mr. Anderson is no longer young is no hindrance to our hope of his growth. Genius in America, if it does not altogether escape America, rises slowly. For it has far to come. The European is born on a plateau. America is still at a sea-level. The blundering, blustering native was thirty-seven before he became Walt Whitman.

YOUNG AMERICA

Van Wyck Brooks

SHORTLY after the outset of the nineteenth century there passed into the intellectual currency of almost every European people a certain phrase which everywhere stood for one substantial, common impulse: a resurgence of national purpose working consciously against a played-out national background. It was the watchword of the new generation—Young Germany, Young Italy, Young Ireland, I mean, to mention a few instances; and in each case it represented a warm, humane, concerted and more or less revolutionary protest against whatever incubus of crabbed age, paralysis, tyranny, stupidity, sloth, commercialism, lay most heavily upon the people's life, checking the free development of personality, retarding the circulation of generous ideas. A little later the phrase and its informing impulse passed beyond the European countries; it emerged in the Orient, first among the Young Turks and finally in Young China and Young India, until within the space of a century the entire Eastern Hemisphere had passed under its rejuvenating touch.

A similar phrase became current at about the same time in our own social history. Who does not remember "Young America," a phrase that served, and continues to serve, though it has long since passed into cant, as a sort of touchstone of American juvenility? Young America blossomed out originally on the covers of innumerable magazines and storybooks, the text of which set forth his ingenious and enterprising career. He was the typical farmer's boy of our national epos, who sought adventure and found success. By shifts and devices that all his contemporaries understood, he came back home from time to time, his pockets bulging with greenbacks acquired somewhere on the other side of the horizon, just in time to save his mother from dispossession or a painful death; and in the end, automatically and by easy stages, he arrived at the White House. The story always stopped just at the point where Young America became the arbiter of our national destinies. He had got his particular plum, that was the climax. How the rest of us fared with regard to the plum, how he himself digested it—everything of that sort was manifestly beside the question.

Now, superficially, of course, there is no basis of comparison between such a conception as this and one so far less easily personified as that of Young Italy, for example, or Young China. But, really, I think, Young America stood for the essential impulse of our post-revolutionary history in exactly the same way that the corresponding phrases have stood for the essential post-revolutionary impulse in every other country. As in China, as in Turkey, as in Italy, as in Germany, it stood for the force that overtoppled the old regime—the colonial regime in our case, the aristocratic, or bureaucratic, or despotic, or alien regime elsewhere, as the case might be, and set up the ferment of modern society. In function it was identical, in quality alone it was fundamentally different, just as the American revolution was fundamentally different from all the revolutions of Europe and Asia.

It was fundamentally different, it was unique, of course, in striking the note of a country where, to reverse the proverb, nothing was to be endured, everything was to be done, where the programme was necessarily one, not of reaction through the mass, but of expansion through the individual. Moral and kindly, bold, callous, and simple, Young America had to do with immense, external, impersonal, wholesale tasks like "developing the West"; it had to fence in lands it had never tilled, filch gold out of mountains it had never lived among, and cover the continent with a sound, rudimentary population. The contest lay all along not between man and society, not between youth and age, as it lay in the Old World, but between the human and the non-human, and it called into play so great an over-plus of will and energy, of self-reliance and self-assertion, that nature, else intractable, was in the end borne under.

That was the quality of our essential historic impulse, the tune to which every loyal American heart in the old days beat high, an impulse that was determined not by the pressure of personality from within, but by the existence, the allure, and the eventual decay of material opportunities outside. For there came a time when the tune began to lag, when the pioneer passed over into the business man and the giants and empire-builders began to lie back among their dividends, spilling right and left in public works the millions they had had a clear title to in the days when everyone felt that their enterprise and prowess were blazing a trail for the race. Well before 1900 Young America gave up dreaming of the White House, not because the White House had become less attainable by everyone at once, but because it had ceased to be in the general regard the merely natural and legitimate prize of the good boy who had made his way best in the world. The hour of the epos had struck.

It had struck, bequeathing to us only one human tradition, by virtue of which we are all "infinitely repellant particles," all too rich in the technique of material enterprise, impoverished and without experience in the technique of society and the intellect. Primitive competition, the competition of the jungle itself, the only mode of life our fathers knew, had left us cold and dumb in spirit, incoherent and uncohesive as between man and man, given to many devices, without community in aim or purpose.

Thus it is that the fierce rudimentary mind of America, like that of some inchoate primeval monster, relentlessly concentrated in the appetite of the moment, knows nothing of its own vast, inert, nerveless body, encrusted with parasites and half indistinguishable from the slime in which it moves. One looks out to-day over the immense vista of our society, stretching westward in a succession of dreary steppes, a universe of talent and thwarted personality evaporating in stale culture, and one sees the inevitable result of possessing no tradition to fill in the interstices of energy and maintain a steady current of life over and above the ebb and flow of individual impulses, of individual destinies. Is it strange that while the spiritual life of the Old World, deep-rooted and all-embracing organism that it is, perpetually blossoms afresh, the spiritual life of America is at the mercy of everything that passes in the air, and that any fresh breeze from a new direction can bowl it over, like a plant sprung up in a sand-waste?

For we are indeed, as Turgeniev said of Russia, *grande et riche, mais désordonnée.* Who can estimate the latent force that inexhaustibly spends itself in the trivialities of our popular fiction and makeshift art, in the search for successful formulas, in aimless theorizing and senseless ingenuity, in advertising and ragtime, in rhetoric, jocosity, and vague sentiment, in half-apprehended culture, and the bogs and fens of theosophy? Our life is like a badly motivated novel, full of genius but written with an eye to quick returns; a novel that possesses no leading theme, in which the style alternates between journalese and purple patches, and every character goes its own arbitrary way, failing of its full effect. So undeveloped we are, save in the little private role we set ourselves, so unhabituated in the more comprehensive relationships of life, that it is as if we lived in relief, as it were, only half cut out. Encircle most Americans and you will encounter nothing but a rough block, plainly not intended to be seen.

Now, I assume that we are all quite aware of these things, that we are all heartily sick and tired both of our own old ways and the old ways of the life about us, quite aware that something fundamental in our national background has played itself out and gone threadbare. To the remotest corners of the country the new generation is putting to itself the question, "What is coming next?" Well, I have spoken of Russian society as at one time, in the one sense at least of possessing no consciously organic life, comparable with ours. And this, not to push the comparison too far, is what happened in Russia at the turn of the tide. The quotation is from Stepniak, on the revolutionary movement of 1873-1874.

> It was a revelation rather than a propaganda. At first the book, or the individual, that had impelled this or that person to join the movement could be traced out; but after a while this became impossible. It was a powerful cry which arose, no one knew where and whence, and which summoned the zealous to the great work of the redemption of country and humanity. And the zealous, heeding this cry, arose, overwhelmed with sorrow and indignation over their past life, and abandoning home and family, wealth and honors, threw themselves into the movement with

a joy, an enthusiasm, a faith, such as are experienced only once in a lifetime, and which when lost are never found again.

I will not speak of the many young men and young women of the highest aristocratic families who labored fifteen hours a day in the factories, in the workshops, in the fields. Youth is proverbially generous and ready for sacrifice. The most characteristic feature of the movement was that the contagion spread even to the people, advanced in years, who had already a future clearly worked out and a position won by the sweat of their brows—judges, physicians, officers, officials,—and these were not among the least zealous.

Yes, it was not a political movement; it rather resembled a religious movement in its contagious and absorbing elements. People not only sought to obtain a distinct practical object, but also to satisfy an inward sentiment of duty, an inspiration, so to speak, leading them toward their own moral perfection.

One can see at a glance, of course, how characteristically Russian all that is, how little it bears, in any specific way, upon anything either existent or potential in the American make-up, in which for one thing the religious impulse has for so long ceased to be organic. I quote it simply as the most perfect example of a psychological phenomenon that appears again and again at appointed moments, in one form or another—the sudden fusion of a race, by which all its elements are miraculously set beating together at the highest pitch. Differing in style and degree, according to the peculiar genius, in response to the peculiar need of the race in question, now literary, now political, now agricultural, now religious, or a combination of two or all of these, it has appeared in all the national movements of Young Europe and Young Asia, from the days of Mazzini to the days of Sun Yat Sen, in the awakening of Ireland, in the re-birth of the submerged nationalities of Eastern Europe, in the sudden tensity of a score of "national cultures" at the outbreak of the war. It is exactly as in the opening and the development of a symphony; a lull succeeds the chaotic din of instruments not yet in tune; in the presentiment of unison, the general dawn of a leading theme, an immense calm descends over all, and then slowly, faintly, at the dropping of the wand, the orchestration begins, weaving its way hither and thither till at last every mind and hand, every thought and sense, every nerve and muscle is aflame, and a whole population is caught up in some supreme system of ideas.

It is vain to look for anything quite like this in America, even if it is this alone, or the less ecstatic and more habitual equivalent of this, which makes a race great and an age great. For we are not a race, to begin with; we are incongruous at once in blood and in culture. Unlike the nations of the Old World, we possess neither a dormant, sub-conscious multitude existing on a common level and capable of responding to a common watchword, nor a student class united in the discipline of common ideals and capable of arousing them. There are centers of our civilization where nothing is real but the future, immense areas of mentality keyed at the Tennysonian pitch, villages in the interior of Virginia, where, they say, Matthew Prior, prince of poets in the age of Anne, is still the reigning favorite in letters, tenacious outposts of culture in Tennessee and Kentucky where the speech of the people remains unchanged from the time of Queen Elizabeth. And this is the tale of the Anglo-Saxon tradition alone. We are a population at sixes and sevens, holding among all classes and at all stages of development scarcely any common conviction save one, that "the essential pre-occupation of youth," as one of our novelists put it the other day, "is organizing a living."

And yet there is one indisputable new fact that has been gradually coming to light these last years, a sort of epilogue to the Young America myth which may in the end put a new face on things, new in a different sense from that of all the other "newnesses" that have befooled and befuddled us from the days of the Transcendentalists down. And this new fact is that material enterprise no longer possesses the infinite horizon and the spiritual *élan* that once justified it in the eyes of all and could alone continue to justify it in the eyes of a "proverbially generous" youth. One stands on perfectly safe psychological ground in asserting that young men will not for long go on committing themselves to a mode of life that has lost its leaven of spiritual conflict and adventure, a mode of life that no longer calls the poetic faculties into play, and offers nothing to the soul; "organizing a living," without that, is altogether too tepid an affair.

One sees how the wind blows in business itself, in the dissatisfaction, so to say, of business with being merely business, in its tendency to pass over its own borders and become a means of expression, an "art-form," as Mr. Gerald Stanley Lee says. But far more significantly one sees it in the tired, baffled expression on the faces of so many middle-aged Americans, bewildered men like Mr. Henry Ford, men who have discovered the inadequacy of business to fulfill their spiritual needs and who, reaching out from it, find themselves lost in a maze of wider relationships with which no technique that they possess enables them to cope.

This is the real disposition of things, and it gives meaning to the painful, insistent, blundering, inarticulate will to exist on a higher plane than that of the domestic animals which manifests itself the country over in so many thousand isolated lives. The poems that all but reach their intention, the novels that never come to market, the religious emotions that never crystalize, the speculations that never quite achieve their master-thought, the political ideas that lose themselves in sentimentality, who can estimate their number, or question the reality of the experience that lies behind them? All this confused, thwarted, multitudinous welter of spiritual impulse is, I believe, the certain visible sign of some prodigious organism that lies undelivered in the midst of our society, an immense brotherhood of talents and capacities coming to a single birth. For we have learned one lesson from our competitive pioneering past—that we human beings are all pretty much, as Balzac said, like the figure O; when another is set beside it we acquire ten times our value.

AESTHETIC FORM

Willard Huntington Wright

IN THE general contemplation of painting many qualities which are regarded as definite signs of greatness have no bearing on the æsthetic worth of the work. These qualities meet certain demands in the individual whose education has been faulty or whose responsiveness is the result of early emotional associations. When the average critic beholds poorly depicted objects of rich and varied colouring, he not infrequently mistakes their ornamental aspect for technical variety. When he sees an effective rendition of a beautiful woman, he is apt to overlook the mediocrity of execution in his rapt contemplation of the desirable subject. Confronted by a rural scene which recalls mellow and sentiment-hallowed vistas of childhood, the critic once more errs by attributing to the artist a high degree of creative reaction to natural beauty. In each of these three instances we find a critical judgment based on considerations which are personal and unrelated to intrinsic artistic merit.

On the technical side of art we find other errors of valuation. Portraiturists who, by exaggerating or idealising certain salient facial characteristics, achieve what is commonly called "character" (after the manner of Frans Hals) are held in high esteem because of some imagined esoteric insight. Again, those painters who practise a careless and economical method of brushing and attain to a free and brilliant technique—the Besnards and the Sargents—are ranked above the profounder men whose surfaces are less masterful. The rich *matière* of a Manet is more admirable in the critics' eyes than the profundities of a Cézanne. Canvases in which the colors are highly neutralised with white; landscapes revealing stiff and airless objects with cold and net outlines;

portraits wherein one may read aloofness, dignity and personal detachment—here, too, are qualities which commonly pass as great. The early primitives have been highly praised for their "austerity"—another quality of accepted greatness. But this austerity was not even the result of an æsthetic impulse. The primitives, just learning the lessons of art, desired, above all, to produce in the spectator a quiet, contemplative and calm emotion, unruffled by any sensuality or memory of life.

These many superficial aspects of art, misunderstood by modern critics, have set criteria of judgment; and not until such extrinsic appeals are ignored shall we be able to approach to a pure æsthetic comprehension of the art of painting. Every enduring quality of great painting—the painting of El Greco, Giotto, Giorgione, Rubens, Titian, Veronese, Renoir and Cézanne—can be explained by the laws of æsthetic form and organisation. One artist is greater than another solely because his form is more perfect. These laws correspond to the laws of life and movement; and the factors of art are the factors of consciousness. Art is a restatement of the whole of life—a bringing to an intense focus the universal will of nature.

The sense of beauty is always related to form. All colours and musical notes are portions of a form which can be completed by other colors and notes. Colors either advance or retreat from the eye; and notes either advance or retreat from the ear. At once there is the implication of a spatial dimension which is a quality of form. A note or a color may therefore be beautiful. A series of notes or a series of colors, so arranged as to give the impression of a balanced form (a picture or a melody), may be doubly, trebly or a hundredfold as beautiful as one note or one color. The beauty increases in proportion to the perfection of the form. But a perfume or a texture never implies beauty. No matter how exquisite a perfume may be, there is no sense of *form* attached to it; and a series of perfumes is no more exquisite than the most exquisite individual perfume in the series. Thus with texture in its tactile (not visual) sense. It may be pleasing to the touch in many different ways—like velvet, satin, flesh polished ivory, or a warm or cold surface. But it lacks the element of beauty because it does not give us the sense of form; nor does a series of tactile experiences produce a formal conception. Only when we project a conception of form into texture (such as visualising a human body when we touch a flesh-like substance), and only when we associate a perfume with an object (calling up the flower, for instance, for which the perfume may be named), does either one of them give us an emotion of beauty.

Form, in the artistic sense, has four interpretations. First, it exhibits itself as shallow imitation in painting, as reportorial realism in literature, and as simple tune in music. (Sorolla, Zola and Rubinstein make use of this type of form.) Secondly, it contains qualities of solidity and competent construction such as are found in the paintings of Velazquez, the novels of Tourguénieff and the music of Liszt. Thirdly, it shows signs of having been arbitrarily arranged for the purpose of volumnear accentuation. (Poussin, George Moore and Wagner represent this development of form.) Last, form reveals itself, not as an objective thing, but as an abstract phenomenon capable of giving the sensation of palpability. All great art—the art of Rubens and Michelangelo, Balzac and Flaubert, Bach and Beethoven—falls under this final interpretation.

But form, in order to be emotion-provoking must be ordered and composed; and here we touch on the vitalising element of art—*organisation*. The natural instinct for order, the desire to have details properly arranged, the pleasure derived from the justness of proportions in the factors of common experience—herein we find the human impulse toward unity. Chaos disturbs the most primitive of intelligences: in all the flux and reflux of existence there is the constant tendency toward law and order, toward the harmonising of divergencies. Even in the minds of pluralistic philosophers will be discovered a process of relationship, which co-ordinates and cements the physical and metaphysical integers. There is a gravity of the mind which attracts to it all intellectual particles; and this mental gravity is no more than the protoplasmic instinct toward unity. All mathematical divisions of one are arbitrary assumptions. The establishment of relationships—which must eventually lead to a unique measure—is our only basis of satisfaction or gratification. A work of art is only perfect in so far as it effects us as a unity—that is, as an ordered and related whole. A demand for this interrelationship in art is analogous to the same demand as applied to the factors of life. In art, however, the unity must be both real and philosophic. It must represent the concentration of the *emotion* of unity—the co-ordination of causes as well as effects.

The form in all the arts must be related in its details as well as in its largest aspects. That is, we must be able, first, to appreciate the mutual dependence of the successive factors of an art (the notes in music, the colors in painting, and the words in literature) ; and, secondly, to co-ordinate all of these dependent factors into a unified whole. The first relationship is established in music by tempo (or accent) ; in painting, by line (or outline) ; in literature, by cadence (or, in poetry, by metre.) The second, and larger, coherence is dependent upon the tonality (or key) in music; upon the lighting (or tonality) in painting; and upon the thought in literature. The laws of progression and coherence are identical with the laws which govern all physiological and psychological activities, and are in harmony with our universal experience.

The demand for symmetry is an expression of the primitive need of static balance. It is the first consciousness of existing. A child learns first to balance itself upright; hence, its initial sensation is symmetry. Later, movement is introduced into this symmetry, and locomotion is acquired. The æsthetic consciousness develops similarly, for we must not lose sight of the fact that art is the expression and projection of life. Herein lies its great philosophic value. It is the reduction of all life to a perfectly composed miniature world. Therefore the reaction to symmetry is anthropomorphically prior to the reaction of movement. Later this symmetry is set into simple action: there is an alternation of balance—a swaying to one side immediately counterbalanced by a swaying to the other side. The primitive art, which followed the making of symmetrical designs, balanced these designs after the manner of the human body in motion. Music was entirely a matter of rhythm, accentuated by the tapping of drums. Still later the rhythms became complicated according to the evolution of bodily movements—running, hopping, skipping, dancing, and so forth. Stimulations of impacts and stress resulted in emphasis on one foot or the other. Because of this rhythmic basis in all consciousness of movement, there exists necessarily a simple rhythm in every work of art which has passed beyond mere symmetry.

There is, of course, in all great art, an underlying and allembracing rhythm which determines the microcosmic life of the work. This profounder rhythm (which, because of the paucity of art nomenclature, we must call æsthetic rhythm) is the result of the perfect organisation of all the qualities of art—linear direction, balance and volume. It has nothing to do with rhythm in the ordinary sense, with tempo, with alternate swaying of curved lines, with action, or with metrics. It is a complete cycle of poised movement presented as a simultaneous vision; and the change of the smallest part would completely alter every constituent. Thus a person may walk or dance rhythmically (in the narrower sense); but one of Michelangelo's slaves, which actually is static, possesses the profounder æsthetic rhythm, for within it is embodied every possible phase of ordinary rhythm of the human body, perfectly related and organised. Likewise a popular piece of dance music may possess rhythm; whereas Beethoven's *C-Minor Symphony* embodies in its four movements a complete world of rhythmic poise which gives itself to the auditor only when the cycle is complete—at the instant the final chord is struck. Again, we find in Swinburne's *Dolores* a melodious rhythm which sweeps us along on its surface; but in Balzac's *Illusions Perdues* we possess a great example of æsthetic rhythm which is developed by the perfect organism of documentary form. Ordinary rhythm extends itself wholly into time, and is the repetition of alternating lines, points or accents. Æsthetic rhythm is poise in three dimensions, wherein all the extremes of movement are related to a center of gravity, giving us the sense of complete satisfaction.

The whole history of art, like the history of all thought, has been directed by a desire to arrive at truth. The first prehistoric scratches on stones, the first crude musical sounds, the first tales and sagas—all have been dictated by some cryptic inner impulse to reproduce and interpret the world of actuality. Along this path, and this path alone, has the search for truth progressed. To many it would seem paradoxical to say that the modern art which aims at an abstract æsthetic effect evolves from the same longing for truth that has given us impressionism, the realistic novel, and illustrative and imitative music. Yet such is the case. From the painting of five hundred years ago, when the artist's only desire was optically to reproduce his model, to the recent art which strikes at underlying causes alone, we have a direct *progressus* of research and aspiration. At first the model was considered merely in its aspect of recognisable silhouette. Next the artist went deeper into the character of the model and subordinated details in order to catch the very essence of what was before him. Then he studied the light surrounding the model, and, dissecting it, made it vibrate even as in nature. Later he discovered the formal qualities of color, and his chief desire was to reproduce the rotundity of the model. As a result of these more or less technical considerations he became acquainted with his medium, and was able to mould it to his own ends.

Needless to say, his progress toward a sure knowledge was not so simple and smooth as it appears set down in a brief statement, for other struggles occupied his thoughts and at times distracted him from the problems directly concerned with his medium. At certain stages in his development he was necessitated to depict figures of the church and the court, or to describe events of past epochs in which he had no interest. But despite these retards he acquired, in turn, resemblance, character, objective reality, color, and volume. It was then that he felt the need of a philosophical element which would express subjectively the laws of life just as his figures and shapes expressed the objects of life. Here entered composition—that quality which, by means of certain laws of line and mass, welds together all parts of the picture and makes of the work a symbolic replica of man's obedience to the laws of nature. After the Renaissance, the knowledge of composition died down, and many minor schools of painting sprang into life; but after a short period of experimentation in methods, composition came back to art with renewed vigor.

More and more the serious creator is coming to realise that there is but one element in all deep and significant expression—*complete order,* and that this element is like a seed out of which every other element and attribute in an art work grow. After all, this complete order is what holds life together—the unseen order which dictates our every thought and action, the energetic and dynamic order of which our separate personalities, our very bodies and brains, are merely the inconsequential result. Just as the truth in life is hidden deeply under the visual and material world, so does the truth in art lie far beneath the document and imitation.

THE STRONG YOUNG MODERN

James Oppenheim

RECENTLY one of our strong young moderns made a frontal attack on utopia. He showed an appetite for "reality" which was immense and satisfying. He showed likewise that he was a disciple of H. G. Wells, who believes not in contorting and twisting the facts of life so that they fit into a vision, but in accepting the facts, breaking them open, following their inside possibilities, and constructing a vision out of them. This is a courageous asking of courage, and the picture presented is of a man of tough nervous system, whose feet know the earth, and who refuses to accept the stars save from a spectroscopic standpoint. In short, we have the picture of a de-sentimentalized Liberal. "What's to be done now?" he asks, and adds, "You cannot legislate for a hundred years hence. Life changes, and we don't know what our descendents may need. Let us turn to the instant pressure, take it, see what we can do. And let us abolish the utopia phantasy, raze it out of the minds and hearts of men. Let us, in short, be realists."

My dear Walter Lippmann! Don't you know that your scheme is both utopian and idealistic? You might as well decide to abolish fairy-tales for children. For fairy-tales are not something which parents have presented to children, but something children have presented to parents. If you abolished fairy-tales, rooted them out to the last Grimm tale, children would merely create them all over again: not out of perversity, but out of need, the need of the symbol. The child's desire outstrips immeasurably his power, and since this desire, a dynamic force, can have no adequate outlet in reality, it takes the road of phantasy. But more is gained than an outlet, a safety valve: there is gained a picture that attracts the child toward growth, toward heroism, and power, and manhood. He identifies himself with the Prince, he takes on the mantle of the Hero. Now of course, this is a childish mechanism for getting ahead. It would be better if he could measure what was actually possible, now and in his child's state. But since he can't, what are we going to do about it?

Utopia-vision and the fairy-tale belong to the same category, and spring from the same needs. For the truth of the matter is that most people are childish and undeveloped, and you can no more take their utopias, heavens, holy Maries, resurrections and immortality from them, than you can ask them to write H. G. Wells novels. Their real need produces the symbol which sustains them, and not only sustains them, but is actually a bridge toward maturity. For the Cross or the Crescent, or the Socialist State, for Nationality and the Flag, for the Home—or any symbol you will that has sprung from and stirred the heart of the race—men have suffered, struggled, created and died in a discipline which has given us the best human nature we have. If you could abolish all the utopia-drive of the past, you would blot out the host of the great. Fired by a false dream, they that bore us achieved a true growth. Who then can deny the pragmatic value of utopias? And cannot we truly say that the symbol was merely a convenient focusing point, an object outside of self by which a man could take hold on the future and so surpass what he was? He raised himself by an idea.

Curiously enough the symbol is not only the essence of art: it is the essence of science. It is the mechanism through which we can advance. Faust and the Superman are artistic symbols of human possibilities: patterns to which we may attempt to mould ourselves. But no less a symbol is the theory of the conservation of energy, or the postulates of the atom, the electron, the evolution of species. Each of these is something experientially unprovable: merely convenient focal points by which we may think and live. Their dynamic value is vitally great, just because of the vistas opened, the possibilities disclosed. "Evolution" as knowledge means nothing to us: as a basis for philosophy or religion it means a right-about-face toward life. It means finally "conscious evolution"—the making of life, the direction and control of it. And of course our strong young modern wouldn't abolish all these symbols: he would merely abolish those which are *more remote*.

Well, he is right when it comes to himself, perhaps, and all strong young moderns. To be able to dispense with heaven and survival after death and the dream of heaven on Earth shows that a certain stage of growth is reached, and that a hero has emerged. But since so few of us have reached this stage of growth, since the mass of mankind is still merely these children, these pitifully blind, overworked, overwrought and needy beings, these desirers and seekers who need so greatly and find so meagerly, our demand that they cease to be childish will be of little avail. They may promise faithfully, but let a Billy Sunday appear, or a Bill Haywood, or the Day of Armageddon, or Defense of Liberty and England or the Fatherland, and they will flock to the dream.

And not only they, my strong young modern: but certain others who seemed so much above such things! Have we not seen this happen in the present war? Have not tough-minded gone maudlin, even as the tender-minded were, ever and ever? And if we really want, right now, to be non-utopian and realistic, yes, if we really want to face the facts of life, shall we not have to allow utopias to others?

DAVID'S BIRTHRIGHT

Edna Wahlert McCourt

WHEN David was six, his friends could not tell whether he was going to evolve into poet or pugilist. There were periods of abstraction and a casual quivering of his upper lip which, together with a dreamy darkening of his grey eyes, suggested the poet. But then, there was the square jaw, sturdy body, ready fists, queer little frown line between his brown brows, and above all a passion for physical activity that made his mother hide the green sheets of the evening paper.

"I can fight anybody," David would declare. "I—I can knock down any feller—even if he's ten. An' I can—I can almost kill girls—even— even if they're twelve! I can pretty *near* kill 'em."

When he came home from a boy-fight he was merely exultant, naturally flushed. But after he had pulled a girl's hair until she howled for mercy, after he had kicked a girl's shins or torn her clothes or twisted her wrists, his eyes burned queerly.

"I—I can almost *kill* girls!" he'd vow.

Of course his mother, being a decent lady with the loftiest of ideals, always sent him to bed, supperless and unkissed, when he voiced his ability and desire to mutilate or annihilate the members of the fair sex. She even shed tears over his ungentlemanliness, his unnaturally brutal tendencies; and she worried terribly. David would weep in his little bed, too—hot blinding tears that quite dampened the pillow. But they were tears of happiness.

"I can whip 'em all I" he'd sob. "Every feller an'—an' *every* girl I know! Oh, I'm so glad I can fight 'em all! If I couldn't I'd—I'd *die,* I would. When I'm a man I'll—I'll fight *mother!*"

And with dizzy visions of that delicious millenium, he would forget to obey her commands, and, jumping from the bed, would run to her like a mad thing and almost smother her with kisses, quite dampening her with his tears.

David's father came from a long line of southern gentlemen. He had never struck a girl in his life, and the mere fancy of physically hurting a woman made his head swim a little. But the defect in his boy's character did not trouble him.

"There are thousands of fine boys that fight. He'll get over it. He'll outgrow it. I don't want to punish him yet. There are thousands of boys who love to fight."

"But there aren't thousands of nice boys who love to fight girls," his wife would reply sadly. And of course he had no answer to make to that. "I can't bear to think he's just a coward—just glorying in fighting the weaker element. It seems more like a disease."

And when David was seven, as he still loved to beat up little girls and to tell of his conquests with quivering lips and queer fanatical gleams in his eyes, she actually took him to a physician. But the doctor only laughed.

"He's a fine boy," he assured the troubled woman. "Don't worry for five or six years. Do what you can to influence him to like girls, or at least to be indifferent to them. But I am sure there is nothing abnormal about your child. There are more youngsters in the world than you imagine with natural perversities. That is all David's passion for superiority is. He'll outgrow it."

But David did not outgrow his so-called natural perversity. His relation to small girls continued to be very much like that between serpent and bird, lion and prey, bull and red rag.

II

It was a warm Spring afternoon, two or three years later, that a very white little boy with blue lips and dilated pupils that made his eyes appear abnormally round, crept into his mother's room.

"David!" she almost screamed. "What has happened! Are you sick?"

The voice that answered her was hoarse and the grey eyes that gazed at her with a sort of inhuman fascination were almost black.

"No, I'm not sick," he said. "I'm just—I'm just—wicked."

It flashed through her mind that at last the thing she had been fearing had come to pass; he had seriously hurt someone or perhaps . . . She would not permit herself to imagine the logical possibilities of her fear.

"What have you done?" she cried.

The far-away voice answered dreamily, "Nothing."

"Don't lie to me, David," she commanded. "Tell me exactly what has happened. What have you done?"

"I—I don't know," he told her. "He just said—he just said I hurt the girls. He just said I was—too wicked to come to school any more."

"You are not——"

He said the word for her bravely: *"Expelled."*

He handed her the note from his principal. She read things about her son she knew and yet did not know; she read judgments she had never permitted herself to formulate; she read prophesies that made her teeth chatter a little. The fact emerged, as unsuspected mountain peaks emerge when the mist lifts, that her son—her son and her gentlemanly husband's son—was too cruel to girls to be allowed to associate with children in the public schools. She would a million times rather have read that he had the small-pox.

During the eternal afternoon hours before the father came home, they two sat silently, and every tick of the clock was stentorian.

Without a word she handed her husband the principal's letter, and, as David watched him read it and realized, for the first time in his little life how handsome his father was and how white his blue veined temples and hands were, tears came to his eyes, quite unconsciously.

David's father whipped him, terribly, that night.

"I want you to understand," his white lips managed to tell the boy, "that I am only doing this because your mother's and my reasoning with you during all these years has been of no avail."

But after it was all over, the boy threw his arms about his father's neck passionately, and, kissing him all over the front of his shirt, sobbed: "Oh, Daddy! Daddy! It was a grand fight you put up! How long will it be before I'm a man like you?"

The father's lower jaw dropped then, foolishly. He had intended to lock the boy up and keep him on the frugalest of diets until he promised never to touch a little girl again. But instead he talked—carefully. He explained to the very best of his ability the sanctioned and conventional attitude of man towards woman and the wisdom of forming chivalrous habits during boyhood. When he exhausted his supply of admonitions and inspirations and warnings, David gazed at him adoringly.

"You talk—Oh you talk beautiful, Daddy!" he sobbed. "But still—Oh Daddy!—it seems *right* for me to—to fight girls! It seems *right* for me to make 'em do what I—want 'em to do—if I—want to. Oh Daddy," he cried earnestly, his white, tear-stained face all a-quiver, "can't you see?"

III

They put him in a boy's school and practically isolated him from the society of little girls; so that, as the years passed, he seemed to develop into quite a normal youth. They even grew able to smile over their fears as to his future, and the youngster came to be able to pass a girl with the same indifference with which he would pass a gate post.

But when he was fourteen, David fell in love.

The object of his young passion was a blonde girl about his own age with long silly curls that her mother, and kids, manufactured over night. She had a simpering little face and affected manners, and her skinny body was togged out in all the ridiculous fluff-fluffs and fashionablenesses and incongruities of the absurd ruling mode. You cannot imagine a greater contrast than that between her useless white hand, bedecked as crudely as any savage's, and David's great baseball-hardened paw. In fact, hers was the last type of girl his parents would have expected him to take for his first sweetheart.

But how he adored her! He carried her books to and from her school (although his gallantry caused him to be repeatedly tardy himself, for which offense he was assigned tremendously long extra exercises, which he performed, however, without batting an eyelash). He fetched her all the books she wanted from the library; she had a passion for reading absurd novels, but was too lazy to go after them herself. He spent all his allowance taking her to moving picture shows and providing her with candy, hot-waffles, and ice-cream. And once, when she told him how she loved to wear chains and things around her neck, he broke open his nickle-and-penny-bank and, with the savings of years, purchased every string of beads in the 5-and-10-cent store for her. He would have died for her or slaved for her or starved for her. Which really means a great deal, for David was enamoured of living and of loafing and above all of eating.

While David's fourteenth year marked the glorious culmination of an inspired childhood, Jessie's ushered in all the false standards, all the hardness, selfishness and illogicalness of budding womanhood. Although she basked, like a cat at the hearth, in the deliciousness of David's devotion and purred her absolute satisfaction inwardly, yet she manifested her complacency in a fashion that David could no more correctly interpret than a fervent bull could the struttings and coquetries of a peacock.

When their courtship was four or five months old, Jessie began to make eyes at and call trivialities to a fellow who lived across the street. But David had a physical interview with his near-rival and, although what transpired between them has not been recorded, his opponent ever afterwards, whenever Jessie entered his line of vision, pulled his cap hastily over his eyes and rapidly disappeared beyond the horizon.

But after a few weeks of peace, Jessie commenced Dancing School where David, of course, scorned to go. For a while the boy was not suspicious of the constancy of his sweetheart, and was absolutely content escorting her to and from the academy. One day, however, a certain Joseph Jones walked home with them. Jessie was in her element, mincing along between the boys, and she laughed and giggled and simpered and frolicked deliciously. David had really no conscious disturbing thoughts; but when, after the next lesson and the next, Joseph again accompanied them homeward, his face became very white and he frequently stumbled. For things swam before his eyes and the bright sunshine cavorted about in purple-blue spirals. Jessie understood intuitively that he was in an unusual mood, but did not aggravate him. Wisely she devoted her entire attention to Joseph.

David did not hear a word of their conversation; he was solving his problem. He figured out that there wouldn't be any sense in fighting Joseph, because he and Joseph were good friends and because Jessie had evidently asked Joseph to walk home with her. He recalled the difficulty with the boy across the street and realized that, even if he did away with

Joseph in like manner, Jessie would probably get interested in yet another fellow. And, he couldn't spend the rest of his life beating up his rivals, could he? He decided that there was only one way to settle his eternal firstness in Jessie's heart for all time to come, and that way was to subdue Jessie.

When they reached the girl's home, he picked up a bit of wood and, whittling carefully, whistled meaningly. Joseph took the hint and left, in what an outsider would have termed unnecessary haste. But then, Joseph had heard of the episode of the boy across the street.

Jessie hummed a frivolous tune. And, "Isn't Joseph a grand looking fellow?" she asked.

David closed his knife carefully and put it in his pocket. Then he stood up, and, as magnificently as though he were throwing the discus at an athletic contest, hurled the piece of wood far down the street. He caught the admiration that leaped to Jessie's eyes, but instead of following his impulse to josh her and forgive her, he listened to something in his brain which kept repeating: *It's got to be settled for good!* He kicked the steps rhythmically and avoided meeting her coquettish glance.

"You've got to quit dancing school," he said slowly.

Her heart fluttered delightedly. "Oh, do I?" she inquired pertly. "Why?"

His breath was sucked backwards and his fists clenched. "Because—I—want—you—to," he answered, and this time he looked at her steadily.

She laughed nervously and flirted with the ruffles of her pretty frock. "Why should I do what *you* want?"

"Because," everything turned perfectly black to him as, for the first time, he uttered the glorious words, "because you're my girl."

She walked across the veranda to her front door with ridiculous dignity. "Oh, is *that* so?" And she tossed her head with the offended pride of her favorite tragedy queen of the movies.

He sprang to her and grabbed her wrists. "Ain't you——" he choked, "ain't you—my girl?"

With the intuition of a seasoned flirt she answered prissily, without meaning a word that she said or implied, "If your eyes'd been open, lately, you wouldn't have to ask that."

David's brain grew clear as ether, and the words whirled through his heart: "She's *my* girl—if I want her. No matter what she thinks or says. Whatever I want her to do, she's got to do. She's got to *want* to do what I want her to. Because I'm a boy!"

And with all his strength, and David was an unusually strong boy, he twisted her wrists. She screamed at the top of her voice. He covered her mouth with his hand. She bit his fingers and screamed louder than before. Then he shook her,—not furiously, but so violently and passionately, that she fainted in his arms.

As inmates of the house rushed to the door in response to her cries, he handed her over to—someone.

Then he was seized with a nervous chill; but somehow he managed to stumble home and to his mother.

"I—I've killed Jessie," he moaned. "She wouldn't do what I wanted—her—to. She got the—best of me. And I'm a boy..."

And he crumpled up at her feet.

IV

I might consume the pages of a good sized novel recounting the conditions and adventures of the next ten years of David's life.

He emerged from a long seige of illness into an epoch distinguished by ardent poise and extreme intellectual activity. He endeavored, almost feverishly, to imitate the good manners of his parents, and he read and studied voraciously, chiefly science and anthropology. Again he seemed dead, dumb, and blind to the existence of womankind. But during his third year at the secondary school he read an original oration on *Woman's Place in Nature* that quite electrified the institution. Teachers listened in astonishment, wondering if it were possible that he had read Nietzsche, and students forgot to applaud.

That night he ran away from home and joined the army. He was only seventeen, but easily passed all tests. In less than a year, however, he returned, having learned very little of patriotism but a great deal of life. He kissed the grey hairs that had come to streak his mother's head during his absence, and studiously prepared himself for college.

When he made Sophomore Honors, a tremendous fury seized him.

"What good is it!" he cried to himself. "Any girl could do as much! *I* want to do something that is manly! I want to be a *man!* Why didn't I live a hundred years ago? Studying is well and good for girls and for fellows who want to live like women and for great men. I—I shall never be great. I don't want to be! I want to be just a man—an ordinary man—but a *man*. All this studying is the absorbing of a feminine type of knowledge. My professors are no different from my mother. Everything is saturated with this feminism,—the newspapers are mere organs for women, sanctioned literature is what the women approve of, the professions, commerce, even politics . . . O, I must live a life that is manly as life used to be! I shall! I will!"

He joined the navy, and for two years sailed the high seas and carved his way through the life of the ports. With the militia he had learned of life. Now he lived it. And he came to know all types of women well, though chiefly the lower orders. He worshipped beauty and kindliness in women: everything else he despised. Not very clearly, not very logically, not with reason, but wholly because he was fiercely jealous of womankind and her perpetually evident superiority, or at least, her importance.

The twenty-three year old boy who finally returned to his mother looked thirty. But he told himself he was a hundred.

"Is there no place in the world for me?" he asked himself, bitterly. "The world today is a world for women and for feminine men who are afraid to be manly, and for men who could be manly if they did not prefer to cater to the women. I am greater than any woman ! I was born knowing it . . . "

He started for "Out West," and though "Out West" is no particular spot on earth, but is only a spirit of freedom and a significance, yet he did gravitate to the Rockies, and he took to ranching and to loving it.

V

But he chose his ranch in empty country, empty save for a tawny road, a blue-gold river, the green glory of the pines, and an infinite wave of violet hills backgrounded by tall massive peaks whose white uplifted faces kissed the sky. Such cabins as were in his neighborhood were scattered far apart. In fact, he grew so out of the habit of expecting to see indication of human life that, frequently, he mistook white smoke from a chimney for cloud or mist or forest fire. His gentle cattle and pretty sheep flocked his hills rhythmically. He loved them. "Because I control their destinies," he told himself.

He rode five miles each day for his mail, and when the ground was firm returned by way of Blue Bell Canyon. The scenery there was of unparalleled beauty, and besides, his good friends, the Waltons, had their cabin near the head of the ravine. Mr. Walton was an ex-college-professor whose library had been conveyed to the mountains in spite of the fact that the professorial savings account had been considerably depleted thereby. The library attracted David as much as the Waltons did.

On a late Spring morning, as the intoxicating odor of new life dilated David's nostrils, his mare, Peggy, from force of habit, slowed her pace as a bend in the road revealed the Walton's whitewashed cabin and fences.

Now David, for more than seven years, had ridden by this, place about three hundred times each twelve months and he knew it well. He stared at the stranger who was calmly sitting in the orchard.

She was quite young, about twenty, and not especially beautiful. But an unusual serenity lay upon her delicate features that ennobled them with something that struck David as more beautiful than beauty. Her lap was full of flowers,—wild flox, the mariposa lily, galardia, harebells, lupine, sulfur, bedstraw... and her white fingers touched them caressingly. David had not the faintest idea who she was, but so well was he acquainted with the Waltons that, just as though he had encountered her on his own verandah, he raised his hat.

She lifted her calm face, as Peggy pranced gently at the gate, but, as though David were an invisible thing, she gazed past him to the farther wall of the canyon. There could be no doubt from the expression of her face that she was aware of his presence, but her calm eyes ignored him. No woman had ever before ignored David, and he winced as though he were ashamed. Then his eyes blazed at her; he turned perfectly white, and wheeling Peggy with a terrible pull, dashed up the trail.

"She—she looked *through* me! I might have been an insect! She was more concerned with the weeds in her lap!"

Peggy caught his mood and galloped furiously.

The next day Mrs. Walton phoned an invitation to come to dinner and "meet her niece."

"I didn't tell you I expected her to visit me," she said, "because I was afraid you would manufacture a pretext for a visit to the hills. And I want you to know her."

But David excused himself. It was the end of the month... he would be busy with his accounts... He changed the subject abruptly, then longed to hear more of her. Mrs. Walton volunteered no information, but in the midst of a discussion on crops he blurted out, angrily.

"Can she sing?"

"Very beautifully."

Like an overwrought child he brought the conversation to a close.

"I've hunted all over the world for that face," he whispered. "It has the expression I have always longed to see on a woman's face. I've so often been afraid she wouldn't sing. To think that she can... and then to have her ignore me." The thought was very bitter.

One cannot disapprove without approving; nor can one censure without appreciating. And so because of the anger and the jealousy and the contempt for women that he had felt in his youth, and, too, because of the poignant antagonism he had experienced in his maturer years, David had formed a more vivid picture of his ideal than most men do. He knew just what his perfect woman should be and what she should not be. He had dreamed of meeting her a million times. He knew he would not fail to recognize her and he had never even vaguely suspected that she would not recognize his superiority. One of the essentials of his ideal woman was that she should know him as her mate and as, if not the creator of her destiny, the chiefest determining factor.

Everywhere he turned, in all his day dreams, all his nightly visions, he saw the calm face of the girl in the Walton's orchard, saw her expression of awareness yet of ignoring, of seeing and yet of looking beyond and through him. He was ashamed. It was as though he had found himself wanting.

He dreaded meeting her. "If she should look at me like that again, I don't believe I could control myself."

He got out his camping outfit and went, with Peggy, to the high hills for a week, in order to "forget her." But when he returned home he could not do that, or stay away from Blue Bell.

He rode down the canyon. Peggy tried to slow up as they approached the Walton's ranch, but when he swore she galloped by, all too swiftly. Yet she had been in the orchard! She had dropped her sewing as he flew by! She had smiled at him! There was something in the smile even that made his heart leap—not shyness but rather humility. O, fool that he had been, wasting all these days when he might have had that smile sooner, that shy, humble smile!

For days he hung around the telephone hoping, almost praying for Mrs. Walton to invite him to her home again. But when he realized that she would not, he made up his mind to visit her unasked. No sooner was his mind made up than he was on Peggy's back. For David never yet had failed to obey an impulse, nor had he ever first procrastinated.

Mrs. Walton met him at the gate.

"I'm glad you've come, David."

"I—I wanted to hear her sing."

"It is a rare treat to hear her. By the way, David, I want to tell you she is blind."

VI

Indian summer: the white beards of the mountains have grown longer; the angiosperms below have turned lemon color; and Blue Bell canyon has donned her most gorgeous array.

"I never thought I should ask a woman to marry me," David told Mary Catherine.

"You probably planned a sort of Young Lochinvar ceremony. Now didn't you?" she questioned.

He laughed a little, but the eyes that watched her white fingers crotcheting swiftly were serious.

"I want to tell you about myself," he answered.

"Haven't you told me a good bit about that person already?"

"I want to tell you logically, before I ask you to marry me."

"I'm all ears, Sir Knight."

"When I was a little shaver, I used to—fight girls. I hurt them like everything. I was expelled from school, even, because I treated them so abominably. I guess I really tortured them."

She caught her breath. David could not tell whether from surprise or dismay.

"When I was fourteen," he went on, "I had a—girl. Because she wouldn't do just what I wanted her to, I hurt her so and frightened her so that—she fainted."

He was afraid to look into her expressive face.

"I hope you won't hate me," he continued quaintly, "but I'm not even ashamed of—all that. The superior airs they assumed seemed *wicked* to me, when I was a boy. I fought girls as the Crusaders did the Heathen, I suppose. They were, they seemed the usurpers of the Temple, you know—the Temple of Manhood."

"What made you that kind of a child, David?"

"I haven't the faintest idea." He fell into a bit of musing.

"Go on," she urged.

"I was thinking of Mother. Father, too. Of course I was a terrible disappointment to them."

"Why 'of course'?" she demanded proudly, for her, almost defiantly.

"They are very modern, very conventional people, you see. It hurt them to have a freak for a son. All during my youth … I hope you won't laugh at me … but it was like Jeanne d'Arc. I always heard Voices crying out for freedom,—crying out against Woman the Tyrant, the usurper of that superiority which had been wholly man's. I heard Voices calling for the old conditions when men were the acknowledged Masters of the Earth."

"You were just a poet."

He kept on with his confession.

"I had a fair amount of brains, but all my school work and all my college work was tainted. For I knew that every realm of knowledge, all learning, the sphere which during all the ages has been the sanctuary, the holy of holies of man alone!—it had been besieged, stormed, conquered by," he smiled, "the enemy."

"Such thoughts robbed book learning of all its pleasure for me. Mother and Father wanted me to be a great physician or a professor of philosophy. But I—I just couldn't. Women could do that. I longed to work at something that was imbued with the old time spirit of manliness. There was the army and the navy. I—I learned them both by heart. There were many women in my life, at that time, too. But I did not find what I was seeking for. It was not until I was twenty-five that I realized the fact had to be accepted: Man was no longer the Czar of the Earth ; Woman had come to stay."

"David," she began.

But he had made up his mind to confess everything.

"I haven't told you the worst. Listen. Of course I know that woman has been evolving according to her god-given rights, even though mistakes have been made in the evolving. I know that hurting her body as I did when a youngster, and hurting her, as I did when I was older, is futile. But … but I still believe men should be, I still wish men were, the more complete. A man ought to confess that before he asks a girl to marry him."

She gave a little cry.

"David—please! You are too wonderful. Don't ask me."

He caught her hands.

"Why not?" he demanded. "I've been honest always. Every honest man may ask."

"You don't understand, I mean … if I were like others, I should be so proud. But, David … I cannot *see*. I cannot *see*."

Her words seemed to reach him like a joyous announcement. "You are my birthright, Mary Catherine," he said.

THE UNTOLD LIE

Sherwood Anderson

WHEN I was a boy and lived in my home town of Winesburg, Ohio, Ray Pearson and Hal Winters were farm hands employed on a farm three miles north of us. I can't for my life say how I know this story concerning them, but I vouch for its truth. I have known the story always just as I know many things concerning my own town that have never been told to me. As for Ray and Hal I can recall well enough how I used to see them on our Main Street with other country fellows of a Saturday afternoon. Ray was a quiet, rather nervous man of perhaps fifty with a brown beard and shoulders rounded by too much and too hard labor. In his nature he was as unlike Hal Winters as two men can be unlike.

Ray was an altogether serious man, as I remember him, and had a little sharp featured wife who had also a sharp voice. The two, with half a dozen thin legged children, lived in a tumble-down frame house beside a creek at the back end of the Wills' farm, where Ray was employed.

Hal Winters, his fellow employee, was a young fellow. He was not of the Ned Winters family, who were very respectable people among us, but was one of the three sons of the old man we called Windpeter Winters, who had a sawmill over near Unionville, six miles away, and who was looked upon by everyone in Winesburg as a confirmed old reprobate.

People from my town will remember old Windpeter by his unusual and tragic death. He got drunk in Winesburg and started to drive home to Unionville along the railroad tracks. Henry Brattenburg, the butcher, who lived out that way, stopped him at the edge of the town and told him he was sure to meet the down train, but Windpeter slashed at him with his whip and drove on. When the train struck and killed him and his two horses, a farmer and his wife who were driving home along a nearby road saw the accident. They said that old Windpeter stood up on the seat of his wagon, raving and swearing at the onrushing locomotive and that he fairly screamed with delight when the team, maddened by his incessant slashing at them, rushed straight ahead to certain death. I myself remember the incident quite vividly because, although everyone in our town said that the old man would go straight to hell and that the community was better *off* without him, I had a secret conviction that he knew what he was doing and I admired his foolish courage. Like most boys I had already had my seasons of wishing I might die gloriously instead of just being a grocery clerk and going on with my humdrum life. I know now that many in our town must have felt the same way.

But this is not the story of Windpeter Winters nor yet of his son Hal who worked on the Wills farm with Ray Pearson. It is Ray's story. But I must tell you a little of young Hal so that you will get into the spirit of it.

Hal was a bad one. Everyone said that. There were three of the Winter's boys in that family, John, Hal and Edward, all broad shouldered big fellows like old Windpeter himself and all fighters and woman-chasers and generally all-around bad ones.

Hal was the worst of the lot and always up to some devilment. For example, I can remember how he once stole a load of boards from his father's mill and sold them in Winesburg. With the money he bought himself a suit of cheap, flashy clothes. Then he got drunk and when his father came raving into town to find him they met and fought with their fists on Main Street and were arrested and put into jail together.

Hal went to work on the Wills farm because there was a country school teacher out that way who had taken his fancy. He was only twenty-two then but had already been in two or three of what we used to speak of as "woman scrapes." Everyone who heard of his infatuation for the school teacher was sure it would turn out badly. "He'll only get her into trouble, you'll see," was the word that went around.

And so these two men, Ray and Hal were at work in a field on a day in the late October. They were husking corn and. occasionally something was said and they laughed. Then came silence. Ray, who was the more sensitive and always minded things more, had chapped hands and they hurt. He put them into his coat pockets and looked away across the fields. He was in a sad distracted mood and was affected by the beauty of the country. If you knew our country in the fall and how the low hills are all splashed with yellows and blacks you would understand his feeling. He began to think of the time, long ago when he was a young fellow living with his father, then a baker in Winesburg, and how on days like this he wandered away to the woods to gather nuts, hunt rabbits or just to loaf about and smoke his pipe. His marriage had come about through one of these days of wandering. He had induced a girl who waited on trade in his father's shop to go with him and something had happened. He was thinking of that afternoon long ago and how it had affected his whole life, when a spirit of protest awoke in him. He had forgotten about Hal and muttered words. "Tricked by Gad, that's what I was; tricked by life and made a fool of," he said in a low voice.

As though understanding his thoughts, Hal Winters spoke up. "Well, has it been worth while? What about it, eh, what about marriage and all that?" he asked and then laughed. Hal tried to keep on laughing but he too was in an earnest mood. He began to talk earnestly. "Has a fellow got to do it?" he asked. "Has he got to be harnessed up and driven like a horse?"

He didn't wait for an answer but sprang to his feet and began to walk back and forth between the corn shocks. He was getting more and more excited. Bending suddenly down he picked up an ear of the yellow corn and threw it at the fence. "I've got Nell Gunther in trouble," he said. "I'm telling you, but you keep your mouth shut."

Ray Pearson arose and stood staring. He was almost a foot shorter than Hal and when the younger man came and put his two hands on the older man's shoulders they made a picture. There they stood in the big empty field with the quiet corn shocks standing in rows behind them and the red and yellow hills in the distance and from being just two indifferent workmen they had become all alive to each other. Hal sensed it and because that was his way he laughed. "Well old daddy," he said awkwardly, "come on, advise me. I've got Nell in trouble. Perhaps you've been in the same fix yourself. I know what everyone would say is the right thing to do but what do you say? Shall I marry and settle down? Shall I put myself into the harness to be worn out like an old horse? You know me, Ray. There can't anyone break me but I can break myself. Shall I do it or shall I tell Nell to go to the devil? Come on, you tell me. Whatever you say, Ray, I'll do."

Ray couldn't answer. He shook Hal's hands loose and turning walked straight away toward the barn. As I've said he was a sensitive man and there were tears in his eyes. He knew there was only one thing to say to Hal Winters, son of old Windpeter Winters, only one thing that all his own training and all the beliefs of the people he knew would approve, but for his life he couldn't say what he knew he should say.

At half past four that afternoon Ray was puttering about the barnyard when his wife came up the lane along the creek and called him. After the talk with Hal he hadn't returned to the cornfield but worked about the barn. He had already done the evening chores and had seen Hal, dressed and ready for a roistering night in town, come out of the farm house and go into the road. Along the path toward his own house he trudged behind his wife, looking at the ground and thinking. He couldn't make out what was wrong. Every time he raised his eyes and saw the beauty of the country in the failing light he wanted to do something he had never done before, shout or scream or hit his wife with his fist or something equally unexpected and terrifying. Along the path he went scratching his head and trying to make it out. He looked hard at his wife's back but she seemed all right.

She only wanted him to go into town for groceries and as soon as she had told him what she wanted, began to scold. "You're always puttering," she said. "Now I want you to hustle. There isn't anything in the house for supper and you've got to get to town and back in a hurry."

Ray went into his own house and took an overcoat from a hook back of the door. It was torn about the pockets and the collar was shiny. The wife went into the bedroom and presently came out with a soiled cloth in one hand and three silver dollars in the other. Somewhere in the house a child wept bitterly and a dog that had been sleeping by a stove arose and yawned. Again the wife scolded. "The children will cry and cry. Why are you always puttering?" she said.

Ray went out of the house and climbed a fence into a field. It was just growing dark and the scene that lay before him was lovely. All the low hills were washed with color and even the little clusters of bushes in the corners by the fences were alive with beauty. The whole world seemed to Ray Pearson to have become alive with something just as he and Hal had suddenly become alive when they stood in the cornfield staring into each other's eyes.

The beauty of our country there about Winesburg was just too much for Ray on that fall evening. That's all there was to it. He couldn't stand it. Of a sudden he forgot all about being a quiet old farm hand, and throwing off the torn overcoat began to run across the field. As he ran he shouted a protest against his life, against all life, against everything that makes life ugly. "There was no promise made," he cried into the empty spaces that lay about him. "I didn't promise my Minnie anything and Hal hasn't made any promise to Nell. I know he hasn't. She went into the woods with him because she wanted to go. What he wanted she wanted. Why should I pay? Why should Hal pay? Why should anyone pay? I don't want Hal to become old and worn-out. I'll tell him. I won't let it go on. I'll catch Hal before he gets to town and I'll tell him."

Ray ran clumsily and once he stumbled and fell down. "I must catch Hal and tell him," he kept thinking and although his breath came in gasps he kept running harder and harder. As he ran he thought of things that hadn't come into his mind for years—how at the time he married he had planned to go west to his uncle in Portland, Oregon—how he hadn't wanted to be a farm hand but had thought when he got out west he would go to sea and be a sailor or get a job on a ranch and ride a horse into western towns shouting and laughing and waking the people in the houses with his wild cries. Then as he ran he remembered his children and in fancy felt their hands clutching at him. All of his thoughts of himself were involved with the thoughts of Hal and he thought the children were clutching at the younger man also. "They are the accidents of life, Hal," he cried. "They are not mine or yours. I had nothing to do with them."

Darkness began to spread over the fields as Ray Pearson ran on and on. His breath came in little sobs. When he came to the fence at the edge of the road and confronted Hal Winters all dressed up and smoking a pipe as he walked jauntily along, he couldn't have told what he thought or what he wanted.

I suppose Ray Pearson lost his nerve and that this is really the end of the story of what happened to him. It was almost dark when he got to the fence and he put his hands on the top bar and stood staring. Hal Winters jumped a ditch and coming up close, put his hands in his pockets and laughed heartily. He seemed to have lost his own sense of what had happened in the cornfield and when he put up a strong hand and took hold of the lapel of Ray's coat he shook the old man as he might have shaken a dog that had misbehaved.

"You came to tell me, eh?" he said. "Well, never mind telling me anything. I'm not a coward and I've already made up my mind." He laughed again and jumped back across the ditch. "Nell ain't no fool," he said. "She didn't ask me to marry her. I want to marry her. I want to settle down and have kids."

Ray Pearson also laughed. He felt like laughing at himself and all the world.

As the form of Hal Winters disappeared in the dusk that lay over the road that led to Winesburg he turned and walked slowly back across the fields to where he had left his torn overcoat. As he went, some memory of pleasant evenings spent with the thin legged children in the tumble-down house by the creek must have come into his mind, for he muttered words. "It's just as well. Whatever I told him would have been a lie," he said softly and then his form also disappeared into the darkness of the fields.

THE SCAR

Elizabeth Stead Taber

I N a certain remote road valley among the foothills of the North Woods country, the Wild Cat Road forms a jagged, unsightly scar upon the otherwise lovely face of Nature,—a scar which is the more hideous by its contrast to the wild, alluring beauty around it. The law of Nature works here in harsh ways which are in accord with the grim aspect of the place.

Bald, rocky steeps; gaunt, struggling pines; and in the lower ground, tall grey corpses of trees still standing upright in the swamps that had brought death to them,—it was on such an outlook that Rilly Ward gazed from the doorway of the tar-papered shanty that was her home. The dead trees stood in a ghastly company on the opposite side of the straggling road which here and there took a turn around a rocky outcrop on its way; beyond the swampy ground Big Elephant Mountain reared its bulky mass; back of the shanty the dry fields were covered with the pale greenish-yellow of the coarse bent grass; upward from them sloped the seared and scarred form of Little Elephant Mountain which had burned over the year before.

The woman in the doorway possessed a certain dull comeliness. The dark, cheap wrapper which she wore hung in shapeless folds; her brown hair had no lights and shadows but was all the dun color of earth; her hands were coarse and large; yet there was an air about her that was almost pleasing. Her eyes were lustreless but they brightened as she stepped down to the broad flat stone in front of the door and called, "Almy."

In response to her call, a strange-looking little creature of six or seven years crept from behind the big tamarack tree, carrying in her hands cones which she had been gathering. Dark hair encircled her colorless face, the eyes were hidden by lowered lids; it was when she raised her glance to her mother's and held out the cones that a foolish smile broke over the face which had, at first glance, seemed almost pretty. It was a smile singularly like the silly grin of a drunken man.

"You set here, Almy, and watch for your pa to come; I'll be makin' supper."

The child sat down on the high doorstep and the woman went within the shanty. A moment later a tall young giant swung into view around the bend of the road. He was dark and roughly handsome with an animal beauty; uncouth and like an untrained animal he looked as he came nearer with lounging strides.

The child in the doorway shrank aside as he reached her, but if he was aware of her presence he ignored it, and passed on into the shanty. The little girl entered when her mother called out, "Almy," and the three sat down to eat from the thick plates on the bare table near the door.

The furniture was scanty and rude; a worn-out stove was at one side of the room, a rough bed stood in the darkest corner, and a homemade cot close beside it.

A deep dish of raccoon meat in thick greasy gravy was the chief food. Joe Ward ate for some time in silence, his wife glancing at him furtively. She was wondering "what ailed Joe" tonight; he had not been drinking, but there was a subdued excitement and unnatural manner about him which disturbed her.

"First coon I've got in a year and it'll be the last for a while, I guess," announced Joe. "Can't nobody else do nothin' huntin' with Ruddy Munroe gettin' it all." He shook back the dark hair from his forehead, and looked at the woman facing him. "Ruddy Munroe's got luck," he continued; "he won't never lack skins to sell nor meat to eat."

"He's been fixin' a new house up the Wild Cat Road," ventured Rilly; "he does get along."

Almy remained silent most of the time, but occasionally she glanced at her mother, the same silly grin disfiguring her face. She was strikingly like her father; it was when that expression came over her countenance that he avoided looking at her.

"Yes, a four-roomed one, all sided up and painted, lookin' off to Blueberry Pond," Joe was saying. "Do you suppose he'd be livin' in a place like this? Neither would I be if I'd ever had any luck. Can't raise nothin' on land that'll only grow hell-bent grass; can't do trappin' where Ruddy Munroe's gettin' rich on it. If it hadn't been for the sawmill comin' in this year, I'd cleaned out before this. But we're windin' up the clearin' and that'll be movin' soon."

Rilly had heard Joe talk against his luck before, although perhaps not quite so fiercely. "Why, Joe, you ain't never tried no farmin'," she said. "Huntin' or farmin' or whatever, Ruddy Munroe's got along because he's a smart man and—"

"Ruddy Munroe don't drink. How'd you like it if he'd chose you for his woman?"

"Why, Joe, Ruddy Munroe wouldn't 'a' looked at me. He's fine set up; but maybe I wouldn't be so bad off," she said musingly.

Rilly had risen and stepped to the door. She was emptying the greasy gravy outside where it fell on the broad stone. She turned back into the room as Joe went on,

"That's the last grease gravy you'll be emptyin' out o' this door, Rilly."

Almy's big eyes looked at him wonderingly and the woman, too, did not seem to understand.

"Yes, Rilly Ward, how'd you like to live up to that new house of Ruddy Munroe's?" Before she could speak he continued, "Well, that's where you're goin'. Ruddy wants a woman,—been havin' his eye on you for some time, he says,—ain't you pleased?"

"Why, what do you mean, Joe? You ain't been drinkin' again?" she questioned, for he spoke with a reckless laugh.

At her words he gave a quick glance at the child, who was still gazing at him with wide open eyes, but he quickly looked away. "No, I ain't been drinkin'. I mean you're goin' to be his woman, Rilly. He don't mind takin' her"—he jerked his head at Almy without looking at her—"for the sake o' gettin' a good woman like you. It'll be a big thing for you."

"Why Joe," she protested, "you ain't tired o' me?"

"It ain't no new idea; I've been thinkin' of it for a long time." His eyes wandered back again to Almy for a moment. "It's no more'n Billy

Tompkins and Jud Camp done,—didn't they swap wives? I'm goin' to clear out, Rilly. I'm goin' down to the Falls, and I'm goin' to get me another woman down there." He said the last words with an air of bravado.

"Ruddy Munroe don't drink, neither," he repeated grimly, keeping his eyes upon her.

"Oh Joe," she cried, "I don't mind your drinkin'. I mean," ——she looked at Almy, "I'd rather live with you anyhow."

"Well, I wouldn't, so that's settled," he declared flatly. "Ain't it enough for you that I'm goin' to get me another woman?"

The woman seemed to sense this thought for the first time. The dog-like look of submission passed from her face, and in its place came a sort of boldness, as with a quick toss of her head she said, "Well, course I ain't wantin' to stay much."

"The bargain's all made and you'll like it first rate," he said.

"Ruddy Munroe!" she muttered. "It's awful sudden, Joe; I wish you'd told me before. But it's real excitin' and I'm glad to go," she declared.

"Ruddy ain't bad if you aim to please him," Joe responded weakly.

Just then they heard the sound of wheels outside. Joe's name was called in a hard ringing voice. He turned to Rilly saying:

"You ain't got much to leave and you ain't got much to take, so it won't take you long to get ready."

"Yes, I'm goin', Joe," she answered as he went out of the door.

Rilly looked around her in a dazed way and then, seeming to awake to the situation, she spoke to the child who all the while had been staring in wonderment at her father.

"Almy, we're goin'. Pick up them things. Goin' for good." She added to herself, "Your pa won't never have to see your face again."

The things were an old cape and a cap which the child sometimes wore. There was indeed but little to take; Rilly soon made a bundle of their only clothes, and with no other preparation she was ready. No looking glass was in sight but she smoothed her hair back with her hands, as if she stood before one.

"He's goin' to get another woman," she muttered. "But it ain't me so much as it is Almy,—he never could stand her, and I might 'a' known he'd do somethin' like this some day. Well, he never treated her bad, and Ruddy Munroe shan't neither."

Grasping the child tightly by the hand, she stepped to the doorway. Joe was entering and Rilly saw that there was green money in his hand, which he placed on the shelf, setting a heavy dish from the table over it. Then he went out after Rilly into the dusk of the evening.

The short stocky form of Ruddy Munroe was dimly outlined in the half light as he sat in the buckboard; his face could not be clearly seen, but Rilly Ward knew the full straight line of his thick lips, and the bulging eyes that almost seemed to hang over his cheeks. She felt those eyes upon her even in the darkness.

"Well, so long, Joe," Ruddy said in an easy tone, while Joe was awkwardly pushing Almy into the buckboard after her mother. "Don't forget your old friends, Joe, when you get down to the Falls."

Rilly was holding her head high.

"When you leavin', Joe?" she asked casually.

"Day or two," he answered, adding shortly, "Goodbye." His tone sounded relieved.

They drove off in the darkness, Almy clinging close to her mother. They went some distance in silence; then the man spoke in a natural manner.

"Well, Rilly, we're goin' to hitch up all right, I guess, eh?"

Rilly gave an almost unintelligible murmur. It sounded like assent. Almy nestled closer to her.

" 'Course nobody could be sorry for leavin' that place. Even Joe's glad to get out." The man's voice rang out loudly in the night air.

Rilly thought, "It ain't that, he's glad to be gettin' away from," but she did not speak.

"I knew you'd be glad to leave," he went on with assurance. " 'Course we all know Joe's a good sort, but he gets drunk most too much sometimes, eh?"

Rilly tightened her hold on Almy's small form. She seemed to see that white face even in the blackness of the night, the face which was to Joe Ward a constant reminder that he was drunk "most too much."

With a real physical effort she tried to master her feeling of undesire. It was not that she wished to hold to Joe,—no, if he was to get another woman, she could put him out of her thoughts and let someone take his place. She did not know why she should mind much leaving Joe, but it had all happened so suddenly, and a feeling of blackness oppressed her, as heavy as the darkness of the night.

Once Ruddy gave the horse a sharp cut with the whip. Rilly winced and she felt the child cringe. While he talked and Rilly joined in now and then with acquiescence, the two miles along the Wild Cat Road were covered. They drew up to the new house which was only a square black spot in the dark night.

When they had entered Rilly saw that the room in which they stood was clean but bare-looking; it seemed to invite a woman's care. She looked around her at the white plaster walls, and thought of the dark discolored sides of the room she had left, but Ruddy, standing awkwardly nearby, interpreted her glance in his own way.

"Pretty good lookin', ain't it?" he questioned.

She nodded approval and then glanced down at the child who still clung to her.

"Almy, you're getting sleepy." Then she looked questioningly at the man.

"She's so quiet she gets forgot," he said. "But that's all right,—she won't be no bother then. Here you,"—he turned to the child, speaking not roughly but without any feeling—"you sleep there tonight." He indicated a couch in the room. "We'll fix up a place in the loft for you later."

Then he turned to the woman. "You ain't never had no real bedroom to sleep in, livin' with Joe, have you? Well, this ain't no tar-papered shanty."

He was close to her; his cheeks were flushed with cold passion. He caught the woman roughly in his arms, and his kisses were as brutal as blows.

He had forgotten Almy, but while he held her mother he felt the small strong hands of the child upon him. They were like claws ready to tear him. He turned and caught her by the arm, twisting it in his strong grasp. As she gave a low cry he flung her aside.

"You damn brat!" His hard voice was shrill. "You fool-face like your drunken daddy! No wonder he wanted to get rid of you!"

The woman caught up the child in her arms and he went on calmly, "Come now, Rilly, you and me have took each other, and she ain't goin' to be no trouble. I paid a price for you and I ain't goin' to go back on my bargain now. But you little devil,"—he paused and looked at the little creature whose eyes evaded him, "you take yourself to sleep and you and me'll get along all right tomorrow." His full lips loosened into a smile that was meant to be friendly.

Almy was already on the couch, as far as possible from him. Submissively Rilly followed him into the bedroom, but the air of dumb coquetry which she had tried to assume was gone.

Hours later she lay, wide-eyed and wakeful, beside the form of the man now sunk in deep slumber. One thought only filled her mind,— that he had laid his hands on Almy to hurt her, but gradually this gave place to the desire to get away. Brutality to herself she would have taken and borne as a part of her new life, but to Almy—no, she should not be touched. They must get away before it could happen again. They must go while the creature beside her slept.

But where? Back to Joe? No, he was going to get another woman, he had said, and she herself had told him that she was glad to go. No, they could not go back there. Presently she thought that it was the remembrance of the money she had seen which made her thoughts go back to him. She saw him as when he had entered the door of the shanty, the money in his hand, the money which he had put on the shelf under the heavy dish. Her crude mind grasped the idea of the money as a possibility of escape.

She could not formulate any clearly conceived plan, but she felt that if the money could only be secured, they might use it in some way to get away. She thought of reaching Stormytown,—it was only six miles away and there was a stage from there to the railroad at Thurston. Her thoughts ran wild; she had no aim in mind but to get away before Ruddy Munroe awoke. The only thing which she saw clearly was that the money might help,—the money which had been paid for her.

Slowly and stealthily she slid from the bed, and passed into the room where Almy lay on the couch. At her mother's touch she rose without a sound, and in a minute more they were out upon the Wild Cat Road.

No words were spoken until they were far from the house, when Rilly said, "We're never goin' back there, Almy, never." After a pause she went on, "We'll go somewhere away, I don't know where, but we'll aim first to Stormytown. We can get there by mornin'."

The child asked no questions but trudged along by her mother's side with her hand tightly clasped in the woman's. Neither thought of the dense blackness of the night that surrounded them, but a sudden sound broke the stillness and brought terror to their hearts. A cry mingling the wail of human agony with the laughter of fiendish glee sounded from Blueberry Pond.

For a moment the woman shivered with fear, but as the child cowered closer to her she said, "It's only a loon, Almy."

They hastened on, at times almost breaking into a run.

The familiar smell of the swamp greeted their nostrils as they approached the little shanty. They slackened their pace and finally they stopped, until their quick breathing had quieted somewhat.

"It's goin' to rain," Rilly murmured, sniffing the air.

Then they went closer toward the doorway, stepping soundlessly. Upon the intense blackness around them the big tamarack tree seemed to cast a still heavier shadow. The sound of Joe's heavy breathing came through the open doorway.

Rilly dropped the child's hand from her tight grasp and seemed to tell her, without words, to stand still while she went forward.

She was within the doorway, her ears sensing the regular breathing, her mind reaching forward to her grasp upon the money which was now almost within her reach. She raised her hand to the shelf and lifted the dish.

As she took it up and her other hand closed upon the money, the cry of the loon rang out again more faintly like a hideous distorted echo of the earlier sound still ringing in her ears. She gave a nervous shiver and the heavy dish dropped to the floor with a crash.

She started toward the doorway but Joe, aroused by the sound, was before her.

"What!" he thundered. "Who's there?"

She could feel his nearness although she could not see him. She thought of Almy, crouching in the night outside, and she spoke calmly.

"It's only me, Joe,—Rilly. I come—"

"Rilly! You come back?" He was touching her. "What—why—where's Almy?"

"I didn't mean to wake you, Joe. I just come back. I—I somehow knocked the dish off when I heard the loon. Almy!" she called from the doorway, and in an instant the child was beside her.

Joe was making a light. Almy's pale face was chalky white in the yellow glare; the fear in her eyes and the ghastly grin of her mouth made a picture of sickening horror. Joe turned from it and looked into Rilly's eyes.

"How—how—" he stammered, bewildered. "Where is he?" and he peered into the night as if expecting to see Ruddy Munroe enter the doorway.

"Him!" she exclaimed fiercely. "Him! God curse him! He laid his hands on Almy; he hurt her and I'll never go back to him. I was a fool to go!" Her strong ejaculations seemed to have spent her force and her voice trailed off weakly. "He didn't let us come away,—no, we come while he was sleepin'."

"You come back to me?" Joe questioned.

"No, we ain't come back. We're goin' to Stormytown and take the stage out—we just stopped—" she faltered.

"But, Rilly, where'd you go? You can't go on," he protested.

"Well, we ain't comin' here, you needn't fear," she answered shortly. She failed to bring disdain into her words.

Joe's thoughts went back to the cause of their appearance. "Ruddy Munroe! He'll be huntin' for you," he exclaimed, "and he'll be comin' here, I bet!"

At these words Almy reached out her thin nervous fingers and caught her mother's hand again.

"We'll rest a bit," Rilly soothed her. "I can't go on just yet. You don't mind our stayin' a while, Joe? We'll go on before Ruddy Munroe should come."

"We made a bargain, Ruddy and me, and I wouldn't want him to think I'd gone back on it," Joe responded. "But you can't go on, Rilly."

"Well, I've said we was goin' and that's all there is to it."

" 'Course you must rest a while, Rilly, and we'll talk it over. I don't see what you're goin' to do," he ended, going to the door again.

He stood there a long time while Almy and her mother sat within. Not a word was spoken. Rilly glanced now and then at Joe's broad back, but for the most part she sat silently in a dejected attitude of fatigue and despair.

When streaks of grey dawn began to show over the dark outline of Big Elephant Mountain, and the tamarack tree showed its huge shape dimly, Joe turned and said:

"Well, Rilly?"

As he spoke new force seemed to straighten her figure. But before she could answer they heard the sound of wheels on the Wild Cat Road, and in another moment a horse and wagon showed obscurely at the turn of the road. It stopped, and Ruddy Munroe jumped out and approached the shanty. Joe filled the doorway as Ruddy stood on the ground outside.

"Has she come back here?" Ruddy's loud voice rang out. "Didn't I pay for that woman, and didn't she come o' her own accord? What's she get up and leave me in the middle o' the night for?"

Rilly, with Almy clinging to the back of her skirts, had come up to the door. She saw only the big bulging eyes of the man before her as she pushed past Joe. She started to answer Ruddy but Joe spoke first.

"It means that Rilly don't choose to stay, that's all. There ain't no law against it, as I know of, if she wants to."

"Huh!" the man sneered. "So she's come back to you!"

"No, I didn't come back to Joe," Rilly spoke up. "But you shan't never touch Almy again. Why, her own father—" she hesitated—"her own father, what can't bear the sight o' her face, ain't never been mean to her."

"Rilly," Joe interrupted her quietly, "hand back that money to Ruddy, and he can go."

It was the only intimation Joe had given that he knew Rilly held the money and she stared at him in surprise. Nevertheless she held out the money to Ruddy. He reached out his hand for it, and as he did so something in the face of the woman seemed to call the passion of cold anger within him.

The money dropped to the ground as he seized her arm; he held her face back and laid his full lips roughly against it.

"I guess that was comin' to me," he said as he stepped back.

But the words were scarcely spoken when Almy was upon him. Her fierce little hands were reaching for his face and her big eyes were blazing. Only for a moment, however, did she expend her force upon him, for he hurled her from him with a strong thrust that sent her falling back into the shanty doorway.

"You little devil, born of a drunken—". He started to speak, stepping forward as he did so, when Joe's arm struck out. It did not touch him, for Ruddy dodged the blow, but Almy, starting to rise as her lips twisted in a half-frightened, half-pained whimper, caught the spent force of it. She fell, slipping on the spot of greasy gravy which Rilly had thrown from the doorway the night before. Her temple struck the edge of the doorstep and she sank in a little sprawling heap upon the big stone.

She lay strangely still in the grey light of the morning that was dawning.

For a moment Joe stepped back within the doorway, and Ruddy stood outside, a bulky mass of indecision. But Rilly was picking up Almy from the broad stone. The little body sagged as she raised it. Joe stooped beside her and, looking into his face, Rilly spoke dully.

"She's dead, Joe."

"Dead!" breathed Joe, and as he leaned down he saw that it was so.

He took the body from her arms, and carried it to the cot in the dark corner within. The small face looked whiter than ever before, and the thin lips smiled at him fixedly. Rilly sank down on the rough floor beside the cot and hid her face in the old cape which Almy had worn.

She moaned quietly once or twice, and Joe looked down at her helplessly. Ruddy had stepped inside the doorway and stood there awkwardly. He cleared his throat with a thick sound a few times, and then he spoke.

" 'Twasn't your fault, Joe, you know. She sort o' slipped on the step."

"I guess it wasn't nobody's fault," Joe answered weakly. "But what's goin' to be done?"

Rilly raised her head. "There ain't nothin' to be done; nothin' but a pine box now, Joe."

She looked at the quiet face. "Just a little bruise on the temple," she whispered. "We'll tell 'em she slipped. We don't want no trouble. It wouldn't do no good now," she muttered.

Ruddy's hard tones became a little lower as he said, "An' what about after the—the—?" He motioned his hand loosely toward the cot, without looking at it.

"Maybe Rilly won't mind comin' now," said Joe.

"No, I don't mind comin' now," she repeated. "After it's over."

A few minutes later she heard the sound of wheels growing fainter on the Wild Cat Road, and she saw in her thoughts the four-roomed house on the shore of Blueberry Pond, white in the cold morning light, awaiting her.

VICARIOUS FICTION

Waldo Frank

OUR centers of civilization differ from those of Europe in this: that they are cities not so much of men and women as of buildings. The imperious structures that loom over us seem to blot us out. And if our life is vital, we win our knowledge of it rather in what oppresses us than in ourselves. Indeed, we have lavished our forces altogether on the immensities about us, turned our genius into steel and stone, and to these abdicated it. There is a chasm between the created thing and the creator; and everywhere we are the underling and the unformed. We find ourselves smaller than our buildings, and yet we know that until we are greater than the vastest of these, we shall be no true nation. The march of our struggle to win back our power is the American drama.

To an astonishing degree, we have objectified our lives. And we have failed to hold within us the power to experience what we put forth. The results of this have been far-reaching. Not alone our buildings crush us: the laws that we so prodigally spin are shackles; the traditions which in our old homes were the ground beneath our feet, here weigh upon our heads. For all the splendor of our achievements, we have not approached that mastering consciousness which alone can make man greater than the parts of his existence.

The old visions, focussed to old lights, that we brought with us, seem to have been unequal to the task of knitting our American welter of unrelated facts. So, as the chaos cools and the specific groups congeal, we find ourselves inexorably set within them. Each of our little clusters of activity has become a world.

And we are now where the process leads. We have become powerful in particular technics; we have studied the materials of living. But politics and trade and human law are not pivots of existence; and to exalt them so, is to lower ourselves; to become, like them, the creatures and symptoms of uncharted forces. If we stand today more submerged than ever in the American Fact, the reason is that all of us are clinging to some part of it that lies cluttered with the rest.

We have the insufferable sense of a wide futility, of the want of sensitive reaction between ourselves and the whole. But we escape our chaos, not by steeping it with an inclusive vision, but by making ourselves comfortable in it. Our intellectuals are no exception. With a religious earnestness, they fix on whatever element in life is sweetest to their mental habit. They pore over the sentimental or the mechanical or the political man. They deny the existence of what moves beyond their radius and so wall themselves into a smug seclusion. So that today, the superb American opportunity is threatening to break into a wilderness of purposes, tangled, unfriendly, sterile; to shrink into a herd of little men, cowed by the unleashed grandeur of their forces.

What we require is vision. Man is the culmination of the blind life that spews him up, only when he has *felt* that life, when it is fused into his consciousness. His power of vision is his power to experience; to make the boundaries of existence the boundaries of his spirit. Only insofar as he feels infinitude within himself is he a master. And all the elements of nature, all the materials of his hand are hard things indeed to make his own. Intuitively, man has felt this issue and realized that he must be forever re-creating life into a form that he can grasp, if he would not be submerged. And one of the ways of his effort is religion; and the other way is art. By art, he lifts up the more hidden bases of existence and makes them his experience; he achieves that sense of unity and *at-homeness* with an exterior world which saves him from becoming a mere pathetic feature of it.

In all ages, this conduit to mastery seems to have been open to mankind. It is not an intellectual thing. We make our own not what we think, but what we feel. And since through art, the essence and depth of being enters our senses and is absorbed by us, the scope of a people's mastery over life may be indeed the scope of a people's art. Moreover, there have been primitive races rich in these conduits to dominion, even as there have been others, deft and powerful in the mechanics of existence, yet helpless to control them.

The tragic thing is that art also can lose itself in the surface complexities of a civilization; can end by becoming a mere expression of the materials from whose tyranny it rightfully should free us. This, in fact, is the situation that confronts America. And it is amply typified by the contemporary English Novel which today holds so large a place in the American mind.

There is no mystery in the strategic power of the novel. The palette of the novelist is substantially the life around him. This he directs to the aesthetic end, quite as the painter handles pigment. An industrial world turns naturally to that art whose language is so near to its industrial pre-occupation. Moreover, it seems right enough that of all novels, those of contemporary England should appeal to the cultured reader of America. The one formed tradition of our past that has not altogether gone in the diffusion of many races, is the English. And all these novelists write competent, timely and engaging works in a language which is our own. We have no rivals for them here.

But Americans are attracted to these writers not through their inspiration but because of the material that they employ. And they confound the two. At all times, the artist takes what is at hand. If he is a painter of the Renaissance, he will use the conventions and symbols of his Church. If he is a novelist of New York, he will depict the frangor of machinery, the strident unrest of man beneath the tyranny of men. These are his stuffs. But if his art is great, it will have its source in truths of which these are symptoms. If it fails in this, it is bad art: for it lacks the roots by which the vitality of life's source can reach us. And its influence is ill, for it comes to us lacking the sustenance that we require of it.

In this light, consider H. G. Wells. Somewhere in "Tono-Bungay"—somewhere near the book's conclusion—Mr. Wells has his hero say: "I might have called this novel *Waste*." Now, the canvas of "Tono-Bungay" is a wide one. On it are flung (ostensibly) the color and line of modern enterprise: the passion of the struggle, the pathos of the victor. And at the end, Mr. Wells thinks that all of it is *waste*. The reason is not far to seek. Mr. Wells has one engrossing thought: to lay low the capitalistic state. His purpose is commendable. Most of us share it with him. Most of us would have agreed that "all of it was *wrong.*" In fact, the true artist would have made this one hundredfold more clear, simply because he must have made his picture one hundredfold more true. The point is, that to no artist can life be waste however far, in its present symptoms, it fail of a specific economic doctrine. And the point is, farther, that with this attitude, no novelist can present life at all. Mr. Wells does not. If he can sensibly say that the thing he shows is waste, the reason is that this thing is not life but merely a certain surface, a certain result of living. It is this alone that occupies him. Nor do we quarrel with him, because of his concern with political mechanics. When Mr. Wells writes "New Worlds for Old," he is strong. But his novel is an anaemic, superficial semblance, concocted mentally, of life. And it is this because it is altogether wanting in what marks off a work of art from the most compelling tract.

It is the same with his other novels. As a work of art, "Mr. Polly" is a feeble thing; its method and color are plainly acquired from Dickens. We rush unchallenged through mild pages of genre-work; and then betimes Mr. Wells strikes to his true occupation and holds us with a paragraph quoted from some enlightened economist in London, and put there to illumine that external and unfortunately necessary thing, his story. The idea of "Mr. Polly" is not impregnate in his book; the conclusions forced on us are not the integral results of Mr. Polly's life. On the one hand is the weak creative gesture; on the other is the acute political theory. The consequence is an unfused novel, warped from the meager composition it does possess by the thrust-in of quite excellent political doctrine. And without these isolated paragraphs from the economist of London, no educated person would have bothered twice about the book.

The later novels sin still more flagrantly, since with an unflagging journalistic instinct, Mr. Wells has increased his canvas. As politics bellied out and burst in the World War, so "The Research Magnificent" transcribes the globe—and "Mr. Britling Sees It Through." This last novel leaves one amazed at how maturity has puddled the fine early style of Mr. Wells. If, in this book, one gropes through three hundred pages of journalistic writing that sound like a hasty handbook clipped together from a thousand daily columns, one arrives at last at the one thing Mr. Wells was interested in, from the beginning. This thing has been the subject of many serious volumes: Lowes Dickinson's "The European Anarchy," Romain Rolland's "Audessus de la Mêlée," Walter Lippmann's "The Stakes of Diplomacy" among them. One wonders why Mr. Wells felt himself constrained to brush through so much tiresome depiction of the humanities, before he allowed himself his thesis. For in the process, he has maimed his material and missed his goal. The splendid subject of the state of England turns, in his hands, to *impedimenta.* And his political faith falls down, simply because he has pivoted it, not on an honest mental base, but on a falsely motivated novel. "The Research Magnificent" is even a worse hybrid. It holds several striking pictures—a mob in China, warfare in the Balkans. But its grasp of source and impulse is really on a level with that of a cinema like "Intolerance," where, with a like good purpose of pursuing an idea, five continents and thirty centuries are flashed before us. The same grandiose externality, the same blindness to the deeper dimensions of life stamp and shrivel these two works. In the films a false ethical view, in the novel a splendid political passion, excuses the panorama. But in both there is the same untrue divorce between idea and material which is the unfailing mark of falsity in art.

Now, it is plain not alone that novels may include the political factor, but that great novels are unlikely to escape it. Rabelais and Cervantes summed up scholasticism and the Feudal Age, foretold the sweep of individualism, projected a whole vast human epoch. Similarly Stendhal called his "Le Rouge et le Noir," which appeared in 1830, a *chronicle of the Nineteenth Century;* and in a way so deeply prophetic was this true, that France herself was not aware of the grandeur of the book until the century was done. In his book, Stendhal traced the bitter aftermath of individualism, its rise and fall, told the tragedy of post-Napoleonic France, and furnished an undying commentary, a hundred years at least before the fact, for socialism. But the political factor in the works of these great artists sprang—like politics itself—from a deeper source. Their need was to create life in a sensory mold. And such a formulation of the complete human impulse may well include the political in art, as indeed it must, in life. But all this is totally removed from Mr. Wells who starts not with the intuitive need of creation, but with the intellectual program of discussion; who begins with the end-symptom where art may incidentally leave *off*.

Mr. Wells in his books is like ourselves in life. He has failed to impregnate his materials with his ideas. He flounders through his works and ends adrift, because his impulse is not channeled from a source beneath the confusion of his senses, but is itself a symptom of that confusion.

Consider another of our favorites: Arnold Bennett, who, also, is a force thrown out by the industrial hysteria of Great Britain. Mr. Bennett would seem the antithesis of an uprooted aesthete like George Moore, but this deep quality unites them: that they have both discovered the realists of France. Mr. Bennett has read these masters carefully. And he has observed that their outstanding character is a profound devotion to details. Mr. Bennett thinks he can "do" detail himself. He finds plenty of it—and finds it master—in his own "Five Towns." His one error is in his understanding of why detail abounds in the novels of his patterns: and of what he should have done with his own crop of it, at home.

It is impossible here to trace the genesis of French realism: to show how thoroughly it expressed the post-revolutionary search for consciousness, and the revolt from the sort of search that the Encyclopedia set up. France, in her recurrent bewilderments—the intellectual mechanism of Voltaire, the accession of the *bourgeoisie,* the body-blow of Prussia— needed an Inventory. While England was still mulling over Dickens, the art of France passed on to an evaluation of what that Inventory gave her: to impressionism, and in the novel to such masters of it as Charles-Louis Philippe and Anatole France, André Gide and Jules Romains. But the point is, that the accumulations of *genre* notings in Balzac, the Goncourt brothers, Flaubert and Zola were simply fuel for their inspiration. Details occupied their novels because their impulse toward orientation had need of them; because their spirit required material, as a furnace requires coal. If the *Comédie humaine* narrates more details than any other work, the reason is the consuming vastness of the spirit of Balzac. They are the means by which the need of light in Balzac could burst to flame. The details in Balzac are incandescent. The details in Mr. Bennett are sodden. In the case of the one, creation glows through his pages and transfigures them. In the case of the other, the detail is everything. It serves nothing. It proclaims itself master in his books, as it is master in his world. It lacks the interstices of light. ...

With John Galsworthy, however, we have a direct artist, one in whose better work the aesthetic impulse is unrefractedly at play. But if we look deep enough, we find that here also, the creative need is weak. Mr. Galsworthy is inspired by the malady of his own senses, by the fragility of his own sinew rather than by the lush urge of a race spirit coursing through him. Often, he reaches into pleading and propaganda—as in his plays: we find him sinning the sin of the school of Mr. Bennett, reliance on unquickened incident, emphasis on massed detail. But when Mr. Galsworthy is most authentic, he lapses into an extended and exotic dirge that gives him quite away: he dwells on the withering of lopped-off social limbs, the iridescent whirlings of secluded problems. His spirit is a gorgeous, past-nourished flower, uprooted and athirst and rotting with the fair glow of putrefaction.

At bottom, these men are one—and supplement each other. They fail to cut below the upper levels of life. And in consequence, their readers cannot win from them the vision which profound experience affords. Mr. Galsworthy weaves from his helplessness an expression that is at least sincere. The others escape theirs, by ponderous and specific study of the chaos that has overwhelmed them—by an obsession with the mechanics and details of existence. All of them create not out of strength, but weakness.

Indeed, it would look ill for the English Novel, were it not for two men who stand out clearly as exceptions. D. H. Lawrence, author of "Sons and Lovers" and J. D. Beresford suggest at last the vital rebirth of an art which in England has been largely given over since the Eighteenth Century to unquickened spirits. In the novels of Mr. Beresford, a superb sense of the present moves with a pregnant racial restlessness. We feel in him that England is once more to be strong. But while Mr. Lawrence and Mr. Beresford indubitably point to a potential England, they do not primarily concern us here: for they are practically without influence in our country....

America needs, above all things, spiritual adventure. It needs to be absorbed in a vital and virile art. It needs to be lifted above the harry of details, to be loosed from the fixity of results. And it is devoted to an art whose chief attribute is abdication of what it most requires.

We are bound to England by our childhood, by our traditions and habits. We are bound to England by our weaknesses. And we glean from our alliance chiefly the weaknesses of England. Their reflected form of art we choose to reflect once more. Their momentary surrender to the chaos of new industrial conditions, we gladly lean on and make to justify our own. The artists of England who are here most in vogue are precisely those artists who have begged their own spiritual question.

The truth is that we shun the artists who would force us to face ourselves, who might inspire us to work upon ourselves. It is easy at any rate to read about the troubles of other countries; to make remote lands suffer and vicariously solve, to the exclusion of our own reality. Devoted as we are to the consideration of surface parts of our dilemma, we find great joy in books that repeat the tendency. Our spiritual lack makes us read, as theirs makes these authors write. We go to them, since they flatter our weakness, and save our effort. We go to them because, spiritually and geographically, they are remote enough not to prick our bubbles. It would be experience to read Theodore Dreiser; it is only the witnessing of a gladiatorial combat to read Mr. Wells.

Similarly, we ignore Walt Whitman. For Whitman offers no help in the mechanics of existence. His political ideas are inadequate to our immediate problem. And this lack in our greatest poet is the touchstone of his disfavor. We have a consuming fondness for the pat and special seer—be he political or scientific. We cannot forgive the man who would drag us into grips with the entire, uneasy problem.

Our sickness is the kind that resists cure: our symptoms are the sort that crave encouragement. The naive find their opiate in the magazines; the more sophisticated find theirs in the contemporary English Novel. A smaller group, more highly sensitized, achieve their mood of righteousness by reading of reality as it exists in Russia. But all alike, we seek the comfort of the Limit, the ease of what is at once specific and remote. We weaken our receptivity for a provocative and a dynamic art. ...

GROPING

Helen R. Hull

"**W**AS that really true, what you said?"

"What?" Cynthia leaned against the wall, tucking her gray kimono about her feet. From that position she could watch the girl who stood before the mirror, braiding her dark hair. She could even catch glimpses in the glass of the girl's face and firm neck, very white as it rose from the folds of the scarlet bath-robe. "What did I say?" she asked again, although she knew exactly what Mary meant.

"That you'd never kissed any—man?"

"Yes, it's true." Cynthia clasped her thin arms about her knees. "I didn't suppose you did unless you were engaged."

"Bless the child!" Cynthia caught a flash of white teeth in the mirror as Mary flung a long braid over her shoulder. "How'd anybody ever know she wanted to be engaged?"

"I've not been engaged," said Cynthia.

Into her eyes and stubborn little mouth had come an intensity which rested in curious presaging on the thin, sober face with its high forehead. She was thinking that here was another of the things she didn't know about, another of the things she had never talked about until tonight. She hadn't talked much tonight; she had listened. The little dormitory room had taken on an atmosphere of midnight confessional, with youth offering all it knew of life, before the other girls, friends of Mary, had pulled themselves sleepily from their chairs and couch corners and said good-night. Shut in alone with Mary, warm, vivid Mary, Cynthia expanded delicately, pushing out from bonds of reticence. Perhaps Mary would tell her more about love and being engaged after they were in bed. She thrust the question aside, and returned to her delight in Mary's intricate preparations for the night. The crisp rustle of the red ribbon Mary was tying about her head pleased Cynthia; she loved the curve of the white arms, with the loose sleeves flaming back from them.

Mary dropped her brushes and turned.

"There! I'm ready. Tired waiting?"

Cynthia jumped from the couch to help eagerly in the process of despoiling it of cover and reducing it to an ordinary bed.

"Pretty narrow," said Mary, as she slid one of the cushions into a pillow-case. "Guess we can manage, though."

"Oo—it's cold!" she cried, pushing a window open and running back to the bed. "Turn off the light there and hurry!"

In the darkness Cynthia climbed between the covers, trying to make herself as small as possible at the edge of the cot.

"Cuddle up, Goosey!" exclaimed Mary, thrusting an arm under Cynthia's shoulders, and Cynthia thrilled to breathlessness in the warm embrace.

"Didn't anybody ever try to kiss you?" demanded Mary after a moment.

"Once." For some reason Cynthia was glad she could say once, at least. "But I didn't like him to try."

Mary drew her more closely against herself, laying her free hand on Cynthia's cheek.

"How cool your hand is." Cynthia snuggled against it.

"Dear!" murmured Mary, and then, impetuously, "You ought to know how it feels, I think." She lifted Cynthia's face to hers, and her full lips closed on Cynthia's. Cynthia lay very still, but within her slender, inert body something began to whirl and whirl, up to the sweet soft lips of Mary. Suddenly, with a shiver, she pulled away, hiding her face against Mary's throat.

"It's like that," Mary whispered, "love is, only far, far more wonderful. You—you don't mind?" she asked, as Cynthia trembled in her arms.

"Oh, no!" Cynthia drew away from her. "But it frightens me."

"That's just that you didn't know," said Mary. Under the practical tone was a note of uneasiness. "I thought you ought to know." She settled herself more deeply into the pillows. "There's so much a girl has to find out for herself. I did."

"I guess—" Cynthia felt toward Mary with a timid hand. "I guess I have a great deal to find out."

Mary seized her hand and pulled her again into the fragrant curve of her shoulder.

"You're a dear!" she said, and a moment later, sleepily, "If I were a man I'd love you." Her drowsy lips brushed Cynthia's forehead.

Cynthia clung to the hand, full of the delight and the pain of mysterious quickening. More wonderful, Mary had said, and instinct-driven, blind, she yearned for that promise of great wonder. She felt beneath her cheek the slow, regular breathing, as Mary slept. Something rustled. She raised her head cautiously; only the curtain blowing in against the desk. The cold wind tingled in her nostrils, and she dropped back into her shelter. The faint, sensuous odor of white flesh made her glow, and in the dark warmth she drowsed, her mind full of new imaginings that hurried after her into her dreams.

She woke the next morning with a start, wondering what it was she was trying to grasp. Suddenly she remembered; as she looked over at Mary, who was stirring reluctantly, she flushed. Then she pushed the thing away from her thoughts; it didn't belong to the bright morning, someway. Behind her thoughts, however, it still worked, so that she jumped out of bed without minding the chilly room, lowered the window, brought Mary her bathrobe, all in a mood of impersonal gratitude.

Breakfast in the big dormitory dining room was a hasty performance; after that Cynthia helped Mary straighten her room. Then she hurried into her coat and hat, while Mary, grumbling because she must spend the morning in a laboratory, gathered her notebooks.

"I'll walk to the car with you," she told Cynthia, "for a breath of air. Wish you lived in the dormitory instead of home."

They walked briskly across the campus, the snow crunching under their heels. Cynthia slipped her hand in Mary's arm with a little skip.

"Aren't things bright this morning!" she said. "Bright blue, bright black—" they were passing a line of pointed firs—"bright white!"

"Cold, too." Mary pulled her sweater about her throat. "Guess I'll run back here."

Cynthia looked up at her. She was wishing she had Mary's bright color; it fitted into the clear winter day.

"I've had a beautiful time," she said. Then she added quickly, "I'm going to the Assembly tonight."

"With Clark?" Mary's eyes met hers, flashed sudden meaning, and dropped.

"Yes." Cynthia hesitated. At a distant rumble she withdrew her arm. "There's my car. I'll have to run. Goodbye!"

Breathless, she dropped into a seat at the rear of the yellow car which connected the college with the town. She bent her head, adjusting her hat and searching her purse for a handkerchief as several girls followed her into the car. In their furs and velvet hats they made her feel awkward; she didn't know them well, anyway. They seated themselves in seats ahead of her, and as the car jangled its starting bell, Cynthia relaxed comfortably. She could watch them now, without having to strain for some answer to their chatter. For a time she did watch them, wistfully; they were much cleverer than she, much prettier. One of them tucked up a lock of hair with a smoothly white-gloved hand, and Cynthia resented bitterly her own clumsy woolen gloves. Her usual solace, that she could outstrip them in her classes, failed her. They were all beautifully gowned young ladies, and she, outside the pale, a queer, awkward girl. She turned her face toward the frosty window. A whiff of air as the door behind her opened to admit a passenger caught her nostrils, and she slipped into the night before. Half guiltily she lingered a moment at the verge of definite recalling. Was it wicked, when it was so beautiful? Even if it was! Slowly she let herself down into the pool of memory, amazed that she could thrill so at things cool over night. Through the memories came, somehow, the last glance Mary had given her, and swift, uncalled pictures of Clark, the boy with whom she went occasionally to dances. The car's jerk as it swung into a switch aroused her, and she hurried off and up the short block to her home, whipping on an air of great nonchalance as she ran up the steps.

In the entry she stopped, to hang her coat and hat on the rack. As she opened the door into the hall she heard her mother's "Is that you, Cynthia?" and smelled the spicy odor of baking. She followed the voice into the kitchen.

"Well, you're here!" Her mother looked up from the pile of dishes she was drying, the habitual irritation of the tired house-keeper in her tone.

Cynthia glanced about the kitchen, with a vague expectation that she might find something changed; she felt as though she had been gone for a long time. Everything was quite the same, however, even to the oatmeal kettle soaking at the back of the range.

"I came right after breakfast," she defended herself against an imagined reproach.

"There's lots to do," replied her mother.

Cynthia took the long-sleeved apron from the hook and slipped her arms into it, turning for her mother to button it at the neck. She still had a feeling of remoteness; for a moment she had lost her continuity with the familiar routine of home life. Her mother patted her shoulder.

"Did you have a good time?" She put the question in a casual way, and Cynthia answered "Yes" in the same tone. "What shall I do?" she asked quickly, to prevent her mother's keen glance from developing into words.

"I don't know." Her mother sighed. "I've had a bad time with the range. There's everything to do."

"You go and sit down. Let me finish the dishes." Cynthia tried to brush her away from the table.

"No, indeed. If you're ready to work, you can see to the upstairs. And the sitting room's got to be brushed up. Was it a nice meeting?"

Cynthia stopped in the doorway. "Very nice." In a little rush of pity for her mother she added, "And afterwards some of the girls came up to Mary's room and had a spread. The best cake! One of their mothers sent it. And they stayed and talked."

"So you did have a good time." Cynthia walked on into the dining room to hide the accusing flush which had run up into her face. Vaguely in her mind flashed the justification, "Mother doesn't want me to know anything. She thinks I'm just a little girl yet."

"Your father was put out because I let you stay," her mother was saying. "I told him you'd have a better time." The note of satisfaction deepened Cynthia's guilt, and she caught her lip between her teeth to keep back a reflection on her father.

Upstairs it was too cold for loitering. As Cynthia hurried about, spreading the fresh Saturday linen, setting the rooms in order, the pleasant indefinite mood of hands busy with a task and thoughts relaxed came to her. She swept, frosted the cake, helped with the lunch, and waved her mother off for a shopping trip. After she had cleared the luncheon things away, she hung her apron behind the door, and went through the quiet house to the library. Always she found it a pleasant adventure to be left alone in the house, and today! She curled up on the couch under the window, and with a little sigh, slipped into the warm flood of thoughts, of half-imaginings, of trembling dreams.

Late in the afternoon her mother returned, and the two hastened the preparations for supper. Cynthia was filling the water tumblers when her father, after much stamping of feet on the porch, came in. He was a stocky, heavy-shouldered little man, with an obstinate chin.

"Well!" he called out. "Thought you'd make us a little visit, did you?"

Cynthia frowned; it was difficult not to take her father's jokes too seriously. Through supper she was silent, eating listlessly, saying nothing, except in answer to questions. At the end, she pushed back her chair.

"I'll have to go and dress, mother."

"Why?" Her father gazed at her sharply. "Where are you going tonight?"

"Just to the Assembly," said the mother quickly.

"What for? You were out all last night."

"Last night," Cynthia said, struggling to speak in a very dignified tone, "was only the literary society at college. I haven't been to a dance for a long time."

"Humph. Who are you going with? That college fellow?"

"Yes." With an imploring glance at her mother, Cynthia fled up the stairs. She heard the protesting murmur of her mother's voice as she shut herself into her own room.

Her father certainly could be most unreasonable! But the deeper concern of dressing for the evening drove her father out of mind. First she brushed her fair hair, trying to fluff it out about her temples, and sighing as it proved too fine and soft. She tied a blue ribbon about it, leaning forward anxiously to peer at the result. She bit her lip; was the ribbon better than no ribbon? She decided to wear it, turning from her reflection with a flush of distress that she was so plain. From the closet she brought her blue dress, slipping it over her head, and fastening it with a little shrug of resignation. How could anyone be pretty who wore always the same clothes?

She waited an eager minute after the bell rang at eight. Perhaps it wasn't Clark. But she caught his "Good evening, Mr. Bates," and laughed to herself in pleasure at his deep formality. As she reached the foot of the stairs her mother sent her an anxious glance; she may have seen a hint of new flowering in the palely flushing face. Cynthia extended her hand, her eyes seeking the face of the boy, as though she thought to find it altered. He looked exactly as he always had; a clear, high-cheekboned face, with practical eyes and immature lips. Cynthia lingered in the doorway while her father asked a grave question concerning the tariff. She didn't hear Clark's answer; she thought, instead, how strong he looked, in his rough overcoat. Finally they were free to go. As they ran down the steps Clark seized her arm.

"I feel in jolly shape," he said. "Let's dance every dance."

Cynthia swung up to tiptoe and laughed. How he towered above her in the crisp dark! She could just see the outline of his face and the puffs of white steam his words made.

"Let's dance them all—together!" she exclaimed.

"That's the stuff. Let's hurry!"

The Assembly Hall was only a few blocks from the house, in the second story of an office building. Never had its windows shone more brightly, Cynthia was sure.

"Oh, I'm glad I can dance." Cynthia didn't know she had spoken aloud, until Clark pressed her arm more firmly.

"You feel good, too, don't you? Let's hurry!"

And they ran together up the wide wooden stairs to the second floor. The hour for the dancing lesson was just over, and a few of the more venturesome beginners were trying their steps on the polished floor, while the orchestra—a pianist and two 'cellists—tried their strings and hunted for the music of the first number of the real assembly. Cynthia hung her coat in the stuffy little cloakroom, sent a swift glance at her blue ribbon in the tiny mirror, for once indifferent to the other girls about her, and sped back to the hallway. Clark was there; she appraised quickly the other waiting males. Not one so tall, so straight, so clean as he, she thought.

It was a new, gay Cynthia that evening, so light that Clark declared she was nothing but the music itself. Her former sober delight in dancing had vanished; she herself did not know how she had come into possession of cajoleries, of daring words, of glances more daring, of eyes swiftly averted. When they swung out to the last waltz, Clark's hand tightened over hers.

"I wish we needn't stop." He bent over her, his breath fanning her cheek.

Cynthia's eyelids drooped; she was nothing but a reed through which the rhythmic motion ran. When the music stopped she went silently for her wraps, something within her hurting a little that the end had come.

They were both silent as they went out into the dark, frosty street. Cynthia shook her head at Clark's "Are you cold?" Her shoulder touched his arm, and in the dark her eyes widened. She slipped on the crusty walk, and Clark caught her hand. "You're shivering!" he exclaimed. "Here!" Then his arm was around her waist. Cynthia felt the rough coat almost against her cheek, felt her heart whirling within her. They crossed the street and mounted the steps of her home. At the door Cynthia pulled away.

"You—you might come in—" she said faintly.

"I might." Clark had a brusk nonchalance in his voice. "I'd like to get warm before I take my car."

They pushed the door softly open and entered. Cynthia's lips parted with a quick breath as she saw the empty sitting room. Her mother had not sat up for her.

"Let me take your coat." Clark's fingers were at her throat, unhooking the collar. She couldn't lift her eyes, but she wheeled, eluding his arms. She shook off the coat, and ran across the room.

"It's warmer over here by the register."

She faced him, leaning back against the wall, her hands outspread. With fluttering wings within her breast, she watched him as he came slowly toward her. Something made her raise her heavy hands to pull the pins from her hat and drop it at her feet. The boy brushed it to one side and stood close to her. The fluttering wings ceased, and Cynthia thought in swift panic that she could even yet stop, could rush back to the old safe ground. This was happening because she had wished it. But Clark whispered "Cynthia! Cynthia!" and she lifted her tender, wishing face. Then he had her in his arms, his lips eager against hers; her heart was molten quicksilver, escaping from her. Clark drew her down into a chair, and knelt beside her, lifting her quivering fingers to his lips and cheek. For a moment they remained thus, Cynthia in a silent ecstacy, pouring herself out through her finger tips. At a sound somewhere above them in the house, Clark got quickly to his feet.

"I suppose I ought to go," he said, listening uneasily. "It's pretty late."

Yes, it was late. Cynthia held her breath to listen. Her father might come to the stairs to call her up to bed. There was no sound again. But Clark moved toward the door.

"I'd better go."

Cynthia rose. Go? Now—? Her eyes alone made protest. At the door the boy stopped.

"Aren't you going to say good-night?" he asked softly.

Cynthia clasped her cold hands. He was going, and in that way!

"Good-night."

"That's not the way, Cynthia." He held his hands to her. "Here!"

She swayed, staring at him, held by a thread of sudden fear. With a sigh she broke the thread and ran to him, clinging to him, swinging up, up against his lips. Her own intensity frightened her, and she thought she was falling, until Clark released her, and she found herself standing in the entry, back in her own body. He was opening the door; she tried to say, "You will come again, soon—" but her lips would not move to the words.

"Good-night," he whispered, and was gone.

She set the night-latch, snapped off the light, and climbed the stairs quite without volition. A voice as she reached the hall above startled her so that she stumbled. "Did you lock the door, Cynthia?" "Yes," she answered, terrified lest her voice might betray her. But her mother called "Good-night," and Cynthia, gaining her room, pushed the door shut and waited in the darkness for her heart to cease pounding in her throat. She undressed rapidly, her mind yearning ahead to the kind shelter of her bed. Finally she lay there, straight and motionless. She would go over the evening moment by moment. Deliberately she returned to the beginning. Suddenly through her body flickered this new emotion, and she turned, hiding her face in the pillow, pulling herself against the bed to quiet the frightening quivers that ran through her. This—this must be love itself! She felt the pillow wet under her cheek; she hadn't known she had cried. She pressed her lips against it, moaning a little. It was wonderful, but terrifying, not to be understood. A crumpled leaf, she whirled up and up in the strong wind of desire she could neither see nor resist, until she slept.

Cynthia, the next day, struggled across the hours of a humdrum Sunday in a valorous attempt to pretend she was the same Cynthia. She was afraid someone would discover her secret; it glowed within her breast until she knew it must shine out and betray her. Not until after the late Sunday dinner, when under pretext of studying, she could retreat to her room with her books, was she free. Sitting by her window, her chin propped on her hands, she drifted quite clear of the tedium of the day.

In the early winter evening the doorbell sounded in the house below. Cynthia jumped to her feet, and flinging open her door, ran to the head of the stairs. Could it be—it was! She heard Clark ask for her. She was downstairs in an instant, flashing past her father into the entry. In a moment she was again in the sitting room, her head thrown high.

"Clark can stay just a little while." Her voice defied her family. "We're going out for a short walk."

"You'll freeze to death," remarked her father, who was settling himself with his book.

"I've not been out all day." Cynthia spoke quickly. "I'll not be gone long."

She pulled a cap over her hair, wound a scarf about her throat, and shaking herself into her coat, joined Clark in the little entry.

"Quick!" she whispered. "Before they decide it's too cold."

Out in the street the lassitude of the day lifted from her. She walked provokingly at the far edge of the sidewalk, chattering of everything which drifted into her head. At the corner she turned into a street recently laid out, and but little built up. Clark, his hands in his pockets, gave sulky answers to her flitting queries. Then her chattering snapped off, and there was no sound but the cold talk of snow under their feet. A man passed them, peering over his shoulder before he disappeared into the night. The snow-covered fields were faintly luminous, with here and there a light picking out the window of a distant house. Cynthia felt Clark moving more closely toward her; they were alone in the bare little street. He touched her arm, and then their cold lips, clinging together, grew warm and moist. They walked on again, Cynthia's hand tight in Clark's. She glanced shyly at him; she was saying to herself, "I love you—I love you." Her lips tingled in the cold air; she felt radiant, as though her singing blood illumined her. She held her face up for a swift little kiss, laughing.

"I say——" Clark pressed her hand. "I've wanted to kiss you for a long time. I didn't know you were like this."

"Like what?" Cynthia wished she could see his face as he bent over her.

"Oh—liking to be kissed, you know."

"I never have!" Cynthia drew back from his face, her voice low with an instinctive pride in the value of her gift to him.

"What? Never? Oh, come!"

Cynthia was troubled; he shouldn't jest about this, even if he did wish to tease her. "Certainly not," she said, gravely.

"Oh, well! Most girls do."

"Do the girls you know?" Cynthia flung out the question as a recoil from the pain of his words.

"Why, yes." Clark paused, and then blundered ahead. "It's more fun going together then. Isn't it?"

Cynthia shrank away from his arm.

"You mean——" and her voice was thin and white like her breath in the winter air—"You mean you do it—for fun?"

"Well, don't you?" Clark demanded. "You let me," he added uncomfortably.

Cynthia was hurrying along, head bent; she wanted to escape the ogre of realization which pursued, close at heel.

"Don't go so fast!" Clark grasped her arm. "You—are you cross?"

"Cross?" Cynthia jerked out a little laugh. "I'm just cold. Let's hurry home. It seems much colder."

"Well, if you want to go home, that isn't the way." Clark failed in his attempt at facetiousness, but his words halted Cynthia. The slight wind drove the cold all into her heart. She couldn't see where they had come.

"It's back this way." Clark wheeled. "If you are cold—"

Without waiting for the end of his sentence, Cynthia turned and ran past him, her scarf fluttering over her shoulder. "It's warmer—running—" she panted, as she heard his feet close behind her.

"All right, come on!" She was scarcely aware that Clark thrust his arm through hers. The air stung her throat; her breath seemed to freeze before it reached her lungs. She ran and ran; where was the corner? The sidewalk began to lurch up to meet her feet. She stumbled, and Clark dragged her up.

"You're all out of breath," he gasped, but she only shook her head.

Just as her feet grew so heavy that she knew she couldn't lift them, she saw ahead the dark mass of the elm which reached up to her window, and then across the snow, patches of light from the sitting room windows. Wrenching her arm free, she whirled ahead, up the steps to the door, where, her fingers clutching the handle, she faced the boy. Stronger than her need to escape, now, was her need to send him away unwitting, to fill his eyes with dust of some untruth, that he might not see her wound.

"I——beat——you!" She shrank against the door.

"You have to pay for that!" His quick breathing burned her cheek.

Her spirit doubled and twisted like a cornered wild thing. What could she say so that he would go—would go, not knowing? His hands were on her shoulders; she pushed them off.

"No! Not any more!" she cried. "You—you'll have to run for your car. I hear it coming."

"But Cynthia—little girl!" The throaty humoring protest was close in her face.

She turned the knob, and stepped into the open door.

"You can't kiss me," she said, distinctly. "I don't think it's much fun. It's rather stupid. Good night."

She closed the door and listened, in panic lest he follow her. After a moment she heard his feet, thoughtful, pausing once, and then descending the steps to the street.

She wheeled with a start as the inner door opened.

"I thought I heard you, Cynthia. What you doing here in the cold?" Her mother held the door wide. "Clark gone?"

"Yes." Cynthia clenched her hands, as though to gather all her emotions there, secure from suspicion, until she could be alone. "Yes. He had to go. I'm just taking off my things."

"Was it pretty cold?" Her mother lingered.

"Dreadfully."

"You shouldn't have gone out again tonight."

Cynthia plunged desperately into the bright sitting room; there was no way to avoid the light. She was afraid to sit down there, where everything had happened last night. Her father and mother would guess!

"I think I'll go to bed," she said. The stairs beckoned to her. "I'm tired."

"Are you sick, Cynthy?" Her mother's voice came after her.

"No. Not a bit." Cynthia was already halfway to the head of the stairs. "Just tired. Good-night."

She wished to lock her door, but she feared lest someone discover that she had done that and demand her reason. So she turned on the light and began to undress, thankful as many older people have been, for the reprieve of a moment through an habitual act. Her shoestring had knotted; she pulled at it with a little sob, and it broke. At length she stood by her bed buttoning her flannel nightgown. Her body felt cold as she touched it with her hand; that was strange, when waves of heat were beating in her head. She climbed slowly into bed letting herself down into the cold sheets with a shudder.

Out of the confusion of emotions that blurred and moved at the horizon of her consciousness, one emerged, expanded, grew distinct, and scorched through her. She was ashamed, ashamed. "You let me!" Clark had accused her, and she had let him. More than that, she had wished him to love her—had worse than asked him. And he had thought it fun! She would have this shame to hide all her life. She must be very sinful, a girl who liked that—she could not think the word for the caresses—when there was no love behind them. Was this the way one's heart broke? She pressed her fingers against her small breasts. She wouldn't hide her face in her arm; that would be childish—she might even cry then. This was no young sorrow, to be melted in tears. Why had she been so shameless? Through her body quivered a poignant memory, unbidden, of Clark's flushed face close to hers, of his lips. She drove the recollection away, the hot shame running up into her very eyelids.

"Oh, I don't love him!" she cried. In a moment of white penetration, she caught back her former attitude toward the boy; she had accepted him with a thoughtless tolerance because he was jolly, and tall, and personable. She sat up in bed, her lips moving. "Oh, I don't know why I did it!" Within her worked an inarticulate bewilderment that things without reality could seem so beautiful, could cause such emotion.

At the sound in the hall she dropped back against the pillow pulling the clothes up to her chin. As the door opened carefully she held her breath; she would pretend to sleep.

But her mother came in and sat down on the bed.

"I've brought you some hot cocoa, Cynthy," she said, and Cynthia knew she was peering anxiously through the dimness. "You'll sleep better."

Cynthia could see the swirl of steam from the cup held toward her. She didn't want it! But drinking it might be the quickest way to regain solitude. Propping herself on an elbow, she gulped recklessly choking a little as she tasted the thick sweetness. It brought tears into her eyes, but that, and the hot pain in her chest after she had swallowed, gave her a curious relief, as if she suffered in atonement for a sin. She lay down again, shrinking from her mother's hand as it touched her forehead.

"You aren't sick, Cynthia?"

"No, I said I wasn't."

"Is anything the matter?"

Cynthia's heart gave a jump, and then ran into quick beating, in her breast, in her throat, in her temples. Had her mother heard—last night? Had she guessed?

"Why, no!" she exclaimed, and then added hastily, "What made you think so?"

"You haven't had a quarrel with Clark?" Her mother's voice was a worried, repressed caress.

"No." Cynthia bit off her laugh suddenly; it felt as if it were about to run up into a scream. "We—we never quarrel. What would we quarrel about?"

"Well," her mother sighed. "You aren't going too far with him, are you? He isn't worth it. Your father says he's just a light-weight fellow."

"I don't know what you mean. You want me to have some fun, don't you?"

She hadn't meant to say quite that, and the phrase "some fun" was a hot wind, shrivelling her against the pillow. Remotely she heard her mother.

"Of course. But I don't want anybody to make you unhappy. You're too young for that sort of thing."

Cynthia stared at her mother's face, just visible in the streak of light from the hall lamp. "That sort of thing!" Then her mother knew—had some knowledge about things. Unconsciously Cynthia groped toward her; perhaps she would explain. Before her hand touched that of her mother, however, it dropped, checked by the old habit of inhibition. Her mother would not understand. She would say, "You are too young to think of such things."

And when the mother, a little wistfully, brushed the hair from Cynthia's forehead, and leaning over, kissed her cheek, Cynthia lay very still, struggling with a resentment which seemed disloyal, a resentment that these older people had knowledge they concealed so carefully.

Her mother rose.

"Good-night, dear. You were up too late last night, I guess. And you probably talked all the night before. Go right to sleep. I'll call you in time tomorrow."

In the doorway for an instant she paused, a rather weary silhouette; then Cynthia was alone again.

She was sleepier; the brief contact with her usual life had dulled the edge of her emotions. At any rate, no one knew. Clark didn't know; he would think she had been playing with him. And her mother didn't guess. She turned curling her arm under her head. Mary wouldn't ask her questions. She opened her eyes for a moment. Did Mary know things, she wondered, except the feeling of them? She closed her heavy eyelids. "Am I very sinful," she thought. Turning a little more, she pressed her eyes against her arm wondering dimly why the gold and blue spots danced about on her eyelids. Perhaps, if she understood more, she would become better. With a faint sigh she slept.

THE ESCAPE

J. D. Beresford

1.

ALBERT HIGGS was beleaguered by all the circumstances of his life. He even found a word for his condition. "I'm *beset*," he thought, as he travelled home in a third-class compartment of the North London Railway, six a-side.

The discovery brought him a momentary relief. Since four o'clock in the afternoon, more than two hours before he had left the office, he had been increasingly harassed by the necessity to find some word for his condition. The trouble and strain of it came between him and his work. As he almost automatically copied figures into the ledger, some part of his mind had been wearily, perpetually engaged in a hopeless struggle to find this world. He had visualized it quite distinctly as an enormously active beetle that traversed complicated figures with a horrid vivacity. If only he could have held it still, for one moment. ... And, now, he had it. It was no longer a beetle,—although the resem blance was quite obvious,—but a plain line of black sans-serif capitals BESET.

He knew that he was in for another attack of influenza. That knowledge was the latest ally to join the beleaguering forces. Some men in Albert Higgs' position might have raised the siege, have laid down their arms and weakly submitted to the inevitable. Higgs was not that sort of man. He meant to flap impotent hands in the face of Fate until he was too weak to lift his arms; after that he would put his tongue out.

For ten years he had been braced to the struggle and resistance had become a habit with him.

Nothing had ever gone right. He was the most conscientious worker in the office, but other clerks had been promoted over his head. The manager was always finding fault with him for being so slow. Perhaps he was slow. He liked to be absolutely certain about every detail connected with his work.

Then he was the only tenant in Golden Oak Road who appeared to have trouble with his landlord. He liked a house to be sound; and he was at considerable pains to see that defects did not go too far before they were remedied. He often wished that he had never taken No. 69. It was without doubt the worst house in the road; and an altogether disproportionate amount of his spare time was occupied in looking after it.

Worst of all, his marriage could hardly be counted a success. Emily was a good wife in many ways, but she was so abominably careless about vital details. She could not realize the importance of method and accuracy either in housework or cooking. He was always being forced to remonstrate with her, but she never improved.

And all these worries seemed to be steadily accumulating. He never had a moment, now, that was not filled by the necessity to counter some new difficulty. He was in no way daunted; he had no intention of relaxing his immense fight with adverse circumstances for a single instant, but he felt that it was very hard that he of all men should have been thus singled out for perpetual persecution. ...

"I've got a temperature," he announced as his wife came out of the kitchen to meet him.

"Then you'd better get off to bed at once," she said with her usual disregard of the practicalities.

"How can I get off to bed?" he asked, patiently. "You know there's that pipe in the kitchen to be seen to; and the loose board in the spare bedroom; and I'm going round to catch the landlord if I can. Being a Jew, he's sure to be in on a Friday night."

"Oh! them things can wait," Emily said.

"You'd let the house fall down if you had your way," he replied without temper.

"No fear of that yet awhile," she said with a laugh. "Now you get off to your bed and I'll make you some nice hot gruel."

"I've got them things to see to first," replied Albert Higgs.

But even as he was struggling to investigate an imaginary leakage in the waste-pipe of the kitchen sink, his influenza that had seemed so much better as he was on his way home began to attack him again. He had forgotten his splendid key-word, and there was the beetle come back, gyrating in the flicker of the candle-end he was holding.

His wife found him squatting on the floor. She took the candle-end from him and helped him to his feet. She was cheerful but very determined.

"Now, my lord, you come along with me," she said, "or I'll be having *you* on me hands next."

He did not resist her, then. He was intent on renaming the beetle, and everything else had temporarily lost importance. But when he had eaten the hot gruel his wife brought him, he remembered the word.

"I'm beset, Emily," he said.

"You won't be in the morning," she replied foolishly. "You have a good sleep and you'll be right as rain by tomorrow."

He shook his head. "I've always been beset," he said.

"It'll wear off," she said; and left him before he could find a suitable reply.

For a time he tried against his will to turn "beset" into "bested," but some letter evaded him, and then "bedstead" presented itself as a still more worrying alternative.

"It's no good lying here," said Albert Higgs aloud to the spaces of the room. "I'd better get up and see to that sink; it's got to be done some time."

2.

He got up at once, but his feet would not touch the floor. At first this intriguing phenomenon was decidedly exasperating, but little by little a great calm settled upon him.

He found that he was suspended over the bed regarding the image of a man who lay on his back and stared fixedly up at the ceiling. He was not an attractive person, this interloper who had settled himself into Albert Higgs' bed. He had a look of bigoted obstinacy, as if he had set himself some perfectly futile task and meant to go through with it no matter who suffered in the performance. He was a small, rather weedy man, Higgs noticed, with high cheek bones and a narrow forehead; he was getting bald, too, and had a little scrubby moustache. Higgs found him almost repulsive, and moved up a few yards to get away from him.

From his new position, he could see the whole of number 69, Golden Oak Road; not only the front of the house but the four walls, the roof and the interior of every room; one comprehensible fragment of building. The sight of it, thus separated and complete, interested him for a time. He saw that it was ugly and badly built, that it could not hold together for many years; but even as he fiercely criticized it, the house became fused with all the other houses in the road; and he saw the long line of them as an indivisible whole. They were all alike, all equally ugly and with the same defects; and little figures moved about them, some satisfied and careless, others anxiously attempting useless repairs.

Then his sight of the road became merged into a vision of the district of Gospel Oak, which lay below him in strong relief as if he saw it from a high roof. He could look down into the channels of the streets, picked out from the general gloom by the regular points of their little rows of lamps. And thousands of tiny figures swarmed in the streets and in the houses, all apparently precisely alike, moving hither and thither, tracing some indefinable pattern on a background, which continually increased in area so that the black spaces of Hampstead Heath were becoming included in his vision and the glare of Camden Town High Street....

Presently he was able to locate Oxford Street and Piccadilly Circus, the outlined, threaded darkness of the Parks, and the wide curves of the river; but the great spread of London was rapidly falling to a mere discoloration on a shallow saucer tipped by the hills of Buckinghamshire and Surrey....

And the saucer was losing its concavity as it steadily grew in extent, slowly flattening, even reversing itself so that it was faintly convex. Round the edges of it a paler darkness crept, indenting the blackness of the land, outlining a section of the irregular but curiously familiar shape of the map of England. The wedge-shaped strip of the English Channel swam up until a silhouette of the French Coast pushed into the horizon; the German Ocean encroached and spread to the right; Scotland and Ireland curved down in the vague distance, dwindling before the invasion of the Atlantic. The panorama filled the field of vision like a dark sky that was turning itself slowly inside out, becoming continually more convex as it receded. And in the East a white full moon rose over Europe and the edge of the sun showed a brilliant scimitar on the verge of the Atlantic. ...

The immense convexity of the earth was flattening again, and the vast bulk of it no longer filled the universe. The sun and moon seemed to be drawing apart, and the moon was no longer full; an irregular clipping had gone from its upper edge as if a piece of it had been jagged away by Titanic pliers. The earth, itself, was in its last quarter, a gigantic crescent stretching across two-thirds of the arc of the heavens; the faintly moonlit mass of it showing as a gloomy circle against the blackness of space, pierced now by innumerable points of light, the steady brilliance of infinitesimal stars.

But as it fell into the depths of space, the Earth waned. The sun that had so miraculously risen was eclipsed behind its western edge; and the moon grown to the apparent size of its primary was rushing up to obscure in turn the whole width of the heavens. For a time it loomed as an enormous sphere, shutting out all sight of earth and stars, and then it, too, dwindled, became a void circle among the constellations of the Milky Way, and so vanished into the abyss. ...

The sun shone one brighter point among the myriads that enclosed the spirit of Albert Higgs.

3.

"Well, you have had a sleep," said the voice of Mrs. Higgs. "I tried to wake you up an hour ago, but you was so heavy I thought I better let you lie. Do you know what the time is? It's past eight. And you'll be late at the office unless you'd like me to send a telegram to say you're ill."

Higgs stared at her. He felt curiously peaceful and still.

The morning sunlight lay across the foot of his bed.

"I'm only just awake," he remarked.

"Well, I can see that for myself," said his wife. "Only as you're so particular about little things perhaps you'll just tell me whether you mean to go to the office today or not."

"It isn't of the least consequence," replied Albert Higgs.

LIFE, ART AND AMERICA

Theodore Dreiser

I DO not pretend to speak with any historic or sociologic knowledge of the sources of the American ethical, and therefore critical, point of view, though I suspect the origin, but I, personally, am at last convinced that, whatever its source or sense, it does not accord with the facts of life as I have noted or experienced them. To me, the average or somewhat standardized American is an odd, irregularly developed soul, wise and even froward in matters of mechanics, organizations, and anything that relates to technical skill in connection with material things, but absolutely devoid of any true spiritual insight, any correct knowledge of the history of literature or art, and confused by and mentally lost in or overcome by the multiplicity of the purely material and inarticulate details by which he finds himself surrounded.

As a boy in the small towns, in which I, at least, was raised, I personally had no slightest opportunity to get a correct or even partially correct estimate of what might be called the mental A B abs of life. I knew nothing of history, and there was not a book in any of the schools which I attended labeled either history, or science, or art, called to my attention, which contained the least suggestion of the rationale which I subsequently came to feel to be relatively true, or at least acceptable to me.

If I remember correctly, in the history of the world which was labeled Swinton's, the defeat of Napoleon, not his career, was pointed out as having had a great moral, if not Christian, value to the world. His end on St. Helena (not the code Napoleon, or the hieratic and ultra economic arrangement of his material forces) was supposed to have achieved something for society! Similarly Socrates and his death were descanted on as having almost a religious, if not a Christian import. His death was painted as having been brought about by his higher moral views—not his private deeds! The true significance of the man as illustrated by the exact details of his life were utterly ignored. I could go on by the hour, the day, the week.

Personally, because my father was a Catholic, and I was baptized in that faith, I was supposed to accept all the dogma, as well as the legends of the Church, as true. In the life around me I saw flourishing the Methodist, the Baptist, the United Brethren, the Christian, the Congregationalist, the what-not churches, each one representing, according to its adherents, the exact historic and truthful development and interpretation of life or the world. As a fourteen or fifteen year old boy, I listened to sermons on hell, where it was, and what was the nature of its torments. As rewards for imaginary good behavior I have been given colored picture cards containing exact reproductions of heaven! Every newspaper that I have ever read, or still can find to read, has had an exact code of morals, by the light of which one might detect at once both Mr. Bad Man and Mr. Good Man, and so save one's self from the machinations of the former! The books which I was advised to read, and for the neglect of which I was frowned upon, were of that naive character known as pure. One should read only good books—which meant, of course, books from which any reference to sex had been eliminated and what followed as a natural consequence was that all intelligent interpretation of character and human nature was immediately discounted.

A picture of a nude or partially nude woman was sinful. A statue equally so. The dance in our home and our town was taboo. The theater was an institution which led to crime. The saloon a center of low, even bestial, vices. The existence of such a thing as an erring or fallen woman, let alone a house of prostitution, was a crime, hardly a fact to be considered. There were forms and social appearances which we were taught to wear, quite as one wears a suit of clothes. One had to go to church on Sunday whether one wanted to or not. It was considered good business, if you please, to be connected with some religious organization, and, by the same token, this commercialized religiosity was transmuted into a glistening virtue! A young man who went to church for that reason was not a low mountebank or shameless interloper, but an individual of moral worth! We were taught persistently to shun most human experiences as either dangerous or degrading or destructive. The less you knew about life the better. The more you knew about the fictional heaven and hell, the same. People walked in a form of sanctified maze or dream, hypnotized or self-hypnotized by an erratic and impossible theory of human conduct, which had grown up heaven knows where or how, and had finally cast it amethystine spell over all America, if not over all the world.

Now, I have no particular quarrel with this, save that it is so impossible, so inane. In my day there were no really bad men who were not practically known as such to all the world, or at least quickly detected, and few, if any, good men who were not sufficiently rewarded by the glorious fruits of their good deeds! Positively, I stake my solemn word on this, until I was between seventeen and eighteen, I had scarcely begun to suspect that any other human being was so low as to harbor the erratic and sinful thoughts which occasionally flashed through my own mind.

At that time I was actually beginning to suspect that some of the things which had been laid down to me by one authority and another, and which I have here previously indicated in a brief way, were not true. All so-called good men were not necessarily good, I was beginning to suspect, and all bad men not hopelessly bad. There were things in cities and towns which, as I was beginning to see, did not accord with the theories of the particular realm from which I sprang, and seemed to indicate another kind of human being, different to the type among which I had been raised. My mother, as I was beginning to suspect—admire her as much as I might—was a mere woman, not an angel; my father a mere, mere crotchety man. My sisters and brothers were individuals such as I soon began to find were breasting the stormy waters of life outside, and not very different to all other brothers and sisters—not perfect souls set apart from life, and happy in the contemplation of each other's perfections. In short, I was beginning to find the world a seething, stormy, bitter, gay, rewarding and destroying realm, in which the strong and the subtle and the charming and the magnetic were apt to be victors, and the weak and the homely and the ignorant and the dull were apt to be deprived of any interesting share, not because of any innate depravity but rather because of the lacks by which they were handicapped and which they could not possibly overcome.

Furthermore, there were other phases which I had previously scarcely suspected. The race, if you please, was to the swift, and the battle to the strong. All great successes, as I was beginning to discover for myself, were relatively gifts, the teachings of the self-helpers and the virtue mongers to the contrary notwithstanding. Artists, singers, actors, policemen, statesmen, generals, were born, not made. Sunday school maxims, outside of the narrowest precincts, did not apply. People might preach one thing on Sunday or in the bosom of their families or in the meeting places of conventional social groups, but they did not practise them except under compulsion, particularly in the stores and wholesale houses and the marts of trade and exchange. Mark the phrase "under compulsion." I admit a vast compulsion which has nothing to do with the individual desires or tastes or impulses of individuals. That compulsion springs from the settling processes of forces, which we do not in the least understand, over which we have no control, and in whose grip we are as grains of dust or sand, blown hither and thither, for what purpose we cannot even suspect. Politics, as I soon found (working as a newspaper man and otherwise), was a low mess; religion, both as to its principles and its practitioners, a ghastly fiction based on sound and fury, signifying nothing; trade was a seething war in which the less subtle and the less swift or strong went under, while the more subtle succeeded; the professions were largely gathering places of weaklings, mediocrities or mercenaries, to be bought by, or sold to, the highest bidder.

The individual, as I found, was trying to do one thing: make himself happy, principally. Life was plainly trying to do another, or at least what it was doing involved no great concern for the welfare of any particular individual. He might live; he might die; he might be well fed; he might be hungry; he might accidentally, or by taking thought, ally himself with successful movements, or he might inherently, by some incapacity or fatality of disposition, involve himself in the drifts toward failure; he might be weak; he might be strong; he might be wise; he might be dull or narrow. Life in the large threshing sense in which we see it to move about us cared no whit for him. Why so many failures? I was constantly asking myself. Why so many stores closed for want of business? So many fires? So many cyclones? So many destroying epidemics? So many failures in health or in trade or by reason of vice or crime? So many, many individuals going down into the limbo of nothingness or failure, so few attaining to that vast and lonesome supremacy which all were seeking? Why? Why? I persistently asked myself, and I have yet to find the answer in any current code of morals or ethics or the dogma of any religion.

However, it is not a picture of my own mental development that I am trying to put forward; rather one of life. My concern is with the mental and critical standards of America as they exist today, and of England, from which they seem to be derived. England—the home of bourgeois art and bourgeois accomplishment. The average American, as I have said before, has such an odd, such a naive conception of what the world is like, what it is that is taking place under his eyes and under the sun.

If you should chance to consult a Methodist, a Baptist, a Presbyterian, a Lutheran, or any other current American sectarian, on this subject, you would find (which, after all, is a dull thing to point out at this day and date) that his conception of the things which he sees about him is bounded by what he was taught in his Sunday school or his church, or what he has stored up or gathered from the conventions of his native town. (His native town! Kind heaven!) And, although the world has stored up endless treasuries of knowledge in regard to itself chemically, sociologically, historically, philosophically—still the millions and millions who tramp the streets and occupy the stores and fill the highways and byways, and the fields, and the tenements of the city, have no faintest knowledge of this, or of anything else that can be said to be intellectually "doing." They live in theories and isms, and under codes dictated by a church or a state or an order of society, which has no least regard for or relationship to their natural mental development. The darkest side of democracy, like that of autocracies, is that it permits the magnetic and the cunning and the unscrupulous among the powerful individuals, to sway vast masses of the mob, not so much to their own immediate destruction as to the curtailment of their natural privileges and the ideas which they should be allowed to entertain if they could think at all, and, incidentally, to the annoying and sometimes undoing of individuals who have the truest brain interests of the race at heart—Vide! Giordano Bruno! Jan Huss! Savonarola! Tom Paine! Walt Whitman! Edgar Allan Poe!

For, after all, as I have pointed out somewhere, the great business of life and mind is life. We are here, I take it, not merely to moon and vegetate, but to do a little thinking about this state in which we find ourselves. It is perfectly legitimate, all priests and theories and philosophies to the contrary notwithstanding, to go back, in so far as we may, to the primary sources of thought, *i. e.*, the visible scene, the actions and thoughts of people, the movements of nature and its chemical and physical subtleties, in order to draw original and radical conclusions for ourselves. The great business of an individual, if he has any time after struggling for life and a reasonable amount of entertainment or sensory satiation, should be this very thing. A man, if he can, should question the things that he sees—not some things, but everything—stand, as it were, in the center of this whirling storm of contradiction which we know as life, and ask of it its source and its import. Else why a brain at all? If only one could induce a moderate number of individuals, out of all that pass this way and come no more, apparently, to pause and think about life and take an individual point of view, the freedom and the individuality and the interest of the world might, I fancy, be greatly enhanced. We complain of the world as dull, at times. If it is so, lack of thinking by individuals is the reason. But to ask the poor, half-equipped mentality of the mass to think, to be individual—what an anachronism! You might as well ask of a rock to move, or a tree to fly.

Nevertheless, here in America, by reason of an idealistic constitution which is largely a work of art and not a workable system, you see a nation dedicated to so-called intellectual and spiritual freedom, but actually devoted with an almost bee-like industry to the gathering and storing and articulation and organization and use of purely material things. In spite of all our base-drum announcement of our servitude to the intellectual ideals of the world (copied mostly, by the way, from England) no nation has ever contributed less, philosophically or artistically or spiritually, to the actual development of the intellect and the spirit. I shall have more to say concerning this later on. We have invented many things, it is true, which have relieved man from the crushing weight of a too-grinding toil, and this perhaps may be the sole mission of America in the world and the universe, its destiny, its end. Personally, I think it is not a half bad thing to have done, and the submarine and the flying machine and the armored dreadnought, no less than the sewing machine and the cotton gin and the binder and the reaper and the cash register and the trolley car and the telephone, may, in the end, or perhaps already have, proved as significant in breaking the chains of physical and mental slavery of man as anything else. I do not know.

One thing I do know is that America seems profoundly interested in these things, to the exclusion of anything else. It has no time, you might almost say, no taste, to stop and contemplate life in the large, from an artistic or a philosophic point of view. Yet, after all, when all the machinery for lessening man's burdens has been invented, and all the safeguards for his preservation completed·and possibly shattered by forces too deep or superior for his cunning, may not a phrase, a line of poetry, or a single act of some half forgotten tragedy be all that is left of what we now see or dream of as materially perfect? For, after all, is it not a thought alone, of many famous and powerful things that have already gone, that alone endures—a thought conveyed by art as a medium?

But let me not become too remote or too fine-spun in my conception of the ultimate significance of art itself. The point which I wish to make here is just this: That in a land so devoted to the material, although dedicated by its constitution to the ideal, the condition of art and intellectual freedom is certainly anomalous. Your trade and your trust builder, most obviously dominant in America at this time, is of all people most indifferent to, or most unconscious of, the ultimate and pressing claims of mind and spirit as expressed by art. If you doubt this, you have only to look about you to see for what purposes, to what end, the increment of men of wealth and material power in America is devoted. We have something like twenty-five hundred colleges and schools and institutions of various kinds, largely furthered by the money of American men of wealth, and all devoted to the development of the mental equipment of man, so we are told, yet all set with the most flinty firmness against anything which is related to truly radical investigation, or thought, or action, or art.

As a matter of fact, in spite of the American constitution and the American oratorical address of all and sundry occasions, the average

American school, college, university, institution, is very much against the development of the individual in the true sense of that word. What it really wants is not an individual, but an automatic copy of some altruistic and impossible ideal, which has been formulated here and in England, under the domination of Christianity. This is literally true. I defy you to read any college or university prospectus or address or plea, which concerns the purposes or the ideals of these institutions, and not agree with me. They are not after individuals, they are after types or schools of individuals, all to be very much alike, all to be like themselves. And what type? Listen. I know of an American college professor in one of our successful state universities who had this to say of the male graduates of his institution, after having watched the output for a number of years: "They are all right, quite satisfactory as machines for the production of material wealth or for the maintenance of certain forms of professional skill, now very useful to the world, but as for having ideas of their own, being creators or men with the normal impulses and passions of manhood, they do not fulfill the requisite in any respect. They are little more than types, machines, made in the image and likeness of their college. They do not think; they cannot think, because they are bound hard and fast by the iron band of convention. They are moral young beings, Christian beings, model beings, but they are not men in the creative sense, and by far the large majority will never do a single original thing until by chance or necessity the theories and the conventions imposed or generated by their training and their surroundings are broken, and they become free, independent, self thinking individuals."

I know of one woman's college, for instance, an American institution of the very highest standing which, since its inception, has sent forth into life some thousands of graduates and post graduates, to battle life as they may for individual supremacy or sensory comfort. They are, or were, supposed to be individuals, capable of individual thought, procedure, invention, development, yet out of all of them, not one has ever even entered upon any creative or artistic labor of any kind. Not one. (Write me for the name of the college, if you wish.) There is not a chemist, a physiologist, a botanist, a biologist, an historian, a philosopher, an artist, of any kind or repute, among them, not one. No one of them has attained to even passing repute in these fields. They are secretaries to corporations, teachers, missionaries, college librarians, educators in any of the scores of pilfered meanings that may be attached to that much abused word. They are curators, directors, keepers. They are not individuals in the true sense of that word; they have not been taught to think, they are not free. They do not invent, lead, create. They only copy or take care of, yet they are graduates of this college and its theory, mostly ultra conventional or, worse yet, anaemic, and glad to wear its collar, to clank the chains of its ideas or ideals—automatons in a social scheme whose last and final detail was outlined to them in the classrooms of their alma mater. That, to me, is one phase, amusing enough, of intellectual freedom in America.

But the above is a mere detail in any chronicle or picture of the social or intellectual state of the United States. No country in the world, at least none that I know anything about, has such a peculiar, such a seemingly fierce determination, to make the Ten Commandments work. It would be amusing if it were not pitiful, their faith in these binding religious ideals. I, for one, have never been able to make up my mind whether this springs from the zealotry of the Puritans who landed at Plymouth Rock, or whether it is indigenous to the soil (which I doubt when I think of the Indians who preceded the whites), or whether it is a product of the federal constitution, compounded by such idealists as Paine and Jefferson and Franklin, and the more or less religious and political dreamers of the pre-constitutional days. Certain it is that no profound moral idealism animated the French in Canada, the Dutch in New York, the Swedes in New Jersey, or the mixed French and English in the extreme south and New Orleans.

The first shipload of white women that was ever brought to America was sold, almost at so much a pound. They were landed at Jamestown. The basis of all the first large fortunes was laid, to speak plainly, in graft—the most outrageous concessions obtained abroad. The history of our relations with the American Indians is sufficient to lay any claim to financial or moral virtue or worth in the white men who settled this country. We debauched, then robbed and murdered them. There is no other conclusion to be drawn from the facts covering that relationship as set down in any history worthy of the name. In regard to the development of our land, our canals, our railroads, and the vast organizations supplying our present day necessities, their history is a complex of perjury, robbery, false witness, extortion, and indeed every crime to which avarice, greed and ambition are heir. If you do not believe this, examine at your leisure the various congressional and state legislative investigations which have been held on an average of every six months since the government was founded, and see for yourself. The cunning and unscrupulousness of American brains can be matched against any the world has ever known, not even excepting the English.

But an odd thing in connection with this financial and social criminality is that it has been consistently and regularly ac companied, outwardly at least, by a religious and a sex puritanism which would be scarcely believable if it were not true. I do not say that the robbers and thieves who did so much to build up our great commercial and social structures were in themselves inwardly or outwardly always religious or puritanically moral from the sex point of view, although in regard to the latter, they most frequently made a show of so being. But I do say this, that the communities and the states and the nation in which they were committing their depredations have been individually and collectively, in so far as the written, printed and acted word are concerned, and in pictures and music, militantly pure and religious during all the time that this has been going forward under their eyes, and, to a certain extent, with their political consent. Why? I have a vague feeling that it is the American of Anglo-Saxon origin only who has been most vivid in his excitement over religion and morals where the written, printed, acted, or painted word was concerned, yet who, at the same time, and perhaps for this very reason, was failing or deliberately refusing to see, the contrast which his ordinary and very human actions presented to all this. Was he a hypocrite? Oh, well!—is he one? I hate to think it, but he certainly acts the part exceedingly well. Either he is that or a fool—take your choice.

Your American of Anglo-Saxon or any other origin is actually no better, spiritually or morally, than any other creature of this earth, be he Turk or Hindu or Chinese, except from a materially constructive or wealth-breeding point of view, but for some odd reason or another, he thinks he is. The only real difference is that, cast out or spewed out by conditions over which he had no control elsewhere, he chanced to fall into a land overflowing with milk and honey. Nature in America was, and still is, kind to the lorn foreigner seeking a means of subsistence, and he seems to have immediately attributed this to three things: First, his inherent capacity to dominate and control wealth; second, the especial favor of God to him; third, to his superior and moral state (due, of course, to his possession of wealth). These three things, uncorrected as yet by any great financial pressure, or any great natural or world catastrophe, have served to keep the American in his highly romantic state of self deception. He still thinks that he is a superior spiritual and moral being, infinitely better than the creatures of any other land, and nothing short of a financial cataclysm, which will come with the pressure of population on resources, will convince him that he is not. But that he will yet be convinced is a certainty. You need not fear. Leave it to nature.

One of the interesting phases of this puritanism or pharisee-ism is his attitude toward women and their morality and their purity. If ever a people has refined eroticism to a greater degree than the American, I am not aware of it. Owing to a theory or the doctrinaire acceptance of the Mary legend (Mary-olotry, no less), the good American, capable of the same gross financial crimes previously indicated, has been able to look upon most women, but more particularly those above him in the social scale, as considerably more than human—angelic, no less, and possessed of qualities the like of which are not to be found in any breathing being, man, woman, child, or animal. It matters not that his cities and towns, like those of any other nation, are rife with sex; that in each one are specific and often large areas devoted to Eros or Venus, or both. While maintaining them, he is still blind to their existence or import. He or his boys or his friends go—but—.

Only a sex blunted nature or race such as the Anglo-Saxon could have built up any such asinine theory as this. The purity, the sanctity, the self-abnegation, the delicacy of women—how these qualities have been exaggerated and dinned into our ears, until at last the average scrubby non-reasoning male, quite capable of visiting the gardens of Venus, or taking a girl off the street, is no more able to clearly visualize the creature before him than he is the central wilds of Africa which he has never seen.

A princess, a goddess, a divine mother or creative principle, all the virtues, all the perfections, no vices, no weaknesses, no errors—some such hodgepodge as this has come to be the average Anglo-Saxon, or at least American, conception of the average American woman. I do not say that a portion of this illusion is not valuable—I think it is. But as it stands now, she is too good to be true: a paragon, a myth! Actually, she doesn't exist at all as he has been taught to imagine her. She is nothing more than a two-legged biped like the rest of us, but in consequence of this delusion sex itself, being a violation of this paragon, has become a crime. We enter upon the earth, it is true, in a none too artistic manner (conceived in iniquity and born in sin, is the biblical phrasing of it), but all this has long since been glozed over—ignored—and to obviate its brutality as much as possible, the male has been called upon to purify himself in thought and deed, to avoid all private speculation as to women and his relationship to them, and, much more than that, to avoid all public discussion, either by word of mouth or the printed page.

To think of women or to describe them as anything less than the paragon previously commented upon, has become, by this process, not only a sin—it is a shameful infraction of the moral code, no less. Women are too good, the sex relationship too vile a thing, to be mentioned or even thought of. We must move in a mirage of illusion. We must not know what we really do. We must trample fact under foot and give fancy, in the guise of our so-called better natures, free rein. How this must affect or stultify the artistic and creative faculties of the race itself must be plain. Yet that is exactly where we stand today, ethically and spiritually, in regard to sex and women, and that is what is the matter with American social life, letters and art.

I do not pretend to say that this is not a workable and a satisfactory code in case any race or nation chooses to follow it, but I do say it is deadening to the artistic impulse, and I mean it. Imagine a puritan or a moralist attempting anything in art, which is nothing if not a true reflection of insight into life! Imagine! And contrast this moral or art narrowness with his commercial, or financial, or agricultural freedom and sense, and note the difference. In regard to all the latter, he is cool, sceptical, level-headed, understanding, natural—consequently well developed in those fields. In regard to this other, he is illusioned, theoretic, religious. In consequence, he has no power, except for an occasional individual who may rise in spite of these untoward conditions (to be frowned upon) to understand, much less picture, life as it really is. Artistically, intellectually, philosophically, we are weaklings; financially, and in all ways commercial we are very powerful. So one-sided has been our development that in this latter respect we are almost giants. Strange, almost fabulous creatures, have been developed here by this process, men so singularly devoid of a rounded human nature that they have become freaks in this one direction—that of money getting. I refer to Rockefeller, Gould, Sage, Vanderbilt the first, H. H. Rogers, Carnegie, Frick. Strong in all but this one capacity, the majority of our great men stand forth as true human rarities, the like of which has scarcely ever been seen before.

America could be described as the land of Bottom the Weaver. And by Bottom I mean the tradesman or manufacturer who by reason of his enthusiasm for the sale of paints or powder or threshing machines or coal, has accumulated wealth and, in consequence and by reason of the haphazard privileges of democracy, has strayed into a position of counsellor, or even dictator, not in regard to the things about which he might readily be supposed to know, but about the many things about which he would be much more likely not to know: art, science, philosophy, morals, public policy in general. You recall him, of course, in "A Midsummer Night's Dream," unconscious of his furry ears and also that he does not know how to play the lion's part—that it is more difficult than mere roaring. Here he is now, in America, enthroned as a lion, and in his way he is an epitome of the Anglo-Saxon temperament. All merchants, judges, lawyers, priests, politicians—what a goodly company of Bottoms they are. Solidified, they are Bottom to the life.

Bottom is so wise in his own estimation. He never once suspects his furry ears or that he is not a perfect actor in the role of the lion—or (if you will take it for what it is meant) the arts. He is just a dull weaver, really, made by this dream of our constitution ("an exposition of sleep" come upon him) into a roaring lion—in his own estimation. No one must say that Bottom is not: he will be driven out of the country—deported or exiled. No one must presume to practise the arts save as Bottom understands them. If you do, presto, there is his henchman Comstock and all Comstockery to take you into custody. Men who have come here from foreign shores (England excepted) have been amazed at Bottom's ears and his presumption in passing upon what is a lion's part in life. Indeed he is the Anglo-Saxon temperament personified. He is convinced that liberty was not made for Oberon or Peaseblossom or Cobweb or Mustard, but for bishops and executives and wholesale grocers and men who have become vastly rich canning tomatoes or selling oil. We must be "marvelous furry about the face" and do things his way, to be free. The great desire of Bottom is for all of us to have furry ears and long ones and to believe that he is the greatest actor in the world. He is bewildered by a world that will not play Pyramus his way. Quince, Snug, Flute, Snout, and Starveling (all those who came over with him in the Mayflower) agree that he is a great actor, but there are others, and Bottom is convinced that these others are in error—trying to wreck that dream, the American Constitution, which brought this "exposition of sleep" upon him and made him into a lion—"marvelous furry about the face" and with great ears.

Alas, alas! for art in America. It has a hard, stubby row to hoe.

But my quarrel is not with America as a comfortable industrious atmosphere in which to move and have one's being, but largely because it is no more than that—because it tends to become a dull, conventionalized, routine, material world, duller even that its reputed mother, sacred England. We are drifting, unless most of the visible signs are deceiving, into the clutches of a commercial oligarchy whose mental standards outside of trade are so puerile as to be scarcely worth discussing. Contemplate, if you please, what has happened to one of the shibboleths or bulwarks of our sacred liberties and intellectual freedom, i. e., the newspaper, under the dominance of trade. Look at it. I have not time here to stop and set forth *seriatim* all the charges that have been made, and in the main thoroughly substantiated, against the American newspaper. But consider for yourselves the newspapers which you know and read. How much, I ask you, if you are in trade, do the newspapers you know, know about trade? How much actual truth do they tell? How far could you follow their trade judgment or understanding? And if you are a member of any profession, how much reported professional knowledge or news, as presented by a newspaper, can you rely on? If a newspaper reported a professional man's judgment or dictum in regard to any important professional fact, how fully would you accept it without other corroborative testimony?

You are a play-goer: do you believe the newspaper dramatic critics? You are a student of literature: do you accept the mouthings of their literary critics or even look to them for advice? You are an artist or a lover of art: do you follow the newspapers for anything more than the barest intelligence as to the whereabouts of anything artistic? I doubt it. And in regard to politics, finance, social movements and social affairs, are they not actually the darkest, the most misrepresentative, frequently the most biased and malicious guides in the world of the printed word? Take their mouthings concerning ethics and morals alone and contrast them, if you please, with their private policy or their financial connections—the forces by which they are directed, editorially and otherwise. I am not speaking of all newspapers, but never mind the exception. It is always unimportant in mass conditions, anyhow. Newspaper criticism, like newspaper leadership, has already long since come to be looked upon by the informed and intelligent as little more than the mouthings or bellowings of mercenaries or panderers to trade, or, worse still, rank incompetents. The newspaper man, *per se,* either does not know or cannot help himself. The newspaper publisher is very glad of this and uses his half intelligence or inability to further his own interests. Politicians, administrations, department stores, large interests and personalities of various kinds, use or control or compel newspapers to do their bidding. This is a severe indictment to make against the press in general. Is it not literally true? Do you not, of your own knowledge, know it to be so?

Take again the large, the almost dominant religious and commercial organizations of America. What relationship, if any, do they bear to a free mental development, a refined taste, a subtle understanding, art or life in its poetic or tragic moulds, its drift, its character? Would you personally look to the Methodist, or the Presbyterian, or the Catholic, or the Baptist church to further individualism, or freedom of thought, or directness of mental action, or art in any form? Do not they really ask of all their adherents that they lay aside this freedom in favor of the reported word or dictum of a fabled, a non-historic, an imaginary ruler, of the universe? Think of it. And they are among the powerful, constructive, and controlling elements in government—in this government, to be accurate—dedicated and presumably devoted to individual liberty, not only of so-called conscience, but of constructive thought and art.

And our large corporations, with their dominant and controlling captains of industry, so-called. What about their relationship to individuality, the freedom of the individual to think for himself—to grow along constructural lines? Take, for instance, the tobacco trust, the oil trust, the milk trust, the coal trust—in what way, do you suppose, do they help? Are they actively seeking a better code of ethics, a wider historic or philosophic perspective, a more delicate art perception for the individual, or are they definitely and permanently concerned with the customary bludgeoning tactics of trade, piling up fortunes out of which they are to be partially bled later by pseudo art collectors and swindling dealers in antiques and so-called historic art and literature? Of current life and its accomplishments, what do they actually know? Yet this is a democracy. Here, as in every other realm of the world, the individual is permitted, compelled, to seek his own material and mental salvation as best he may. The trouble with a democracy as opposed to an autocracy, with a line of titled idlers permitted the gift of leisure and art indulgence, is that there is no central force or group to foster art, to secure letters and art in their inalienable rights, to make of superior thought a noble and a sacred thing. I am not saying that democracy will not yet produce such a central force or group. I believe it can and will. I believe when the time arrives it may prove to be better than any form of hereditary autocracy. But I am talking about the mental, the social, the artistic condition of America as it is today.

To me it is a thing for laughter, if not for tears: one hundred million Americans, rich (a fair percentage of them, anyhow) beyond the dreams of avarice, and scarcely a sculptor, a poet, a singer, a novelist, an actor, a musician, worthy of the name. One hundred and forty years (almost two hundred, counting the Colonial days) of the most prosperous social conditions, a rich soil, incalculable deposits of gold, silver, and precious and useful metals and fuels of all kinds, a land amazing in its mountains, its streams, its valley prospects, its wealth-yielding powers, and now its tremendous cities and far-flung facilities for travel and trade, and yet contemplate it. Artists, poets, thinkers, where are they? Run them over in your mind. Has it produced a single philosopher of the first rank—a Spencer, a Nietzsche, a Schopenhauer, a Kant? Do I hear someone offering Emerson as an equivalent? or James? Has it produced a historian of the force of either Macauley or Grote or Gibbon? A novelist of the rank of Turgenev, de Maupassant, or Flaubert? A scientist of the standing of Crooks or Roentgen or Pasteur? A critic of the insight and force of Taine, Sainte-Beuve or the de Goncourts? A dramatist the equivalent of Ibsen, Chekhov, Shaw, Hauptmann, Brieux? An actor, since Booth, of the force of Coquelin, Sonnenthal, Forbes-Robertson, or Sarah Bernhardt? Since Whitman, one poet, Edgar Lee Masters. In painting, a Whistler, an Inness, a Sargent. Who else? (And two of these shook the dust of our shores forever.) Inventors, yes. By the hundreds, one might almost say by the thousands. Some of them amazing enough, in all conscience, world figures, and enduring for all time. But of what relationship to art—the supreme freedom of the mind?

I have been asked to comment on the moral, the social, drift of America, as this relates itself to mental freedom. Look at it for yourself. What is there to say really? What?

The most significant and, to me, discouraging manifestation in connection with the United States today, is the tendency to even narrower and more puritanic standards than have obtained in the past. In all conscience, up to this year of our Lord nineteen hundred and seventeen, they have been bad enough. As a matter of fact, America, in its hundred years of life, has not even reached the intellectual maturity that goes in individual cases with a stripling of eighteen.

I am constantly astonished by the thousands of men, exceedingly capable in some mechanical or narrow technical sense, whose world or philosophic vision is that of a child. As a nation, we accept and believe naively in such impossible things. I am not thinking alone of the primary tenets of all religions, which are manifestly based on nothing at all, and which millions of Americans, along with the humbler classes of other countries, accept, but rather of those sterner truths which life itself teaches—the unreliability of human nature; the crass chance which strikes down and destroys our finest dreams; the fact that man in all his relations is neither good nor evil, but both.

The American, by some hocus pocus of atavism, has seemingly borrowed or retained from lower English middle-class puritans all their fol de rol notions about making human nature perfect by fiat or edict—the written word, as it were, which goes with all religions. So, although by reason of the coarsest and most brutal methods, we, as a nation, have built up one of the most interesting and domineering oligarchies in the world, we are still by no means aware of the fact.

All men, in the mind of the unthinking American, are still free and equal. They have in themselves certain inalienable rights; what they are, when you come to test them, no human being can discover. Your so-called rights disappear like water before a moving boat. They do not exist. Life here, as elsewhere, comes down to the brutal methods of nature itself. The rich strike the poor at every turn; the poor defend themselves and further their lives by all the tricks which stark necessity can conceive. No inalienable right keeps the average cost of living from rising steadily, while most of the salaries of our idealistic Americans are stationary. No inalienable right has ever yet prevented the strong from either tricking or browbeating the weak. And, although by degrees the average American everywhere is feeling more and more keenly the sharpening struggle for existence, yet his faith in his impossible ideals is as fresh as ever. God will save the good American, and seat him at His right hand on the Golden Throne.

On earth the good American is convinced that the narrower and more colorless his life here the greater his opportunity for a more glorious life hereafter. His pet theory is that man is made useful and successful and constructive—a perfect man, in short—by the kinds and numbers of things he is not permitted to do or think or say. A pale, narrow, utterly restrained life, according to his theory, is the perfect one. If one accepted St. James's version and kept utterly unspotted by the world, entirely out of contact with it, he would be the perfect American. Indeed, ever since the Mayflower landed, and the country began to grow westward, we have been convinced that we were destined to make the Ten Commandments, in all their arbitrary perfection, work. One might show readily enough that America attained its amazing position in life by reason of the fact that, along with boundless opportunities, the Ten Commandments did not and do not work, but what would be the use? With one hand the naive American takes and executes with all the brutal insistence of nature itself; with the other he writes glowing platitudes concerning brotherly love, virtue, purity, truth, etc., etc.

A part of this right or left hand tendency, as the case might be, is seen in the constant desire of the American to reform something. No country in the world, not even England, the mother of fol de rol reforms, is so prolific in these frail ventures as this great country of ours. In turn we have had campaigns for the reform of the atheist, the drunkard, the lecher, the fallen woman, the buccaneer financier, the drug fiend, the dancer, the theatregoer, the reader of novels, the wearer of low-neck dresses and surplus jewelry—in fact, every human taste and frivolity, wherever sporadically it has chanced to manifest itself with any interesting human force. Your reformer's idea is that any human being, to be a successful one, must be a pale spindling sprout, incapable of any vice or crime. And all the while the threshing sea of life is sounding in his ears. The thief, the lecher, the drunkard, the fallen woman, the greedy, the inordinately vain, as in all ages past, pass by his door, and are not the whit less numerous for the unending campaigns which have been launched to save them. In other words, human nature is human nature, but your American cannot be made to believe it.

He will not give up the illusion which was piled safely in the hold of the Mayflower when it set sail. He is going to reform man and the world willy nilly, and, while in his rampant idealism he is neglecting to build up a suitable army and navy wherewith to defend himself, he is busy propagating little cults whereby man is to be made less vigorous, more the useless anaemic thing that he has in mind.

Personally, my quarrel is with America's quarrel with original thought. It is so painful to me to see one after another of our alleged reformers tilting Don Quixote-like at the giant windmills of fact. We are to have no pictures which the puritan and the narrow, animated by an obsolete dogma, cannot approve of. We are to have no theatres, no motion pictures, no books, no public exhibitions of any kind, no speech even, which will in any way contravene his limited view of life. A few years ago it was the humble dealer in liquor whose life was anathematized, and whose property was descended upon with torches, axes and bombs. Now comes prohibition. A little later, our cities growing and the sections devoted to the worship of Venus becoming more manifest, the Vice Crusader was bred, and we had the spectacle of whole areas of fallen women scattered to the four winds, and allowed to practise separately what they could not do collectively. Then came Mr. Comstock, vindictive, persistent, and with a nose and a taste for the profane and erotic, such as elsewhere has not been equaled since. Pictures, books, the theatre, the dance, the studio—all came under his watchful eye. During the twenty or thirty years in which he acted as a United States Postoffice Inspector, he was, because of his dull charging against things which he did not rightly understand, never out of the white light of publicity which he so greatly craved. One month it would be a novel by D'Annunzio; another, a set of works by Balzac or de Maupassant, found in the shade of some grovelly bookseller's shop; the humble photographer attempting a nude; the painter who allowed his reverence for Raphael to carry him too far; the poet who attempted a recrudescence of Don Juan in modern iambics, was immediately seized upon and hauled before an equally dull magistrate, there to be charged with his offense and to be fined accordingly. All this is being continued with emphasis.

Then came the day of the White Slave Chasers, and now no American city, and no backwoods Four Corners, however humble, is complete without a vice commission of some kind, or at least a local agent or representative, charged with the duty of keeping the art, the literature, the press, and the private lives of all those at hand up to that standard of perfection which only the dull can set for themselves.

Several years ago, when the White Slave question was at its whitest heat, the problem of giving expression to its fundamental aspects was divided between raiding plays which attempted to show the character of the crime in too graphic a manner, and licensing those which appealed to the intelligence of those who were foremost in the crusade. Thus we had the spectacle of an uncensored, but nevertheless approved, ten-reel film showing more details of the crime and better methods of securing white slaves, than any other production of the day, running undisturbed to packed houses all over the country, while two somewhat more dramatic, but far less effective distributors of information in the way of plays were successfully harried from city to city and finally withdrawn.

Shakespeare has been ordered from the schools in some of the states. A production of "Antony and Cleopatra" has been raided in Chicago. Japanese prints of a high art value, intended for the seclusion of a private collection, have been seized and the most valuable of them held to be destroyed. By turns, an artistic fountain to Heine in New York, loan exhibits of paintings in Denver, Kansas City, and elsewhere, scores of books by Stevenson, James Lane Allen, Frances H. Burnett, have been attacked, not only, as in the case of the latter, with the invisible weapons of the law, as might be expected, but, in regard to the former, with actual axes. A male dancer of repute and some artistic ability, has been raided publicly by the Vice Crusaders for his shameless exposure of his person! No play, no picture, no book, no public or private jubilation of any kind, is complete any more without its vice attack.

To me this sort of thing is dull, and bespeaks the low state to which our mental activities have fallen. When it comes to the matter of serious letters it is the worst. In New York a literary reign of terror has been and is now being attempted. The publisher of Mr. D. H. Lawrence's latest novel is warned before he brings it out that he will be prosecuted—a work that probably has no more defect than being intelligent and true. Similarly, Mr. Przybyszewski's "Homo Sapiens"—a by no means pornographic work—was at once seized on its appearance, and the publishers frightened into withdrawing it. This was true of "Hagar Ravelly," "Tess of the d'Urbervilles," "Sapho," "Jude the Obscure," "Rose of Dutchers Cooley," "A Lady of Quality," "A Summer in Arcady," and indeed scores of others. Imagine banning a book like "A Summer in Arcady" from the public libraries! And now "The Sexual Question," by the eminent August Forel, has been banned also. Think of it—the work of a scientist of Forel's attainments being banned!

This sort of interference with serious letters is, to me, the worst and most corrupting form of espionage which is conceivable to the human mind. It plumbs the depths of ignorance and intolerance; if not checked, it can and will dam initiative and inspiration at the source. Life, if it is anything at all, is a thing to be observed, studied, interpreted. We cannot know too much about it, because as yet we know nothing. It is our one great realm of discovery. The artist, if left to himself, may be safely trusted to observe, synchronize, and articulate human knowledge in the most palatable and delightful form. Human nature will seek and have what it needs, the vice crusaders to the contrary notwithstanding. There is no compulsion on any one to read. One must pay to do so. What is more, one must have taste inherently to select, and a brain and a heart to understand. With all these safeguards and a double score of capable critics in every land to praise or blame, what need really is there for a censor, or a dozen of them, each far less fitted than any of the working critics, to indulge his personal predilection and opposition, and to appeal to the courts if he is disagreed with?

Personally, I rise to protest. I look on this interference with serious art and serious minds as an outrage. I fear for the ultimate intelligence of America, which in all conscience, judged by world standards, is low enough. In our youth and conceit we think ourselves wise. Intelligent cosmopolitans actually know that our ignorance is appalling. In the main we are unbelievably dull and wishy-washy. Now appears a band of wasp-like censors to put the finishing touches on a literature and an art that has struggled all too feebly as it is. Poe, Hawthorne, Whitman, and Thoreau, each in turn was the butt and jibe of unintelligent Americans, until by now we are well nigh the laughing stock of the world. Where is it to end? When will we lay aside our swaddling clothes, enforced on us by ignorant, impossible puritans and their uneducated followers, and stand up, free thinking men and women? Life is to be learned as much from books and art as from life itself—almost more so, in my judgment. Art is the stored honey of the human soul, gathered on wings of misery and travail. Shall the dull and the self-seeking and the self-advertising close this store on the groping human mind?

THE THIMBLE

D. H. Lawrence

S HE had not seen her husband for ten months, not since her fort-night's honeymoon with him, and his departure for France. Then, in those excited days of the early war, he was her comrade, her counter-part in a sort of Bacchic revel before death. Now all that was shut off from her mind, as by a great rent in her life.

Since then, since the honeymoon, she had lived and died and come to life again. There had been his departure to the front. She had loved him then.

"If you want to love your husband," she had said to her friends, with splendid recklessness, "you should see him in khaki." And she had really loved him, he was so handsome in uniform, well-built, yet with a sort of reserve and remoteness that suited the neutral khaki perfectly.

Before, as a barrister with nothing to do, he had been slack and unconvincing, a sort of hanger-on, and she had never come to the point of marrying him. For one thing they neither of them had enough money.

Then came the great shock of the war, his coming to her in a new light, as lieutenant in the artillery. And she had been carried away by his perfect calm manliness and significance, now he was a soldier. He seemed to have gained a fascinating importance that made her seem quite unimportant. It was she who was insignificant and subservient, he who was dignified, with a sort of indifferent lordliness.

So she had married him, all considerations flung to the wind, and had known the bewildering experience of their fortnight's honeymoon, before he left her for the front.

And she had never got over the bewilderment. She had, since then, never thought at all, she seemed to have rushed on in a storm of activity and sensation. There was a home to make, and no money to make it with: none to speak of. So, with the swift, business-like aptitude of a startled woman, she had found a small flat in Mayfair, had attended sales and bought suitable furniture, had made the place complete and perfect. She was satisfied. It was small and insignificant, but it was a complete unity.

Then she had had a certain amount of war-work to do, and she had kept up all her social activities. She had not had a moment which was not urgently occupied.

All the while came his letters from France, and she was writing her replies. They both sent a good deal of news to each other, they both expressed their mutual passion.

Then suddenly, amid all this activity, she fell ill with pneumonia and everything lapsed into delirium. And whilst she was ill, he was wounded, his jaw smashed and his face cut up by the bursting of a shell. So they were both laid by.

Now, they were both better, and she was waiting to see him. Since she had been ill, whilst she had lain or sat in her room in the castle in Scotland, she had thought, thought very much. For she was a woman who was always trying to grasp the whole of her context, always trying to make a complete thing of her own life.

Her illness lay between her and her previous life like a dark night, like a great separation. She looked back, she remembered all she had done, and she was bewildered, she had no key to the puzzle. Suddenly she realized that she knew nothing of this man she had married, he knew nothing of her. What she had of him, vividly, was the visual image. She could *see* him, the whole of him, in her mind's eye. She could remember him with peculiar distinctness, as if the whole of his body were lit up by an intense light, and the image fixed on her mind.

But he was an impression, only a vivid impression. What her own impression was, she knew most vividly. But what *he* was *himself*: the very thought startled her, it was like looking into a perilous darkness. All that she knew of him was her own affair, purely personal to her, a subjective impression. But there must be a *man,* another being, somewhere in the darkness which she had never broached.

The thought frightened her exceedingly, and her soul, weak from illness, seemed to weep. Here was a new peril, a new terror. And she seemed to have no hope.

She could scarcely bear to think of him as she knew him. She could scarcely bear to conjure up that vivid image of him which remained from the days of her honeymoon. It was something false, it was something which had only to do with herself. The man himself was something quite other, something in the dark, something she dreaded, whose coming she dreaded, as if it were a mitigation of her own being, something set over against her, something that would annul her own image of herself.

Nervously she twisted her long white fingers. She was a beautiful woman, tall and loose and rather thin, with swinging limbs, one for whom the modern fashions were perfect. Her skin was pure and clear, like a Christmas rose, her hair was fair and heavy. She had large, slow, unswerving eyes, that sometimes looked blue and open with a childish candor, sometimes greenish and intent with thought, sometimes hard, sea-like, cruel, sometimes grey and pathetic.

Now she sat in her own room, in the flat in Mayfair, and he was coming to see her. She was well again: just well enough to see him. But she was tired as she sat in the chair whilst her maid arranged her heavy, fair hair.

She knew she was a beauty, she knew it was expected of her that she should create an impression of modern beauty. And it pleased her, it made her soul rather hard and proud: but also, at the bottom, it bored her. Still, she would have her hair built high, in the fashionable mode, she would have it modelled to the whole form of her head, her figure. She lifted her eyes to look. They were slow, greenish, and cold like the sea at this moment, because she was so perplexed, so heavy with trying, all alone, always quite coldly alone, to understand, to understand and to adjust herself. It never occurred to her to expect anything of the other person: she was utterly self-responsible.

"No," she said to her maid, in her slow, laconic, plangent voice, "don't let it swell out over the ears, lift it straight up, then twist it under—like that—so it goes clean from the side of the face. Do you see?"

"Yes, my lady."

And the maid went on with the hair-dressing, and she with her slow, cold musing.

She was getting dressed now to see her bridegroom. The phrase, with its association in all the romances of the world, made her snigger involuntarily to herself. She was still like a schoolgirl, always seeing herself in her part. She got curious satisfaction from it, too. But also she was always humorously ironical when she found herself in these romantic situations. If brigands and robbers had carried her off, she would have played up to the event perfectly. In life, however, there was always a certain painful, laborious heaviness, a weight of self-responsibility. The event never carried her along, a helpless protagonist. She was always responsible, in whatever situation.

Now, this morning, her husband was coming to see her, and she was dressing to receive him. She felt heavy and inert as stone, yet inwardly trembling convulsively. The known man, he did not affect her. Heavy and inert in her soul, yet amused, she would play her part in his reception. But the unknown man, what was he? Her dark, unknown soul trembled apprehensively.

At any rate he would be different. She shuddered. The vision she had of him, of the good-looking, clean, slightly tanned, attractive man, ordinary and yet with odd streaks of understanding that made her ponder, this she must put away. They said his face was rather horribly cut up. She shivered. How she hated it, coldly hated and loathed it, the thought of disfigurement. Her fingers trembled, she rose to go downstairs. If he came he must not come into her bedroom.

So, in her fashionable but inexpensive black silk dress, wearing her jewels, her string of opals, her big, ruby brooch, she went downstairs. She knew how to walk, how to hold her body according to the mode. She did it almost instinctively, so deep was her consciousness of the impression her own appearance must create.

Entering the small drawing-room she lifted her eyes slowly and looked at herself: a tall, loose woman in black, with fair hair raised up, and with slow, greenish, cold eyes looking into the mirror. She turned away with a cold, pungent sort of satisfaction. She was aware also of the traces of weariness and illness and age, in her face. She was twenty-seven years old.

So she sat on the little sofa by the fire. The room she had made was satisfactory to her, with its neutral, brown-grey walls, its deep brown, plain, velvety carpet, and the old furniture done in worn rose brocade, which she had bought from Countess Ambersyth's sale. She looked at her own large feet, upon the rose-red Persian rug.

Then nervously, yet quite calm, almost static, she sat still to wait. It was one of the moments of deepest suffering and suspense which she had ever known. She did not want to think of his disfigurement, she did not want to have any preconception of it. Let it come upon her. And the man, the unknown strange man who was coming now to take up his position over against her soul, her soul so naked and exposed from illness, the man to whose access her soul was to be delivered up! She could not bear it. Her face set pale, she began to lose her consciousness.

Then something whispered in her:

"If I am like this, I shall be quite impervious to him, quite oblivious of anything but the surface of him." And an anxious sort of hope sent her hands down onto the sofa at her side, pressed upon the worn brocade, spread flat. And she remained in suspense.

But could she bear it, could she bear it? She was weak and ill in a sort of after-death. Now what was this that she must confront, this other being? Her hands began to move slowly backwards and forwards on the sofa bed, slowly, as if the friction of the silk gave her some ease.

She was unaware of what she was doing. She was always so calm, so self-contained, so static; she was much too stoically well-bred to allow these outward nervous agitations. But now she sat still in suspense in the silent drawing-room, where the fire flickered over the dark brown carpet and over the pale rose furniture and over the pale face and the black dress and the white, sliding hands of the woman, and her hands slid backwards and forwards, backwards and forwards like a pleading, a hope, a tension of madness.

Her right hand came to the end of the sofa and pressed a little into the crack, the meeting between the arm and the sofa bed. Her long white fingers pressed into the fissure, pressed and entered rhythmically, pressed and pressed further and further into the tight depths of the fissure, between the silken, firm upholstery of the old sofa, whilst her mind was in a trance of suspense, and the fire-light flickered on the yellow chrysanthemums that stood in a jar in the window.

The working, slow, intent fingers pressed deeper and deeper in the fissure of the sofa, pressed and worked their way intently, to the bottom. It was the bottom. They were there, they made sure. Making sure, they worked all along, very gradually, along the tight depth of the fissure.

Then they touched a little extraneous object, and a consciousness awoke in the woman's mind. Was it something? She touched again. It was something hard and rough. The fingers began to ply upon it. How firmly it was embedded in the depths of the sofa-crack. It had a thin rim, like a ring, but it was not a ring. The fingers worked more insistently. What was this little hard object?

The fingers pressed determinedly, they moved the little object. They began to work it up to the light. It was coming, there was success. The woman's heart relaxed from its tension, now her aim was being achieved. Her long, strong, white fingers brought out the little find.

It was a thimble set with brilliants; it was an old, rather heavy thimble of tarnished gold, set round the base with little diamonds or rubies. Perhaps it was not gold, perhaps they were only paste.

She put it on her sewing finger. The brilliants sparkled in the fire-light. She was pleased. It was a vulgar thing, a gold thimble with ordinary pin-head dents, and a belt of jewels around the base. It was large too, big enough for her. It must have been some woman's embroidery thimble, some bygone woman's, perhaps some Lady Ambersyth's. At any rate, it belonged to the days when women did stitching as a usual thing. But it was heavy, it would make one's hand ache.

She began to rub the gold with her handkerchief. There was an engraved monogram, an Earl's, and then Z, Z, and a date, 15 Oct., 1801. She was very pleased, trembling with the thought of the old romance. What did Z. stand for? She thought of her acquaintances, and could only think of Zouche. But he was not an Earl. Who would give the gift of a gold thimble set with jewels, in the year 1801? Perhaps it was a man come home from the wars: there were wars then.

The maid noiselessly opened the door and saw her mistress sitting in the soft light of the winter day, polishing something with her handkerchief.

"Mr. Hepburn has come, my lady."

"Has he!" answered the laconic, slightly wounded voice of the woman.

She collected herself and rose. Her husband was coming through the doorway, past the maid. He came without hat or coat or gloves, like an inmate of the house. He was an inmate of the house.

"How do you do?" she said, with stoic, plangent helplessness. And she held out her hand.

"How are *you*?" he replied, rather mumbling, with a sort of muffled voice.

"All right now, thanks," and she sat down again, her heart beating violently. She had not yet looked at his face. The muffled voice terrified her so much. It mumbled rather mouthlessly.

Abstractedly, she put the thimble on her middle finger, and continued to rub it with her handkerchief. The man sat in silence opposite, in an arm-chair. She was aware of his khaki trousers and his brown shoes. But she was intent on burnishing the thimble.

Her mind was in a trance, but as if she were on the point of waking, for the first time in her life, waking up.

"What are you doing? What have you got?" asked the mumbling, muffled voice. A pang went through her. She looked up at the mouth that produced the sound. It was broken in, the bottom teeth all gone, the side of the chin battered small, whilst a deep seam, a deep, horrible groove ran right into the middle of the cheek. But the mouth was the worst, sunk in at the bottom, with half the lip cut away.

"It is treasure-trove," answered the plangent, cold-sounding voice. And she held out the thimble.

He reached to take it. His hand was white, and it trembled. His nerves were broken. He took the thimble between his fingers.

She sat obsessed, as if his disfigurement were photographed upon her mind, as if she were some sensitive medium to which the thing had been transferred. There it was, her whole consciousness was photographed into an image of his disfigurement, the dreadful sunken mouth that was not a mouth, which mumbled in talking to her, in a disfigurement of speech.

It was all accident, accident had taken possession of her very being. All she was, was purely accidental. It was like a sleep, a thin, taut, overfilming sleep in which the wakefulness struggles like a thing as yet unborn. She was sick in the thin, transparent membrane of her sleep, her overlying dream-consciousness, something actual but too unreal.

"How treasure-trove?" he mumbled. She could not understand.

She felt his moment's hesitation before he tried again, and a hot pain pierced through her, the pain of his maimed, crippled effort.

"Treasure-trove, you said," he repeated, with a sickening struggle to speak distinctly.

Her mind hovered, then grasped, then caught the threads of the conversation.

"I found it," she said. Her voice was clear and vibrating as bronze, but cold. "I found it just before you came in."

There was a silence. She was aware of the purely accidental condition of her whole being. She was framed and constructed of accident, accidental association. It was like being made up of dream-stuff, without sequence or adherence to any plan or purpose. Yet within the imprisoning film of the dream was herself, struggling unborn, struggling to come to life.

It was difficult to break the inert silence that had succeeded between them. She was afraid it would go on forever. With a strange, convulsive struggle, she broke into communication with him.

"I found it here, in the sofa," she said, and she lifted her eyes for the first time to him.

His forehead was white, and his hair brushed smooth, like a sick man's. And his eyes were like the eyes of a child that has been ill, blue and abstract, as if they only listened from a long way off, and did not see any more. So far-off he looked, like a child that belongs almost more to death than to life. And her soul divined that he was waiting vaguely where the dark and the light divide, whether he should come in to life, or hesitate, and pass back.

She lowered her eyelids, and for a second she sat erect like a mask, with closed eyes, whilst a spasm of pure unconsciousness passed over her. It departed again, and she opened her eyes. She was awake.

She looked at him. His eyes were still abstract and without answer, changing only to the dream-psychology of his being. She contracted as if she were cold and afraid. They lit up now with a superficial over-flicker of interest.

"Did you really? Why, how did it come there?"

It was the same voice, the same stupid interest in accidental things, the same man as before. Only the enunciation of the words was all mumbled and muffled, as if the speech itself were disintegrating.

Her heart shrank, to close again like an over-sensitive newborn thing, that is not yet strong enough in its own being. Yet once more she lifted her eyes, and looked at him.

He was flickering with his old, easily roused, spurious interest in the accidentals of life. The film of separateness seemed to be coming over her. Yet his white forehead was somewhat deathly, with its smoothly brushed hair. He was like one dead. He was within the realm of death. His over-flicker of interest was only extraneous.

"I suppose it had got pushed down by accident," she said, answering from her mechanical mind.

But her eyes were watching him who was dead, who was there like Lazarus before her, as yet unrisen.

"How did it happen?" she said, and her voice was changed, penetrating with sadness and approach. He knew what she meant.

"Well, you see I was knocked clean senseless, and that was all I knew for three days. But it seems that it was a shell fired by one of our own fellows, and it hit me because it was faultily made."

Her face was very still as she watched.

"And how did you feel when you came round?"

"I felt pretty bad, as you can imagine; there was a crack on the skull as well as this on the jaw."

"Did you think you were going to die?"

There was a long pause, whilst the man laughed self-consciously. But he laughed only with the upper part of his face: the maimed part remained still. And though the eyes seemed to laugh, just as of old, yet underneath them was a black, challenging darkness. She waited whilst this superficial smile of reserve passed away.

Then came the mumbling speech, simple, in confession.

"Yes, I lay and looked at it."

The darkness of his eyes was now watching her, her soul was exposed and new-born. The triviality was gone, the dream-psychology, the self-dependence. They were naked and new-born in soul, and depended on each other.

It was on the tip of her tongue to say: "And why didn't you die?" But instead, her soul, weak and new-born, looked helplessly at him.

"I couldn't while you were alive," he said.

"What?"

"Die."

She seemed to pass away into unconsciousness. Then, as she came to, she said, as if in protest:

"What difference should *I* make to you! You can't live off me."

He was watching her with unlighted, sightless eyes. There was a long silence. She was thinking, it was not her consciousness of him which had kept *her* alive. It was her own will.

"What did you hope for, from me?" she asked.

His eyes darkened, his face seemed very white, he really looked like a dead man as he sat silent and with open, sightless eyes. Between his slightly-trembling fingers was balanced the thimble, that sparkled sometimes in the firelight. Watching him, a darkness seemed to come over her. She could not see, he was only a presence near her in the dark.

"We are both of us helpless," she said, into the silence.

"Helpless for what?" answered his sightless voice.

"To live," she said.

They seemed to be talking to each other's souls, their eyes and minds were sightless.

"We are helpless to live," he repeated.

"Yes," she said.

There was still a silence.

"I know," he said, "we are helpless to live. I knew that when I came round."

"I am as helpless as you are," she said.

"Yes," came his slow, half-articulate voice. "I know that. You're as helpless as I am."

"Well then?"

"Well then, we are helpless. We are as helpless as babies," he said.

"And how do you like being a helpless baby," came the ironic voice.

"And how do *you* like being a helpless baby?" he replied.

There was a long pause. Then she laughed brokenly.

"I don't know," she said. "A helpless baby can't know whether it likes being a helpless baby."

"That's just the same. But I feel *hope,* don't you?"

Again there was an unwilling pause on her part.

"Hope of what?"

"If I am a helpless baby now, that I shall grow into a man."

She gave a slight, amused laugh.

"And I ought to hope that I shall grow into a woman," she said.

"Yes, of course."

"Then what am I now?" she asked, humorously.

"Now, you're a helpless baby, as you said."

It piqued her slightly. Then again, she knew it was true.

"And what was I before—when I married you?" she asked, challenging.

"Why, then—I don't know what you were. I've had my head cracked and some dark let in, since then. So I don't know what you were, because it's all gone, don't you see."

"I see."

There was a pause. She became aware of the room about her, of the fire burning low and red.

"And what are we doing together?" she said.

"We're going to love each other," he said.

"Didn't we love each other before?" challenged her voice.

"No, we couldn't. We weren't born."

"Neither were we dead," she answered.

He seemed struck.

"Are we dead now?" he asked in fear.

"Yes, we are."

There was a suspense of anguish, it was so true.

"Then we must be born again," he said.

"Must we?" said her deliberate, laconic voice.

"Yes, we must—otherwise—" He did not finish.

"And do you think we've got the power to come to life again, now we're dead?" she asked.

"I think we have," he said.

There was a long pause.

"Resurrection?" she said, almost as if mocking. They looked slowly and darkly into each other's eyes. He rose unthinking, went over and touched her hand.

" 'Touch me not, for I am not yet ascended unto the Father,' " she quoted, in her level, cold-sounding voice.

"No," he answered; "it takes time."

The incongruous plainness of his statement made her jerk with laughter. At the same instant her face contracted and she said in a loud voice, as if her soul was being torn from her:

"Am I going to love you?"

Again he stretched forward and touched her hand, with the tips of his fingers. And the touch lay still, completed there.

Then at length he noticed that the thimble was stuck on his little finger. In the same instant she also looked at it.

"I want to throw it away," he said.

Again she gave a little jerk of laughter.

He rose, went to the window, and raised the sash. Then, suddenly with a strong movement of the arm and shoulder, he threw the thimble out into the murky street. It bounded on the pavement opposite. Then a taxi-cab went by, and he could not see it any more.

THE SEVEN ARTS AND THE SEVEN CONFUSIONS

Joel Elias Spingarn

THERE are as many arts as there are artists,—the number is not seven, but countless as the stars. We group them in constellations for our convenience, not theirs; seven units are more easily handled than a trillion. The confusions in regard to them are countless too; the actual number is far greater; but they may also be gathered for our convenience into seven groups,—"seven" has the perfume of a mystic tradition kept fragrant by the superstition of generations of men. So I begin with a roll-call of them all: Poets write for money; poets are influenced by their environment; poets write in meters; poets write tragedies and comedies; poets are moral or immoral; poets are democratic or aristocratic; poets use figures of speech.

The first of the Seven Confusions, then, is this, that "Poets write for money." This is only one way of stating a misconception of the nature of art that might be phrased in a hundred different ways. The most common form today is perhaps this: "Plays are written to be acted, not read." The confusion remains exactly the same when it is put: "Plays are written to be read, not acted." We are not concerned with the fact (if it be a fact) but with its implication for criticism.

The poet may find that a brisk walk stimulates his writing, or that he can write more easily when he has smoked a cigarette. The walk or the cigarette has not produced the poetry; it has simply served as a stimulus to the personality that creates the poetry. It opens the faucet, but neither produces nor modifies the water that pours out. Other poets find that they cannot write easily without the stimulus of imagined reward,— money, the plaudits of the crowd, the resplendent beauty of theatrical performance. But men with the same ambitions write different poems or plays, and in this difference lies the real secret of art. For after all, whatever the imaginary stimulus, there is only one real urge in the poet's soul, to express what is in him. To trifle with the plumbing, after the faucet has been turned on, instead of drinking the water, is hardly the function of the critic or lover of art. To say, therefore, that poets write for money, that playwrights write for the stage, that painters paint to be "hung," is to confuse mere stimulus with creative impulse.

The second confusion, that "Poets are the products of their environment," is a twisted corollary of the first. We need not quarrel with the statement so long as it remains suspended in the air, as a vague generalization that can do no harm unless it carries with it the further implication that a study of the environment helps us to understand the poetry. Not what the poet's environment may have been, but what he has made out of it, is what interests us in a poem. The secret of a unique personality (if one may use the phrase when personality means nothing but uniqueness) is what the reader enjoys and the critic seeks to discover. Sociologists may trouble themselves about external and superficial resemblances between artists or groups of artists; aesthetic critics are concerned only with the unbridgeable differences. To look for a poet's power outside of his work rather than in it, to assume that his relation to his environment is of any concern whatever to a lover or critic of poetry, is to confuse criticism and sociology.

The most deeply imbedded superstition in regard to art, however, is concerned with its external form. The third confusion, that "Poets write in meters," is therefore one of the oldest of all the confusions. Aesthetic theorists have waged a battle against it, from the days of Aristotle, who said that poetry is distinguished from history by something more essential than meter, and that the history of Herodotus would remain history even if written in verse, to our own day, when Benedetto Croce, the only modern who may be mentioned in the same breath with him, has left the old confusion without any ground to stand on. The fact is that there is no real distinction between prose and verse. Out of the infinite varieties of rhythm in human speech, it is possible, for convenience' sake, to separate the more regular from the more irregular, and to call one verse and the other prose: to say where one ends and the other begins is impossible. But to build a system on these empirical and convenient classifications is to confuse superficial likenesses with the realities of creative art. For after all no two poets write in the same meters. I may imagine that I am writing an iambic pentameter, or a line with a certain succession of beats or accents, but in reality I am creating a new line. If that line is good it is because of some special virtue of its own, and not because of some imaginary and purely external resemblance to something else. Poets do not use old meters, but each poet creates rhythms of his own.

What is true of meter is also true of language itself. To speak of "learning a language" is to risk the danger of the same confusion; we do not learn language, we learn how to create it. That is why it is so wide of the mark to say, as Max Eastman does, that "to sail into a man" is or is not a good expression because it means the same as the Latinism "to inveigh against a man." "Inveigh" may etymologically mean "sail into;" but if language is a living thing,—a form of art, not to be torn from its context or understood outside of it,—the Latin word helps to explain the English as much as the disinterred skeleton of a thirteenth century English yeoman helps us to understand the personality of Max Eastman. It is inconceivable that a modern thinker should still adhere to abstract tests of good expression, when it is obvious that we can only tell whether it is good or bad when we see it in its natural context. Is any word artistically bad in itself? Is not "ain't" an excellent expression when placed in the mouth of an illiterate character in a play or story? To deal with abstract classification instead of the real thing,—versification instead of poetry, grammar instead of language, technique instead of painting,—is to be guilty of confusing form as concrete expression with form as a dead husk.

The fourth confusion may be summed up in the phrase: "Poets write tragedies or comedies." It is true that poets set out with the intention of writing them, although they have only the vaguest idea of what they mean by the terms; and it is equally true that their work may be impeded by false conceptions of these literary forms. But fortunately for us, their real achievement is independent of this confused ambition. Tragedy, comedy, lyric, epic, and other words of this sort, are simply convenient ways of classifying works of art, just as books may be classified as tall or small, cloth-bound or morocco-bound, for the purpose of arrangement in libraries, or men may be classified as tall or small for the purpose of arrangement in a company of soldiers. We shall always find these terms useful, in poetry no less than in libraries or regiments, and the confusion arises only when it is implied (as is almost always implied) that the classification is not merely a matter of convenience, but a law of art by which poems are to be judged. For example, a critic studies a number of poems having a certain resemblance and called tragedies; out of this study he evolves a "law of tragedy" and then attempts to impose it on the first poet who writes another poem of somewhat the same kind. "Sir," we hear him say throughout the ages, "you have disregarded all the laws of good tragedy, and your poem is therefore no good." The poet's answer should be a very simple one: "There are no laws of good tragedy; there are only good or bad poems." No rule, no theory, no "law" coined by critics or scholars has any validity for the poet in the creative act; and when that act is completed and the poem achieved, the critic must make his theory of tragedy chime with the new poet's poem, not the poem with the theory. Only in one sense has any of these terms any profound significance, and that is the use of the word "lyric" to represent the free expressiveness of all art. The Divine Comedy, Lear, Michelangelo's David, a Corot landscape, or a Bach fugue is as truly lyric as any of the scrips of Heine or Shelley.

The fifth confusion, that "Poets are moral or immoral," is also world-old. We should no longer banish poets from an ideal Republic because of the immorality of their art, as Plato did; but most of us still confuse art with morals. To say that poetry is moral or immoral is as meaningless as to say that an equilateral triangle is moral and an isosceles triangle immoral. Surely we must realize the absurdity of testing anything by a standard which does not belong to it or a purpose for which it was not intended. Imagine these whiffs of conversation at a dinner table: "This cauliflower would be excellent if it had only been prepared in accordance with international law." "Do you know why my cook's pastry is so good?

He has never told a lie or seduced a woman." But why multiply obvious examples? We do not concern ourselves with morals when we test the engineer's bridge or the scientist's researches; indeed we go farther, and say that it is the moral duty of the scientist to disregard morals in his search for truth. As a man he may be judged by moral standards, but the truth of his conclusions can only be judged by the standard of science. Beauty's world is remote from both these standards; she aims neither at morals nor at truth. Her imaginary creations, by definition, make no pretence to reality, and cannot be judged by reality's tests. Art is expression, and poets succeed or fail by their success or failure in completely and perfectly expressing themselves. If the ideals they express are not the ideals we admire most, we must blame not the poets but ourselves: in the world where morals count we have failed to give them the proper material out of which to rear a nobler edifice. To separate art and morality is not to destroy moral values but to augment them,—to give them increased powers and a new freedom in the realm in which they have the right to reign.

In modern America it would be strange if our practical hopes did not lead us into a sixth confusion,—that "Poets are democratic or aristocratic,"—as if art were concerned with the political program of the poet any more than with his moral standards. It is easy to sneer at Shakespeare and Dante as "reactionaries," but it is difficult to see what this has to do with the quality of their poetry, unless we are to assume that only men of our own political or economic convictions can be good poets. It is as hard to write a good poem on democracy as on aristocracy; alas, it would seem even harder, if we may judge from the experience of poets. To find fault with the past because it is not exactly like the present is as good a test as one needs of a shallow mind; and to find fault with good poetry because it is not good political science or good sociology is a fairly serviceable test of the incompetent critic. It is not the purpose of poetry to further the cause of democracy, or any other practical "cause," any more than it is the purpose of bridge-building to further the cause of Esperanto. If a poet consecrates himself to the spread of democratic ideals, his work still remains to be tested by the standards of art, not of politics. Criticism is concerned with the question, "Has he written a good poem?" and is not helped in its decision by the answer to a wholly different and indifferent question: "Is he a democrat, a conservative, a Socialist, or a psychoanalyst?"

Somewhat similar is the attempt of critics to determine the subject-matter of poetry, no less than the political convictions of poets. It is an old illusion: in the seventeenth century, for example, Boileau belabored the poets who had the temerity to prefer Christian to Greek mythology. Today the critics are insisting on the use of contemporary material, and are praising the poets whose subjects are drawn from the life of their own time. But even if it were possible for critics to impose subjects on poets, how can the poets deal with anything but contemporary material? How can a twentieth century poet, even when he imagines that he is concerned with early Greek or Egyptian life, deal with any subject but the life of his own time, except in the most external and superficial detail? Cynical critics have said since the first outpourings of men's hearts, "There is nothing new in art; there are no new subjects for the poet." But the very reverse is true. There are no old subjects; every subject is new as soon as it has been transformed by the imagination of the poet.

Finally, there is the confusion which is represented by the statement that "poets write metaphors." Poets write a good many things, so many that it is hard to say what they do write; frequently they even write nonsense; but one thing we may be sure they do not write, and that is the impossible. Metaphors are myths created by grammarians which have no reality in the poet's world or any other. The misconception involved in these "figures of speech" is that style is something separate from the work of art and not part and parcel of its inner being. It is conceived as an ornament to be added to or subtracted from expression instead of as expression itself. If "lion-hearted" be only another way of saying "brave," why use one rather than the other? Or if they mean something different, however slight, why say that one is used for the other at all? We have inherited these figures from the old Greek rhetoricians, and in any theory of style as concrete expression they have no place. Every phrase is a thing in itself, always indefinably new, wherever it may be, never representing anything but itself in the exact context where it is found for the first and only time. It can never be exactly the same, even when it is used again in the same passage; and, it has been well said that the word "love" in Dante's famous line,

> "Amor, che a nullo amato amar perdona,"

is not the same word thrice repeated, but must be considered artistically as three separate and distinct expressions.

The misconception involved in all these "confusions" is the same,—it is to mistake anatomy for personality, the husk for the core, the dead for the living, abstractions for realities, non-art for art.

A POOR THING, BUT OUR OWN

Harold Stearns

SINCE the war the amiable illusions of those who have been so busily announcing the dawn of an American drama have curiously paralleled the naive despairs of those who only a few seasons ago were bewailing the utter mediocrity of our native plays. It is a typical swing of the pendulum, for American prophets seem still to derive a childlike delight from the romantic extreme—in the home of the superlative and the illuminated advertisement popular essayists must cling to the sharp, pure black or white generalization. Of course, if we had ever had an American drama at all, strictly speaking, it would be easier to forgive this perpetual critical adolescence. But the awkward age becomes really such, when prolonged. And the truth is, we have had at the most only a few playwrights, more or less successfully imitative of their English or European superiors, an occasional play redolent of America and its youthful, barbaric, wistful, humorous spirit (usually a farce), a few really fine *genre* pieces, and some first-class melodramas. Surely the post-bellum sentimentalities of the 70's and 80's or the "Shore Acres" and "Sag Harbor" of Herne are not hugged to our collective bosom as the first tender flower of national selfconsciousness, nor can the steady development of our farces from irresponsible burlesque to frank imitation of the humors of the boulevard be said to express the spiritual history of a people. Even when clever or, more rarely, of genuine poetic grace, our abortive intellectualistic dramas, so earnestly admired by absurd, self-conscious "uplift" societies, are dreary unrealities. Literally, they are *déracinés*—homeless. They spring from the top levels of disinherited minds; disinherited, I mean, of national traditions or a strong racial sub-soil.

In a word, we have not yet produced an American drama, and it will be time to despair of it when it exists. Meanwhile, our theater will remain a sort of critical No-Man's-Land, where every dogmatic *dilettante* can discover exactly what it pleases him to discover, and every personal mirage can be called the true dawn. Just now, for example, it is the fashion to be valiantly optimistic and every month to herald the glad tidings of the renaissance.

Yet I cannot but believe that the current optimistic accent is the true accent. Ultimately we are sure to possess a distinctive American drama, just as we already possess a distinctive commercial architecture. In the long run can a nation escape individuality in the theater any more than it can escape individuality in speech? Because we have been bolder and more creative in the externals of life than in the amenities is no necessary sign that our culture, our *vie intérieure,* as Romain Rolland calls it, must always be awkward and selfconscious except when imitating foreign models. Sooner or later we are almost sure to possess a fund of plays and a method of attack which will be everywhere recognized as peculiarly our own. If our individuality seems stifled now, the final release may be all the more thrilling.

But this longed-for transvaluation of values in our theater to American values will most certainly be unduly delayed unless we soon mend our ways. We bring to our stage an incredible amount of cant and intellectual snobbery which has the effect not merely of muddying and thwarting our own interpretation of American plays, but of likewise intimidating our playwrights. They are frightened into furtive imitations of what they have been told is correct in an older and more sophisticated tradition; they are ashamed of that portion of their work which is truly American as flippant or shoddy and hide it, or, goaded by the jeers and indifference of the intelligentsia, parade it in the every-day theater with an over-cynical commercialism. Human nature seems to be extraordinarily simple in those elements which cluster around the instincts of vanity. Even what a mid-Western Browning society would call the most debased and corrupted of dramatists craves intelligent appreciation. Denied everything except big audiences, it is small wonder he becomes strident in his eulogy of the "low-brow" and boasts, since he is allowed to boast of nothing else, of his bank account. Our steadily false Europeanized demand has resulted in almost the final perversion of taste. I am not speaking of our power to recognize the abstractly good from the abstractly bad, nor of the quickness of our response to excellent technique; I am speaking of our power to recognize the play which rests its assumptions on the American assumptions about life, and to distinguish it from the play which emerges from a foreign culture and tradition, or, as so frequently happens, from no culture or tradition at all. Yet it would be truer to say, not that we had lost this taste, but rather that we had never possessed it. We have to rely for our news about the beginnings of our own drama upon reporters who cannot recognize an American play when they see it. Their criteria, like nine-tenths of the pictures in our art galleries, are all imported.

In fact we seem to have completely forgotten certain rudimentary things about the drama—that of all the arts it is the most popular; that when it becomes special or esoteric or too subtle or too intellectually radical it runs the serious danger of also becoming flabby and devitalized. The genius of the drama is the genius of the generality of its appeal. In America there is a distinct tendency to look upon the drama as a cultural agent rather than as what it is, a cultural expression. The true function of the drama does not lie in guiding and controlling and setting the pace for our emotional life, but in revealing and expressing that life. Its business is disclosure, not discipline. Every expression of life is, too, an educative force. But every generalization is only partly true, and I am arguing for an emphasis and an attitude, as it seems to me, of genuine pragmatic value. It involves certain critical commonplaces. Yet the infinite harm done to our playwrights by the coldness of the academicians and by the false cleavage established between the play of "popular" and the play of "special" appeal have together worked twice the damage so generally put upon the already sagging shoulders of stupid producers. There is a sophomoric mood of generous and impulsive idealism which hopes to exploit the drama for its big dividends in culture, which sees in playwriting a facile instrument for the propagating of new ideas. It is extraordinary how this mood persists and with what speed it acquires rigidity and intolerance. We simply will not be humble about the stage. We insist on the borrowed plumage of other traditions, because we are impatient at what we consider the barrenness of our own. Without the sympathy or insight to discover our own life, we cavalierly dismiss it as shabby and superficial and lean upon the fullness of emotional experience which is some one's else. Dimly we recognize that we cannot have a great drama until, in one sense at least, we have a great life. But we are suspicious and skeptical of ourselves. We are afraid of what too many people like. Other nations' masterpieces, wrought out of the fullness of time and tradition, lie ready to our hand, and it is easier to expatriate our taste.

This confusion of our desires with reality, this expectation from our theater of what only foreigners may legitimately expect of theirs, has had certain very definite and vicious consequences. We long for the sophistications of Schnitzler from the movie-bred young playwrights of Indiana, or force the accent of Synge lyric tragedy from the Ford-owning Kansas litterateur. We expect the wit and realism of Shaw from the writers who have heard nine-tenths of their jokes in the Pullman smoker. That blending of mind and soil, that saturation of personality with the color and shape of its environment which comes from years of loving localism we also expect from a generation that moves every spring and spends a fair share of its life on trains. All the pageantry and romance and spiritual experiences of a slow, cumulative national life are invoked to the bitter bewilderment of the dramatist. We laud Clyde Fitch when he writes like W. S. Maugham at his drawing-room comedy best, and ignore the unpretentious, true middle-class Americanism of a tiny farce like "Too Many Cooks." We sniff at such really indigenous products as "Broadway Jones," to grow ecstatic over the exotic prettifactions of a "Yellow Jacket." Van Wyck Brooks has admirably described that easy optimism of an America which hardly dares do other than grow proud of its material success, but we scorn in the theater those flank sentimental attacks on it—attacks which, for all their fluff and sugarcoating, do suggest an honest emotional discontent. Even in the most conventional of the "relief from ordinary life" or mere wish dramas there is some expression of the fermenting forces stirring in the country, thin and timid though that expression be. Because of our polite shudders at their crudeness and newness these unfinished and inchoate rebellions receive no appreciation or encouragement. Indeed, no true-born American is supposed to experience any emotion deeper than the skin affection of the couples on the covers of cheap magazines or the thrill of justified satisfaction which comes from the worsting of business rivals in the approved manner of a guide-to-success. The emotional break-down of the "strong" man on the stage should be welcomed with cheers as a confession of our common clay with the rest of the world. Yet when, in a crisis, any American hero is other than whitecheeked, thin-lipped and determined, the critics sadly shake their heads and mutter "unreal." We are snobs about the theater almost in spite of ourselves.

I am not attempting to eulogize American life as it is. I do not defend our vulgarity, our emotional inflexibility, our pre-occupation with material things, the immature pruriency which is expressed in the dare-devil titillations of our musical comedy. There are better if less articulate aspirations beneath these traits, but at present these are the predominant traits, and I defend the drama that springs from them—defend it not because it satisfies the soul of man, but because it is ours. If we wish really to encourage an American drama, we must resolutely accept what we already have. We must cease to be ashamed of our medium, and cease to long so intently for alien gold that we cannot complete the original statue in clay. The deeper fineness will come only with the time that will make our whole national life finer.

Discontented with over-advertised, cheap, third-rate "road" companies in over-advertised trivialities, cities like St. Louis, San Francisco, Chicago, Los Angeles, Baltimore, Philadelphia and St. Paul have all built their own "little" theaters. Many of them are operated successfully on a sort of community basis. These enterprises still cater to the snobs. They produce the plays of Ibsen and Sudermann and Maeterlinck and Galsworthy, because those are the plays which the subscribers now want. The courage of their imagination extends to only what they are certain is good. Gradually, however, the lure of foreign excellence will conflict, I believe, with the curiosity which directs itself to the immediate and actual life. Our own drama and the creative spirit to forge it will emerge bit by bit as the need for self-interpretation becomes urgent. These community theaters may well be the *foci* of confused and troubled revolt at an environment which is so stark and unyielding that it has to cross the ocean to find emotional release. The progress of self-interpretation and creation will be hastened or retarded as we flinch or not before our own life.

Possibly we shall never have the racial integrity nor the individuality of the comic point of view which comes with one blood. After all, we are a nation, not a race, and a heterogeneous nation at that. Different sections of the country have sharp and distinct economic and cultural backgrounds; politically we are still split in two by a sectionalism which reinforces a bitter memory by an actual historical "line." It will be difficult and perhaps impossible to transcend these variations in terms of a wider national experience. Nevertheless, I cannot but suspect that we shall discover far greater emotional reaches, far more uniqueness of attitude and mood than we now dare hope for, once we have become unashamed of our own drama, struggling, self-conscious, awkward and trivial. Only the frankness of real welcome will cure the fantasies of our youth. For the soul of man takes many shapes and even in America, once we have the courage to grasp the nettle of our own life, our drama may reveal ourselves to ourselves. We have first to recapture our self-respect. We have a humor that has often dissolved the world in laughter and helped keep it sane. Perhaps, too, we have a pathos.

A DEVIL OF A FELLOW

Wilbur Daniel Steele

HE had always been spoiled, by men, and especially by women. Even in the name they called him in Portuguese Old Harbor, down cape, there was a ring of irrepressible triumph—"Va Di! Va Di!"—as it were, "a devil of a fellow," or "a gay bird."

They had been dead for more than half a year, he and Stiff Peter—dead, that is, in the knowledge of the home world. And as befitting one out of the unknown, he returned more magnificent than ever, stepping down the fruit steamer's plank at the Boston dock dressed in a suit of cream-colored flannels gotten in the tropics, between which and the pale block of the Panama hat above, his face showed more than ever swarthy, rich-toned and clean-drawn, with its crisp black spurs of moustache breaking the line of either cheek, like a brigand on a poster. In his right hand he poised a slender cane, something he had learned in Port au Prince. Stiff Peter came behind, carrying the new, straw suitcase, clothed himself in much the same sort of shoddy in which he and his captain had been picked up from the fisherman's wreckage, seven months before, by a southward-going tramp. Stiff Peter was a small fellow; he had to look up to Va Di; had he had to look down to Va Di, the world would have been quite inexplicable.

The pair stood outside the dock gates, staring about them at the heavy summer city, the vendors of colored fruits, the hot blue elevated trains thundering overhead, the ice-carts sweating long, cold threads across the cobbles.

"Here's the country fer you, eh, Peter?"

Peter nodded, showing his bad teeth. "Betcha!"

The master pointed the tips of his moustache and smiled easily at a passing shop-girl. "Say, Peter, I a'most wisht now I didn't send that letter home. Be some sport now, coming ashore into Old Harbor, like a—miracle."

"Betcha!" The little fellow grinned, thinking that would have been fine. "I wisht you didn't either," he echoed. The fact that Peter himself had sent the letter, Va Di never having learned to read or write, did not obtrude itself upon either of them. Peter waited patiently, eyes on the cobbles.

"Well, Peter, we'll see a night, afore we go down home, anyhow. Wonder who'll be to Schlinsky's? Them boys off the fleet'll be tickled to see me."

"Betcha!"

Outside Schlinsky's place they were confronted by a slovenly-jointed man whose little, red-rimmed eyes seemed to be looking at ghosts.

"Thousand devils!" the fellow gasped in his long throat.

Va Di straightened the left lapel of his coat and flicked a damp curl from his forehead. No one enjoyed this sort of thing more than he.

"Hello, Costa. How's fishin'—good? Any the boys done good this year?"

"But for Gawd's s-a-k-e!" Costa stretched out an absurdly long finger to touch the flannel stuff. "And is that Stiff Peter?" His eyes wobbled about in a grotesque fashion. "Say, you fellahs is *drowned*!"

He closed his eyes tight and mopped the sweat from his brow with the back of a wrist. "I was onto the *Arbitrator* myself las' fall when she picked up your wreckage. Me and Tony Silva catched a dory-load o' corpses ourselves. The hull o' you 's got good granite stones up to the graveyard. And here you come tackin' up to me in broad daylight." He popped his eyes very suddenly at the conclusion, as if to give nature a chance.

"And you never *knowed*?" Va Di demanded, losing his dramatic composure.

"Knowed *what*?"

"Knowed we was picked up, me and Peter, and took to Brazil."

Costa shook his head uneasily, still a little suspicious of them.

"But looky here, didn't—who was it I sent that letter to, Peter? Mamie Cabral? Say, man, didn't Mamie get no letter offa me, eh?"

"N-n-naw." Costa's face changed abruptly from pale brown to brick-color and his unmanageable fingers fussed with his beard. "Mamie's went—"

"*Went?* Went *where?*"

"Nowheres. Only she went an' got married."

"Got *married?*"

"Got married."

"Onto *who?*"

"Onto that old store-keep, Henny Lake—you know."

"Old Henny Lake with the crooked leg? Looky here, Costa——"

Costa backed away a step, licked his lips, fumbled uneasily in and out of his pockets, and after a moment spoke in a voice unnecessarily loud:

"Come on up an' have a drink, Va Di, old fellah." He slapped the other on the back, crying: "There's other fish into the water, man!"

"You go straight to hell!"

Va Di stood for a long time after Costa had retreated up the stairway, scowling into the yellow sun of evening, his teeth playing with his nether lips, his hands tormenting the frail Malacca.

"They—they's other fish into the water," Peter stammered, desperate to shift the great man's humor. Va Di wheeled with out-flung hands.

"Other fish! Well, I *guesso*. Mary Virgin, but I got a dozen girls in town, right here, better'n that run-around slut that jumps after an old man's money the minute I get out o' sight. Fish? I *guesso!* Come on up, Stiff Peter. I'll show 'em."

He mounted the dusty stairs, with Peter sweating after him, and in the wide, many-tabled hall of the Jew, heavy with the arid lushness of a summer night in the city, he drank himself into an heroic insensibility, so that he had to be carried away to dark T Wharf, in the willing hands of the fish fleet, and dumped aboard a schooner bound down on the morning tide for the end of the Cape.

They opened the town around Long Point, a straggling arc of infinitesimal houses and wharves and spires, all colored alike in the sulphur fires of sunset, with here and there a gleam of clear flame refracted from a window pane, a whole broadside from the cold-storage in the western sands.

"Seven month," Peter mused, an eye cornerwise on the silent man beside him in the bows. "Seven month; and it's like yiste'day—er mebby ten, twenty year, lookin' at it another way, eh, Cap'n?"

"They'll be took aback," Va Di muttered, rousing himself from his sour preoccupation. "I'm goin' to see the Silvado girls tonight, Peter. You watch their faces, now. Fish into the water—I guesso." He fell into another silence, broken only by the faint rustle of the cutwater and the tiny crescendo of men's voices as the bow-gang straggled forward to make the anchor ready. The fleet at mooring drifted nearer, spiring purple on a mat of pellucid gold.

"I see Maya's shifted his off-shore trap," Peter struggled patiently.

The tide was low when the dories came ashore, leaving a wide stretch of flats, soggy, half-reflecting. Two of the crew, to tell of it afterward, carried Va Di on their shoulders and saved his white shoes from the wet, their own boots leaving tiny lakes behind, full of yellow sky. A bare-legged girl with a clam-rake in her hand turned curiously as she crossed in front of them, opened her eyes wider, ran away blushing richly, the damp skirts flinging about her knees.

Va Di called after her: "Ai there, you Angie—you watch out for me."

People began to come out on the stranded wharves; some padded across the flats, hallooing to one another. At the "rising," Va Di kicked to be let down, and stood with the great hat held dramatically across his breast, watching the townspeople converging upon him. A party of summer visitors from the East End passed in a motor; one of them, a handsome woman of thirty or so, smiled amusedly at the figure, flushed and tightened her lips as she found her smile returned with a shocking candor, made to pluck her companion's sleeve, thought better of it, lowered her eyes to her lap, and so whirled on into nothingness.

"Le' me alone," Va Di cried with a sudden ferocity. "Peter, gi' me that dress-suit-case." Grasping the shiny thing he wheeled and strode away into the mouth of a lane, leaving mouths and eyes wondering behind him.

The day died very suddenly now. Passing beneath the willows that hung out of Ma Deutra's chicken pen it was almost night already, cool and struck through with the acrid foetal of the roots; and when he came out beyond, the world's color had changed perceptibly, its passion chilled by the faint white influence of the moon. Turning into the back street, he paused before a small weathered building with "Henry Lake, Merchandise & Provisions" lettered across the false front.

"Shut up a'ready," he mused with a hard-won sneer. "Stays home of evenin's *now*—the old bastard. I'll wring his dried-up neck—you watch."

He moved on again, smoothing out his coat-folds and tipping the Panama further back and to the side, for he had to pass the house now. The perfectly inexplicable thing was that he should find himself so upset over Mamie Cabral—*Mamie Cabral*—a good-enough girl, but... He walked along the white pickets of the fence, shoulders squared back, heart-rending chin thrust forward in an heroic preoccupation, eyes fastened on the moon, where Fergus's willows chopped it into ragged white fragments. But, somehow, he could not get past the gate; he faltered there, set down the suitcase, and leaned his elbows on the posts.

Through all the years of his boyhood he had played around that house of Lake's; later he had stalked past it going to or from his various vessels. And yet he could not have told anyone definitely what it looked like. He retained a dim impression of a grape-vine, that was all. Now he looked at it for the first time with eyes of interest, intense glowering interest. The vine, shooting thick and rough from the ground near the front door and sprawling haphazard over the dimming whiteness of the walls till it came to the semi-restraint of a pergola, touched the man's ponderous imagination and made him think of a snake, or a kind of guardian dragon.

"And them two are in there," he mumbled to himself. "Into the dark." He leaned still more heavily on the gate post, his garments melting into the luminous streak of the fence, his dark, working face invisible against a further hedge, only that monstrous exotic bloom of a hat hanging in the dusk, air-sustained.

"Tony! Oh—Oh, Tony Va Di!"

It came from the side of the house where a bay-window sheltered beneath the vine-strangled pergola, a low cry. Va Di stood up rigid, leaning slightly backwards as if before a blow, his tongue running over his lips. He muttered: "Name of God!"

The low cry repeated itself, half in appeal, half-ecstatic.

"Ton'! Ton'!"

Opening the gate, careless now of who might see or hear him, he strode along the nasturtium-bordered walk and stood beneath the pergola, staring at the window slightly above the level of his head.

She was kneeling inside, so that no more than her head was visible against the interior darkness, and her forearms crossed on the sill, bare and brown and sweetly modelled. The last dim effulgence of the sunset warmed her right cheek, the other was chilled by the waxing power of the moon—like the two phases of a man's passion. Neither seemed to have any words, save those scared, triumphant articulations of their eyes. So they gazed at one another for a long time, while the knotted shadows of the vine established themselves upon the ground and the house-side, austere and grotesque.

A slow bewilderment took hold of Va Di; something began to flutter in the back of his brain, an intolerable, weightless thudding, and the pupils of his eyes dilated curiously. He could not understand. He had an instinctive desire to huddle down or to turn and run away, as a coral-islander might feel, put down miraculously in the midst of the Himalayas.

"Where—where is he?" he whispered by and by.

"He's dead, Tony."

"Dead!"

"Three days, Ton'."

The man took off his hat and stared into it; vaguely astonished at a jewel shining on the brim, he raised his hand to find tears rolling out of his eyes. He had an almost uncontrollable impulse to pray.

"Old Lake's dead," he echoed in a shallow, vacant voice. Sluggish visions tumbled through his mind as he stared at Mamie's dark, unmoving eyes.

"Wha'—what was ailin' of him?"

"I killed him."

The air about the open window grew dank and old, shot with a faint reek of never-opened rooms, unaired wall-paper, crumbs of funeral cakes and spilled wine, and a memory hanging about it of withered old dead limbs. Va Di shrank back till his shoulders touched an upright of the pergola. His face was yellow in the half-light and one yellow finger scratched a cross on his breast.

"You—y-y-you——"

"I killed him, Ton'—after I got your letter."

If she would take her eyes away for an instant, then he could run.

"You—got it—then?"

She nodded slowly.

"I didn't tell nobody. Why? I don't know, Ton'. But then I prayed to all the saints that he would die, and to the Blessed Virgin, and even to Christ Hisself—and three days ago he fell off Maya's wharf and drownded."

"O-o-oh!" It was not tears now that wet his cheeks, but sweat, released suddenly from its pores. "They can't git—you—for—*that*."

"They can't. *They* can't. No. But——"

For all the frightful, occult implication of her words, her eyes were still level and unfrightened, full of a deep, transfigured calm. Va Di could not live up to that; without ceasing he crossed himself and looked out of the corners of his eyes, as though fearful of beholding in that moon-checkered nook the form of a black, relentless priest.

"Oh, Ton'," she called softly. He had to look at her, and even the cold exhalations of the night light could not kill the color sweeping her cheeks. He became aware of her hand reaching out to him, wavering close before him; heedless of all things else, earthly and unearthly, he took it in his own and turned it over and kissed the palm—kissed it over and over again till it smothered him.

"Mamie!" he cried, searching her face with his reckless eyes. "You're mine, ain't you, Mame? Ain't you?" He came nearer and stood on tiptoe to draw down her lips, but she went white at that and pulled back, fluttering her free hand over her bosom.

"Ton'—Ton'! Don't! I—I ain't—smart—Tony."

He stood perfectly quiet for a moment, as if struck there in stone by a flash of some Medusa-head. After a time, becoming aware that he still held the girl's hand in his, he let it drop abruptly. He began working his lips, as if they were stiff from long disuse. His face was yellow and hard.

"The hell you say!"

Turning away he walked around the corner of the house, a singular woodenness in his knees. But he returned immediately to lean against the upright and confront her with his blighted rancor.

"You didn't waste no time, did you."

She did not appear to have grasped it yet. Once again he flung off around the corner, and this time he did not return.

When he came into his own lane, gated with clumpy willows and at the further end fading out into the blue-white slope of a dune dotted with rubbish, he saw that the news had run ahead of him and all the neighborhood was out-of-doors, hiding in the dusty thoroughfare, shouting, sobbing, squealing. His mother lunged forward at sight of him, an old, raggedhaired woman, full of fecund years, tripping over the torn hem of her skirt.

Va Di glowered at her, holding her off with his strong hands. She had been handsome once, too; even now there were fine foundation-lines which the folds of her cheeks, red and rutted like a rooster's wattles, could not altogether hide.

"Ma!" he cried of a sudden. "Ma, I'm back." Folding her in his arms, he patted her back with a rough tenderness, and wept. Then all the others, who had come pattering, fell to weeping and screeching and pounding *him* on the back. They got, finally, into the house, a bleak, tall, narrow structure with peeling clapboards without and a pervasion of linoleum within; into the kitchen, full of all the essentials of life, a stove, a pump, a lithograph of the Virgin, a mahogany wardrobe leaking cornmeal and onions, a phonograph, cot bed, chairs and a table.

Eight brothers and sisters had to be heard; a ninth came running in from her husband's house up-street, her stolid velocity not in the least hampered by the protuberance under her shawl, understood to be a nursing infant, miraculously adhesive. "You'll git the house painted," she murmured with a hint of severity to Angelina, seventeen, and in high school.

"Yeh." Angelina had thought of that herself, having callers.

His mother busied herself in an oily nimbus above the stove, frying a *linguisa* and other things, watching her first-born all the while with convulsive tremors about her mouth which made her appear to grin, at intervals, idiotically. Va Di pounded the red table-cloth with the butt of his knife.

"Ma, git a move onto that. Ain't I told you I'm hungry?"

"Well, ain't I hurryin'?" The old woman made the *linguisa* crackle by poking it with a knife. Va Di rubbed the back of his hand across his lips and justified himself. "Well, I'm hungry."

He ate in silence, only once raising his voice, and his hands, to bid the company be quiet. "You make me nervous," he cried. After he had finished he got up and dusted the crumbs off his fine clothes, scratching an old spot with a thumb-nail and rubbing it with his coat-cuff, ran a hand through his straight, black hair, and lounged to the front door. His mother called after him with a curious cluck in her voice. "Where you goin', son?"

"Aw, see the town."

But he got no further than the step to the gate, where he leaned on his elbows and gloomed at the roofs across the lane. Curious ones passed, turned back, cleared their throats, and, seeing his face, did not speak.

"A kid," he mumbled in his throat. "A kid off o' that crooked-legged old sow." And after another sour silence: "I never remembered what a good-looker she was. Say! And crazy about me. But … Hell!"

The moon swam high over the end of the lane, filling the dusty passage with its effulgent silver. The clear notes of Town Hall telling eleven floated across the huddled dwellings, and Va Di, wondering at the hour, looked about to find all the windows dark in the lane, save one toward the street end where a mandolin twinkled an Island melody. A solitary figure moved in the vista, coming nearer, a girl, dark-faced and with her dark hair piled on either side of her ears, wearing a white linen skirt and a crimson sweater. Opposite Va Di's gate she paused to kick a twig lying in the dust and discovered the man with a slight start.

"I heard you're back," she said, drifting easily nearer. "Glad t'see you."

The man smoothed his moustache. "Hullo, Mary. Didn't 'spect to see me again, eh, girlie? How's things?"

"Lookin' up, *now*." She leaned against the other side of the fence, smiling and fussing idly with her hair, her eyes lowered demurely. By and by she raised them, nonplused by his failure to go on, and found him staring at the sky as if he had forgotten she was there. She drifted away, after a time, flinging her shoulders a little, and once looking back with a wounded, malignant expression. Va Di shook himself and stared after her, moved by a faint sensation of regret. "I must be turnin' foolish," he muttered to himself.

For a moment he thought she was coming back, and straightened up with a not unaccountable thrill. But then he sank down again, recognizing old Baldy Minn by a faint flapping of soles, many sizes too large for her, on the dust. Baldy Minn had a wide, gelatinous person, forever billowing and breaking against the precarious dams of her clothing when she moved about; a silky gray beard blurred the contour of her chin; her small eyes floated in a brownish liquor, prying, inquisitorial, continually suspicious of women's figures, seeming to say: "Mmmm—so you're at it again. Don't lie about it, because you can't fool *me*." A most horrible old woman. She came flapping through the moonlight and stopped in front of the gate.

"Ai, Ai!" she greeted in a strong, bubbly voice. "They told me you're back, Va Di. Too much f' the devil, was y'u? Well, Blessed Saints take pity onto the maids, if they's any lef' ... Is y'r ma up?"

"I dunno." Va Di was a little afraid of this woman, and disliked her accordingly. "I'll take a look," he mumbled, after enduring her eyes for a moment. He turned to the door and called : "Ma—hey there, *Ma*."

A sudden faint crash sounded from the other end of the house, as if someone had started out of a doze and knocked something over.

"Huh, Tony! That you, Tony?"

"A'right," Va Di grumbled. "You c'n go in, Baldy Minn. ... Say——" He peered at the bundle swinging in her hand, an old shawl stuffed full and exuding ragged ends of things. "Say, what you want, this time o' night?"

The old crone turned within the entry and winked a leering eye.

"That big kettle o' y'r ma's," she bubbled.

"Oh! O-o-oh, I git y'u. Who is it this time, Baldy Minn?"

The woman grinned and flapped a hand at him with a horrible coyness.

"None o' your beezness, *any*how."

After a time, driven by an unaccountable restlessness, he moved into the house, felt his way softly along a wall and stood in what had been meant for the dining-room. The air was heavy and sour with the sleeping of the three younger boys, but the door was open a crack into the kitchen, and in the lean, bright aperture he could see Baldy Minn's face with all its dewlaps shivering.

"I knowed it all along," she was saying. "I knowed she'd never carry it—ugh-ugh—not outa that old crook-leg."

The boards groaned ever so slightly beneath Va Di's heels.

His mother's voice came through the crack, heavy with the burden of ages.

"I've hear of seven-monthers livin'."

"I kep' one myself." The midwife's lips sucked in and exploded with a suggestion of defiance. "Mis' Deutra claims she kep' one oncet, but she never. Sam Raphael's boy 's a seven-monther an' *I* kep' *him*, an' don' you let nobody tell y'u diff'nt, Annie. ... But a six-monther—Ugh-ugh. No."

Va Di's mother had borne sixteen and brought up ten. He heard her now, moaning gently through her apron: "Well, well, I don't know—I don't know. ... I go long with you, Baldy Minn. Poor thing—poor thing. I put my shawl, go long with you, Baldy Minn."

"Naw, ain't no need, Annie. I got Angie Bragg up there now, an' Rosie Courier's there anyhow. Gimme the kittle. She ought to be comin' 'long now. Rosie come down two hour ago." She stood for a moment ringing the huge kettle with a thumb nail. "Won'er what started her up. She ain't fell or nothin' *I* hear of. Well ... "

She flapped away along the dark hall, not a yard from the silent man, humming and bubbling between her gums. There was a long hush, broken only by the snores of the sleepers and the continuous, subdued moaning from the kitchen, like the chant of a vigil. Va Di went out as softly as he had come in, and stood by the gate, fanning his face with the big hat.

"Damn," he mumbled, and after a moment: " 'Tain't none o' *my* fun'ral, though."

Putting the hat on his head, he opened the gate, turned aimlessly toward the back country and mounted the clear, blue slope of the dune, picking his way mechanically amongst the scattered tomato cans and disemboweled bedticks and skeletons of barrels. Sitting down on the crest he became part of it, moon-colored and still. The night was so intolerably quiet that the ground-swell eating the beaches far off on the outside crept in to him, and he ruffled the sand with his feet because it made him think of his mother's moaning and her words: "Poor thing—poor thing."

"God, how that girl looked at me," he remembered out loud. "She l-l——"

He jumped up and shuffled around; rolled a cigarette, wetting it too much with his tongue so that it fell apart; threw it away. "She *l-l-loves* me," he came out, more racked by the word than ever a child by his virgin oath.

He found himself at the foot of the dune on the other side, his canvas shoes sucking up moisture from a bog. He climbed another hill, drawn back toward the town, and waded across it knee-deep in scrub and wild roses that tore triangular rents in his flannel trousers. Descending into the shadow of familiar trees, he hunched himself up to sit on the shingles of a pig-sty, and heard the sluggish animals, whose distant forebears he had beaten with furtive barrel-staves, grunt and roll over in the interior muck.

He took out his knife and whittled the shingles, trying not to look at the house. There was something incredibly fearful about its being awake in the midst of all the sleepers, staring him down with its lighted windows, profligate of kerosene and tallow. The kitchen door was open; by and by a woman came and leaned in the bright rectangle, a silhouette of fatigue. This was Rosie Courier. She had been old Henny Lake's housekeeper as long as Va Di could remember. Sometimes she had served in the store. Va Di could think of her, immensely tall and tight-garmented behind the counter, her lean, brown face with its cheek-cords pressing in the corners of her mouth, hovering over his head, righteous and suspicious. Quite invisible as he was in the shadow, he could not keep from cringing a little against the roof as she stood there in the doorway, breathing and resting.

Town Hall clanged a single note, full and round, and as if in answer another note came and hung among the leaves, a high, unmodulated animal-cry, torn carelessly from the tissues of a throat. The austere silhouette in the doorway straightened and disappeared.

"Oh, my God!" Va Di breathed. As a boy he had always been sent to play with neighbor children on those days when brothers or sisters accrued to his family, and so he did not know. He had supposed he knew; he had had a leg broken once by a jibing boom, and he had seen plenty of men crushed or torn in the bad seconds of ocean fishing. But they had always screamed like human beings.

The distracted ululation was in the trees again.

"Don't," the man whispered. "For Christ's sake, M-a-m-i-e—d-o-n't!"

He got down and tried to walk away, but found himself back again, leaning his crossed arms on the sty roof. He had to be doing something, to dull the blade of that outcry, and so he made up an unearthly anger at those shadows moving against the window-squares.

"God damn you to hell!" he mumbled, shaking his white fists, "Why don't y'u *do* somethin'? Why don't y'u *do* somethin'?"

He was aware of Baldy Minn's figure flapping out of the door, a yawling cat held at arm's length. He watched her slay the little beast, make some horrible business with a kitchen knife, and flap into the house again with the warm liver. He knew well enough that this would soothe the sufferer a little, tied with a cord around her neck, but he became more than ever furious at the shadowy transaction. He did not want Mamie's agony allayed a little; he wanted it stopped, definitely and forever. He stood up and bawled after the retreating midwife: "Ow! Ow! Ow!" Baldy Minn turned and peered into the night, wondering, shook the fleshy pendants of her head, crossed her billowy bosom with the hand that contained the liver and slammed the door shut.

Without any clear transition, his hate shifted from "them" to "it." It was "it" that was tearing and killing Mamie.

"Damn it—I'd like to——" The finger-nails ate into his palms. He hoped that "it" would die—that "it" would be a "six-monther," so there could be no possibility of its not dying. "Her and I would be——" His ravening speculations tumbled on into giddy chaos.

The night was laced with threads of agony, exquisite, racking, prolonged, still prolonged. Va Di reached out and gripped either edge of the roof, as if to keep himself from sliding. He pleaded with it to stop. The interstices among the leaves of the overhanging willows were filled with the gore of imminent day; Ma Deutra's rooster crowed in his hollow house away down a flushing lane. But still that haggard utterance hung over the world.

It ceased. A faint breeze came to life and wandered across the back yards, tumbling papers; a lark, as though bribed and timed, mounted into the sky and whistled his morning triumph; Va Di's head sank down on his arms, his knees caved in to rest against the side of the sty, and his fingers fell out flat on the shingles.

He opened his eyes by and by to find Rosie Courier standing in the horizontal radiance of the sun, regarding him from the other side of the pen. Her face was the color of a dusty boot, lifeless and flabby.

"She wants to see you," she said.

"Who? *Her?*"

She nodded stiffly, allowed the thick, mottled lids to droop over her eyes, and turned back toward the kitchen door. Va Di followed. In the kitchen Baldy Minn sat beside the sink, her hands working in a huge blossom of suds. The tight little nubbin of hair had shaken down off the bald spot, lending her a curious expression of wildness.

"Was it—did——" Va Di groped for words. "Did it live, Baldy Minn?"

"Did it *live?*" Her eyes rolled in their liquor, her whole person quivered and dashed against its margins, and she grinned at him, closing the rent in her teeth with a meaning tongue-tip. "Did it *live?* Ho-ho-ho!"

He turned away and followed Rosie Courier through a dark passage, smelling of life and death, and entered a room full of sunshine. Within the door a profound embarrassment laid hold of him; he shifted from foot to foot and looked down at the great hat revolving in his hands. Mamie was so white and still and all eyes, and the eyes dwelt upon him with such a spent and inscrutable adoration. He was afraid to look at her; he felt curiously like a figure done in clay, destructible and worthless. Her hand, all the opacity burned out of it, lay on the flowered "comfortable," and remembering suddenly how it had come out to him from last night's window, he fell down on his knees and laid his cheek against it and wept the tears of weakness.

"Mamie," he sobbed in the wadding. "You're a good girl, M-m-mamie."

After a little a sound of snickering behind him brought him to his feet, his face flaming. It was Baldy Minn, almost filling the doorway with her oceanic being, against which the bundle in her arms seemed incredibly tiny and helpless. She advanced, undulating and bubbling, to lay it across Va Di's hastily-crooked arms, laughing at his panic.

He held his chin stiff and his eyes desperately horizontal. "Naw, naw," he mumbled, "Somebody come." He turned to Mamie, appealing, and Mamie, moved by that irresponsible humor which is deeper than solemnity, smiled.

"Ton'," she whispered unsteadily. "It's killin', Ton'—how he favors you. It makes me laugh, Ton'—you without the moustache, *exactly*. I wisht you'd look, Ton'."

His knees were no good; he sat down in a rocker and looked around the room for mental help. Rosie Courier, standing, a black, unimpeachable spire, beside the bureau, gave him none. Her lids were lowered and her thoughts had turned inward for refuge. By an irony, he had to come to Baldy Minn. Dirty, evil-fleshed, full of matter prurient, there still endured in her a flicker of that essential fire that lives, somehow, through all the changing winds of orthodoxies. She had to express it, of course, in her own way.

"You old devil," she bubbled benevolently. "I might o' knowed ... "

The bundle in Va Di's arms became articulate, demanding its primal planetary food. The man's muscles suffered a poignant sensation of combat, a gentle struggle with an infinitesimal kicking. His face became pink; his mouth-muscles contracted in that species of self-conscious smirk so hard for others to bear; he opened and closed his lips tentatively, as though they were quite new and uncertain of their powers.

"He's—he's—he's a *s-s-stout* little bastard," he stammered, in all innocence.

A MODERN ACCIDENT

Peter Minuit

I WAS impanelled a few weeks since as juryman in an accident case. I confess I served willingly. The opportunity to observe legal procedure from the safe and impersonal point of view of the jury box seemed most attractive. And so I obeyed the summons gladly, and rendered myself shortly before ten o'clock in the part of the City Court presided over by Justice Harold Rabinowitz.

To my surprise, the courtroom was crowded. There were present when I arrived men of all ages and all degrees, and others filed in continually. A neighbor informed me that all these citizens had been called for jury duty. And for several minutes I reflected on the extreme wisdom of the law, that summoned all ranks and all conditions of men, and made use of their varying experiences and understandings in order to obtain justice. How superior, I thought, is our free and democratic system to the autocratic legal institutions of France and Germany! However, I retained my sentiment of pride but a short while. Hardly had the judge seated himself behind his high desk, when a clerk announced that all jurors who held positions of trust and responsibility, all who were managers of large business enterprises, all who had distinguished themselves in the conduct of affairs of whatever character, in fact, all jurors with ability, energy, and sureness of judgment, would be excused from duty without question. No sooner had this announcement been made than the major portion of those present quit the courtroom, leaving only a handful of timid and depressed men. I and eleven others were impanelled, and sworn in on a small block of wood.

Directly before the jury box there stood a lengthy table. Several men came and seated themselves at it. One of them arose and addressed us, explaining the nature of the case about to be tried.

It was what is termed an "accident case." Suit was being brought by a lawyer against a certain Mr. Napolitano, alleged to be an owner of real estate in the City of New York. This lawyer, whose name was Apponyi, I believe, claimed that a certain Mrs. Peter O'Toole lived in a tenement house, and that this house belonged to the said Mr. Napolitano. He further claimed that, owing to the negligence of the landlord, there was a staircase in the said house, and that one evening Mrs. O'Toole had fallen down it. As a result of this fall, the lawyer claimed that his own wife, Mrs. Elizabeth Apponyi, had suffered severe injuries, had had a miscarriage, was forced to keep her bed for days in succession, and could give him neither her society nor her services, to both of which he was rightfully entitled. Therefore, he brought suit against Mr. Napolitano, charging him with negligence, and demanding a monetary indemnity.

After the jury had been examined and found satisfactory, witnesses were called. The array of evidence was truly imposing. First, several persons were introduced to prove that there was a staircase in the tenement of Mr. Napolitano. This was a grave point, hotly contested by the defence. Then, it was conclusively shown that in order to get from one floor to another, it was necessary to make use of the staircase, and that in descending the steps, it was advisable to hold on to the bannisters. After this evidence had been produced, three physicians appeared in succession. They testified that Mrs. Apponyi had suffered grievously through her miscarriage, that she was ailing, and scarcely able to resume her duties. When asked whether this condition was induced by Mrs. O'Toole's accident, they swore roundly that there could be no doubt of it. At this point, the plaintiff rested his case.

By order of the Justice, counsel for the defense then rebutted.

"Gentlemen of the jury," he said, "my learned opponent has endeavored to persuade you that my client, Mr. Napolitano, owns this tenement. In other words, gentlemen, he wishes you to believe that he owns real estate in the City of New York. Gentlemen, in the name of all fairness, I resent that imputation! There is nothing before you, gentlemen, to prove my client guilty of anything of the sort. In fact, had I thought it necessary, I would have brought before you any number of witnesses to prove that he is in all ways an honorable man, fair in business and upright in all his relationships. The accusation that my learned opponent has levelled against him is absolutely without foundation! Gentlemen, this man does not own real estate! On the contrary, he is in every way worthy of your respect and admiration, and I beg you to dismiss from your minds all prejudice that my opponent's insinuation might have lodged there. Gentlemen, I do not deny that Mrs. O'Toole fell downstairs, nor do I deny that in consequence Mrs. Apponyi came to misfortune. But I do deny that it has been proven that my client owns a house in this city, and, therefore, gentlemen, I ask you to find a verdict in his favor."

When he had concluded, and seated himself, counsel for the plaintiff arose.

"Your Honor, and gentlemen of the jury," he began, "I will not affront your intelligence by pretending that my client, Mr. Apponyi, has a case. I am positive that it would be useless to attempt to mislead you into believing that he has. I see that you are surprised by my candor. Doubtless, you are wondering why I should confess as much to you, and not permit your natural distrust of the propertied classes, your pity for the sufferings of the poor, and especially for those of women, to influence you in favor of my client. Well, the truth is, that I am quite sure that if I tell you the actual facts, you will award him a larger damage than if I suppressed them. Gentlemen, these are the facts:

"The father of Mr. Apponyi, my client, was a bricklayer. Now, as you know, bricklaying is neither a richly paid nor a highly respected trade. The father of Mr. Apponyi often regretted his occupation. And he determined that his son should not have to follow in his footsteps, that he should have a more profitable and respectable business. And so he made him a lawyer.

"Gentlemen, the tragedy of it is that Mr. Apponyi has not the slightest talent for practising law. He has neither the astuteness, the personal presence, the business sense, nor, wanting these, the influential connections that make for success in it. Perhaps, were the profession less crowded, he might be able to perform a certain amount of service valuable to the community. But, since it is so unfortunately overcrowded, he, and all others in his situation, instead of being called upon to serve the purposes of the law, call upon the law to serve their own purposes. And so they bring actions of this kind. What else are they to do? It is too late for most of them to learn a trade, or enter a business house. Most of them have wives and children to support, and cannot begin life anew. Their one means of livelihood consists of whipping up processes of this sort.

"I do not blame them. In fact, I am always glad to accept their cases for very small remuneration. For, after all, it is society that put them into the positions they now hold, by underpaying the skilled trades, by giving such valuable occupations as bricklaying scant respect, and by permitting parents to do with their children as they will. And, in the last analysis, it is society that pays for the wrong it has done. The property owners who are sued to keep this man and his family alive are well insured with insurance companies. In order to cover their premiums, they raise the rentals of their tenements. Their tenants, forced to give more for housing, join unions and so increase their wages. And the public at large pays their wages. In this way, justice is done, and society makes good again its errors. Therefore, gentlemen, I ask you to make use of the power that is yours, and right the wrong done my client by an inefficient state, by returning a verdict in his favor."

After he, in his turn, had seated himself, the Justice arose and addressed the jury. He told us that the question before us had nothing whatsoever to do with the evidence. The question before us—in fact, the only question before any jury—was whether we wished to remain in the jury-room in the interests of justice. He reviewed the aspects of the question. There was much to be said on both sides. If, on the one hand, we wished to remain in the jury-room, we would probably have to go without our dinner, and might even be locked up for the night. If, on the other, we did not, we would be able to reach home well in time for the meal. He left it to the insight of the jury to see the truth of the matter. As for the case actually before us, he begged us not to worry unnecessarily over it. He had fully weighed the evidence, and had quite firmly decided the merits himself. He was not to be shaken in his opinion that we ought to find a verdict in favor of the lawyer for the plaintiff, who was personally sympathetic to the court. He was obviously a gentleman, never intricated the court in difficult situations, quoted the choice legal axioms gracefully, in fact, was the very type of man the court was most anxious to see at the bar. In the light of his personal opinion, the Justice asked us to return a verdict in favor of the plaintiff.

This we did. We filed into the jury-room, put our feet up on a table there for that purpose, and listened to several of the more experienced members of our little group of serious thinkers recount some of the cases on which they had sat. From their stories it was easy to glean that General Sessions was the only court in which it was at all amusing to serve, for there alone cases of rape and murder came to hearing. Finally, when it became late, we decided to find a unanimous verdict in favor of the judge. The court had adjourned at three o'clock. So we handed in a sealed verdict, were presented with twenty-five cents, and returned home proudly as servants of the City of New York, and engines of human justice.

YOUNG JAPAN

Seichi Naruse

(ED. NOTE: *Mr. Naruse is the former editor of Shin-Sicho, "The New Tide of Ideas," a monthly magazine published in Tokio which, he tells us, corresponds in general purpose with* THE SEVEN ARTS. *He is the author of plays and stories expressive of the new spirit in Japan and has translated a number of the works of Romain Rolland into Japanese. Mr. Naruse is at present in America and this paper is his first work written in the English language.)*

WHEN a spiritual creed or tradition, which has ruled the soul of man for a certain length of time, comes to be questioned and threatens to dissolve, a period of transition more or less anarchic in its aspects inevitably comes about before the establishment of a new order. The awakening of the contemporary younger generation in Japan, of which I am going to give a short sketch in this essay, may serve as a remarkable example.

It is natural that the more sudden and sweeping the change, the more terrible and intense will be the disorder. Prior to fifty years ago when their country was at last forcibly opened to the world, no science worthy of the name was known to the Japanese people. Their total possession was a small stock of experiential knowledge, objective, primitive and inadequate, accumulated and handed down through the generations. On their spiritual side the Japanese were even poorer. Buddhism and Confucianism were the prevailing religions; but they had gradually been Japanized in their transmission from India and China, and were almost totally different from the original forms. The Japanese were too caught up in themselves to have gone out and discovered the realities of life and nature. Thus, it was not the theological aspect of Buddhism, not the consequence of a serious and ardent quest for the truth, which commended that religion to the Japanese. Rather they took that direction as the result of some temporal unhappiness or calamity which made the renunciation of pleasure and the retirement to a convent the natural reaction. People became Buddhists because they were disappointed in love or because they had lost a parent or because they had failed to rise in the world. They did not care for the high and unattainable ideal of Nirvana; religion was for them a simple means of escape from present suffering. Confucianism in Japan became formal and artificial. The criteria of good and evil were looked on as purely external and absolute. The nature of the individual mind was not considered. In other words, virtue and vice alike were founded on objective behavior. Loyalty and filial piety were in all cases looked on as the loftiest things in the world, even as their contraries were in all cases looked on as vicious. It was a primitive morality little concerned with subjective motive or personal character. And the literary productions of Japan, although valuable in their own way, were for the most part the expressions of this attitude. Of course there was much writing that did not deal with religion or morality. But this sort also did not seek beyond the actual world. It was the surface expression of calm and contented minds. Even fantastic and romantic works, which are very rare in Japanese literature, were unmistakably matter-of-fact. The prevailing note of all Japanese life was a contentment with the superficial aspects of reality.

It would be wrong to give the name of realism to such an attitude; for it was nothing like a conscious creed. It was a simple tendency of mind. The Japanese had not even taken positive steps to justify their state or to compare it with possible alternatives. This may seem strange to you. But the explanation lies in the national isolation which had been maintained for so many centuries and which had prevented spiritual contact with any of the civilized nations of the world. The Japanese lacked a measure to put their thoughts to the test and to stimulate deeper thinking. They were self-sufficient in their own culture.

What confusion must necessarily follow the sudden opening of a country under such conditions! Naturally Japanese civilization could not cope with that of Europe, which had been tempered to its present state after incessant test and exercise. There was a tremendous distance between the intellectual development of the Japanese and the Occidental mind. It was obvious that even if the younger men wished to keep their own traditions, they would need some standpoint that was less dogmatic and less hostile to their new demands. But the power of foreign civilization was too great for such a compromise. The conflict with their fathers' creed was inevitable at the first contact of the two cultures, and at once some of the old real treasure of Japanese thought was swept away.

Of course, the old modes of living had enclosed the people's souls for many centuries. However absurd they seemed in the new light, they were still powerful. And since absolute obedience to elders was of the very stuff of Japanese culture, the struggle rose to a quick intensity. Both new and old believed too blindly in their own point of view to go out and study that of the opposition. There was a deep gap between the two, over which neither side attempted to build the bridge of mutual understanding.

The first state was one of extreme chaos. The two factions were content simply to abuse each other. It was the prelude to revolution. For the young people, Occidental culture was something like a star in heaven. They admired it without really knowing what it was. And their rejection of past authority was like the insubordination of self-willed children, emotional yet not entirely without reason.

But it was not long before the stage of chaos was lived through; and the first period of conscious reformation followed. With the importation of concrete examples of western culture came an advance in mental understanding. The classic authors of Europe were translated; and books on spiritual subjects entirely new to Japan began to appear. The inevitable change took place in the spiritual tendency of the young men. For a sound appreciation of things one must have a definite axis of one's own, an established individuality on the basis of which the new knowledge may be related up. This of course was lacking in the Japanese. The young men took to reading everything without preference or judgment. The result was a confusion of mind caused by the blind appreciation of many great works which, although very impressive, were apt to be contrary in teaching and in nature.

Still no conclusions seemed achievable. The chaos became more intense, more terrible because a new enemy had appeared in the Japanese soul—a bitter scepticism. As they became aware of the unfathomable depth and remoteness of the Truth they sought, a profound oppression stole over the Japanese like that of a traveler lost in the desert who after a weary walk finds at the day's end that he has not reached the longed-for oasis. Doubt was their enemy from within; and from without, to heighten their misery, they had to suffer the tyranny of the past which weighed all too heavily upon them. Desperate pessimism, which is the strongest note of young Japan, had invaded their souls.

This pessimism, the first known to the Japanese people, broke out at last in the suicide of a young student of philosophy at the Tokio High School. A young man named Misao Fujimra jumped down from the high cliff of the Kegon waterfall after carving the following words on a tree-trunk at the edge of the precipice:

"How mightily and steadily go Heaven and Earth! How infinite the duration of Past and Present! Try to measure this vastness with five feet? A word explains the Truth of the whole Universe—*unknowable*. To cure my agony I have decided to die. Now, as I stand on the crest of this rock no uneasiness is left in me. For the first time I know that extreme pessimism and extreme optimism are one."

These words, written in 1903, found their way into many young hearts, even as the act of the suicide brought to the surface many smouldering emotions. To the older generation this suicide was not a call but rather a sudden peal of thunder. To kill oneself because of a philosophical dilemma or a view of life was beyond the reach of their imagination. The episode was taken up by the conservatives. Grave fears were expressed for the spiritual welfare of the younger men. It was pointed out that western culture was poisonous and that there was need of returning to the ancient soul of Japan. But the outcry was too feeble to turn back the powerful trend of the times.

The suicide was only too symbolic of the spiritual state of the Japanese youth. The heavy flood of European culture was too overwhelming. It laid bare the vacancy of the old way of living and at the same time supplied no concrete ground for the building of the future. The ignorant goodwill of the older generation only made matters worse. Young Japan had learned too many things, had become too intellectual to seek the solaces of the ancient order.

Meanwhile, suicides increased. Death was exalted. The Kegon waterfall where Misao Fujimra killed himself became a popular sanctuary and the name grew to be a slogan for spiritual revolt. At last, however, the light of faith began to dawn. One writer declared that there were but three ways open to the Japanese:—madness, suicide and faith. The *laisser-aller* of traditional Japan was rigidly condemned. But more and more, madness and suicide were passed by and faith was looked on as the goal.

From this situation emerged the two main currents of contemporary Japan. The first is aspiration for religion and philosophy; the second is an extreme dilettantism and decadence. The hunger for philosophy and an adequate religion was sincere and serious, although of course rudimentary. The youth of Japan sought a key to release them from their agony, a fulcrum to support them. But they were too ardent to care for purely scientific philosophy, which seemed to them, to use their own term, as a play of logic. What they really aspired for was not the system itself, but metaphysical emotion. Schopenhauer, Nietzsche, Pascal, Leopardi, the Bible, the Buddhist gospel, and the Koran were read with passionate love. It was in this epoch that all the great names of Russian literature were introduced. The somber, heavy touch of these masters was entirely in harmony with the tendency of young Japan.

On the other hand there were those who quickly tired of the quest for authority and truth. These denied the cogency of religion and insisted on the impossibility of knowledge. They were the decadents and the a-moralists. The most remarkable trait of this group of writers was their devotion to the dark side of human nature—a side which had been entirely absent up to this time in Japanese literature. The *fin de siècle* culture of Europe found its way to Japan. Wilde and d'Annunzio, Baudelaire and other French writers of the sort were prevalent at this time.

The old morality of Japan had been pragmatic. The one spiritual activity it had recognized was that which served the needs of sheer existence. Japanese religion, morality and literature were largely utilitarian. But now all this was changed. These qualities ceased to be regarded as merely useful things. Their intrinsic value, their power of exalting man to a wider life came to be recognized. In the old times religion, morality and literature were subordinate to tradition; now they were regarded as guides by which tradition could be measured. Another remarkable change was the individualistic tendency. The old heteronomic conceptions were cast aside. Thinking became subjective; and its emotional impulse was heightened by the great mental suffering which clouded Japan. The young men seemed to find no energy for thinking of the past; nor for planning the foundations of the future. Doubtless, the tyrannical oppression of past authority was responsible for this. But this double side of the struggle in which the young men were engaged, destruction and construction, gives a vivid picture of the revolution.

Finally several theaters were founded in which plays of the new tendency were to be produced. Ibsen, Hauptmann, Maeterlinck, Sudermann, and Shaw were among the favorites. Of course, these plays were directly subversive of the old authority of Japan, and it is quite natural to find the censor active. An interesting example is the episode that took place on the production of Sudermann's *Heimat*. The teaching of this play is of course opposed to the ideal of filial piety. It was suppressed and only permitted to go on, with Magda repentant of her revolt in the last act. The subsequent prohibition of the publication of many European and Japanese works intensified the struggle. So that today the young men are openly hostile to the government censorship. This is carried so far that many writers intentionally publish work which they are sure will be suppressed. For it is known that if an issue of a magazine is confiscated the demand for the following number will be very great.

Unfortunately this same tone of distrust and complete isolation is found in the relations of the young men among themselves. They are split up into various hostile groups and their polemic is often shafted against each other. It is the custom today for each little company of men to publish a magazine of its own. The majority of the Japanese cultural papers are on this order. And they seem to have overlooked the great kinship which ought to unite them. They struggle not only against their elders but equally against all the young men outside their group.

This condition of revolutionary chaos may be called the second stage in the awakening of Japan. Its notable characteristic is the elevation of philosophy, religion and literature to something higher than utilitarian aims; to the recognition of them as valuable in themselves. This moralistic tendency has a deep resemblance to the movement in France of "art for art's sake." It may have been a necessary stage, but obviously it could not stand for long.

A new spiritual basis—the realization of the need of spirit in actual life—was not slow to come. We find a remarkable example of this development in the new appreciation of Tolstoi, who was previously regarded simply as a great writer. Now his admirers, who are increasing more and more, have begun to transfer his doctrines into real life. The eccentric and absolutist literary tendency is slowly passing away. Similarly, in religion, transcendentalism has come to be justified only in so far as it is deeply rooted in reality. The individualistic and philosophic tendencies remain; but now the young men of Japan are exerting themselves to carry their ideals over into action. And this effort has made the struggle still more tragic. They were already at grips with all the emotional and ideal tenets of Japan; now they are at grips with daily life.

The revolution has reached the stage of practice. Evasion of military service is becoming more and more prevalent; opposition to family life is becoming more and more bitter. The serious younger men are bewildered with their quandary: whether to be true to their convictions or to the affection of their parents, whether to devote themselves to truth or to love. The literary productions of the day are steeped with this dilemma. The new ideal and the old morality which requires them to sacrifice even their ideal out of loyalty are in constant struggle.

Out of this conflict have been born the socialist and feminist movements of Japan. The sudden appearance of a group of extremely violent socialists in 1910 threw the nation into a panic. An attempt was made to do away with the great Figure whom all the people had always worshipped as a demi-god—the Figure for whom the language provided a special pronoun. How the undertaking was received may easily be imagined. It was called *Dai-Gyaku*—great treason. With no discussion, all the social-ists were put to death. Their execution, however, did not end the life of socialism in Japan. It is impossible to deny its ever increasing power over the younger generation. The young men are becoming more and more democratic and cosmopolitan. An interesting result of this may be seen in the social position of the nobles, once looked upon with envy and now regarded with contempt.

The feminist movement, another remarkable phenomenon of the reformation, aims at the individual freedom of women who, in the old regime, were confined strictly to home life. The Bible of this revolt is Ibsen's *Doll's House*. What distinguishes it from similar movements in Europe and America is the stress on women's free growth as personalities and human beings, rather than on their political and economic rights. This propaganda also has its magazines, but it must be said that the women have had a hard battle to fight, for they are pitted against society and against the time-worn custom which demanded blind obedience to men. Some of the women have taken extreme steps. The marriage laws have been disregarded and the idea of chastity scoffed at. Although their progress has not been great, the mere birth of an idea of this kind marks an amazing change in Japan.

This is the present transitional stage. Its keynote is the passionate effort to place the new ideals in complete harmony with life. It is difficult to foretell the end. The reactionary and conservative tyranny is gradually dying down. The younger men are being left more to their own faith. But it is safe to say that any new authority which would become strong enough to prevail in the future must, as its necessary condition, regain a deep intimacy with Japanese and Oriental culture. This must be the basis of any permanent assimilation of European thought. For, after all, the Japanese are the Japanese. It is impossible to change the color of their hair and skin; it will remain impossible to change the constant fundamental quality of their souls.

A great leader must appear to bring about this marriage of Occidental and Oriental cultures. Indeed the tendency has already made itself felt. Indian, Chinese and Japanese learning is regaining its hold and the comparative study of these cultures with those of the West is being taken up. The latest germination of humanism among the young men of Japan is in this direction. The strong note of pessimism still prevails among them; but at least the new feeling for internationalism no longer assumes the exclusion of their native culture.

It may, then, be said that the first step of preparation has been achieved; that the real awakening of Japan, a renaissance in the true sense of the word, is at hand. Of course, the way is still long, but, if my opinion is right, and I am not too patriotic in saying so, the future rôle of Japan in the spiritual life of the world will be great indeed. For it is the Japanese who are in the most favorable position to understand the two great currents of world-civilization—that of the West and that of the East; it is they who must harmonize these currents into one great life. I have the firm belief that this vision will come to them before long. And it is my great wish to live to see it.

THE PURITAN'S WILL TO POWER

Randolph S. Bourne

TO THE modern young person who tries to live well there is no type
so devastating and harassing as the puritan. We cannot get away
from him. In his sight we always live. We finish with justifying our
new paganism against him, but we never quite lose consciousness of his
presence. Even Theodore Dreiser, who always revolted from the puritan
clutch, finds it necessary now and then to tilt a lance against him. If there
were no puritans we should have to invent them. And if the pagan Mr.
Dreiser has to keep on through life fighting puritans, how much more
intrigued must we be who are only reformed puritans, and feel old dangers stirring at every aggressive gesture of righteousness? For the puritan
is the most stable and persistent of types. It is scarcely a question of a puritanical age and a pagan age. It is only a question of more puritans or less
puritans. Even the most emancipated generation will find that it has only
broken its puritanism up into compartments, and balances sexual freedom—or better perhaps a pious belief in sexual freedom—with a cult of
efficiency and personal integrity which is far more coercive than the most
sumptuary of laws. Young people who have given up all thought of "being
good" anxiously celebrate a cult of "making good." And a superstition like
eugenics threatens to terrorize the new intelligentsia.

Every new generation, in fact, contrives to find some new way of
being puritanical. Every new generation finds some new way of sacrifice. Every new triumphant assertion of life is counterbalanced by some
new denial. In Europe this most proud and lusty young generation goes
to its million-headed slaughter, and in America the social consciousness
arises to bewilder and deflect the *essor* towards life. Just when convention

seemed to be on the run, and youth seemed to be facing a sane and candid attitude towards sex, we find idealistic girls and men coming out of the colleges to tell us of our social responsibility towards the race. This means not only that our daily living is to be dampened by the haunting thought of misery that we cannot personally prevent, but that our thirst towards love-experience is to be discouraged and turned aside into a concern for racial perfection. That is, we are subtly persuaded against merely growing widely and loving intensely. We become vague and mystified means toward nebulous and unreal ends. This new puritanism will not let us be ends in ourselves, or let personality be the chief value in life. It will almost let us sometimes. But it always pulls us up somewhere. There is always a devil of inhibition to interpose before our clean and naive grasping of life. (You see, my puritanism takes the form of a suspicion that there may be a personal devil lurking in the universe.)

This is why the puritan always needs to be thoroughly explained and exposed. We must keep him before our eyes, recognize him as the real enemy, no matter in what ideal disguise he lurks. We must learn how he works, and what peculiar satisfactions he gets from his activity. For he must get satisfaction or he would not be so prevalent. I accept the dogma that to explain anybody we have to do little more than discover just what contentment people are getting from what they do, or from what they are permitting to have happen to them, or even from what they are flinging their will into trying to prevent have happen to them. For, if life is anything positive, it is the sense of control. In the puritan, of course, we have the paradox how he can get satisfaction from ruggedly and sternly subjecting himself and renouncing the world, the flesh and the devil. There is a popular superstition that the puritan has an extra endowment of moral force, that he reverses the natural current of life, that he resists the drag of carnality down toward hell, that his energy is thrown contra-satisfaction, that his control is a real straddling of the nefarious way. But, of course, it is just this superstition that gives the puritan his terrific prestige. In the light of the will-to-power dogma, however, this superstition fades. The puritan becomes just as much of a naturalistic phenomenon as the most carnal sinner. Instincts and impulses, in the puritan, are not miraculously cancelled, but have their full play. The primitive currents of life are not blocked and turned back on their sources, but turned into powerful and usually devastating channels. The puritan is just as much of a "natural" man as you or I.

But we still have to explain how this lustful, headstrong creature called man, spilling with greed, could so unabatedly throughout the ages give up the primitive satisfactions of sex and food and drink and gregariousness and act the ascetic and the glumly censorious. How could an animal whose business was to feel powerful get power from being in subjection and deprivation? Well, the puritan gets his sense of power from a very cunningly organized satisfaction of two of his strongest impulses,—the self-conscious personal impulses of being regarded and being neglected. The puritan is no thwarted and depleted person. On the contrary, he is rather a complete person, getting almost the maximum of satisfaction out of these two apparently contradictory sentiments,—the self-regarding and self-abasing. The pure autocrat would feed himself wholly on the first, the pure slave would be only a human embodiment of the second. But the pure puritan manages to make the most powerful amalgam of both.

What we may call the puritan process starts with the satisfaction of the impulse for self-abasement, (an impulse as primitive as any, for in the long struggle for survival, it was often just as necessary for life to cower as it was to fight.) It is only the puritan's prestige that has attached moral value to self-sacrifice, for there is nothing intrinsic in it that makes it any more praiseworthy than lust. But its pragmatic value is immense. When the puritan announces himself as the least worthy of men, he not only predisposes in his favor the naturally slavish people around him, but he neutralizes the aggressive and self-regarding who would otherwise be moved to suppress him. He renounces, he puts on meekness, he sternly regiments himself, he makes himself unhappy in ways that are just not quite severe enough to excite pity and yet run no risk of arousing any envy. If the puritan does all this unconsciously, the effect is yet the same as if he were deliberately plotting. To give his impulses of self-abasement full play, he must, of course, exercise a certain degree of control. This control, however, gives him little of that sense of power that makes for happiness. Puritan moralists have always tried to make us believe in this virtue of self-control. They forget to point out, however, that it does not become a virtue until it has become idealized. Control over self gives us little sense of control. It is the dreariest of all satisfactions of the will-to-power. Not until we become *proud* of our self-control do we get satisfaction. The puritan only begins to reap his satisfaction when the self-regarding impulse comes into play.

Having given his self-abasing impulse free rein, he is now in a position to exploit his self-regard. He has made himself right with the weak and slavish. He has fortified himself with their alliance. He now satisfies his self-regard by becoming proud of his humility and enjoining it on others. If it were self-control alone that made the Puritan, he would not be as powerful as he is. Indeed he would be no more than the mild ascetic, who is all abnegation because his self-regarding mechanism is weak. But in the puritan, both impulses are strong. It is control over others that yields him his satisfactions of power. He may stamp out his sex-desire, but his impulse to shatter ideas that he does not like will flourish wild and wanton. To the true puritan the beauty of unselfishness lies in his being able to enforce it on others. He loves virtue not so much for its own sake as for its being an instrument of his terrorism.

The true puritan is at once the most unselfish and the most self-righteous of men. There is nothing he will not do for you, give up for you, suffer for you. But at the same time there is no cranny of your world that he will not illuminate with the virtue of this doing of his. His real satisfaction comes not from his action of benevolence but from the moral of the tale. He need not boast about his renunciation or his altruism. But in any true puritan atmosphere, that pride will be prevalent. Indeed, it is the oxygen of that atmosphere. Wherever you come across that combination of selfless devotion with self-righteousness, you have the essence of the puritan. Should you come across the one without the other you would find not the puritan but the saint.

The puritan then gets the satisfaction of his will-to-power through the turning of his self-abasement into purposes of self-regard. Renunciation is the raw material for his positive sense of power. The puritan gets his satisfaction exactly where the most carnal of natural men gets his, out of the stimulation of his pride. And in a world where renunciation has to happen to us whether we want it or not, the puritan is in the most impressive strategic position. In economy of energy he has it all over the head that is bloody but unbowed. For the puritan is so efficient morally that he can bow his head and yet extract control both out of the bowing and out of the prestige which his bowing gives him, as well as out of the bowing which he can enforce on others. The true puritan must become an evangelist. It is not enough to renounce the stimulus to satisfaction which is technically known as a "temptation." The renouncing must be made into an ideal, the ideal must be codified, promulgated, and, in the last analysis, enforced. In the compelling of others to abstain, you have the final glut of puritanical power. For in getting other people to renounce a thing, you thereby get renewed justification for your own renouncing. And so the puritan may go on inexhaustibly rolling up his satisfactions, one impulse reinforcing the other. The simultaneous play of these two apparently inconsistent personal impulses makes the puritan type one of the stablest in society. While the rest of us are longing for power, the puritan is enjoying his. And because the puritan is so well integrated, he almost always rules. The person whose satisfactions of control are more various and more refined is on the defensive against him.

The puritan gets his sense of power not in the harmless way of the artist or the philosopher or the lover or the scientist, but in a crude assault on that most vulnerable part of other people's souls, their moral sense. He is far more dangerous to those he converts than to those he intimidates. For he first scares them into abandoning the rich and sensuous and expressive impulses in life, and then teaches them to be proud of having done so. We all have the potentiality of the puritan within us. I remember suffering agonies at the age of ten because my aunt used to bring me candy that had been wickedly purchased on the Sabbath day. I forget whether I ate it or not, but that fact is irrelevant. What counted was the guilt with which the whole universe seemed to be stained. I need no other evidence for the irrational nature of morality than this fact that children can be such dogged little puritans, can be at the age of ten so sternly and intuitively righteous.

The puritan is a case of arrested development. Most of us do grow beyond him and find subtler ways of satisfying our desire for power.

And we do it because we never can quite take that step from self-abasement to self-regard. We never can quite become proud of our humility. Renunciation remains an actual going without, sacrifice a real thwarting. If we value an experience and deliberately surrender it, we are too naive to pretend that there are compensations. There *is* a loss. We are left with a vacuum. There is only depression and loss of control. Our self-regard is not quite elemental enough to get stimulation from wielding virtue over others. I never feel so degraded as when I have renounced. I had rather beat my head rhythmically and endlessly against an unyielding wall. For the pagan often breaks miraculously through the wall. But the puritan at his best can only strut outside.

Most of us, therefore, after we have had our puritan fling, sown our puritan wild oats as it were, grow up into devout and progressing pagans, cultivating the warmth of the sun, the deliciousness of love-experience, the high moods of art. The puritans remain around us, a danger and a threat. But they have value to us in keeping us acutely self-conscious of our faith. They whet our ardor. Perhaps no one can be really a good appreciating pagan who has not once been a bad puritan.

AMERICAN INDEPENDENCE AND THE WAR

A MONTHLY MAGAZINE is not the best place for discussing political problems in days of rapid change; and surely a magazine devoted to that phase of nationality which is expressed by a nation's arts, would seem to overstep its function in such discussion. But we are face to face with so grave a crisis, that we can very well afford to forget the rules and dogmas we have laid down for ourselves; and remember only that a democracy has no one to do its thinking for it. It must think for itself. At a moment when a decision and a line of policy will determine a whole future epoch, it is necessary to press into service every organ of publicity, to mobilize, as it were, every medium of discussion. Action already outstrips our thinking: let us consider well then before that action becomes, first, a policy, second, a tradition, and third, the very spirit and structure of our nation.

We have taken steps against Germany because of the submarine menace: and in so far as this is an accomplished fact, it becomes necessary for us to put the country on a warlike footing. To take steps against Germany is to invite war, and with the coming of war must be expected an increase of peril from other directions. It may be alarmist to consider seriously the German scheme to embroil us with Mexico and Japan, and the remote possibility of the defection of Russia from the Allied cause, with a realignment in which we should find ourselves exposed East and West. But if we are to be caught in this great conflict, we shall have to take the consequences of the shifting fortunes of the combatants. In short, we cannot expect to make a sortie, deliver a blow at Germany, and then safely retire to American shores. If nothing else happens, we are lucky—but not more than lucky. Preparedness then becomes a safeguard against such possibilities, and if we are strong in defense, we may be able to deal with the present problem with a larger measure of justice and wisdom.

For the present predicament has elements in it more grave and more fraught with profound consequences than appear on the surface. It is not too much to say of these, that not only are our physical well-being and our fortunes staked on their handling, but our spiritual growth as well. A nation is nothing more than a collective personality, a multi-man, and its growth and development parallels the growth and development of the individual. There comes a time then when it must leave its childhood and its youth, and strike out alone, with a measure of autonomy and power, and with an achieved maturity. Nations in all stages of growth exist: old-age nations like China and India, childish nations like the South American Republics, mature powerful nations like England, Germany and France—and adolescent nations like the United States. What we are, we know now : the truth has been coming slowly home to us. We stand at the beginning of our own manhood.

Nor need we comfort ourselves with the illusion that because we had grandiose ideals, and because we are kindly and peace-loving, and because we have allowed unhindered immigration and have set the slaves free, that therefore we are a land of destiny, and can sit idly by while some god-in-the-machine prepares our crown of power. A nation, like a man, may come to nothing. It is the fate of many precocious youngsters. And certainly in the sort of world we live in, we have yet done little to earn a high place. Even if we are carrying on a worthy experiment, the experiment of democracy, we are not necessarily carrying it on worthily; and if we stood in the van twice in our history, where do we stand now when it comes to personal development, as compared with England and France, and to social organization, when it comes to Germany?

It is pertinent here to point out that our lack of great art is an index of our poverty of life, as well as of the prodigality of our possessions. We are like a sleek smooth-faced boy of nineteen, who is well-fed and has an easy job, and has the best intentions in the world (as well as an insufferable pride and an eye to profits), but who looks rather shabby when placed side by side with the mature manhood of France, or Germany, or England. The experience of life, which, fused into character, is what we call a man's soul—that is lacking. On the sort of nation we are, depends then whether we are to be great in society, in experience, in art, in personality. Or to put the question inversely, is the great intention to take on a measure of reality or not?

We must clarify then why we are going into this conflict and what we are seeking to gain from it. President Wilson stated in his second inaugural that the conflict is a private affair between Germany and the United States over the submarine menace. The United States is going to protect its ships from attack; but in no way is this to be construed as a joining of our forces to those of the Entente. We are not, in other words, to become one of the Allies against the Central Powers. We are going to settle a dispute of our own with Germany, and when that is disposed of, our interest in the matter is ended.

This seems plain enough, but it is not as simple as it appears. It has been pointed out cogently and clearly by varied parties, Anglo-Americans as well as German-Americans, that at no time have we taken an exclusively neutral stand in the war. We proclaimed neutrality, but this neutrality was in fact "differential"—a neutrality benevolent to the Entente. Both sides broke international law: but we have chosen to discriminate only against the Central Powers. The case is epitomized with remarkable clarity by *The New Republic* in its issue of February 17:

"All along the Germans have seen two great truths: first, that British command of the sea has become absolute, and has abolished the neutral rights which interfere with it; second, that America's policy has been to protest feebly and without effect against Britain while Germany has been held by threat of war from using the submarine fully to relieve the pressure. The Germans have pointed out quite accurately that the result of this policy has been to close the road to Germany and hold open the road to Britain and France. The German highway we have allowed the Allies to bar, the Allied highway we were ready to keep open at the risk of war. We have not merely been committed theoretically to selling munitions and supplies to any one who can come and fetch them. We have in fact permitted the Allies to cut off Germany, we have been in fact prepared for war to deliver munitions and foodstuffs to the Allies. Stripped of all its technicalities this is the issue, and the Germans have not been slow to recognize it.

"A number of things have obscured the issue. The first and most spectacular is that no American lives have been lost by the action of the Allies, and consequently their illegalities have never seemed monstrous to most of us. Nevertheless inhumanity is not the real difference. No American lives would have been lost had we acquiesced in Germany's policy as we have in Britain's. American lives would almost certainly have been lost had we refused to agree to Great Britain's 'blockade' as we have to Germany's 'war-zone' decree. If Britain said we must put into a certain port we have put into it, if Britain said we must not use certain areas of the North Sea we have not used them, if Britain said we could do only a certain amount of trade with Holland, that is all the trade we have done. Nor is there any reason for regarding the submarine war as more deadly than the blockade of Germany. It is well to remember that the German people are suffering anguish as a result of it, that their children's vitality is being sapped, that there is an alarming increase of tuberculosis within the German Empire. The blockade and the submarine are both terrible weapons, and the blockade is the more effective of the two. In choosing between them we are not choosing between legality and illegality, nor even perhaps in the last analysis between cruelty and mercy."

With this as a basis, the conclusion is inevitable, and *The New Republic* makes it, that if such was our neutrality, just such will be our participation in the war. Of course, it is added that we shall go in, not fully—go in merely with ships, supplies and money for the Allies—for to go in fully would be to get entangled in the national schemes of the combatants, and first we shall have to have guarantees of a just settlement, and later a reform of English sea-power In the meantime, to pierce to the truth of the matter, our going in, if we yield to the pressure of such an attitude, means actually that we are entering the war on the side of England. Or, in other words, we are not to fight for the freedom of the seas, but for England's supremacy on the seas. The President then is obscuring the issue with his words, and Germany has some right in calling us hypocritical.

Now why are we to help maintain the English sea-supremacy, and why, in this venture, must we help cripple Germany's effort to break that supremacy? Not only because we have already been doing so with our "benevolent neutrality," but also, as *The New Republic* says further, "A victory on the high seas would be a triumph of that class which aims to make Germany the leader of the East against the West, the leader ultimately of a German-Russian-Japanese coalition against the Atlantic world." In other words, we are to fight to maintain in the world the sort of civilization we are accustomed to, the sort that England has given us through her supremacy. We must in effect fight for the status quo before the war, for any other kind of world would not be inhabitable.

Let us consider first this problem, before we proceed to examine the question of benevolent neutrality with its appendix, benevolent war.

It is true that England has not only been the Mother of Parliaments but also the Mother of the World. A third of the Earth's territory is hers, so scattered and disposed, that she may very well feel that she has the planet under her wing. And wherever England has gone, her speech, her tradition, her law, her aspirations, have followed. On the whole, she has treated her children well, and spread liberal and humane thought throughout the world. And her children have felt their dependency upon her—their dependency for trade, and also for protection, in their weakness, against aggressive neighbors. This protection was in the form of a superb and supreme Navy.

All this is admitted. But we must make a further admission. We look upon ourselves as a real nation ; we have spoken much of our isolation and our independence. But there is a difference between physical and spiritual autonomy. The mere fact that a boy leaves his parent's house is not a sign that he has achieved his own independence: we know well enough those subtle and deep-lying ties of emotion and memory, of habit and sympathy, which may bind him in his familial bonds enough to condition his every thought and action. He has severed himself only physically from his childish tie to the parents. He goes among strangers, and betrays by everything he does as well as by everything he leaves undone, that he is still his mother's boy.

Such in some ways is our position as a nation in relation to England. We have, it is true, attained a large measure of autonomy in dealing with internal problems; but internationally, as a nation among nations, a man among men, we are to a large extent dependent on the strong arm of England. But we are colonial in a deeper, a more insidious, way: all that part of our life, which for want of a better word, we must call spiritual, derives from the Mother Country. Through that hidden, uncut nexus come those emotions, those attitudes and prejudices, those habits of thought which betray us as provincials in everything we do and say. The Puritanism which obsesses us, the emotional repressions to which we subject ourselves, the externality of which we are so proud, the lack of authentic and native art, the masking of egoistic enterprise under the guise of beautiful moralities and fine-sounding ethics, our fear that what we do is incorrect, and at the same time our feeling of moral superiority over the rest of the world—all these are the mother in the son, England in us. Our serious writers slavishly follow the English models of style and theme, our serious thinkers take their thought from London.

Do we not know, and have we not said again and again, that until we lean to our own soil, and humbly get down in our own dust, yes, until we go to our own selves to find ourselves, that not until then shall we be a nation and have a soul of our own? And how shall we do this until we cut the cord that binds us to our childhood—the cord with England? Born of England we must be reborn into ourselves.

This may seem to some as an unimportant problem to intrude in a national crisis. But in this problem lies the crisis itself. We met one great test to free ourselves from England, and we did achieve a sort of physical freedom. But now an enemy lies not overseas but in ourselves. We must overcome that which is England in us.

We have been fortunate, it now appears, in our immigration policy, for beyond a doubt our strength to break free has increased with the influx of Continental immigrants. They have leavened the English lump with other traditions and other bloods, and if for the time being, they have divided us against ourselves, in that very inner conflict lies the hope of our freedom. Out of this added blood has risen some of our most characteristic expression, with the promise of a genuine American art. For our dominant expression was New England, and the words themselves give away the case. *New* England was *Old* England transplanted, and weakened in the transplanting. Against it have appeared such figures as Walt Whitman, and the strongest of our younger men.

Events have so converged now that we may choose to deepen our ties with the Mother Country, as the rest of the Colonies have done, or follow a course which will loosen these ties: which will, in the end, throw us more completely on ourselves. If we follow the first course we may help to maintain an English world, and go on for another epoch under the wing of England. It is, possibly, the safer and easier way. But if we follow the second course, the risk is great.

It is, however, the sort of risk that any man must take if he is to be true to himself and wants to be strong enough to stand alone.

However, we need not swallow whole the reactionary fears of our Colonials. It is quite probable that the war will end in a draw and that the realignment will bring either a League for Peace, or a combination, as Shaw suggests, of Germany, England, France, and America. At least this is the present outlook, and it is nothing less than utopian and fantastic to take action on any other basis.

However, even if events turned out otherwise, in spite of everything, it is well to remember some plain facts. If we are to live in a hostile world, we have means to make ourselves feared. It is true that we have gone unarmed because England was doubly armed, but why should we continue to be pacifist at England's expense? For if we are pacifist at England's expense, we know well enough that England will make us pay for it. Have we not the means and the men to make our country so strong in its defensive power that the offender may beware? With our splendid position, our two oceans, our self-sustaining continental soil, there is ample opportunity to meet any risks that may arise.

But when a lad grows up he does not necessarily make ready for some melodramatic crisis that may emerge a decade or two later. He prepares in a more average way; and until this nation is faced with more fearful threats than those we are meeting, a wise middle policy is possible.

We must now face the real problem that *The New Republic* poses—namely, that of "benevolent neutrality." Surely if we have been twofaced in our neutrality, if we have actually been one of the Allies while protesting that we favored neither side, and if, as a result, we are about to go to war with Germany for a wrong no greater than that which we have suffered at the hands of England, then it is time we dropped our hypocrisy, and came out clearly with our purpose. And if we *are* one of the Allies, then surely we ought to aid as thoroughly and wholeheartedly as, say, Canada has aided. We ought to send men, ships and money, and take steps to join the battle-line.

In this light, to say that we are fighting separately, merely to get American ships through the war-zone, is to cloud our purpose and our action with hypocrisy. And, indeed, if we did merely fight for such a purpose, would we not convoy ships, not alone through the submarine barrier, but also through the barrier of the English blockade and see that we reached both sides with our cargoes?

This is the dilemma. We are siding with the Allies, when our expressed intention is to protect American rights. We even use the phrase "armed neutrality."

Now undoubtedly the contention of the President is that illegality might be condoned, but "frightfulness" is a crime which we must seek to punish—that there is no comparison between what England has done and what Germany has done—that we have in fact endeavored to remain neutral, that we have protested to both sides, and have only met Germany with resistance because Germany has physically attacked us. So far as trading is concerned, we have traded where we could, and when a German commerce submarine reached us, we received it with open welcome and sent back a cargo.

Such arguments, however, fail to shatter the contention which is made by Germany, by German sympathizers here, and by Anglophiles no less. To repeat:

"No American lives would have been lost had we acquiesced in Germany's policy as we have in Britain's. American lives would almost certainly have been lost had we refused to agree to Great Britain's 'blockade' as we have to Germany's 'war-zone' decree."

This is certainly irrefutable, and hence the policy of our Government can only be approved by those who misunderstand it. To our Anglo-Americans it is hypocritical, and falls short of effective action; to our German-Americans it is only the latest breach in our declared neutrality ; and to those who really desire a new and greater America it offers no hope for the great aims we cherish.

Hence, we are with our Colonials in so far as they demand that the issue be clarified and brought out honestly into the light. The American people must know, and know fully, why they are being swung out into the madness and suffering of this great war. And the world, no less, must know why we are appearing on the scene.

We must begin then by disavowing that this is an action for America only; and by admitting, that whatever the cause—whether profits in munitions, or genuine sympathy, or a drifting policy on the part of our government—we have on the whole been pro-Ally and anti-German. To admit this, however, does not automatically pledge us to a continuance of such a policy. In fact, President Wilson transcended this policy by a much greater one when he asked the combatants for a statement of peace terms, and declared that each nation was, in effect, fighting for the same cause, and that a peace without victory was the best way to end the war. This logically went hand in hand with his declaration in favor of a League for Peace after the war, wherein both sea-supremacy and land-supremacy would be laid aside, and all nations would, like our several states, pool their police power and so safeguard the world from such another catastrophe.

These facts remain as much in force today as they did then. This is not a pro-Ally policy nor a pro-German policy: it is a world-policy, and one worthy of the greatest sacrifice and efforts. A victory of either side would be a genuine calamity. A victory of Germany would place Europe in jeopardy and in the end align a large part of the world against the United States. A victory of the Allies would maintain England in her supremacy of the sea, with the full danger of her present absolutism continuing.

There is no doubt that we should have shown real greatness, had this larger policy resulted in our keeping out of the war; but the provocation was great, we were already in full swing toward action, and the pressure of events, added to the grave diplomatic stupidity of Germany, have been too much for us. It is quite human for us to be in it—perhaps, all too human. But if we are in it, we owe it to the great aim we have before us, to keep from being stampeded by the Colonials and our frenzied militarists from putting our whole weight on the side of the Allies. We must, above all, attempt to keep the action narrowed down : we must not add such strength to the Allies that Germany is crushed.

If we can succeed in doing this, we shall be in a position later, at that time when both sides share equally the great longing for peace, to help to bring them together in the faith, on their part, that we care much more for a just peace than for the victory of either side.

But we shall not succeed in this, unless we know from the start just what we are doing. We shall not succeed in this if we remain blind to our relationship with England and the fact that we have no great future unless we achieve a new independence of our Mother Country. With this steadily held before us, we shall be able to deal with this relationship, through making effective, in the end, our world-policy, and thus escape the grave peril of being bound faster than ever in the bonds that hold us. In this lies our chance of a new release, a new autonomy, and the coming of a greater national consciousness.

But we shall show ourselves a flabby people indeed if we vent the white heat of this crisis only in this action and this attitude. There is a task for us, a task greater than mounting guns on our merchantmen. Do we not see now, in a sudden shock of realization, how helplessly we lie scattered before danger, and how inefficiently and blindly we stumble into the future? Are we not able to unmask our sentimentality—the good-natured dream of the pacifists who think they can handle life by evading it, and the equally kind phantasy of those who believe we are neutral—and remember our own history, recall that if we had faced a modern power in '61, our two years of amateur fighting would have undone us ? We are here, confronted by the harsh facts of a dangerous world, and by the discovery of our own weakness and childishness. At this moment it so happens we are roused, an emotion of nationality raises us, a realization of ourselves is brought home to our hearts. But we know how swiftly our great moods pass and leave behind them little more than idle words and wishes.

Let not this great hour go from us without its achievement in sound and sure action. Let us get ourselves ready, take stock, gather our resources and put ourselves under discipline. Let there be a preparation of our spirit and of our forces. Let us take measures to make ourselves for the first time thoroughly independent. America must begin a steady and slowly increasing mobilization in resource and in spirit, so that the day may come when we may go about our business assured that we need turn to no one when danger threatens us.

If out of our crisis this emerges, then we have converted a spasmodic reaction into a lasting good, and transformed a mood into living national power. Out of our momentary plight there may be born then the much-heralded, the long-dreamed-of, America.

IN A TIME OF NATIONAL HESITATION

John Dewey

WERE I a poet, this should be, even at the dangerous risk of comparisons invited, an ode. But, alas, the passion as well as the art is lacking. I can but set down a blurred perception of immense masses stirring across great spaces. There is not even the assurance that the fogged outlines mark a thing beheld. They may be only felt, and felt with too much of an observing curiosity to find out what they mean to permit them to kindle into passion.

It is likely that our national hesitation will outwardly have been swallowed up in act before these words appear upon the printed page. But if I read the hesitation aright such a resolution of uncertainty will be but partial. We shall have decided a small thing, what to do, but the great thing, the thing so great as to cause and perpetuate our hesitation, may remain. We may still be uncertain as to our will to be. In the course of doing, we may, it is true, learn something of what we would be. But also it may turn out that even while doing deeds which are imperatively demanded of us our hesitation may grow into a greater doubt. For the hesitation which I see is that of a nation which knows that its time has not come, its hour not struck. The ripening forces have not yet matured, and like all vital processes they are not to be forced. The time of national hesitation is the time of slow and certain growth to an end which is not to be anticipated nor prevented. The day of fate tarries and not till it arrives will the authentic direction be spoken. Meantime suspense.

This is not the usual rendering of our course. The most vocal among us tell us that our hesitation is at best the provincialism of ignorance and at worst a slothful cowardice bred of mammon-serving peace; that we hesitate from inner division and distraction; because we are not a nation, but a boardinghouse of aliens; because we have been corrupted by overmuch prosperity and a sentimentally humanitarian pacifism. Our fiber is gone: we are spineless. We have been told that we are justly the objects of universal scorn and contempt, that our national hesitation is a national humiliation. When a fellow-citizen said, after the dismissal of the German ambassador, that now for the first time in two years could he stand straight and look others in the eye, he only said what the more vocal elements have been reiterating day after day, week after week. Such has been the obvious, not to say clamorous, explanation of our prolonged and penetrating hesitation.

Such statements are not material for argument or disproof. One only sees what one sees, and it is hard to tell even that. But these accounts prove too much. We are told that the nation pauses for lack of leadership, when heaven knows our ears have ached from the roarings of those who have told us what to do and who have exhausted the fishwives' vocabulary in scolding us because we have not done it. We have bowed our heads, and allowed the tempest of words to pass over. We have waited listening for something, just what we have not known, but assuredly for something else than what platform and press are dinning into us. Hordes and aggregates of accident do not wait and hesitate in this fashion. They respond with a stampede. The strident tone of our critics in its increasing shrillness is evidence that the inertia, the solidity of a people was there; for only those who are fused into a single being can wait enduringly in the midst of such clamor and world stir. We have continued to be uncertain just because we were certain that our destiny had not declared itself. Those who have offered themselves as prophets have shown that they were rather historians, reminiscent of a colonial age out of which the people, the masses, had slowly grown. Those who lamented the lack of leadership proclaimed by their laments that a fused people had assumed its own leadership and was waiting in silence to issue its directions. Never has the American people so little required apologizing for, because never before has it been in such possession of its senses.

If there has been such impressive unification, why the prolonged hesitation? Because though we have become a single body—hence the inertia which the unknowing have taken to be apathy—and are in possession of our senses, we have not yet found a national mind, a will as to what to be. It is easy to be stampeded; it is easy to be told what one's mind is, and humbly to accept on trust a mind thus made up. It is not easy to make up the mind, for the mind is made up only as the world takes on form. We have hesitated in making up our mind just because we would make it up not arbitrarily but in the light of the confronting situation. And that situation is dark, not light.

This is itself proof that a New World is at last a fact, and not a geographical designation. We no longer can be spoken to in the language of the old world and respond. We must be spoken to in our own terms. I do not say this in a complacent or congratulatory mood, but record it as a fact. It is a disagreeable fact to many, and especially disagreeable to those with whom we feel most friendly. It cannot fail to be in some measure disagreeable to ourselves that we should have attained a state which is bound to be intellectually and morally unpleasant to those who are our near spiritual kin and who have, as against anybody but ourselves, our warm sympathies and best wishes. That the gallant fight for democracy and civilization fought on the soil of France is not our fight is a thing not to be realized without pangs and qualms. But it is a fact which has slowly disclosed itself as these last long years have disclosed us to ourselves. It was not ours, because for better or for worse we are committed to a fight for another democracy and another civilization. Their nature is not clear to us: all that is sure is that they are different. This is the fact of a New World. The Declaration of Independence is no longer a merely dynastic and political declaration.

For this reason I hold that a termination of hesitation so far as to engage in overt war against Germany will not be of itself a conclusion of our hesitation. There is such a thing as interests being affected vitally without a vital interest being affected. As I write, we seem to be on the point of arriving at the conclusion that we cannot aid, by means of a passive compliance, the triumph of a nation that regards its triumph as the one thing so necessary that all means whatsoever that lead to that triumph are not only legitimate but sacred. Such a future neighbor we do not wish to be developed, certainly not by our aid as passive accomplices.

So far our hesitation gives way to action, because so far the situation has declared itself. We but meet a clearly proffered challenge.

But it is vain to suppose that thereby our deeper hesitation is concluded; that on this account we join with full heart and soul even though we join with unreserved energy. Not until the almost impossible happens, not until the Allies are fighting on our terms for our democracy and civilization, will that happen. And so we shall still hesitate, for the huge slow-moving body does not see its goal and path. When the President spoke his words as to the conditions under which the American people would voluntarily cooperate in fixing the terms of future international relationships, something stirred within, but the whole bulk did not respond, not even though the appeal was couched in that combination of legal and sentimental phraseology which is our cherished political dialect. At the Russian revolution there was a more obvious thrill. Perhaps through some convulsion, some rearrangement still to come, there will be a revelation of the conditions under which the world's future may be wrought out in patient labor and fraternal comity, a disclosure so authoritative that in it we shall see and know ourselves and recognize our will. More likely there will be partial events and partial conclusions. But one thing has already happened. The war has shown that we are no longer a colony of any European nation nor of them all collectively. We are a new body and a new spirit in the world. Such at least is the impression which has been forming in me, unbidden and unforeseen, concerning the time of our national hesitation.

THE SONG OF ARIEL

S. N. Behrman

VIOLET, the winter dusk filtered down between the towering files of office-buildings and pressed against the golden light from a thousand windows. Behind the windows desks closed, weary clerks shuffled from their seats, dragged on drab coats over soiled shirt-sleeves and crowded into the dingy elevators which bore them to the street.

Dave Soule moved slowly up lower Broadway to the Subway. But before the entrance he stopped uncertainly, hesitant. For the first time in years he did not join the stream that flowed into it but moved on past. Then he stopped again. At home they would be expecting him. Supper was waiting. And he had promised Ann to come over immediately after. Sooner or later he would have to tell her.

Nevertheless he moved on up Broadway. He wasn't hungry and he must have a little time to think. What would he tell Ann? Already she had waited two years for him. The extra expense of keeping his invalid mother and fourteen-year-old sister in school had made it impossible for them to marry. And now he must tell her that they would have to put off their wedding again. The raise he expected that day had not been forthcoming. The head clerk had just told him so.

Soule moved on up Broadway with the crowd. Ahead of him Madison Square opened like a fan rimmed by fairy buildings glowing through the purple veiling of the dusk. Motors curved and squirmed, crammed busses bumped and waddled past. More of grotesquerie and magic here than in any city of olden times colored by the imagination of the antiquarian. A tidal wave of humanity spewed from the spiring abodes of commerce and shot, fifty miles an hour by Subway and Elevated, to the infinite cubby-holes of the Bronx and Harlem.

But Soule, drifting along, was scarcely conscious of the teeming vistas through which he moved. With a few matter-of-fact words the man from whom he took his orders at the office had destroyed the planning of months. "How shall I say it to Ann?" he was asking himself. Uppermost in his mind was a perplexity about how to phrase to Ann this news, so unexpected, so fraught with disappointment. She had so counted on this. She lived in a home that she hated, with a step-mother and too many children. To sentence her to further imprisonment there when she had caught so near a glimpse of freedom, a home of her own,—how could he do it? And he himself who so wanted her—how could he go on this way? And yet he knew that he would go on; that he would refuse Ann when she asked him to let his sister go to work so they might marry. That he would never allow. Ella must keep on at school, must grow up educated, must be given the chance he never had—.

Symbolized in stone or in words Commerce and Industry are gods or goddesses (depending on whether strength or fecundity is the attribute emphasized) ; they have the titan limbs of a figure by Michelangelo; often they carry cornucopias, streaming bounties. But to the multitudes of lowlier workers in the service of these heroic deities such apotheosis must occasionally seem far-fetched. David Soule, known to be a faithful, earnest, unvaryingly reliable worker, was filled with a bitter resentment against his firm, against the whole fabric of his world. For the first time in his life he cursed the servitude that bound him.

But only for a moment. The habit of years reasserted itself and his mind reverted to its normal adjustment. Things were this way—there was nothing to be done.

He plodded on. Suddenly he found that he was no longer thinking of his disappointment. He tried to prod it back, but his mind refused to focus. He was very tired: the long day, the uncustomary walk, the strain and worry, were telling on him. His mind was filled with a vague conglomerate of impressions; he was conscious of the rush about him, the occasional pretty face of a girl; he wondered at the confident, eager stride of some of the men. Behind the plate glass windows of motors profiles showed. But these impressions had no real meaning for him: actually they were as far-away, as mythical, as non-existent as things in a story. Were these people really living in the same world as he?

In front of a shop a knot of people was gathered. Mechanically Soule stopped too. Through the doorway came the full, rich sound of a woman's voice singing something on a phonograph. It was the *Vissi D'arte* from "Tosca." Something in the voice thrilled through Soule, stirring him out of himself. A painful nostalgia swept over him. The luxurious tones made him conscious of something beyond himself which he could never reach.... A vision of Ann came into his mind. He suddenly felt a great longing for her. So poignant and strange and overpowering was this new desire that he became for the moment faint and weak. The singer's voice rose powerfully, with a joyous mastery of strength. The melody fell over Soule as cascades of water play over a figure in a fountain. He wished that Ann were there so that she too might listen. Then she would understand what he was feeling. A great pity for her welled up in him—she meant so much to him, he wanted so much to make her happy and he could do so little! After a moment the singing stopped! It was as though a super-presence had been near him, touching him. He stood still, waiting. But the voice did not come again. Then he turned away and trudged wearily to the Subway.

Fred Rudnor, journalist, getting no answer to his knock on the door of Soule's sitting room, opened the door gently and peered within. Sitting at the table, hunched over a book, a girl was reading aloud and Rudnor stopped still a moment to listen.

"Where the bee sucks, there suck I,
In a cowslip's bell I lie;
There I couch when owls do cry.
On the bat's back I do fly
After summer merrily.
Merrily, merrily shall I live now
Under the blossom that hangs on the bough."

As she reached the last line the girl was startled by a pair of hands clasped suddenly around her eyes.

"Who is it?"

"Mr. Rudnor."

"Guessed it the first time." He relinquished his hold and patted her on the cheek.

"You're reading Lamb's Tales, I see."

"Thank you so much for it, Mr. Rudnor."

"Like it?"

"I *love* it. I'm on 'The Tempest'. Isn't Ariel lovely? Does the prince marry Miranda?"

"Shouldn't be surprised—"

"Really?"

"Surest thing you know."

The small head dove back to the book in a flurry of light brown curls.

"Where's David?"

"He hasn't come home yet. He's awful late."

"Guess I'll wait for him—how's mother?"

"About the same."

Rudnor sat down in a rocking-chair, tipped as far back as he could, and directed the smoke from his pipe at the ceiling. Just outside the frowzily curtained windows the elevated trains thundered; it was a room such as you may see any evening from the "L" platform. Only secondarily did it convey the sense of poverty: the salient impression was of a mean insignificance—furniture with chipped, varnished surfaces, a glazed table-cover stamped with a pictorial presentment of the Brooklyn Bridge—the ugly factitiousness of the machine. On the mantel-shelf a vagariously tinted, papier-maché plant grew directly out of a round piece of wood, its tenderness protected from bacterial attack by a fly-speckled glass cylinder completely covering it. This ornament failed of decorativeness. But it achieved much more than that; it possessed the dignity and pathos of a symbol.

From the next room a querulous voice, calling her, disturbed Ella at her reading. Reluctantly, almost without lifting her head from the book, she rose and went out. Rudnor, left alone, improvised a little tune for Ariel's song. He was rather short and given to stockiness and had lively black eyes with a gleam of humor in them. He wore a shiny, black, loosefitting suit and a soft-collared shirt with a carelessly made four-in-hand tie. To the Socialist meetings and the editors of the radical press in the city Mr. Rudnor was not unknown. Even the critics of immaculate Eastern journals had patronised his stories of East Side life. This amused Rudnor vastly.

Soule, looking tireder than usual, interrupted the tenth variation of Rudnor's song.

"Hello, Fred," he said listlessly.

"How are you, Dave?—where've you been?"

"Walking."

"What's up?"

"Nothing—"

"Everything all right at the office?"

"Expected a raise today. Didn't get it."

"Make much difference?"

"Puts Ann and me off again."

"Tough!"

"Hard on Ann."

"Hard on you too."

"Wait a minute—I'm going in to see mother."

"Eaten yet?"

"I'm not very hungry."

Soule went into the next room and Rudnor walked about the room, his face serious. Soule came back and slumped into a chair. Ella appeared at the door.

"Don't you want your supper, Dave?"

"I've had a bite down town. Go back to mother."

Rudnor looked out of the corner of his eyes at Soule staring ahead of him absently.

"What are you doing tonight?" he asked briskly.

"I was going over to see Ann. But I guess I won't. I'm thinking—"

"What?"

"Perhaps I oughtn't to stand in her way any longer."

"Beats all how the girls do want to get married! As a child wants a new toy—want to go with me tonight?" Rudnor broke in abruptly on his generalization.

"Where to?"

"I'm meeting some girls. We're going to Miller's for a dance or two."

"And a drink or two—"

Rudnor smiled. "It's not impossible. Want to come?"

"No."

"Why not! Do you good—"

"You know I don't do that sort of thing."

"The trouble with you is you lead too pious a life. You never have any fun."

"I'd be a nice one to go out with your crowd—when I'm going with a girl—"

"'Going with a girl' as you call it isn't doing you much good, Dave," said Rudnor quietly.

Soule seemed not to hear,—at any rate he made no response. Rudnor was emboldened to continue.

"The way I feel about it is this. Here you are thirty and over. Mother and little sister to support. You ought to be married but you can't. Now what's the answer—?"

"No use, Fred. It wouldn't be fair to Ann—"

"If girls like Ann weren't so damn respectable—"

"Cut that out!" said Soule sharply.

"All right. Sorry you won't join me in my Saturday night festivities. It's my one chance in the week to see you and the kid and I thought I'd step in.—You know she's bright, that sister of yours—"

Something lit up in Soule's face.

"Think so?"

"You bet she is. Well, I'll be running along. Really going to stay in tonight?"

"I don't know."

"Well, so long, Dave."

"So long, Fred."

Rudnor stopped at the door.

"If you should change your mind about tonight—"

"I won't."

"I was going to say—you might come over to Miller's. You'll be welcome. So long."

The door shut to. As he heard Rudnor's steps retreating in the hallway Soule rose suddenly and started for the door. Half-way he stopped short. After a moment he turned and went back to his chair, sitting motionless, staring at the floor.

A faint knocking roused him. "Come," he called, and turned. A woman stood in the doorway, a woman of about twenty-five, pale, thinnish, with tightly-coiled dark hair and tense eyes.

"Ann!"

"What's wrong, Dave?"

"Why—nothing—"

"I've been waiting for you. I thought perhaps your mother—she isn't—worse?"

"No."

"Then why—?"

"It's just that—I was coming over in a few minutes, Ann."

"I was sure it must be your mother. This is the first Saturday night in a year, I guess—something *is* wrong."

"It's that—"

"What?"

"That raise—"

"You didn't get it?" But she read the answer in his face.

Soule raised his arms in a helpless gesture.

"I'm sorry, Ann."

"Surely you don't mean—that we can't be married—even now?"

"If we wait a little longer—till the war is over—"

"Till the war is over!"

"I'm sorry, Ann."

There was a silence. She came close to Soule, her hands clenched at her sides, her eyes flashing.

"I wish she were dead!" she whispered passionately.

"Ann!" He threw a horrified glance toward his mother's room.

"I do. I do. Her life is over. She sits on there in that room, hanging on, eating up your money, robbing me of my chance—"

"You mustn't, Ann—"

"How long do you think I can go on this way?—while you keep spending your money for doctors and medicines that don't do her any good."

"You don't know what you're saying—"

"Don't I? When I came here tonight it was hoping she had died—so help me God!"

She stopped, staring at him defiantly. He looked back at her mute, agonized.

"I can't help it, Ann," he said finally, "I can't do anything. If you want you don't have to keep your promise to wait—"

She laughed bitterly.

"You're willing enough to break it off now, aren't you? After everyone knows I've been going with you and no one comes near me—"

"You know I love you, Ann—like anything—"

"Then why don't you show it? If you let Ella go to work—"

"We've been over all that. Ella must have her chance. Besides—she's not strong. She couldn't stand the grind."

"I stand it!"

"But, Ann," he pleaded, "Ella's only fourteen—"

She came near to him and put her arms around his neck.

"Don't you love me any more, Dave?"

"You're all I've got, Ann,—you're everything—"

"We could be so cozy together—." Her upturned face almost touched his. He clasped her to his breast, his lips pressed against hers.

"I'll make you so happy," she whispered, "so happy."

"You darling—"

"I'll take such good care of you, dear—we'll be so cozy together—"

"Ann! Ann!"

"My boy!—You will do what I ask, won't you?"

"If I only—"

"I'm so tired of waiting, dear. We'll get married right away—promise me. I so want my own little place—and you. After all it will only be for a little while that Ella will have to work. As soon as you get your raise she can stop. Won't you, Dave—won't you?"

Her lips and the touch of her shut away from him the trouble and menace of the world.

"Yes," he whispered.

A laugh broke from her, a laugh almost fierce in its triumph. Something of its harshness broke the spell she had woven. He drew away from her sharply.

"We'll have to wait," he said.

"But you just promised—"

"It wasn't—fair," he said simply.

"Then this is good-bye."

"Ann—please—"

"You must choose between us—"

"But don't you see—?"

"It's between me and them," she said finally.

"I can't do differently, Ann."

"All right. I'm going."

She had reached the door. He called her name. She turned.

"Which is it to be?"

He said nothing but his arms lifted in the old helpless gesture.

"I hate you," she cried. "You hear—I hate you! I never want to see you again—"

He wanted to stop her, to run after her but could not. He stood motionless staring at the door through which she had disappeared. Then he walked uncertainly to a chair and sat down. His face worked convulsively with the effort to master himself. Suddenly a low cry escaped him, and he leaned forward over the table, his head bedded in his arms.

For a long time he sat so—till he heard an uncertain stumbling step on the stairs and a voice calling his name. He rose quickly and opened the door to admit a new Rudnor, a Rudnor with flushed face and eyes aglow.

"There you are, old man! Saw the light and thought I'd come in to find out if you'd changed your mind. Met Ann on the street. She snubbed me. What's the matter? Quarrelled? Well, don't mope. Life's too short to mope. Come on with me. Cheer you up. Two ladies waiting outside—what do you say?"

"Leave me alone, will you?"

"Oh, come. Don't be so upset. Lots of sweethearts in the world. Come on along with me. Saturday night! Life—joy—romance—"

"You're drunk."

"Not much. Just enough to soften the edge of reality. Just enough to make the world beautiful. Just enough to make the ladies beautiful. Even if they're thin and their noses are sharp, a few drinks and they become round and misty and beauteous. Don't stand there like a stick. I tell you the ladies are waiting. A few drinks and the world will change—"

"All right," said Soule suddenly. "I'll come!"

"Get your coat."

"In a minute—"

He went into the next room and rushed out pulling his coat on as he ran.

"Let's go," he cried, "let's go."

Ella's voice calling her brother stopped them at the door.

"Where you going?"

But Soule had already disappeared and Rudnor followed him. Ella ran to the window and watched them till they were lost to her sight in the crowded street. Then she turned slowly away, a sadness in her eyes that made her look strangely old. The book Rudnor had given her was still in her hand. She sat at the table and started to read. But her attention wavered.

"Mother," she called.

"Yes."

"Are you all right?"

"Yes."

"I'll be in here reading if you want me."

Silence in the room save for the intermittent jangle of the "L" and the faint hum from the street. Lilting the lines in a hushed wistful voice she began reading aloud the gladsome song of Ariel :—

"Merrily, merrily shall I live now
Under the blossom that hangs on the bough."

Her voice trailed off—the book fell to her lap; she sat staring ahead of her, her eyes a-dream.

BREAD-CRUMBS

Waldo Frank

WHICHEVER way she moved—if it was possible with a turn of her head—Mrs. Silvester looked out on the street. Three children were romping there. They rolled and screamed and twisted gaily. Behind their fragile note was the thick texture of the City.

"I'd give them more sensible clothes to play in," she decided, "if they was mine. And just as nice, too!"

It was closing time—early. But the day had been good, the five o'clock bake was gone, and Joseph Silvester's leg was troubling him again. So she had sent him home, and the boy away. And as she worked, absently dusting, tidying, locking up, her eyes and her heart dwelt with the romping children. The impress of them was not glad, but it was sharp. Their fascination hurt her.

Still aloof from what she did, she went to the cash-drawer and lifted out the day's receipts. And then, as if by force, she turned her eyes from the children to the money. She counted it. She was smiling vaguely at what it told of success and comfort.

The children's laughter lay above the gray street like a little field of flowers. The woman made a bundle of the coins and bills. Then, she took two quarters from it and slipped them into the pocket of her skirt. Then, she completed the package and bolted the door behind her. She brushed past the children without attention. Quite suddenly they were uninteresting and annoying.

It was a walk of three minutes to her flat—one on the avenue, two on the block. The warm Spring evening tinged the clamorous movement of the City, made it somehow gentle and glad and clean. Its smile was stronger than the street's stridency. Helene Silvester went unconsciously along. The crowd that clotted and upset her way with its thick drab was nothing to her. It was like inconsequential mud beneath her feet. She walked through the Spring evening. She was aware of nothing else. A thought of what she had so inexplicably done in the store strove to be noticed. But the part of her that thought was mute and impotent. She did not care, she did not care to know that she had taken the two quarters. The impulse that had caused her deed kept her from questioning its purpose. It seemed sure of itself. Altogether it ruled her, so that she was in no way troubled.

She found her husband ailing. She cooked his supper, and then made him go to bed. It was too early for her to follow. She put out the light. She sat by the window of her front room. Her eyes and that part of her that dreamed took their course outward through the window.

She semed strangely strong and her reach had no sense of limitation. Directly before her was the brown mass of buildings, deep in a faint purple haze. Below, the street seethed with its myriad energy that drew in as it rose, and struck her like the sharpened crest of a wave. Her window had a slight square frame, and somehow she perceived herself within it, dull and small in her gray dress, with her cheeks pale against the air. And yet the sky welling above the street, which huddled like a swarming thing beneath it, was a more real measure. The sky seemed to catch her with its gleam that fell upon her window; seemed to carry her up and to unfold her. The frangent street was lost in the silence of her outspreading self. And now she no longer saw her little figure framed by the window. She saw a serene sweep of world, slowly murmurous; and of it she saw her life, a pulse in the wide rhythm...

She had been married five years and she had been unhappy. Their trade had thriven. She had seen children romping like flowers in gray soil. She had stolen two silver quarters from herself. And in six months, she was to have—at last—a baby of her own...

The great sky rocked the world like a calm mother cradling an infant. The torn noises of the open windows and the block became a cry. Helene Silvester sat without further thought. And then she roused herself. She had been slumbering away, her face sheer to the air. And in her silly dream, she and the sky were one, the playful turmoil of the street was a single voice for which she waited.

Carefully, the young woman closed the window.

"It might rain," was her thought.

Then, she went to bed.

The following day, Joseph Silvester remained at home. Helene kept the store herself. The curious impulse of the day before did not return. She brought back her little bundle of money undespoiled. But the two quarters had stayed where she had tucked them.

Joseph was feeling better, so there were two that evening beside the window. The silence was no less. Helene's thrill had become her monotone.

"I feel so glad—so glad..." she had said half-aloud. "It's two lives, husband: my own—and—" she stopped.

Joseph sat there, gripping his black pipe with white teeth. They showed behind the dark droop of his moustache. Also faintly as he puffed, his mouth showed and his lips were thin. He was a tall and heavy man. He was ten years older than his wife: a silent man, knotted by his power, stifled in his lack of an outlet. As he sat there, languid and slow, he was the portrait of a veteran, retired and cluttered up in the kind parsimony of the present. His energy was the sort that longs to slumber. Now, he blinked at Helene's words. They were the nonsense that had made him love her.

"He'll be a good, strong lad," he said with effort—the reach of his imagination.

"Husband—husband!" she was disturbed by the prosaic forecast. A good strong lad—? Others had merited that term.

The silence came again. Outside, the street was a harsh pagan a-frolic in the shadow of a church. But Helene's spirit chimed on. She had been thinking of her son. And now, she was reminded of the two quarters she had stolen from herself.

Light burst on her act. She was not amazed by it, now that she understood. But she was caught by the glamor of her impulse, as it came to her, radiant with her deed. That silver was for her son! Everything that she did and had was hers and her husband's together. The child also would be theirs together; and the clothes he wore and the care of him and the hope for his success. But the money was not theirs; it was hers! It was a bond with her child that birth would not sever.

She went no farther in her planning. She had no will to sound the sense of it. Why steal for her child, when everything that was theirs would be his? It was indeed a mute, foolish, guilty impulse. But Helene knew she would abide by it. Merely, since it was foolish, she would put it away. Since it was guilty, she would protect it. Since it was mute, she would love it.

The next day a quarter went into her skirt. At the month's end, Helene secretly opened an account in her own name, at the nearest bank for savings.

By no other thing was her life stirred from the course of waiting and of working. There had been one reason for her unhappiness. And it was going; each day it was going farther. And in its stead, there were a thousand reasons for being glad. Every detail of existence was quick now with a new throb of gladness; was like herself with the early throb of a new being. All life was tense and proud, was reticent and sweet with its sap of birth. She and all life were sisters. The baking and selling of bread, the brushing of her hair at night, the clothing of her breasts at dawn, the preparing of food, the gossip of her neighbors, the gentle pleasure of her husband—in everything was an unuttered song. A melody had come of the clatter and the travail of existence.

Helene walked through the cold sounds of life, outwardly quiet, inwardly a flame. But it was the flame that moved her. And the flame needed fuel. This was the reason of the now regulated theft.

The child was born in October. They baptized him William. It was Joseph's choice.

Helene's mood changed.

More and more, the business of the bakery devolved on her. During the early months of the child's life, Joseph was grumbling in his subterranean way. It was clear to Helene that she must overcome the tense hope of mothering more children. The peace of their life seemed to call for her unfailing presence. Joseph was lovable only when she allowed him to be passive. And only then did he appear to love her child.

He would say: "Work—worry—work—worry—for *him!*" when Helene had wished to stay at home. And such talk was unbearable to her.

Besides, it seemed just that her husband should provide the color, the moral standard of their home; and that she should be its life. Gladly, she accepted whatever turn of events made him more the figure-head, herself more the burdened one. And it was not long before this unlevel distribution seemed a part of her comfort. For Helene was a woman with loyal faith in her own hands. Those whom she loved, she loved to feel dependent. Those whom she loved, she did not care to look on as dependable.

But with these full days she had changed. The wistful, the dreamful in her grew more covert. All her activity was an outward feature of her dream. But as work amassed, that gentle strain retired from the surface. At marriage, she had been a girl with tender lines, frail almost—a soft curve to her forehead, and a petulant wave to her hair, and nervous hands. Now, she was ample, sturdy. She had seemed tall with her slenderness; she was now short with her solidity. Only the glamor of her tilted eyes and the elusive tremble of her lips remained as tokens of her nature.... And her eyes looked mainly at accounts; and from her lips came capable commands.

It was not hard for Helene to manage a safe arrangement for her secret Fund. It had become an altar with its daily offering. To serve it, Helene had taken over complete charge of the bakery's accounts. The store was entirely her husband's. But even Joseph knew that he no longer ordered it. His was the credit and the atmosphere. Helene held command; and, since the bakery throve, she took her tithe.

The boy grew also, and the boy's Fund, as she now always thought of it. Helene was a careful mother. She was not lavish in attentions which warp and spoil a child. Strictly she measured her boy's nature, and planted a word or a sentiment, where, in her absence, it would grow. In a real way, William was her own. It was her taste and intuition that took root in the soil of his will. And yet, a great part of the mother went yearning and hungry. Helene did not have enough of her son. Almost, it seemed that her son was not enough for her. There were periods of rebellion against the store; hectic flights of her passion beyond life's meticulous plod; times when it was hard not to be altogether mother. But Helene held herself. The bakery needed her; life gripped her and reined her in. Her eager arms straightened against their fever to enclose her son; guarded against the lover in her breast. She remained housewife, manager, the restrained and careful parent. But in such phases, she heightened the daily toll for her secret Fund. This was a way of outlet.

It had sprung from a mute source. It had grown to be a field for all the mute things in her—where they could play, where they could meet a sort of sun, where they could be.

For Helene would not have been so indispensable a helpmeet, had she not been many more things first. Into this pent shell she crowded a maze of murmurous life. She was a symbol of the stifled city. Athrob with a deep stream of power, she ran a bakeshop; all woven up in a panoply of dreams the least of which had a bright tip in the stars, she robbed small coins from her own cash-box. Her vision was that the dun streets were strewn with pied and playing flowers, yet she lacked force to win the communion that she needed with her child, to dare the venture of another. In all things, it is her like that had turned the glad fields into dolorous cities; and that give their golden lilt to the shambled gutters.

The Fund grew then; and into it, swelling also, flowed her thought and her impulse. But the sign of all this was merely her more rapt interest in the Fund. She knew of nothing else. She was a quite ordinary woman. Yet, it was the Fund that made her cramped life bearable. It was a way of revolt and of adventure: a way of having a separate life and of doing a silent thing. It had been Romance; it became Reality.

Joseph sat in his rocker and it was Sunday and he was unable to suggest their going anywhere.

"Don't you feel like an outing?"

"I'm tired, Helene. You go—with the boy."

She did not think of the drouth of her husband's life. A dart of pleasure at the fruitful sum she had put away tinged through her. This was enough.

Joseph plied her with questions, in the store.

"We must get another place for the cakes. Why don't the Martins never come here any more? By the way, Helene, can you send our William with that extra delivery to number 393? I forgot it with the boy's orders."

William went. Helene answered all the questions.

"Ten cents extra for my child's having to do errands," she adjudicated grimly, as she made her theft that evening. So the inner rebellion was sloughed off.

Life was a dead thing. But her live fingers worked on it. Its dross was quick with her spirit.

After ten years, there was the Fund grown to four figures!

And then, Helene fell sick.

Once more her life was unlit, unwoven dross. Its emptiness had a painful, echoing reverberation. And then, all of her limbs were lead; and her thoughts weighted her body which they had lifted up. And the air choked her breathing; and the pavements of the street struck hard against her walking. And her work was a tedium and love was an irony...It was the sort of illness Helene could be made to admit—the one sort. It sank her to her bed. And there it held her stricken for half a year, while the world slumbered and dreamed outside, and her spirit beat within. And only her hands were flecked with life, as if life had run down and low to that extremity.

Finally, she was washed up, a blanched shred of herself, with all of world and spirit to be made anew.

For twelve months, Joseph had the store and his son in his unaided hands. The task was beyond the man. Gradually, all these years, he had let his initiative dry away. He had settled into a state of half-decrepitude, of sweet inertia. It had been as much Helene's fault as his.

He strove heroically. He was all caught up in the stern business of command, and did not know that he was failing. He worked incessantly; he nursed his wife; he tried to be an active father; he got up at dawn. And while he worked, his mind was stiff with fear and worry—mute to recording....When Helene came to herself, the bakery had fallen off from its prosperity. And Joseph Silvester was in debt.

Her healing was a sharp, slow birth. Her illness had been a guilty night. While her senses slumbered there was her household fallen away! All of it was like a mad interlude from faithfulness.

But now she was able to sit in her chair, while Joseph laid the events before her. Not until then was he sure himself of what had happened.

What he knew best was that he had fought hard, admitted no breach in his hope. He stood beside her, a large, gentle man with his hair greying and his eyes poignantly moist and his lank hands faintly moving.

"Sit down, dear," she had to tell him. He sank awkwardly, and faced her. They looked calmly at each other. They seemed closer together than they had been. This dread thing, life, had played them an irreverent trick. It had tried to lay silence on them. But they were above the silence.

"I tried, Helene, to keep strict accounts of the business. But I was worried—I was so tired!" He gave her a batch of crumpled papers, blurred over with his pencil.

"Here are bills; I haven't paid them yet." He gave these to her, also.

She took them. "Go back to the store," she said, "while I study these."

Joseph got up and lingered. At the door he spoke.

"Helene——"

"Yes, husband——?"

"I—I wanted to say—it don't matter—none of the trouble—now; when I see you gettin' well."

"Of course, it don't!" she answered. And then she laughed.

The story of the crumpled sheets was an easy one for her trained eyes to read. The business of the bakery was dwindling. At the first outlay due to her illness, Joseph had retrenched. He had forced a diminution of his sales by a curtailment of his supplies. It had been the one way he knew of to save money. And it had its logical result. His trade had shrunk. He had let it shrink. At each reverse, he had cut down the amount and the quality of what he had to sell. The vicious process had gained momentum. Expenses had risen. Everything else had lessened. And for each drop, the foolish man had had no wiser answer than to add a willed retrenchment of his own.

Helene shook her head.

"It's my fault," she said. "If he had been that silly when I married him, he could never have had a bakery at all! I've spoiled him." And then, "I had no business getting sick."

She got up from her chair to see if she was strong enough to walk. A pain shot through her temples; her mind sickened in a swirl of nausea. But her feet held her. She walked the length of the room, three times.

Then she sank down in her chair. She wanted to rest on her bed. She had resisted that. That had been giving ground, not gaining it.

"In a week, I'll be good," was her decision. It had no link with the pain in her temples.

She nursed herself carefully, meanwhile. She knew that she was preparing for a battle. And all of that week, she laid her plans, she went over the conditions she would have to cope with, she marshalled her resources. During that week no thought or fact of her life seemed to escape her. All of her was quickened by the sharp emergency of her affairs. All of her was attuned to meeting it. Yet, she did not dream, one moment, of touching her secret Fund.

"If only we had saved some money," Joseph said to her, with a low shake of his big head, looking away. "We should have, wife. We have been foolish."

"It is a pity, husband," was her answer.

And then, the battle.

Her eagerness swept her along. She was content, being full-handed. She had no eye to gauge the direction of her struggle. But even hope had to stop to breathe; and in the pause Helene looked about her. What she found was strangely different from her hope.

The way of their life had been increase. Now, it was loss. To bring about that change, there had come a violent event—her illness. No effort seemed strong enough to turn them back to the old way. Helene learned that there was stubborn growth in a bad direction, even as in a good one. The tide was going out.

And while she labored, hands beating against the ebb, hope weaving a frail garb against the onslaught, her Fund was fat and peaceful with its interest.

There were five years of battle. Into it Helene flung all of her diligence and craft. For it her husband found a new bloom of obdurate resolution. They served merely to prolong the battle.

She had begun to fight, for her health's sake, too soon. She did not regain the full vigor she had lost. Once more, she was pale and thin, and her hands were nervous. Her work and worry ate up each new shoot of strength as it appeared. Again the dreamful fiber of Helene stood at the surface—stripped, like her life, of its substance. Without blossom of youth and lilt of growth, there she was as she had been at the naked outset. Only she had her son beside her, and the secret Fund in the bank for savings.

These, then, served in place of the hope and passion and power of fifteen years before. These alone remained. She clung to them with desperation. And her grip was that of a spent, scared creature in the dark. For Helene did not know what life was fashioning. But, although she did not understand, she thought no more of giving up her Fund than she did of giving up her boy. In some way, one group of feelings bound them.

And inexorably, failure had crept up.

They had worked body to body—she and her husband. The old easeful state of Joseph had shrivelled and gone away. He was a strong man, now. His will had burst forth. But the long sleep had atrophied his powers. He was intent on doing; he did not know what to do. He was more helpless in his blindness, because he was more active. His energies were new, but his skill was old. And, after all, even the Helene who had been, the woman merged into the substance of her will, with all of her vigor athrob and her strength unthwarted, had done no greater thing than this: to make a prosperous bake-shop prosper a little more.

But the blight of the year when she lay blighted also, had sunk too deep into the source of their affairs. About them had been too much life, strained to catch the sun where they drooped to the shadow. So now, at last, the time of deferring debts was over. The battle of five years swerved suddenly to a decision.

They sat facing each other, their hard stiff chairs against two walls. Joseph's rocker was empty. He was in no mood for it. Before them, in the center of the room, was a bare table. Their flat was darker, poorer than any they had occupied before. It was a Sunday afternoon. The morrow was the last day for paying certain creditors who had placed their ultimatum on legal paper. Joseph had the paper in his hands. It was his, because the property was his.

Beyond the window was a sordid street that stretched like a funnel to a little treeless park. Here their son was playing.

"Wife," Joseph said, "these are what's going to ruin us. Eight hundred dollars. If we could meet them——"

"The store is picking up."

"Yes; that's the sneering part of it. All of this fight, and the store picking up. And then—" he stirred the paper languidly, "then this."

"What can we do, Joseph?" Only her mouth moved as Helene spoke.

"Yes; that's it—what can we do, Helene?" He seemed to be tracing her words, with a tired care, in order to comprehend them.

"We'll have to go to work," she said.

The big man trembled. He rose partly from his seat. And then, gripping himself, he rested back.

"You mean a job—for *us?*" Still he seemed to grope, fingering over her words.

"What else is there to do!"

Helene left her chair. She wanted to walk.

"Sit down, wife." His tone was an unmistakable command.

Helene caught it, amazed, and her seat found her.

"Do you know what you've said, Helene? Do you know what that'd mean? Do you understand——?"

His voice was shaken, but it was strong. He had outstretched his hand. It also was both strong and shaken.

"Joseph," Helene said, "how can I help knowing? Have I been outside? You talk——!"

All of her feeling ravelled into pain. After his wreckage, had she not given the sinew of her body?

"Listen, Helene. I'm over fifty years old. I've been a sober man. I've been a decent man. Do you want me to go out, like a laborer, now? Could you stand for me to do that, Helene——?"

"I'll be going with you, Joseph."

"Listen some more, Helene. Have I ever harmed you? Have I ever interfered with all you wanted. I know you was clever. I know I was lazy. You was the boss, Helene. And when you was sick, don't you think I was ashamed how I spoiled what you had done? Do you think, wife, I liked to see myself for what I was? This is my fault. That ain't easy, knowing!"

"We're in it together, like one, husband. We'll face it."

His words hurt her. They had driven tears to her eyes. There was a tragic anger in this man's grief which she had never seen; which—of all of him—she could not master.

"You can stop it, Helene."

"What!"

He was standing over her. His big hands were clenched. And his body seemed alive in his flat clothes.

"I'm speaking, now! I watched you. I've known all along. I said nothing. Why should I? You deserved what you took. You would do no harm with it. I trusted you. I trust you, now, Helene. But save us! What's it all been piled up for, else? It's a heap of money, if you ain't spent it!"

His voice had been low. His words came ponderously. Helene was watching his clamped hands.

"Is it spent, Helene?"

"No, husband, it ain't spent."

Joseph lurched back, loosing his hands. "Thank God," he breathed.

"It ain't going to be spent! It ain't mine to spend! It's Willie's!"

Her words were quick. They were more shattering to him than all of his surprise had been to her. Rather than meet them, he contrived to doubt them.

"Then you don't understand."

"I do, husband. Who should understand, if I did not?"

"It's ruin! It's disgrace!" he was shouting now. "Here, with that bank-book!"

He thrust forth his palms. She was also on her feet.

"No."

"Here!" he once more lowered his voice.

"It's Willie's, I tell you."

"It's my money. Where did you get it from? My store—"

"You can't take it, Joseph."

"I don't mean to take it. You'll give it here."

They swayed close to each other. And then, she smiled. She had mastered him again.

"Sit down, husband. And let's talk."

Bewilderment was foremost in his senses. Long he had known of this. But always he had had two habits: a profound respect for the woman that he loved, a profound silence for what was close-woven in his life. He was ready, with the wreck of that life upon him, to listen to her words. With another, doubtless, all his slumbering mute strength would have flamed high with passion and a blind violence. He sat now, his body strained and aquiver, while his wife spoke, slowly.

"I never guessed you knew. Well, you do know. I thought it was my secret. I'm glad you never spoke to me about it. Thanks for that, husband. Your speaking would have spoiled it. I don't know why," she shook her head, "but it would. And it's true. And it's three thousand dollars"— She paused.

He measured his hope with her words, not daring to know their strangeness one to the other.

"Joseph," she went on, "think what it is—all that money—think what it means. It's the difference between you and Willie; it's what you never had. I love you, but what are you? What are either of us? It's what is goin' to make him stronger, better!"

"You see us on the edge of nothing. And you insult your husband."

"I don't. But our life's done. We can plod through, somehow. What'll that money do for us? Pay our debts—yes; and run our bakery. What's that to Willie? And what can it do for him? The money can give him an education! It can send him to college! Oh, don't you see?"

"And we——?"

"We'll work. It's your store. It's my money. I don't have to pay your debts with it. But Joseph, am I forsaking you? Have I done that yet? I'll work with you, husband. I'm yours, even if this money ain't. I'll care for you. Oh, what won't I go through with you!"

"You can save us."

"At his expense?"

Her face had been soft. It hardened.

"No, I tell you! That's his. That's his chance. If we got to go down, so he can keep on goin' up—why down we got to go!"

She stopped. There was an austere ring in her voice.

Joseph looked at his wife. He came up close to her, in order to look close. She seemed, this moment, the clear, single summary of all that she had been to make him love her:—all this, in what appeared to him the moment of betrayal.

Still, he said: "You're heartless, wife. You steal from me; years, you been stealing from me. And now, you think of making your son better than I was."

"It's true."

"You don't care for me. All your love's there." He waved to the street.

"I'm yours, husband," was her answer.

"Is this honest—for them we owe to?"

Helene smiled: "It's his, now. We'll work to pay off, if that's your will."

"You mean it, Helene."

"What do we count, Joseph? *We* can work—until we die."

The man's face flamed a moment; and from the fire came hardness.

"Where's your love o' life? Are we that old?"

She smiled at him again—a smile this time flushed with a great knowledge that hurt. Her mind raced back. She saw three children romping in the street before the window of her shop. She saw herself, grasping two silver coins. And now, her hands moved vaguely in the direction of the window near which she stood.

"Where's your love o' life?" he had asked her. Her waving was her answer.

She sank into her chair. She held her head in her two hands. She sobbed. For it seemed that she had understood.

Her husband wavered before the agony of her vision. He was disarmed. He, also, understood—but as one separate from life, seeing it, feeling its horrid beauty across a gulf. He stood there, silent.

And then, in Helene's grief-bathed mind the vision came, and her tears made it gleam. She saw herself and her husband. They were aged and bowed, and stained and stricken with dull toil. And they were clad as are the men and women who labor with their hands. And they were going forth through a black swamp. And before them was nothing. But behind them—impelling them to go, driving them on, was a child dressed all in white. It was their child.

AMERICAN OPTIMISM

Leo Stein

THE obviously insistent fact about the expressions of the American spirit is their optimism. The stories, read by the upper ten million of the community, the plays they see, the things they say, the phrases on their lips, all correspond. And what is true of them is in an almost equal measure true of those who aim at finer and more carefully selected things. Not only the cheap literature, but the better and the best, is predominantly optimistic. The contradictory note is on occasion struck, but it becomes at once a matter for comment, and is by most critics noted, as un-American. There is of course in general a recognition of much and many evils, but beneath there is a sanguine hope. Every book almost, that is not frivolous, ends on the note of amelioration, and when, as in some of the modern poetry, there is no positive temper of expectancy, the spirit is that of enthusiastic, all-including, and impartial observation. Things either can be made good or else the moral values are ignored in recognition of the values of mere existence. To be, and to be alive, is then considered a sufficient justification. What, on the other hand, one rarely finds, is the note of utter tragedy, the note of stoicism, of mere acceptance, of renunciation. The optimism is inveterate and all but universal. It is also, it must be admitted, in general ignorant and biased. It accepts much without a rigorous examination of credentials, and minimizes the obstacles that it finds. In spots it shows itself courageous in acceptance, though on the whole it does avoid the test of a close examination of the facts that it should confront. Its cheerful carelessness is therefore something less than convincingly heroic, and its prevailing blindness makes one doubt its full validity; and one is forced to ask whether the courage is not in part a result of just that blindness. Could American optimism hold its own, if it would fairly measure the facts it has before it? Has it a deeper justification than inexperience? Do time and progress tend toward its endorsement or its refutation?

This note of persistent optimism in American letters, even at their best, contrasts sharply with the temper of the world's classic literature, in which the optimistic accent even when present is rarely dominant or exuberant. Rather one finds in it when it plumbs deeply the spirit of life and is not crushed by what it finds, the note of resignation, of noble submission to an overmastering fate. There is despair, there is serenity that surmounts despair, there is stoicism that accepts, there is ecstasy that exults in the mystery-enclouded, scarcely-revealed splendors of the divine wisdom, but in general for the life of man there is the felt term, the tomb that marks the boundaries of mortality, and confines the noblest flights of the spirit. The order of life is delimited and fixed, and the soul of man can, for a short while only, rejoice in the garden. Against the fate that ever threatens to turn paradise into a desert, there is a refuge in a heaven beyond, a life beyond life, where the spirit is made whole, from the bruises of this world of pain. Tragedy has at all times except the present, and especially the present of America, been looked on as the supreme expression in art, the deepest, fullest manifestation of man's sense of his life's meaning, the statement of his closest and most naked contact with the problem of his destiny. The only great transcendence of the tragic was the resurrection, the upspringing on the farther side of the tomb's horizon, the compensation for the woeful journey through the world. From lightning and tempest, from plague, pestilence and famine, from battle, murder and from sudden death, good Lord, deliver us, was the prayer of those who lived under an earlier order. To them nature was inexorable and supreme, the rule of things mysterious and inflexible, and they themselves the moment's tenants of the clay, beaten upon by all the forces of the world, and held upright only by the benignant finger of God. Such has been man in his deep and self-revealing moments.

To keep the balance true he has had the feeling of the flesh. If his tragedy was full of agony and despair, his comedy was not deficient in joy and radiance. The sculptors of Greece and the painters of Italy, of France and Flanders loved the body's sensuous magnificence as those of Holland the body's indulgence. Tragedy was only in small part the artist's concern, for the chisel and brush were better suited to illustrate the pleasures than the lacerations of the soul. The pageantry of earth was their greater theme, and they were soaked in the sunshine and shadow of a world of sense. Their subject was the obverse of the spiritually tragic realm of the great poets, and only rarely, as with Michelangelo, did they wrestle with the spirit's agony. For the poet as for the philosopher, nature was in large part the spirit's vestment and the means to its interpretation, for both laid their stress upon its inner meaning; but to the painter and the sculptor, nearer in spirit to the constructive genius, the engineer, the builder, and the man of science, nature was treasured more for its bodily values and for the beauty of its outward side.

Of this sensuousness, as of the tragic spirit, there is but little in American art. Its world of plastic forms is thin and bloodless, and its tragedy is only make-believe—a sighing reminiscence. It has been optimistic in the main and sensuously reticent—in matters of the spirit, and the flesh as well, it has stopped short of full acceptance of the facts before it. Optimism, as Walt Whitman has shown, can be robust; perhaps in time it may become both robust and rich, and wise. Its future hopes depend upon this consummation.

The optimism that prevailed in former days in America was very different from that which we know today, and differently conditioned. It took its rise when the decline of the New England Puritanism that had carried heavily, and painfully, its burden of sin, permitted the emergence of a more expansive spirit. Puritanism, as long as it continued to be seriously regarded, was essentially a denial of the spiritual value of opportunity, since it really meant that as long as destiny held the keys of salvation, no freedom and success could be genuinely real. It was only with the rise of Unitarianism and the greater range of spiritual experiment that culminated in the typical literature and social endeavor of New England that the optimism born of the American opportunity came into being. Men were then free for inner expansion, in consonance with their practical conditions. They came to realize the significance of their economic possibilities, and pitied Europe because of its kings, its crowds, and its poverty. In striking contrast, free land and free opportunity were to make of America, or for that matter had made of America, a uniquely favored world. Of course there were plenty of drawbacks and limitations, but these were more than compensated for by the sense the people had of citizenry in a chosen land, and the free movement determined by the vast ranges of unoccupied soil intensified the feeling of option and independence.

In Benjamin Franklin, the first important American writer, political and economic optimism voiced themselves, but there was in it nothing of the American scale. Except for the greater opportunity due to the fact that everything was still in the making, and to a certain freshness due to the variety of interests in a community in which a man of conspicuous practical intelligence had plenty of scope, Franklin was sufficiently typical of the highest grade of self-made man in any Anglo-Saxon society. It was the opportunity that seems singularly American, rather than the man and his ideas. With Emerson, however, this was not so. He conceived the type of American optimism as something quite particular, and though himself a New England villager, he had the vision of the American continent. He felt the originality of the occasion, and of the opportunities that it offered, and he demanded the freedom to avail himself of it. His thoughts were those of a philosophical idealist, conditioned by the economic, political and social outlook of America, not that America only which his countrymen had up to then discovered, but, more extensively, that which the American scene made possible. He felt so strongly the greatness of the occasion, the fulness that life offered to him who would put out his hand and take, that he on the whole ignored the difficulties of the enterprise, and assumed a perfectibility that he could not prove.

Next came Walt Whitman, the Parsifal of American literature, who drew in eloquent terms the picture of the perfect America, not perfect in the sense of perfected, but perfect rather in the sense that all of it was good. The imperfect equally with the perfect he sang, and everything was good for the mere reason that it was. He radiated with delight over the great length and breadth of the continent, over everything that grew on it, or walked or scampered across its surface. Never before had there been such an undiscriminating ecstasy, such an exuberant wallowing in the actuality, not of existence as such, but of the existence of things. Things were good, any old thing, and the more things there were the better, and hence a large part of his verse is not even description—it is a mere catalogue of things, a list of all the things that memory could recall or fantasy suggest in enlargement of the original theme.

This tone, which Walt Whitman made effective in art for the first time, had long been characteristic of American political and social oratory. The notion of munificent plenty and all of it admirably and wonderfully American—the little red school house with its range of democratic promise outreaching far the hopes of the old world, the hampered generations of Europe, with their limitations in the present and the future, contrasted with the optimism-inspiring reaches of America—all this was continually held up to view.

There was, however, an important difference in the reception accorded to the Fourth of July oratory, and that accorded to the poetry of Whitman. The oratory really represented public sentiment on matters social and political, whereas Walt Whitman's self-styled "barbaric yawp" represented nothing that the public recognized or wanted. What stood between him and his countrymen was simply the fact that in matters of the soul's utterance, Americans did not want America. They hungered for romance, for the grace and charm of Europe, for its color and its emotional riches. Lectures and clubs for the dissemination of culture were found throughout the land, and culture always meant the culture of Europe. The attitude toward it was largely sentimental and its passion was attenuated in transmission, for people did not really feel their own identity in kind with the men and women overseas. They yearned for Europe as a Mecca, as the bearer of emotional values utterly different from the commonplace of home, and in their more acceptable art they echoed its expressions. America was felt to be too new, too raw, to be the matter and stuff of beauty, and when as in the case of Cooper and Irving the American scene was utilized, it was done in the spirit of related English forms. Hawthorne's tragedy was romantically remote and sentimental rather than real. Except in spots our literature has been in spirit a translation. Americans felt themselves to be, culturally, expatriates, and their souls yearned for their spiritual home. They could not yet conceive of freedom otherwise than as political or economic.

In the course of time, however, it was found necessary to revise the primitive attitudes towards the economic and social freedom, and the optimism that they had inspired, for this older optimism had gone on the assumption that America had shortcircuited many of the deepest difficulties of European life. It assumed that such economic and social troubles as afflicted America were the results of crudity, of hurry, and of imperfect assimilation; but that all this would correct itself in time, and that in the main America was safe. But after the decades of expansion and corruption succeeding the Civil War, things got worse instead of better, and in the nineties many persons, who before had been self-confident, began to doubt whether America was really the paradise that had been so extensively advertised. It began then to be felt that the Topsy period was over and that America would not grow to beauty, virtue and goodness, unless some one took it in hand. This was the period of Bryanism and of the beginnings of sustained efforts to achieve administrative reform. Even the Constitution, which, till then, had enjoyed an almost undisturbed reverence, fell under suspicion, and the Fathers began to totter a little on their altars. A newer optimism was grafted on the old, but its roots had grown in a very different soil, and it had had a very different history.

This root was science, and the history was that of invention and discovery. I am of course not at all concerned to trace this history, but only to consider some of the ways in which its progress affected the temper of the last century and our own. And this was done not merely by the positive achievement of the sciences, and by the products that they put at man's disposal, but rather by the way that the mere fact of solving difficulties which up to then had either not been looked upon as matters for solution or had been utterly beyond solution, altered the character of thought and feeling with respect to man's range of faculty and his relation to nature.

Before the end of the eighteenth century science had been essentially a subject for men of science, and except for its philosophical implications, of very little interest to others. Outside of a few applications of mathematics and astronomy to navigation and to engineering, its results affected very little the daily life of men. Opinion and authority, modified by the results of direct rule-of-thumb practical experience, ruled men's lives. But with the invention of the steam engine and the discovery of modern chemistry, conditions were entirely changed, machinery and innumerable substances of value to industry became rapidly available, and from then on, instead of haphazard and occasional progress, the advance in the mastery and control of material conditions became orderly and continuous.

The natural consequence of this has been the greatly increased power over nature that has in large part determined specifically the temper of our time; and since the wireless and the aeroplane have been invented and radium discovered, it is almost impossible for skepticism to prevail against our quite unlimited confidence in the range of scientific understanding and utilization.

But though the rate of scientific progress has vastly outstripped all that the wildest prophecies could have anticipated, another of the benefits from the machine that was as hopefully expected has not been realized at all. The social benefits that were so confidently predicted have failed of realization, and a disillusioned century learned that not alone the engine, but the engineer also, would have to be transformed, in order that a social revolution should keep society advancing at a rate proportionate to the progress in mechanics. The mastery of matter was triumphantly achieved, but a victorious science was halted at the threshold of society; and its pretended advance into that further field was only the pseudo-science of political economy. In reality, authority, tradition, prejudice, continued to rule, as they had always done.

This was the social tragedy of the nineteenth century, that such increase of power should have come about and that so little should have been achieved to make intelligent direction of that power possible. There was no lack of interest in the subject, but those who took one side or those who took another in the endless controversies that arose were helpless to adduce decisive reasons. Nothing was available except opinion illustrated rather than proved by fact, and even if at some moment the movement was in a right direction, it could never be depended on to continue so. What opinion can at one moment do it can in the next moment undo, and so the older cultures were a series of progressive and recessive movements, wherein the beliefs developed, at one moment, were overthrown and rendered invalid and incapable of function by beliefs that happened to come after. Good theories could be overwhelmed by bad, good practices forced from the field by worse, because these were for temporary reasons more in harmony with some prevailing conditions or emotional trends.

To this continual flux of capricious alteration, science opposes a vital contrast. Its results are verified and in part experimentally determined, and eventually embodied in utilities. They prove their value or their lack of value in use, and either go into the scrap-heap as unavailable or else remain in service on their merits, and it is only in so far as genuine test and understanding can be rendered applicable to things that the irresponsible mutations of opinion can be succeeded by the cumulative reasonableness of growth. The early optimists of the nineteenth century did not reckon with the fact that unilluminated egotism would defeat the nobler aspirations that had no warrant except nobility, and that the road to better things could not be successfully charted simply because of the possession of more perfect instruments. Science which had been embodied only in material utilities and had left man individually and socially as he had always been, had fulfilled only the lesser of its possibilities. The greater and more important task was still before it.

It was already in the middle of the last century, the time of Ruskin, Dickens and Carlyle, that the failure of a society built up on machines and political economy was getting to be recognized, but though many fulminated against it they developed nothing that could effectually oppose it. Mechanical invention was a fact, absolute and irremovable, not to be done away with but to be supplemented by increase of knowledge and such a mastery of conditions as should make an effectual science of society possible; and the beginnings of such an extension of our understanding were already on the way. It was by no direct road that one could pass from mechanics to sociology, and the approaches attempted from philosophy and ethics did not lead to much. Another and more humble subject which had come to be attacked with serious effort, and which the biological sciences were then transforming, offered a more effective opening. This was hygiene which has since then in its various aspects come to stand quite in the forefront of contemporary interest, which has in many ways, by its conquests, revolutionized our attitudes, and is as yet only on the threshold of its achievement. Indeed so infinitely various and so dominating are the influences of hygiene on the conduct of life in our time that ours might well be called the age of hygiene, of constant and deliberate concern with health. The services of the medical profession have been at all times great in forwarding the subjects with which they were but indirectly concerned, but in no field has their co-operation had a tithe of the importance that it has had in making possible a real and serviceable science of society.

However, it is not our affair to follow these achievements but to take count of some of their significant consequences in the life of the contemporary spirit. And in fact these consequences are enormous. Hygiene has freed the human spirit from some of its most oppressive horrors and rendered less fearful others that it could not utterly remove. Death and decay, the loss of power, and the loss of life, these have been endless themes of thought and objects of solicitude. "How death came into the world and all our woe," the mystery of pain, the aspirations of eternal youth ... than these no matters have more profoundly stirred the minds of men. Nothing has more deeply worked on their imagination than pestilence, that terror that walked by night and ravaged away the life of thousands. The image of death has shadowed the life of man and has moved him to many of his richest utterances and therefore there is no irrelevance in bringing into close connection with the consideration of contemporary feeling, in which are rooted all creative impulses, the influence of that hygienic progress which has made disease, especially the imaginatively most appalling forms, plague and in general, infectious disease, recede and become less and less a terror. We have now, thanks to Lister, Pasteur, and a host of others, reached the point where in our normal life neither death, disease or pain is felt, as genuinely impending, and their incidence is occasional and not constant. They have come to mean in turn adventure and regret rather than passionate fear and horror, and our spiritual atmosphere has altered accordingly. Many things have changed because of this, although we do not always recognize the close connection. The removal of an ancient incubus has made possible new constructions, that would have found no place on the old blood-encumbered soil.

Among these products are America's only creative contribution to religion, the new thought creeds of which the best-established is Christian Science. The older religions offered compensations for the pain and death that weighed so heavily upon mortality, when sin also was made effectively awful because its wages were death, but now that dangers of all kinds are normally becoming more remote, that disease is more controlled, and death no longer felt to lurk in ambush, we feel less need of the ancient comforts. Optimism in the present takes the place of resignation, tempered by a distant hope, and the new thought religions build their temples where Calvary once stood. The religious cheerfulness that wars upon neurotic symptoms and despises the lumbering steps of a material science, stands on the ground which that science has prepared.

And what is true of religion is true likewise of philosophy, which in this country has two characteristic tendencies. Pragmatism, the immediate child of scientific method, is, in its moral aspects, a philosophy of risk, and differs from the older philosophies, which were predominantly philosophies of assurance. When life was more dangerous, men sought in philosophy tranquillity and security or at the least an ideal progress, and only now when the unsought risks are relatively small have they substituted for the ideal of the peace that passeth understanding, the ideal of the turmoil that invites the soul.

And with the other movement in philosophy, the realistic, it is likewise true that its acceptance of the facts, its feeling for the objective real, so strikingly accordant with the tendency in much modern literature to accept reality simply and to describe it, is a recognition of the lack of terror in the facts. The realist, unlike the pragmatist, rejoices less in movement and adventure than in mastery and control. Realism means the spirit of fact predominant, and the sheer acceptance of reality.

So far then as hygiene, the control of pain and disease cooperating with the products of mechanical science, has helped to build up and sustain the characteristic cheerful hope of progress and increasing mastery, it has acted as a powerful determinant of contemporary life. It has let the sun and air into the recesses of disease and as a consequence a large amount of mental sun and air have followed.

But individual hygiene is a limited field and is a pathway to greater and more important conquests. Its masters were already men of scientific training, and therefore in some measure prepared for scientific methods. Besides they had at their command familiar sciences, chemistry and biology. But for the larger fields of social hygiene, neither the knowledge nor the men were to be had. And yet it was in this field that most was yet to be accomplished if the possibilities growing out of the achieved mastery of matter were to be realized. The hopes that grew and flourished in the early days of scientific progress and invention were disappointed, for the society that wielded the instruments that science had devised, were controlled entirely by the methods of authority and opinion. A democracy however, a true democracy, must be more free than that; it must have better ground for action than tradition, and cannot trust to the wisdom of the men possessed of talent for political leadership to determine what its course should be. Nor is majority opinion adequate for such determinations, for though the tyranny of a majority may be in some sense more democratic than some other kind of tyranny still it does not truly serve as a solution.

A true democracy might be defined as a society where men have opportunity according to their talents, and rewards according to their services, and to discover the value of such services we need to know the worth of things. We cannot judge this worth by reliance on traditional taboo or primitive feeling, but only by long and carefully, critically studied effort. Only a social science that through knowledge leading to mastery can give us social health and clarify intentions, can give us also unity of purpose, that unity in matters on which men must agree, in order to live and work harmoniously together. Unless we can get that, authority and opinion which divide will rule, rather than understanding which unites.

Nothing has pointed out more sharply than our experience in social hygiene how far the values of opinion must yield to knowledge, how many things, generally considered matters of irreconcilable opinion, have proved in the long run to be matters of determinable fact. And so our social legislation and eventually a thousand other things that democracy requires and which may ultimately justify our optimism, will depend on ever widening circles of enlightenment. The notion of method and of ordered intelligence in affairs of public interest has become a very real issue, and though of course it is not commonly thought of in terms of science, yet it continually implies the science that it disregards. Our political reformers are not usually scientific men, but the new spirit of investigation, the conviction that it is possible by methodic and impartial effort to find right ways of doing things, has communicated itself far beyond the confines of the laboratory. The conception of the expert who experiments and learns instead of the amateur who guesses and prefers, is a contribution from the scientific spirit, and has helped to overcome the pessimistic hopelessness of those who realised that impulses expressing themselves merely in terms of authority and opinion, have their flux and reflux, without any assurance of eventual stable progress. But with knowledge in application something is progressively gained and fixed.

It has been characteristic of this country that a great part of the social amelioration which in Europe is matter for the attention of a paternal bureaucracy has required initial effort from the public, and that this interest and occupation has helped to give to those who read, and that means all the more or less educated millions, an acquaintance with the facts of the social and material world about them. There is in consequence no lack, in books and magazines, of vigorously effective description, in which the color, form, and outward aspect of body and mind are illustrated. This reportorial work is admirable, yet no one reading this literature can escape the conviction that in spite of its buoyancy, its husky energy, and its wide-flung intelligence, its interest in fact is only an interest in externals and that beneath the surface it is traditionally elementary. The outer aspect for mind and body both is realistic, but within we find the spirit of the fairy tale.

The fairy tale employs elementary situations, and deals with the large, basic objects of desire: wealth, power, love, and life. It deals with these in terms of simple conflicts between patently hostile agents. The hero ends in the possession of riches, kingdom, princess and eternal felicity. It is a perfectly coherent scheme, and the simplicity of the formulation is entirely in harmony with the simplicity of the desires. There is in consequence no effect of triviality. But in the American story this coherence is lost. The souls of hero and heroine are only a trifle more complicated than those of the fairy tale, but the scene has become realistically elaborate. North, South, East and West, all classes and all occupations are pictured for us, and the picturing is admirably done. Unfortunately these simple souls do not belong in a world so complex and so strained. The scene is studied from the life, but the people are, in Kipling's phrase, "just-so" people, cast in a simple mould of spiritual consistency, and undisturbed by inner contradictions. Their conflicts, when they have them, are sometimes as deep as are the outer layers of the skin, and one can go quite to the bottom without danger of drawing blood. The soul of man is treated as though it were a simple thing, as though what one did not know would never hurt one, as though an optimistic faith required the sustaining force of ignorance and fatuity.

However modern science is showing with quite convincing power that it is precisely what we do not know that can hurt us most, and if we are to have a valuable democratic society and a significant democratic art we must learn to realize this terrifying truth. Nor must it be supposed that democratic is here used as a mere catch-word. It has a definite relevance and an intimate relation to the tendencies of modern social movement.

A democratic art in the conditions of modern life must differ profoundly from most of the art of former times, for that has been in the main of two kinds: peasant art and aristocratic art. A peasant art implies a stationary society, one where by slow and gradual modifications, motives derived from any source whatever were made effective and specifically relevant to the traditional feeling of the craftsmen that produced them. The craftsman himself was furthermore one of the group for whom he worked, and through the intimacy that prevailed between the workman, the material and the public, there developed that appropriateness, that rhythmic coherence, which we find so commonly in the art of peasants, barbarians and traditional workmen in general. We find there the same naively direct rhythmical adjustment that we find in children's drawings, and which can only be achieved when the disturbance due to complex solicitation of experience can be withheld. We all know how the child whose drawings are so marvellously just may show no taste whatever in selection, and that the peasant is notoriously at fault outside of his customary range.

We cannot have a peasant art. We have no stationary society, comparatively remote from foreign influences, nor is the desire for such a thing at all reasonable. The peasant and his art also belong to the past, to a time that can never more return; besides that, always, except among barbarians, it implied its opposite: an aristocratic art.

An aristocratic art depends upon the existence of a leisure class, a group of men born to consume the fruits of toil. They themselves produce nothing except occasional lyrics, but they are patrons and critics. Their need of a luxurious extravagance as part of their class manifestation leads to a corresponding need of variety and novelty. They require art to deck their own superiority and the artist to produce it. The artist is a craftsman and therefore drafted from the ranks of the middle classes, to which he is moreover so often maladjusted. In former times he was directly dependent on the aristocrat, but in time this close connection was dissolved, and there grew up the normal correlate of the aristocratic patron, i.e., the bohemian artist. Peasantry, aristocracy, whether noble or bourgeois, and bohemia, these are, roughly speaking, the conditions of modern European art production, and those that we, with very moderate success, have sought to acclimatize among us. The purpose has essentially miscarried, for we have in America neither the peasantry, the aristocracy, nor the bohemia, nor do we really tend toward their production. If we are to have a native art we must look elsewhere.

Our culture and our social tendencies, our larger hopes and aspirations, point rather toward broader, leveling characters. We tend rather toward the large appeal and wider distribution. The smaller currents of esotericism, of delicate selection and choice exclusion, are not things of primary importance. They are pleasant as minor poetry is pleasant, but if they are to count in larger measure they must find a way for their currents into the main stream of national life. The kind of thing that we are energetically and commonly doing, but doing badly, must be done well. The parochialism of our soul's outlook must be enlarged, and we must get more insight and more understanding. The range of intelligent investigation must be extended, and we must add to the courage that is leading us to grapple with the hygiene of society, the greater courage that is needed to grapple with the hygiene of the soul.

This means, I take it, that just as hygiene of the body necessitated the admission of intelligence, and then of light and air, those greatest of purifiers and antiseptics, as hygiene of society required investigation, progressively more fearless and circumstantial, into those hidden regions, obscured behind a veil of social, economic and political conventions, which passed for those who profited and for those too supine or too stupid to protest, as necessary, so the soul's hygiene will require the admission of light and air into our individual depths. Hypocrisy means their exclusion, and whether conscious or unconscious, is the stupefier of the soul. We cannot move backwards to the innocence of childhood, and therefore we must move forward to a full maturity. We must learn to face the complexity of our inner life. A European with his older culture and his more mature experience is familiar with it. He knows that the only escape from hypocrisy is the recognition of his own inner multiplicity. He knows and has adapted his life to this variety of outlook, and he knows that he must have numerous standards, social, political and economic, if he is going to be honestly and truthfully oriented with reference to the vicissitudes of daily life. He is not afraid to let his right hand know what his left hand is doing, because he knows that the complexity of human relations is so great that what the left hand may be justified in doing the right hand may refuse to do, or do it differently. His recognition of his differences makes self-criticism possible, for self-criticism is nothing but the criticism of one of our selves by another. The American, however, pretends to a simplicity that is not real. He manages to think his right hand and his left identical and consequently remains extraordinarily ignorant of both. He cannot genuinely criticise himself, for his false consistency hides his soul from his own observation, and makes for hypocrisy in act and triviality in art. A man who cannot see himself from within can see himself only as reflected in a mirror, and then, of course, he can see nothing but the outside.

If we would reach a true simplicity, that ideal simplicity whose shallow substitute assails us from the pages of an anæmic literature, we must boldly take the last step to attain healthy-mindedness. We cannot go back to a peasant simplicity which as Americans we never had, and the only alternative is full self-consciousness. We must in some way do for ourselves the thing that we are seeking to do with reference to our social structure, that is, we must seek to clarify our individual depths. We should have profited more largely for our art if we had gained this knowledge through the stress and agony of painful growth, but since we failed to get it that way, we must get it any other way we can. And we are getting it in characteristic wise. What our experience did not teach us, for that experience was quite blunted against the armor of our optimistic complacency, we are about to learn from science. The newer individual psychology, especially identified with the name of Freud, is telling us a number of things which in part at least we should have known, and it is probable that one of the reasons why it is being accepted so much more easily here than in the centers of a wiser and more reflective civilization, is that, on the whole, we feel rather less attainted by it. We feel it as dis-coveries in a new and interesting field rather than as something that tears deeply at our vitals. When we have learnt the lesson we may fairly expect some importantly new orientations. In life, our optimism will have to reckon with many radical difficulties that we have hitherto ignored, and in art we then shall find that the things we now produce are inept even for their own trivial purposes. However, if we succeed, upon the basis of such knowledge, in adding to the description of mere outward things an equally successful presentation of the inner, we shall produce a picture of our time, which even in the absence of transcending genius will be vital and sufficient.

And on another range of interest, a deeper insight would have impor-tant consequences, for it is not only in regard to spiritual depths that expression in America has been inhibited by the failure to plumb the soul's demand. It was a similar uncritical simplicity of thought and shal-lowness of feeling that justified the identification of the flesh and the devil. No chance was given to follow either of the two alternative correctives: that of the peasant or barbarian who can indulge freely both the senses and the spirit and find no contradiction or incompatibility, because his mind makes no demand for classification and consistency; or, on the other hand, that of a finer critical insight and experience which makes distinctions with a richer understanding. Our crude uncritical criticism and our dull middle-class moralities, intelligent in form without intelligence in substance, with neither frank brutality nor beautiful refinement, which sought to rule the future with the preconceptions of the past, and chained the deeper levels of the spirit while whipping the surface into an agitated foam, blown up with wind; these have limited our sensuous, as they have limited our intellectual, life. Only a criticism that is intelligent and that ignores pre-established boundaries, and is prepared to drop its searchlight into the deepest recesses of our lives can set us free. There is already notable progress in that direction and our fondness for the dance, the pageant, for more light and color, and greater stretching out into the open spaces, are happy symptoms. They are some first fruits of that greater knowledge, almost the greatest critical insight, that all things are good when not displaced, and that the business of education is not to do away with things, but to find places for them. It is not chaining energy but harnessing it that is desired, and only life when running freely can measure the fulness of its possibilities.

It is not then optimism nor materialism either, as we often hear, that is the crying fault of American life and art, but shallowness. Its superficiality has kept its optimism from the ultimate test, but has not disproved it. And the growing materialism is a fiction. Wherever there is wealth and luxury available, people seek it. Therefore the increase in luxury is only evidence that more can be obtained. There is, however, tremendous increase of interest in physical well-being, in general welfare, and it is often pointed out that even the churches turn more and more to questions of social betterment than to salvation. But materialism is not a matter of geography, and the good old heaven was no less essentially material because it was not to be reached by flesh-encumbered men. For most of us today, heaven, if there be a heaven, must be found on earth, and there are proportionately more people in this country today and their number is growing daily, who give themselves to making such a one as they can manage to conceive. It is such action, when there is no crisis that compels even the money-changer in the temple to turn patriot and lover of his kind, that is the test of social idealism, and this country does not seem to fall short of reasonable expectation. Nor is it of importance that some time ago proportionately more people were interested in Browning clubs than could be gathered together for that purpose today. Browning was for them a way of making larger contacts with life, and the membership was almost confined to women. Today there are a greater number of contacts that women have with living processes in society, which has made it possible for them to leave Browning where he belongs; that is, on the shelf, except, of course, when one is moved to take him down and read him.

Art is a comment, an expression, an extension of life, experience, and not a substitute for it, and it should not be taken with exaggerated seriousness. Real progress in art appreciation comes of dissatisfaction with that art which fails to answer individual needs. Therefore to create a need, and not a mere snobbish desire for profounder and spiritually richer things, we must enrich the soul. When people really need good art, and good art is available, they will take it, but if they take it for any other reason it does not make much difference. If, therefore, the search for social health leading to further social liberation will make the American mind more eager and more apprehensive, we may with confidence await the growth of a larger and more vital audience and an art production to supply their wants.

THE WAR AND THE INTELLECTUALS

Randolph Bourne

TO those of us who still retain an irreconcilable animus against war, it has been a bitter experience to see the unanimity with which the American intellectuals have thrown their support to the use of war-technique in the crisis in which America found herself. Socialists, college professors, publicists, new-republicans, practitioners of literature, have vied with each other in confirming with their intellectual faith the collapse of neutrality and the riveting of the war-mind on a hundred million more of the world's people. And the intellectuals are not content with confirming our belligerent gesture. They are now complacently asserting that it was they who effectively willed it, against the hesitation and dim perceptions of the American democratic masses. A war made deliberately by the intellectuals! A calm moral verdict, arrived at after a penetrating study of inexorable facts! Sluggish masses, too remote from the world-conflict to be stirred, too lacking in intellect to perceive their danger! An alert intellectual class, saving the people in spite of themselves, biding their time with Fabian strategy until the nation could be moved into war without serious resistance! An intellectual class, gently guiding a nation through sheer force of ideas into what the other nations entered only through predatory craft or popular hysteria or militarist madness! A war free from any taint of self-seeking, a war that will secure the triumph of democracy and internationalize the world! This is the picture which the more self-conscious intellectuals have formed of themselves, and which they are slowly impressing upon a population which is being led no man knows whither by an indubitably intellectualized President. And they are right, in that the war certainly did not spring from either the ideals or the prejudices, from the national ambitions or hysterias, of the American people, however acquiescent the masses prove to be, and however clearly the intellectuals prove their putative intuition.

Those intellectuals who have felt themselves totally out of sympathy with this drag toward war will seek some explanation for this joyful leadership. They will want to understand this willingness of the American intellect to open the sluices and flood us with the sewage of the war spirit. We cannot forget the virtuous horror and stupefaction which filled our college professors when they read the famous manifesto of their ninety-three German colleagues in defence of their war. To the American academic mind of 1914 defence of war was inconceivable. From Bernhardi it recoiled as from a blasphemy, little dreaming that two years later would find it creating its own cleanly reasons for imposing military service on the country and for talking of the rough rude currents of health and regeneration that war would send through the American body politic. They would have thought anyone mad who talked of shipping American men by the hundreds of thousands—conscripts—to die on the fields of France. Such a spiritual change seems catastrophic when we shoot our minds back to those days when neutrality was a proud thing. But the intellectual progress has been so gradual that the country retains little sense of the irony. The war sentiment, begun so gradually but so perseveringly by the preparedness advocates who came from the ranks of big business, caught hold of one after another of the intellectual groups. With the aid of Roosevelt, the murmurs became a monotonous chant, and finally a chorus so mighty that to be out of it was at first to be disreputable and finally almost obscene. And slowly a strident rant was worked up against Germany which compared very creditably with the German fulminations against the greedy power of England. The nerve of the war-feeling centred, of course, in the richer and older classes of the Atlantic seaboard, and was keenest where there were French or English business and particularly social connections. The sentiment then spread over the country as a class-phenomenon, touching everywhere those upper-class elements in each section who identified themselves with this Eastern ruling group. It must never be forgotten that in every community it was the least liberal and least democratic elements among whom the preparedness and later the war sentiment was found. The farmers were apathetic, the small business men and workingmen are still apathetic towards the war. The election was a vote of confidence of these latter classes in a President who would keep the faith of neutrality. The intellectuals, in other words, have identified themselves with the least democratic forces in American life. They have assumed the leadership for war of those very classes whom the American democracy has been immemorially fighting. Only in a world where irony was dead could an intellectual class enter war at the head of such illiberal cohorts in the avowed cause of world-liberalism and world-democracy. No one is left to point out the undemocratic nature of this war-liberalism. In a time of faith, skepticism is the most intolerable of all insults.

Our intellectual class might have been occupied, during the last two years of war, in studying and clarifying the ideals and aspirations of the American democracy, in discovering a true Americanism which would not have been merely nebulous but might have federated the different ethnic groups and traditions. They might have spent the time in endeavoring to clear the public mind of the cant of war, to get rid of old mystical notions that clog our thinking. We might have used the time for a great wave of education, for setting our house in spiritual order. We could at least have set the problem before ourselves. If our intellectuals were going to lead the administration, they might conceivably have tried to find some way of securing peace by making neutrality effective. They might have turned their intellectual energy not to the problem of jockeying the nation into war, but to the problem of using our vast neutral power to attain democratic ends for the rest of the world and ourselves without the use of the malevolent technique of war. They might have failed. The point is that they scarcely tried. The time was spent not in clarification and education, but in a mulling over of nebulous ideals of democracy and liberalism and civilization which had never meant anything fruitful to those ruling classes who now so glibly used them, and in giving free rein to the elementary instinct of self-defence. The whole era has been spiritually wasted. The outstanding feature has been not its Americanism but its intense colonialism. The offence of our intellectuals was not so much that they were colonial—for what could we expect of a nation composed of so many national elements?—but that it was so one-sidedly and partisanly colonial. The official, reputable expression of the intellectual class has been that of the English colonial. Certain portions of it have been even more loyalist than the King, more British even than Australia. Other colonial attitudes have been vulgar. The colonialism of the other American stocks was denied a hearing from the start. America might have been made a meeting-ground for the different national attitudes. An intellectual class, cultural colonists of the different European nations, might have threshed out the issues here as they could not be threshed out in Europe. Instead of this, the English colonials in university and press took command at the start, and we became an intellectual Hungary where thought was subject to an effective process of Magyarization. The reputable opinion of the American intellectuals became more and more either what could be read pleasantly in London, or what was written in an earnest effort to put Englishmen straight on their war-aims and war-technique. This Magyarization of thought produced as a counter-reaction a peculiarly offensive and inept German apologetic, and the two partisans divided the field between them. The great masses, the other ethnic groups, were inarticulate. American public opinion was almost as little prepared for war in 1917 as it was in 1914.

The sterile results of such an intellectual policy are inevitable. During the war the American intellectual class has produced almost nothing in the way of original and illuminating interpretation. Veblen's "Imperial Germany;" Patten's "Culture and War," and addresses; Dewey's "German Philosophy and Politics;" a chapter or two in Weyl's "American Foreign Policies;"—is there much else of creative value in the intellectual repercussion of the war? It is true that the shock of war put the American intellectual to an unusual strain. He had to sit idle and think as spectator not as actor. There was no government to which he could docilely and loyally tender his mind as did the Oxford professors to justify England in her own eyes. The American's training was such as to make the fact of war almost incredible. Both in his reading of history and in his lack of economic perspective he was badly prepared for it. He had to explain to himself something which was too colossal for the modern mind, which outran any language or terms which we had to interpret it in. He had to expand his sympathies to the breaking-point, while pulling the past and present into some sort of interpretative order. The intellectuals in the fighting countries had only to rationalize and justify what their country was already doing. Their task was easy. A neutral, however, had really to search out the truth. Perhaps perspective was too much to ask of any mind. Certainly the older colonials among our college professors let their prejudices at once dictate their thought. They have been comfortable ever since. The war has taught them nothing and will teach them nothing. And they have had the satisfaction, under the rigor of events, of seeing prejudice submerge the intellects of their younger colleagues. And they have lived to see almost their entire class, pacifists and democrats too, join them as apologists for the "gigantic irrelevance" of war.

We have had to watch, therefore, in this country the same process which so shocked us abroad,—the coalescence of the intellectual classes in support of the military programme. In this country, indeed, the socialist intellectuals did not even have the grace of their German brothers and wait for the declaration of war before they broke for cover. And when they declared for war they showed how thin was the intellectual veneer of their socialism. For they called us in terms that might have emanated from any bourgeois journal to defend democracy and civilization, just as if it was not exactly against those very bourgeois democracies and capitalist civilizations that socialists had been fighting for decades. But so subtle is the spiritual chemistry of the "inside" that all this intellectual cohesion—herd-instinct become herd-intellect—which seemed abroad so hysterical and so servile, comes to us here in highly rational terms. We go to war to save the world from subjugation! But the German intellectuals went to war to save their culture from barbarization! And the French went to war to save their beautiful France! And the English to save international honor! And Russia, most altruistic and self-sacrificing of all, to save a small State from destruction! Whence is our miraculous intuition of our moral spotlessness? Whence our confidence that history will not unravel huge economic and imperialist forces upon which our rationalizations float like bubbles? The Jew often marvels that his race alone should have been chosen as the true people of the cosmic God. Are not our intellectuals equally fatuous when they tell us that our war of all wars is stainless and thrillingly achieving for good?

An intellectual class that was wholly rational would have called insistently for peace and not for war. For months the crying need has been for a negotiated peace, in order to avoid the ruin of a deadlock. Would not the same amount of resolute statesmanship thrown into intervention have secured a peace that would have been a subjugation for neither side? Was the terrific bargaining power of a great neutral ever really used? Our war followed, as all wars follow, a monstrous failure of diplomacy. Shamefacedness should now be our intellectuals' attitude, because the American play for peace was made so little more than a polite play. The intellectuals have still to explain why, willing as they now are to use force to continue the war to absolute exhaustion, they were not willing to use force to coerce the world to a speedy peace.

Their forward vision is no more convincing than their past rationality. We go to war now to internationalize the world! But surely their League to Enforce Peace is only a palpable apocalyptic myth, like the syndicalists' myth of the "general strike." It is not a rational programme so much as a glowing symbol for the purpose of focusing belief, of setting enthusiasm on fire for international order. As far as it does this it has pragmatic value, but as far as it provides a certain radiant mirage of idealism for this war and for a world-order founded on mutual fear, it is dangerous and obnoxious. Idealism should be kept for what is ideal. It is depressing to think that the prospect of a world so strong that none dare challenge it should be the immediate ideal of the American intellectual. If the League is only a makeshift, a coalition into which we enter to restore order, then it is only a description of existing fact, and the idea should be treated as such. But if it is an actually prospective outcome of the settlement, the keystone of American policy, it is neither realizable nor desirable. For the programme of such a League contains no provision for dynamic national growth or for international economic justice. In a world which requires recognition of economic internationalism far more than of political internationalism, an idea is reactionary which proposes to petrify and federate the nations as political and economic units. Such a scheme for international order is a dubious justification for American policy. And if American policy had been sincere in its belief that our participation would achieve international beatitude, would we not have made our entrance into the war conditional upon a solemn general agreement to respect in the final settlement these principles of international order? Could we have afforded, if our war was to end war by the establishment of a league of honor, to risk the defeat of our vision and our betrayal in the settlement? Yet we are in the war, and no such solemn agreement was made, nor has it even been suggested.

The case of the intellectuals seems, therefore, only very speciously rational. They could have used their energy to force a just peace or at least to devise other means than war for carrying through American policy. They could have used their intellectual energy to ensure that our participation in the war meant the international order which they wish. Intellect was not so used. It was used to lead an apathetic nation into an irresponsible war, without guarantees from those belligerents whose cause we were saving. The American intellectual, therefore, has been rational neither in his hindsight nor his foresight. To explain him we must look beneath the intellectual reasons to the emotional disposition. It is not so much what they thought as how they felt that explains our intellectual class. Allowing for colonial sympathy, there was still the personal shock in a world-war which outraged all our preconceived notions of the way the world was tending. It reduced to rubbish most of the humanitarian internationalism and democratic nationalism which had been the emotional thread of our intellectuals' life. We had suddenly to make a new orientation. There were mental conflicts. Our latent colonialism strove with our longing for American unity. Our desire for peace strove with our desire for national responsibility in the world. That first lofty and remote and not altogether unsound feeling of our spiritual isolation from the conflict could not last. There was the itch to be in the great experience which the rest of the world was having. Numbers of intelligent people who had never been stirred by the horrors of capitalistic peace at home were shaken out of their slumber by the horrors of war in Belgium. Never having felt responsibility for labor wars and oppressed masses and excluded races at home, they had a large fund of idle emotional capital to invest in the oppressed nationalities and ravaged villages of Europe.

Hearts that had felt only ugly contempt for democratic strivings at home beat in tune with the struggle for freedom abroad. All this was natural, but it tended to over-emphasize our responsibility. And it threw our thinking out of gear. The task of making our own country detailedly fit for peace was abandoned in favor of a feverish concern for the management of the war, advice to the fighting governments on all matters, military, social and political, and a gradual working up of the conviction that we were ordained as a nation to lead all erring brothers towards the light of liberty and democracy. The failure of the American intellectual class to erect a creative attitude toward the war can be explained by these sterile mental conflicts which the shock to our ideals sent raging through us.

Mental conflicts end either in a new and higher synthesis or adjustment, or else in a reversion to more primitive ideas which have been outgrown but to which we drop when jolted out of our attained position. The war caused in America a recrudescence of nebulous ideals which a younger generation was fast outgrowing because it had passed the wistful stage and was discovering concrete ways of getting them incarnated in actual institutions. The shock of the war threw us back from this pragmatic work into an emotional bath of these old ideals. There was even a somewhat rarefied revival of our primitive Yankee boastfulness, the reversion of senility to that republican childhood when we expected the whole world to copy our republican institutions. We amusingly ignored the fact that it was just that Imperial German regime, to whom we are to teach the art of self-government, which our own Federal structure, with its executive irresponsible in foreign policy and with its absence of parliamentary control, most resembles. And we are missing the exquisite irony of the unaffected homage paid by the American democratic intellectuals to the last and most detested of Britain's tory premiers as the representative of a "liberal" ally, as well as the irony of the selection of the best hated of America's bourbon "old guard" as the missionary of American democracy to Russia.

The intellectual state that could produce such things is one where reversion has taken place to more primitive ways of thinking. Simple syllogisms are substituted for analysis, things are known by their labels, our heart's desire dictates what we shall see. The American intellectual class, having failed to make the higher syntheses, regresses to ideas that can issue in quick, simplified action. Thought becomes any easy rationalization of what is actually going on or what is to happen inevitably tomorrow. It is true that certain groups did rationalize their colonialism and attach the doctrine of the inviolability of British sea-power to the doctrine of a League of Peace. But this agile resolution of the mental conflict did not become a higher synthesis, to be creatively developed. It gradually merged into a justification for our going to war. It petrified into a dogma to be propagated. Criticism flagged and emotional propaganda began. Most of the socialists, the college professors and the practitioners of literature, however, have not even reached this high-water mark of synthesis. Their mental conflicts have been resolved much more simply. War in the interests of democracy! This was almost the sum of their philosophy. The primitive idea to which they regressed became almost insensibly translated into a craving for action. War was seen as the crowning relief of their indecision. At last action, irresponsibility, the end of anxious and torturing attempts to reconcile peace-ideals with the drag of the world towards Hell. An end to the pain of trying to adjust the facts to what they ought to be! Let us consecrate the facts as ideal! Let us join the greased slide towards war! The momentum increased. Hesitations, ironies, consciences, considerations,—all were drowned in the elemental blare of doing something aggressive, colossal. The new-found Sabbath "peacefulness of being at war"! The thankfulness with which so many intellectuals lay down and floated with the current betrays the hesitation and suspense through which they had been. The American university is a brisk and happy place these days. Simple, unquestioning action has superseded the knots of thought. The thinker dances with reality.

With how many of the acceptors of war has it been mostly a dread of intellectual suspense? It is a mistake to suppose that intellectuality necessarily makes for suspended judgments. The intellect craves certitude. It takes effort to keep it supple and pliable. In a time of danger and disaster we jump desperately for some dogma to cling to. The time comes, if we try to hold out, when our nerves are sick with fatigue, and we seize in a great healing wave of release some doctrine that can be immediately translated into action. Neutrality meant suspense, and so it became the object of loathing to frayed nerves. The vital myth of the League of Peace provides a dogma to jump to. With war the world becomes motor again and speculation is brushed aside like cobwebs. The blessed emotion of self-defence intervenes too, which focused millions in Europe. A few keep up a critical pose after war is begun, but since they usually advise action which is in one-to-one correspondence with what the mass is already doing, their criticism is little more than a rationalization of the common emotional drive.

The results of war on the intellectual class are already apparent. Their thought becomes little more than a description and justification of what is going on. They turn upon any rash one who continues idly to speculate. Once the war is on, the conviction spreads that individual thought is help-less, that the only way one can count is as a cog in the great wheel. There is no good holding back. We are told to dry our unnoticed and ineffective tears and plunge into the great work. Not only is everyone forced into line, but the new certitude becomes idealized. It is a noble realism which opposes itself to futile obstruction and the cowardly refusal to face facts. This realistic boast is so loud and sonorous that one wonders whether realism is always a stern and intelligent grappling with realities. May it not be sometimes a mere surrender to the actual, an abdication of the ideal through a sheer fatigue from intellectual suspense? The pacifist is roundly scolded for refusing to face the facts, and for retiring into his own world of sentimental desire. But is the realist, who refuses to challenge or criticise facts, entitled to any more credit than that which comes from following the line of least resistance? The realist thinks he at least can control events by linking himself to the forces that are moving. Perhaps he can. But if it is a question of controlling war, it is difficult to see how the child on the back of a mad elephant is to be any more effective in stop-ping the beast than is the child who tries to stop him from the ground. The ex-humanitarian, turned realist, sneers at the snobbish neutrality, colossal conceit, crooked thinking, dazed sensibilities, of those who are still unable to find any balm of consolation for this war. We manufacture consolations here in America while there are probably not a dozen men fighting in Europe who did not long ago give up every reason for their being there except that nobody knew how to get them away.

But the intellectuals whom the crisis has crystallized into an acceptance of war have put themselves into a terrifyingly strategic position. It is only on the craft, in the stream, they say, that one has any chance of controlling the current forces for liberal purposes. If we obstruct, we surrender all power for influence. If we responsibly approve, we then retain our power for guiding. We will be listened to as responsible thinkers, while those who obstructed the coming of war have committed intellectual suicide and shall be cast into outer darkness. Criticism by the ruling powers will only be accepted from those intellectuals who are in sympathy with the general tendency of the war. Well, it is true that they may guide, but if their stream leads to disaster and the frustration of national life, is their guiding any more than a preference whether they shall go over the right-hand or the left-hand side of the precipice? Meanwhile, however, there is comfort on board. Be with us, they call, or be negligible, irrelevant. Dissenters are already excommunicated. Irreconcilable radicals, wringing their hands among the debris, become the most despicable and impotent of men. There seems no choice for the intellectual but to join the mass of acceptance. But again the terrible dilemma arises,—either support what is going on, in which case you count for nothing because you are swallowed in the mass and great incalculable forces bear you on; or remain aloof, passively resistant, in which case you count for nothing because you are outside the machinery of reality.

Is there no place left, then, for the intellectual who cannot yet crystallize, who does not dread suspense, and is not yet drugged with fatigue? The American intellectuals, in their preoccupation with reality, seem to have forgotten that the real enemy is War rather than imperial Germany. There is work to be done to prevent this war of ours from passing into popular mythology as a holy crusade. What shall we do with leaders who tell us that we go to war in moral spotlessness, or who make "democracy" synonymous with a republican form of government? There is work to be done in still shouting that all the revolutionary by-products will not justify the war, or make war anything else than the most noxious complex of all the evils that afflict men. There must be some to find no consolation whatever, and some to sneer at those who buy the cheap emotion of sacrifice. There must be some irreconcilables left who will not even accept the war with walrus tears. There must be some to call unceasingly for peace, and some to insist that the terms of settlement shall be not only liberal but democratic. There must be some intellectuals who are not willing to use the old discredited counters again and to support a peace which would leave all the old inflammable materials of armament lying about the world. There must still be opposition to any contemplated "liberal" world-order founded on military coalitions. The "irreconcilable" need not be disloyal. He need not even be "impossibilist." His apathy towards war should take the form of a heightened energy and enthusiasm for the education, the art, the interpretation that make for life in the midst of the world of death. The intellectual who retains his animus against war will push out more boldly than ever to make his case solid against it. The old ideals crumble; new ideals must be forged. His mind will continue to roam widely and ceaselessly. The thing he will fear most is premature crystallization. If the American intellectual class rivets itself to a "liberal" philosophy that perpetuates the old errors, there will then be need for "democrats" whose task will be to divide, confuse, disturb, keep the intellectual waters constantly in motion to prevent any such ice from ever forming.

TOMORROW

Eugene G. O'Neill

I T was back in my sailor days, in the winter of my great down-and-out-ness, that all this happened. In those years of wandering, to be broke and "on the beach" in some seaport or other of the world was no new experience; but this had been an unusually long period of inaction even for me. Six months before I had landed in New York after a voyage from Buenos Aires as able seaman on a British tramp. Since that time I had loafed around the water front, eking out an existence on a small allow-ance from my family, too lazy of body and mind, too indifferent to things in general, to ship to sea again or do anything else. I shared a small rear room with another "gentleman-ranker," Jimmy Anderson, an old friend of mine, over an all-night dive near South street known as Tommy the Priest's.

This is the story of Jimmy, my roommate, and it begins on a cold night in the early part of March. I had waited in Tommy the Priest's, hunched up on a chair near the stove in the back room, all the late afternoon until long after dark. My nerves were on edge as a result of a two days' carouse ensuing on the receipt of my weekly allowance. Now all that money was gone—over the bar—and the next few days gloomed up as a dreary, sober and hungry ordeal which must, barring miracles, be endured patiently or otherwise. Three or four others of the crowd I knew were sitting near me, equally sick and penniless. We stared gloomily before us, in listless atti-tudes, spitting dejectedly at the glowing paunch of the stove. Every now and then someone would come in bringing with him a chill of the freez-ing wind outside. We would all look up hopefully. No, only a stranger. Nothing in the way of hospitality to be expected from him. "Close that damned door!" we would growl in chorus and huddle closer to the stove, shivering, muttering disappointed curses. In mocking contrast the crowd at the bar were drinking, singing, arguing in each other's ears with loud, care-free voices. None of them noticed our existence.

Surely a bad night for Good Samaritans, I thought, and reflected with bitterness that I counted several in that jubilant throng who had eagerly accepted my favors of the two nights previous. Now they saw me and nodded—but that was all. Suddenly sick with human ingratitude, I got out of my chair and, grumbling a surly "good-night, all" to the others, went out the side door and up the rickety stairs to our room—Jimmy's and mine.

The thought of spending a long evening alone in the room seemed intolerable to me. I lit the lamp and glanced around angrily. A fine hole! The two beds took up nearly all the space but Jimmy had managed to cram in, in front of the window, a small table on which stood his dilapidated typewriter. The typewriter, of course, was broken and wouldn't work. Jimmy was always going to have it fixed—tomorrow. But then Jimmy lived in a dream of tomorrows; and nothing he was ever associated with ever worked.

The lamp on the table threw a stream of light through the dirty window, revealing the fire-escape outside. Inside, on a shelf along the windowsill, a dyspeptic geranium plant sulked in a small red pot. This plant was Jimmy's garden and his joy. Even when he was too sick to wash his own face he never forgot to water it the first thing after getting up. It goes without saying, the silly thing never bloomed. Nothing that Jimmy loved ever bloomed; but he always hoped, in fact he was quite sure, it would eventually blossom out—in the dawn of some vague tomorrow.

For me it had value only as a symbol of Jimmy's everlasting futility, of his irritating inefficiency. However, at that period in my life, all flowers were yellow primroses and nothing more, and Jimmy's pet was out of place, I thought, and in the way.

Books were piled on the floor against the walls—and what books! Where Jimmy got them and what for, God only knows. He never read them, except a few pages at haphazard to put him to sleep. Yet there must have been fifty at least cluttering up the room—books about history, about journalism, about economics—books of impossible poetry and incredible prose, written by unknown authors and published by firms one had never heard of. He had a craze for buying them and never failed, on the days he was paid for the odd bits of work he did as occasional stenographer for a theatrical booking firm, to stagger weakly into Tommy's, very drunk, with two or three of these unreadable volumes clutched to his breast—books with titles like: "A Commentary on the Bulls of Pope Leo XIII," or "God and the Darwinian Theory" by John Jones, or "Sunflowers and Other Verses" by Lydia Smith. Think of it!

I used to grow wild with rage as I watched him showing them to Tommy, or Big John, if he was on, or to anyone else who would look and listen, with all the besotted pride in the world. I would think of the drinks and the food—kippered herring and bread and good Italian cheese—he might have purchased for the price of these dull works; and I would swear to myself to thrash him good and hard if he even dared to speak to me.

And then—Jimmy would come and lay his idiotic books on my table and I would look up at him furiously; and there he would stand, wavering a bit, smiling his sweet, good-natured smile, trying to force half his remaining change into my hand, his lonely, wistful eyes watching me with the appealing look of a lost dog hungry for an affectionate pat. What could I do but laugh and love him and show him I did by a slap on the back or in some small way or another? It was worth while forgetting all the injuries in the world just to see the light of gratitude shine up in his eyes.

This night I am speaking of I picked up one of the books in desperation and lay down to read with the lamp at the head of the bed; but I couldn't concentrate. I was too sick in body, brain, and soul to follow even the words.

I threw the book aside and lay on my back staring gloomily at the ceiling. The inmate of the next room, a broken-down telegrapher—"the Lunger" we used to call him—had a violent attack of coughing which seemed to be tearing his chest to pieces. I shuddered. He used to spit blood in the back room below. In fact, when drunk, he was quite proud of this achievement, but grew terrified at all allusions to consumption and wildly insisted that he only had "bloody bronchitis," and that he was getting better every day. He died soon after in that same room next to ours. Perhaps his treatment was at fault. A quart and a half of five-cent whiskey a day and only a plate of free soup at noon to eat is hardly a diet conducive to the cure of any disease—not even "bloody bronchitis."

He coughed and coughed until, in a frenzy of tortured nerves, I yelled to him: "For God's sake, shut up!" Then he subsided into a series of groans and querulous, choking complaints. I thought of consumption, the danger of contagion, and remembered that the window ought to be open. But it was too cold. Besides, what was the difference? "Con" or something else, today or tomorrow, it was all the same—the end. What did I care? I had failed—or rather I had never cared enough about it all to want to succeed.

I must have dozed for I came to with a nervous jump to find the lamp sputtering and smoking and the light growing dimmer every minute. No oil! That fool Jimmy had promised to bring back some. I had given him my last twenty cents and he had taken the can with him. He was sober, had been for almost a week, was suffering from one of his infrequent and brief efforts at reformation. No, there was no excuse. I cursed him viciously for the greatest imbecile on earth. The lamp was going out. I would have to lie in darkness or return to the misery of the back room downstairs.

Just then I recognized his step on the stairs and a moment later he came in, bringing the oil. I glared at him. "Where've you been?" I shouted. "Look at that lamp, you idiot! I'd have been in the dark in another second."

Jimmy came forward shrinkingly, a look of deep hurt in his faded blue eyes. He murmured something about "office" and stooped down to fill the lamp.

"Office!" I taunted scornfully, "what office? What do you take me for? I've heard that bunk of yours a million times." Jimmy finished filling the lamp and sat down on the side of his bed opposite me. He didn't answer; only stared at me with an irritating sort of compassionate pity. How prim he was sitting there in his black suit, wispy, grey hair combed over his bald spot, his jowly face scraped close and chalky with too much cheap powder, the vile odor of which filled the room. I noticed for the first time his clean collar, his fresh shirt. He must have been to the Chinaman's and retrieved part of his laundry. This was what he usually did when he had a windfall of a dollar or so from some unexpected source. Never took out all his laundry. That would have been too expensive. Just called at the Chink's and changed his shirt and collar. His other articles of clothing he washed himself at the sink in the hallway.

I eyed him up and down resentfully. Here was a man who ought always to remain drunk. Sober, he was a respectable nuisance. And his shoes were shined!

"Why the profound meditation?" I asked. "You'd think, to look at you, you were sitting up with my corpse. Cheer up! I feel bad enough without your adding to the gloom."

"That's just it, Art," he began in slow, doleful tones. "I hate to see you in this condition. You wouldn't ever feel this way if you'd—only—only—" he hesitated as he saw my sneer.

"Only what?" I urged.

"Only stop your hard drinking," he mumbled, avoiding my eyes.

"This is almost too much, Jimmy. The water wagon is fatal to your sense of humor. After a week's ride you've accumulated more cheap moralizing than any anchorite in all his years of fasting."

"I'm your friend," he blundered on, "and you know it, Art—or I wouldn't say it."

"And it hurts you more than it does me, I'll bet!"

Jimmy had the piqued air of the rebuffed but well-intentioned. "If that's the way you want to take it—" he was staring unhappily at the floor. We were silent for a time. Then he continued with the obstinacy of the reformed turned reformer: "I'm your friend, the best friend you've got." His eyes looked up into mine and his glance was timidly questioning. "You know that, don't you, Art?"

All my peevishness vanished in a flash before his woeful sincerity. I reached over and grabbed his hand—his white, pudgy little hand so in keeping with the rest of him—warm and soft. "Of course I know it, Jimmy. Don't be foolish and take what I've said seriously. I've got a full-sized grouch against everything tonight."

Jimmy brightened up and cleared his throat. He evidently thought my remarks an expression of willingness to serve as audience for his temperance lecture. Still he hesitated politely. "I know you don't want to listen—"

I laughed shortly. "Go ahead. Shoot. I'm all ears." Then he began. You know the sort of drool—introduced by a sage wag of the head and the inevitable remark: "I've been through it all myself, and I know." I won't bore you with it. Coming from Jimmy it was the last word in absurdity.

I tried not to listen, concentrating my mind on the man himself, my nerves soothed by the monotonous flow of his soft-voiced syllables. Yes, he'd been through it all, there was no doubt of that, from soup to nuts. What he didn't realize was that none of it had ever touched him deeply. Forgetful of the last kick his eyes had always looked up at life again with the same appealing, timid uncertainty, pleading for a caress, fearful of a blow. And life had never failed to deal him the expected kick, never a vicious one, more of a shove to get him out of the way of a spirited boot at someone who really mattered. Spurned, Jimmy had always returned, affectionate, uncomprehending, wagging his tail ingratiatingly, so to speak. The longed-for caress would come, he was sure of it, if not today, then tomorrow. Ah, tomorrow!

I looked searchingly at his face—the squat nose, the wistful eyes, the fleshy cheeks hanging down like dewlaps on either side of his weak mouth with its pale, thick lips. The usual marks of dissipation were there but none of the scars of intense suffering. The whole effect was characterless, unfinished; as if some sculptor at the last moment had suddenly lost interest in his clay model of a face and abandoned his work in disgust. I wondered what Jimmy would do if he ever saw that face in the clear, cruel mirror of Truth. Straggle on in the same lost way, no doubt, and cease to have faith in mirrors.

Although most of his lecture was being lost on me I couldn't prevent a chance word now and then from seeping into my consciousness. "Wasted youth—your education—ability—a shame—lost opportunity—drink—some nice girl"—these words my ears retained against my will, and each word had a sting to it. Gradually my feeling of kindliness toward Jimmy petered out. I began to hate him for a pestiferous little crank. What right had he to meddle with my sins? Some of the things he was saying were true; and truth—that kind of truth—should be seen and not heard.

I was becoming angry enough to shrivel him up with some contemptuous remark about his hypocrisy and the doubtful duration of time he would stay on the wagon when he suddenly digressed from my misdeeds and began virtuously holding himself up as a horrible example.

He began at the beginning, and, even though I welcomed the change of subject, I swore inwardly at the prospect of hearing the history of his life all over again. He had told me this tale at least fifty times while in all stages of maudlin drunkenness. Usually he wept—which was sometimes funny and sometimes not, all depending on my own condition. At all events it would be a novelty to hear his sober version. I might get at some facts this time.

To my surprise this story seemed to be identical with the others I had been lulled to sleep by on so many nights. Making allowances for the natural exaggeration of one in liquor, there was but little difference. It started with the Anderson estate in Scotland where Jimmy had spent his boyhood. This estate of the family extended over the greater part of a Scotch county, so Jimmy claimed, and he was touchy when anyone seemed skeptical regarding its existence.

He loved to dilate on the beauty of the country, the old manor house, the farms, the game park, and all the rest of it. All this was heavily mortgaged, he admitted; and he was not in good standing with most of his relatives on the other side; but he declared that there was one aunt, far gone in years and hoarded wealth, who still treasured his memory, and he promised all the gang in the back room a rare blowout should the old lady pass away in the proper frame of mind. To all of this the crowd would listen with an amiable pretence of belief. For, after all, he was Jimmy and they all swore by him, and a fairy tale like that is no great matter to hold against a man.

But here he was spinning the same yarn in all its details! I looked at him suspiciously. No, he was certainly stone sober. Could there be any truth in it then? Impossible. I finally concluded that Jimmy, after the fashion of liars, had ended by mistaking his own fabrications for fact.

He continued on through his years in Edinburgh University, his graduation with honors, his going into journalism first in Scotland, then in England, afterwards as a correspondent on the Continent, and finally his work in South Africa during the Boer War as representative of some news service.

I had never been able to verify any of this except that relating to the Boer War. An old friend of his had once told me that Jimmy did hold a responsible position in South Africa during the war and had received a large salary. Then the old friend, old-friendlike, shook his head gravely and muttered: "Too bad! Too bad! Drink!" Whether the rest of Jimmy's life, as related by him, had ever been lived or not hardly mattered, I thought. Undoubtedly he had been well educated and what is called a gentleman over there. Of course the Anderson estate was a work of fiction, or, at best, a glorified country house.

"And mind you, Art, up to that time," Jimmy's story had reached the point where he was at the front in South Africa for the news service company, "I had never touched a drop except a glass of wine with dinner now and again. That was ten years ago and I was thirty-five. Then—something happened. Ten years," he repeated sadly, "and now look where I am!" He stared despondently before him for a moment, then brightened up and squared his bent shoulders. "But that's all past and gone now, and I'm through with this kind of life for good and all."

"There's always tomorrow," I ventured ironically.

"Yes, and I'm going to make the most of it." His eyes were bright with the dream of a new hope; or rather, the old hope eternally redreamed. He glanced at the table. "I'll have to have that typewriter fixed up."

"Tomorrow?"

"Yes, tomorrow, if I can spare the time." He hadn't noticed my sarcasm.

"Why, is your day all taken up?" I asked, marvelling at his imagination.

"Pretty well so." He put on an air of importance. "I saw Edwards today"—Edwards was a friend of his who had risen to be an editor on one of the big morning papers—"and he's found an opening for me—a real opening which will give me an opportunity to show them all I'm still in the race."

"And you start in tomorrow?" I was dumbfounded.

"Yes, in the afternoon." His face was alive with energy. "Oh, I'll show them all, Art, that I'm still one of the best when I want to be. They've sneered at me long enough."

"Then you really are about to become a wage slave?" I simply couldn't believe it.

"Honestly, Art. Tomorrow. Do you think I'm spoofing you about it?"

"I must admit you seem to be confessing the shameless truth. Well, at any rate, you seem to be pleased, so—" here I jumped up and pumped his hand up and down—"a million congratulations, Jimmy, old scout!" Jimmy's joy was good to see. There were tears in his eyes as he thanked me. Good old Jimmy! It took him quite a while to get over his emotion. Then, as if he had suddenly remembered something, he began hurriedly fumbling through all his pockets.

"I must have lost it," he said finally, giving up the search. "I wanted to show it to you."

"What?"

"A letter I received today from Aunt Mary." Aunt Mary was the elderly relative in whose will Jimmy hoped to be remembered. "She complains of having felt very feeble for the past half year. She appears to be entirely ignorant of my present condition, thank God. Writes that I'm to come and pay her a long visit should I decide to take a trip abroad this Spring. Fancy!"

"And you've lost the letter?" I asked, trying to hide my skepticism.

"Yes—was showing it to Edwards—must have dropped on the floor— or else he—" Jimmy stopped abruptly. I think he must have sensed my amused incredulity, for he seemed very put out at something and didn't look at me. "I do hope the poor old lady isn't seriously ill," he murmured after a pause.

"What!" I laughed. "Have you the face to tell me that, when you know you've been looking forward to her timely taking off ever since I've known you?"

Jimmy's face grew red and he stammered confusedly. He knew he'd said things which might have sounded that way when he'd been drinking. It was whiskey talking and he didn't mean it. Really he liked her a lot. He remembered she'd been very kind to him when he was a lad. Had hardly seen her since then—twenty-five years ago. No, money or no money, he wanted her to live to be a hundred.

"But you've told me she's almost ninety now! Isn't she?"

"Yes, eighty-six, I think."

"Then," I said with finality, "she's overlingered her welcome, and you're a simpleton to be wasting your crocodile tears—in advance, at that. Besides, I've never noticed her sending you any of her vast fortune. She might at least have made you a present once in a while if she cared to earn any regrets over her demise."

"I've never written her about my hard luck. I hardly ever wrote to her," Jimmy said slowly. His tones were ridiculously dismal, and he sat holding his face in his hands in the woebegone attitude of a mourner.

"Well, you should have written." A sudden thought made me smile. "What will the bunch in the back room say when they hear this? You may give them that long-promised blowout—tomorrow," I added maliciously.

Jimmy stirred uneasily and turned on me a glance full of dim suspicion. "Why do you keep repeating that word tomorrow? You've said it now a dozen times."

"Because tomorrow is your day, Jimmy," I answered carelessly. "Doesn't your career as a sober, industrious citizen begin then?"

"Oh," he sighed with relief, "I thought—" he walked up and down in the narrow space between the beds, his hands deep in his pockets. Finally he stopped and stood beside me. There was an exultant ring to his voice. "Ah, I tell you, Art, it's great to feel like a man again, to know you're done for good and all with that mess downstairs." After a pause he went on in a coaxing, motherly tone. "Don't you think you ought to go to work and do something? I hate to see you—like this. You know what a pal I am, Art. You can listen to me. It's a shame for you to let yourself go to seed this way. Really, Art, I mean it."

"Now, Jimmy," I got up and put my hands on his shoulders. "I say it without any hard feeling, but I've had about enough of your reform movement for one night. It'll be more truly charitable of you to offer me the price of a drink—if you have it. Your day of reformation is none so remote you can't realize from experience how rotten I feel. I can hear polar bears baying at the Northern Lights."

Jimmy sighed disconsolately and dug some small change out of his pocket. "I borrowed a dollar from Edwards," he explained. "I'll pay him back out of my first salary." The self-sufficient pride he put into that word salary!

But his financial aid proved to be unnecessary. As I was about to take half of his change, there was a great trampling from the stairs outside. Our door was kicked open with a bang and Lyons, the stoker, and Paddy Mehan, the old deep-water sailor, came crowding into the room. Lyons was in the first jovial frenzy of drink but poor Paddy was already awash and rapidly sinking. They had been paid off that afternoon after a trip across on the American liner St. Paul.

"Hello, Lyons! Hello, Paddy!" Jimmy and I hailed them in pleased chorus.

"Hello, yourself!" Lyons crushed Jimmy's hand in one huge paw and patted me affectionately on the back with the other. The jar of it nearly knocked me off my feet but I managed to smile. Lyons and I were old pals. I had once made a trip as sailor on the Philadelphia when he was in her stokehold, and we had become great friends through a chance adventure together ashore in Southampton—which is another story. He stood grinning, swaying a bit in the lamplight, a great, hard bulk of a man, dwarfing the proportions of our little room. Paddy lurched over to one of the beds and fell on it. "Thick weather! Thick weather!" he groaned to himself, and started to sing an old chanty in a thin, quavering, nasal whine.

"A-roving, a-roving
Since roving's been my ru-i-in,
No more I'll go a-ro-o-ving with you, fair maid."

"Shut up!" roared Lyons and turned again to me. "Art, how are ye?" I dodged an attempt at another love-tap and replied that I was well but thirsty.

"Thirsty, is ut? D'ye hear that, Paddy, ye slimy Corkonian? Here's a mate complainin' av thirst and we wid a full pay day in our pockets." He pulled out a roll of bills and flaunted them before me with a splendid, spendthrift gesture.

"Oh, whiskey killed my poor old dad! Whiskey! O Johnny!" carolled Paddy dolorously.

"Listen to 'im!" Lyons reached over and shook him vigorously. "That's the throuble wid all thim lazy, deck-scrubbers the loike av 'im.

They can't stand up to their dhrink loike men. Wake up, Paddy! We'll be goin' below." He hauled Paddy to his feet and held him there. Come on, Art. There's some av the boys ye know below waitin'. Ye'll have all the dhrink ye can pour down your throat, and welcome; and anything more you're wishful for ye've but to name. Come on, Jimmy, you're wan av us."

"I've got something to do before I go down. I'll join you in a few minutes," Jimmy replied, wisely evading a direct refusal.

"See that ye do, me sonny boy," warned Lyons, pushing Paddy to the door. I turned to Jimmy as I was going out. "Well, good luck till tomorrow, Jimmy, if I don't see you before then."

"Thank you, Art," he murmured huskily and shook my hand. I started down. From the bottom of the flight below I heard Lyons' rough curses and Paddy wailing lugubriously: "Old Joe is dead, and gone to hell, poor old Joe!"

"Ye'll be in hell yourself if ye fall in this black hole," Lyons cautioned, steering him to the top of the second flight as I caught up with them.

The fiesta which began with our arrival in the bar didn't break up until long after daylight the next morning. It was one of the old, lusty debauches of my sailor days—songs of the sea and yarns about ships punctuated by rounds of drinks.

The last I remember was Lyons bawling out for someone to come down to the docks and strip to him and see which was the better man. "Have a bit av fun wid 'im" was the way he put it. I believe I was Dutch-courageous enough to accept his challenge but he pushed me back in my chair with a warning to be "a good bye" or I'd get a spanking. So the party had no fatal ending.

As you can well imagine I slept like a corpse all the next day and didn't witness Jimmy's departure for his long hard climb back to respectability and the man who was. When he came home that night he appeared very elated, full of the dignity of labor, tremendously conscious of his position in life, provokingly solicitous concerning my welfare. It would have been insufferable in anyone else; but Jimmy—well, Jimmy was Jimmy, and the most lovable chap on earth. You couldn't stay mad at him more than a minute, if you had the slightest sense of humor.

Had he toiled and spun much on his first day, I asked him. No, he admitted after a moment's hesitation, he had spent the time mostly in feeling about, getting the hang of his work. Now tomorrow he'd get the typewriter fixed so he could do Sunday special stuff in his spare moments—stories of what he'd seen in South Africa and things of that kind. Wasn't that a bully idea? I agreed that it was, and retreated to the gang below who were still celebrating, leaving Jimmy with pencil poised over a blank sheet of paper determined to map out one of his stories then and there.

I didn't see him the next day or the day after. I was touring the water front with Lyons and Paddy and never returned to the room. The fourth day of his job I ran into him for a second in the hallway. He said hello in a hurried tone and brushed past me. For my part I was glad he didn't stop. I felt he'd immediately start on a heart-to-heart talk which I was in no mood to hear. Later on I remembered his manner had been strange and that he looked drawn and fagged out.

The fifth day Paddy and Lyons were both broke, but I collected my puny allowance and we sat at a table in the back room squandering it lingeringly on enormous scoops of lager and porter which were filling and lasted a long time. We were still sitting there talking when Jimmy came back from work. He looked in from the hallway, saw us and nodded, but went on upstairs without speaking.

"What's the matther wid Jimmy?" grumbled Lyons. "Can't he speak to a man?"

"He looks like he was sick," said Paddy. "Go up, Art, that's a good lad, and ask him if he won't take a bit of a drink, maybe."

"I'll go," I said, getting up, "but he won't drink anything. Jimmy's strictly temperance these days. He's more likely to give us all a sermon on our sins."

"Divil take him, then," growled Lyons, "but run and get him all the same. He looks loike he'd been drawn through a crack in the wall."

I ran quickly up the stairs and opened the door of our room. Jimmy was sitting on the side of his bed, his head in his hands. I glanced at the typewriter. The keys were still grey with a layer of long-accumulated lust. Then he hadn't had it fixed. The same old tomorrow, I thought to myself.

"Jimmy," I called to him. He jumped to his feet with a frightened start. When he saw who it was a flush of anger came over his face.

"Why don't you scare the life out of a man!" he said irritably. I was astonished. I'd never known him to flare up like this over a trifle.

"Come down and join us for a while. You don't have to drink, you know. You look done-up. What's the trouble—been working too hard?"

He winced at this last remark as if I'd shaken my fist in his face. Then he made a frantic gesture with his arms as though he were pushing me out of the room. "Go! Go back!" His voice was unnaturally shrill. "Leave me alone. I want to be alone."

"Jimmy!" I went to him in genuine alarm. "What's the matter? Anything wrong?"

He pressed my hand and tried a feeble attempt at a smile. There were dark rings under his eyes, and, somehow, in some indefinable manner, he seemed years older, a broken old man.

"No, Art, I'm all right. Don't mind me. I've a splitting headache—"

"Don't be a fool and let them work you to death." He raised his hands as if he were going to clap them over his ears to shut out my words.

"Leave me alone, Art, will you? I'm going to bed," he stammered.

"Right-o, that's the stuff. Get a good sleep and you'll be O. K." I went downstairs slowly, vaguely worried about him, wondering what the trouble could be. In the end I laid his peculiar actions to a struggle he was having with his craving for drink. Paddy and Lyons agreed with this opinion and called him a "game little swine" for sticking to his guns. And as such we toasted him in our lager and porter.

When I went up to the room to turn in he was asleep, or pretending to be, and I was careful not to disturb him. The next morning I heard him moving about, but as soon as he saw I was awake, he appeared in a nervous flurry to get away, and we didn't speak more than a few words to each other. That night he never came home at all. I went to bed early—everyone was broke and there was nothing else to do—and when I was roused out of my slumber by the sun shining on my face through the dirty window, I saw that his bed hadn't been touched. A somber presentment of evil seemed to hover around that bed. The white spread, threadbare and full of holes, which he had tucked in with such precise neatness, had the suggestion of a shroud about it—a shroud symbolically woven for one whose life had been threadbare and full of holes.

I tried to laugh at such grim imaginings. Jimmy had stayed with Edwards or someone else from his paper. What was strange in that? This wasn't the first time he'd remained away all night, was it? If I was to give way to such worries I might just as well put on skirts and be done with it.

But my phantoms, however foolish, refused to be laid. I got dressed in a hurry, anxious to escape from this room, bright with sunlight, dark with uncanny threat. Before I went down, struck by a sentimental mood, I got some water from the sink in the hallway and poured it on his ridiculous geranium plant.

After a breakfast of free soup, I walked with Paddy and Lyons down to the Battery. We spent the afternoon there, lounging on one of the benches. It was as warm as a day in Spring and we sat blinking in the sunshine drowsily listening to each other's yarns about the sea and lazily watching the passing ships.

When the sun went down we returned to Tommy the Priest's. On the way back I remembered this was Jimmy's pay day and wondered if he would show up. He owed me some money which I hoped would be forthcoming. Otherwise the night was liable to prove an uneventful one. And a farewell bust-up was imperative because Paddy and Lyons would have to go on board ship the following day if they wanted to make the next trip.

The evening didn't pass off as dully as we had feared. Old McDonald, the printer, was in a festive mood and invited us to join him. Two of the telegraph operators, out of a job at that time, had borrowed some money somewhere and were anxious to return the many treats they had received from us in the past. So the time whiled away very pleasantly.

It was shortly after midnight when Jimmy came in. As soon as I saw his face I knew that something had happened to him, something very serious. He was incredibly haggard and pale, and there were deep lines of suffering about his mouth and eyes. His eyes—I can't describe them. There was nothing behind them. He nodded and took his place at the bar beside us. Then he spoke, asked us what we'd have, in a strained, forced voice as though it cost him a tremendous effort to talk. He took whiskey himself, poured out a glass brim full, and downed it straight. Big John changed a bill for him, and without looking at me, he held out the couple of dollars he owed me. I put them in my pocket. Jimmy motioned to Big John and called for another round. A spell of silence was on the whole barroom. Everyone there knew him well. They had all joked with him during the week about his being on the wagon, but they had secretly admired his firmness of will. Now they stared at him with genuine regret that he should have fallen. Their faces grew sad. They had done the same thing themselves so many times. They understood.

"Jimmy!" He caught the reproach in my voice and turned to me with a twisted smile. "It doesn't matter," he said. "Nothing matters." His voice became harsh. "Don't forget what you said about my lectures and start in yourself." He immediately felt sorry for having said this. "No, Art, I don't mean that. Never mind what I say. I'm upset—about something."

"Tell me what it is, Jimmy. Maybe I can help."

"Help?" He laughed hysterically. "No, no help please. After all, why shouldn't I tell you now? You're bound to find out sooner or later. They'll all know it." He indicated the others who, feeling that Jimmy wanted to be alone with me, had taken their drinks to a table in the rear and were sitting around talking in low, constrained voices. Jimmy blurted out: "My job, Art, is gone to hell!"

"What!" I pretended more astonishment than I felt. I had guessed what the trouble was.

"Yes, they asked me to quit—politely requested. Edwards was very nice about it—very kind—very charitable." He put all the bitterness of his heart into these last words.

"The rotten swine!"

"Oh no, Art, it wasn't his fault. If they hadn't—fired me—I'd have had to resign anyway. I—I couldn't do the work."

"That's all nonsense, Jimmy. Well, cheer up. All said and done, it's only a job the less. You can always get another for the asking."

He looked at me with a sort of wild scorn in his eyes. "Can't you understand any better than that? What do I care for the job itself? It isn't that. I tell you I couldn't do the work! I tried and tried. What I wrote was rot. I couldn't get any news. No initiative—no imagination—no character—no courage! All gone. Nothing left—not even cleverness. No memory even!" He stopped, breathing hard, the perspiration glistening on his forehead. "It came to me gradually—the realization. I couldn't believe it. I had been so sure of myself all these years. All I needed was a chance. It had been so easy for me in the past—long ago. These last few days I've guessed the truth. I've been going crazy. Last night I walked—walked and walked— thinking—and finally—I knew!" He paused, choking back a sob, his face twitching convulsively with the effort he made to control himself. Then he uttered a cracked sound intended for a laugh. "I'm done—burnt out— wasted! It's time to dump the garbage. Nothing here." He tapped his head with a silly gesture and laughed again. I began to be afraid he really was going mad. "No, Art, it isn't the job that's lost. I'm lost!"

"Now you're talking like a fool!" I spoke roughly, trying to shake him out of this mood.

"I won't talk any more," he said quite calmly. "Don't worry. I'm all shot to pieces—no sleep." He broke down suddenly and turned away from me. "But it's hell, Art, to realize all at once—you're dead!"

I put my arm around his shoulders. "Have a drink, Jimmy. Hey you, John, a little service!" What else was there to do? Life had jammed the clear, cruel mirror in front of his eyes and he had recognized himself—in that pitiful thing he saw. "Have a drink, Jimmy, and forget it. Take a real drink!" I urged. What else was there to do?

After we had had a couple at the bar, Jimmy filling his glass to the brim each time, I led him in back and we sat down at the table with the crowd. More drinks were immediately forthcoming, and it wasn't long before Jimmy became very drunk. He didn't say anything but his eyes glazed, his lips drooped loosely, his head wagged uncertainly from side to side. I saw he'd had enough and I hoped his tired brain had been numbed to a forgetful oblivion.

"Come on to bed, Jimmy," I shook him by the arm.

He stared at me vacantly. "Bed—yes—sleep! sleep!" he mumbled, and came with me willingly enough. I helped him up the stairs to the room and lit the lamp. He sat on the side of the bed, swaying, unlacing his shoes with difficulty. Presently he began to weep softly to himself. "It's you, Alice—cause of all this—damn you—no—didn't mean that—beg pardon," he muttered. He lifted his head and saw me sitting on the other bed. "One word advice, Art—never get married—all rotten, all of 'em—"

This was something new. "What do you know about marriage?" I asked curiously. "Nothing from experience, surely."

He winked at me with drunken cunning. "Don't I, though! Not half! Never told you that, what? Never told you what happened—Cape Town?"

"No, you never did. What was it?"

"Might s'well tell Art—best friend—tell you everything tonight—all over. Yes—married in England—English girl, pretty's picture—big blue eyes—just before war—took her South Africa with me, 'n left her in Cape Town when I went to front. I was called back to Cape Town s'denly—found her with staff officer—dirty swine! No chance for doubt—didn't expect me to turn up—saw them with my own eyes—*flagrante delictu*, you know—dirty swine of a staff officer! Good bye, Jimmy Anderson! All over! Drink! Drink! Forget!" He blubbered to himself, his face a grotesque masque of tragedy.

In a flash it came back to me how he'd always stopped in the stories of his life at the point where he'd commenced drinking. Even at his drunkest he'd always ended the history there by saying abruptly: "and then—something happened." I'd never attached much importance to it—thought he merely wanted to suggest a mysterious reason as an excuse for his tobogganing. Now, I knew. Who could doubt the truth of his statements, knowing all he had been through that day? He was in a mood for truth. So this was the something which happened! Here was real tragedy.

Real tragedy! And there he was sobbing, hiccuping, rolling his eyes stupidly, scratching with limp fingers at the tears which ran down and tickled the sides of his nose. I felt a mad desire to laugh.

"I suppose you and she were divorced?" I asked after a pause.

"No—I couldn't—no proof—no money. Besides, what'd I care about divorce? Never want to marry again—never love anyone else." He wept more violently than ever.

"But didn't she get a divorce?"

"No, she's too cute for that—thinks Aunt Mary'll leave me money—and I'll drink myself to death. No," he interrupted himself hastily, "can't be that—not s'bad s' that—not Alice—no, no, mustn't say that—not right for me to say that—don't know her reason—never can tell—about women. Damn shoes!" He gave up the attempt to get his shoes off and flung himself on the bed, fully dressed. In a minute he was dead to the world and snoring. I left him and went downstairs.

Most of the people in the back room were asleep, but Paddy and Lyons and the operators were still drinking at one table, and I sat down with them. I talked at random on every subject that came up, seeking to forget Jimmy and his woes, for a time at least. His two confessions that night had got on my nerves.

Later on I must have dozed, for I was jolted out of a half dream by a sharp cracking smash in the back yard. Everyone was awake and cursing in an instant. Big John appeared from behind the curtain, grumbling: "Dot's right! Leave bottle on the fire escape, you fellers! Dot's right! Und I have to sweep up."

We heard someone racing down the stairs and Jimmy burst into the room. His face was livid, his eyes popping out of his head. He rushed to the chair beside me and sat down, shaking, his teeth chattering as if he had a chill. I told Big John to bring him a drink.

"What's the trouble now, Jimmy?" I asked him when he'd calmed down a little. He appeared to be quite sober after his sleep.

"The geranium—" he began, his lips trembling, his eyes filling up.

"So that's what fell down just now, is it?"

"Yes, I woke up, and I remembered I'd forgotten to water it. I got up and went to get the water. The window was open. I must have stumbled over something. I put out my hand to steady myself. It was so dark I couldn't see. I knocked it out on the fire escape. Then I heard it crash in the yard." He put his hands over his face and cried heart-brokenly like a sick child whose only remaining toy has been smashed. Not drunken tears this time, but real tears which made all of us at the table blink our eyes and swear fiercely at nothing.

After a while he grew quiet again, attempted a smile, asked our pardons for having created a foolish scene. He stared at his drink standing untouched on the table in front of him; but never made any motion to take it, didn't seem to realize what it was. For fully fifteen minutes he sat and stared, as still as stone, never moving his eyes, never even seeming to breathe. Then he got up from his chair and walked slowly to the door like a man in a trance. As he was going out he turned to me and said: "I'm tired, Art. I think I'll go to sleep," and something like a wan smile trembled on his pale lips. He left the door open behind him and I heard him climbing the stairs, and the slam of our door as he closed it behind him.

A buzz of conversation broke out as if his going had lifted a weight of silence off the roomful of men. Then it happened—a swish, a sickish thud as of a heavy rock dropping into thick mud. We looked wildly at one another. We knew. We rushed into the hall and out to the yard. There it was—a motionless, dark huddle of clothes, a splintered, protruding bone or two, a widening pool of blood black against the grey flags—Jimmy!

The sky was pale with the light of dawn. Tomorrow had come.

THE LITTLE TOWN

J. D. Beresford

I

"IT is quite a small place."

That was all the information I could obtain. I had been referred to the omniscient Joe Shepperton, and this was everything he could tell me. "St. Erth," he had said. "In Cornwall?" And when I had explained that this was another St. Erth, he had said, "Oh! quite a small place." Probably he had never before heard of it .....

As I looked out into the darkness and tried to dodge the reflection of my own face in the window, it seemed that we were passing through country of a kind which was quite unfamiliar to me. I had a vision of mountains and the broad roll of great forests; an effect that may have been produced by clouds. The yellow lighted reflection of the now familiar interior jutted out before me, its floor diaphanous and traversed by two streaks of shining metal. And my own white face peered in at me with strained, searching eyes, frowning at me when our glances met, trying to peer past me into the light and warmth of the railway carriage.

Once we crossed an interminable bridge that roared a sonorous resentment against our passage. I could not explain that bridge. We were not near the sea and no English river could surely have been so wide. Yet the bridge was not a valley viaduct, for I caught the gleam of water below, some reflection of paler shadows from the lift of the sky.

This adventure into unknown country was immensely exciting. It was discovery. I gave up my strained enquiry into the world beyond, and let my imagination wander out into mystery. I was in the midst of high romance when the magnificent energy of our triumphant speed was checked by the sickening grind of the brake....

The little station was a terminus; one forsaken, gloomy platform that stretched a grey finger into the night out of which we had come. I tried to see what was on the further side, across the metals, but beyond was a black void. I received the impression that I was on an immense height, that the dimly seen low stone wall was the parapet of some awful abyss.

I could form no idea of the town during my minute's walk from the station to the rooms I had engaged. The whole place seemed to be very ill-lighted. All I could see was that it hung on the side of a hill.

I went out when I had had something to eat. It was only a few minutes past eight, and I was eager for adventure. I told my landlady that I was going down into the town to explore.

"It's very dark," she said, with a note of warning in her voice.

The street in which I was staying dipped gently toward the town; but as I went on the dip became more pronounced. I congratulated myself on the fact that there would be no difficulty in finding my way back. The lie of the land would direct me, I had merely to ascend again.

My street was longer than I had expected. At first there were houses on one side only, but further down the roadway narrowed and there were houses on each side. I classified my lodgings as being in a sort of suburb grown up round the railway station which was detached for obvious reasons—no railway but a funicular could have been carried down that hill.

I came to the bottom of the street at last and found another narrow street running across right and left. Opposite to me an alley continued the descent in nearly a straight line. Far below a dim lamp was burning. I decided to keep straight on and plunged down the alley.

It was interminably long. At the lamp it twisted suddenly but still descended the hill.

"The place is bigger than I thought," was my reflection. I saw, however, that as the road continually fell before me, I must be keeping a right line.

The town was not deserted. There were movement and the sound of voices all about me; figures loomed up out of the darkness to meet me and clattered past over the rough cobbles. I heard laughter, too, and whisperings in the dim black recesses of courts and doorways, and once or twice I caught the tinkle of some thin high music far away in the distance.

Everywhere I was conscious of the stir and struggle of life, of unseen creatures as careless of my presence as I of theirs.

And still I had not come as yet to the town itself. I had pictured to myself some wider streets, or open market, a place of lighted shops and visible life. I began to wonder if I had not passed by this imagined center. I became a trifle impatient. I hurried on; down, always down, through the wriggling maze of tiny narrow alleys and passageways, lighted only by an occasional flickering lamp, bracketed out from some corner house.

"A small place, indeed," I said to myself. "It is an enormous place." I received the impression that I might walk on forever through that tedious ravel of streets. Yet I knew that I could not be walking in a circle, for I was always descending.

I gave no thought now to the long toil of my return up the mountain—already I thought of it as a mountain—I felt that I must and would reach the bottom.

It was not what I had expected to find, yet the reality, when I came upon it, was so inevitable that I believed it to be the thing I had always anticipated.

I turned at last out of a passage so narrow that my body brushed the wall on either side, into a small square of low houses and the floor of the square was flat. On all sides it was entered by passages such as that from which I had just emerged, and all of them led upwards. About and above me I could vaguely distinguish an infinite slope of houses, ranging up tier above tier, lost at last in the black immensity. I appeared to be at the bottom of some Titanic basin among the mountains; at the center of some inconceivably vast collection of mean houses that swarmed over the whole face of visible earth.

"There is surely no other place like it in the world," I said to myself in wonder.

II.

There was light in the square; two lamps that flanked an open door. Above the door was a faded sign. I guessed the place to be a hall of entertainment, probably a "picture-palace."

I walked over to it and read the sign; it bore the one word "Kosmos."
"Some charlatan," I decided.

No one was taking money at the door, and after a moment's hesitation I went in.

It was a queer little hall. The bareness of the walls was partly hidden by pathetic attempts at decoration; some red material was rudely draped over the raw brickwork; and a few unframed, dingy canvases—the subjects indistinguishable—were hung on this background.

At the end was a rough proscenium opening, and behind it a stage that appeared to me quite brilliantly lighted, after my long sojourn in the darkness.

In the body of the hall some twenty persons were seated on rough benches staring at the still unoccupied stage.

I found a seat near the door and waited. It came to me that the stage was disproportionately large for the size of the hall.

And then out of the wings came wobbling a tiny figure, and I realised that this great stage was set for a puppet-show. The whole thing was so impossibly grotesque that I nearly laughed aloud. ...

Presently I turned my attention for a moment to the vague forms sitting round me, some of them silhouetted against the light of the stage. But none of them returned my stare. "Rustics!" I thought, with a touch of contempt. "Men and women of such small intelligence and narrow experience that even such an amateur show as this amuses them."

I turned back to the performance, though the foolishness of the doll's actions was beneath criticism.

Nevertheless, after a time, a certain fascinated interest began to grow upon me, and I watched the performance, chafing at its slowness—with increasing attention. I tried to disentangle some meaning, some story, some purpose, from the apparently aimless movements of these tiny dolls staggering about their gigantic setting. Every now and again I thought that I understood, and that there was an indication of some sequence of action, some development of a theme. But always the leading figures wavered or fell at the critical moment, and chaos followed; a hopeless, maddening jumble.

One piece of management, however, deserved and received my approbation. I had never in any marionette show I have ever witnessed seen the suspending wires so cleverly concealed. Stare and criticise as I would I could see no sign of any mechanism whereby the dolls were supported and animated. This did, indeed, give me a curious sense of reality, it made me feel that these poor ridiculous little figures had a sentient life of their own. Then some senseless action or helpless collapse reminded me of the invisible wires, and my pity for the feeble dolls was turned to contempt for the ineptitude of the operator.

Dwelling on that ineptitude, I began to lose my temper and I became conscious that other members of the audience were being similarly affected. I heard impatient sighs and half suppressed groans of despair when some doll attempted to strut across the stage and collapsed half way.

I looked round me again and saw that men were twitching their arms, hands and fingers; leaning this way and that as if to influence the movement of the dolls—just as a man will strain and grimace in order to influence the run of a ball over which he has no sort of control.

I discovered that I had been unconsciously making the same foolish movements, and, also, that our attempted directions were not concerted. There was no unison, no characteristic sway in this direction or that. It was plain that we wished to influence the dolls in contradictory ways.

But one feeling, I am convinced, animated us all: we were unanimously and angrily critical of the unseen operator; we were all convinced that we could work the unseen wires far more efficiently than that bungling performer. Indeed, the fact, so far as I was concerned, seemed clearly demonstrable. The actions of the dolls were so infantile, so contemptibly purposeless.

That obsession grew upon me. The mismanagement of the whole stupid affair began to appear of quite transcendant importance.

I could not watch without striving to help, and I was forced to watch. ...

III.

The performance closed abruptly.

The curtain descended without notice, apparently in the middle of the play, unheralded by any grouping or arrangement which might suggest a finale.

The audience, almost in darkness, were left to stumble out as best they could.

I could not find the exit and when I did find a door it was not the right one. It opened on to a flight of steep narrow stairs.

It occurred to me that this must be the way up into the flies, to the place in which the operator sat and controlled his dolls. In a sudden mood of determination I decided to seek him out—I would give him some primitive instruction. He must be some ignorant countryman. I would give him a few useful hints in the conduct of his business; suggest a story for his dolls to act, some sequent, purposeful story moving toward a climax. . . . .

I stumbled upwards in the dark, one hand on the cold rough wall, the other stretched out before me to guard against any obstacle which might be in my path. It was a very long staircase, for the proscenium opening was a high one. When I was nearly at the top, the stairway twisted unexpectedly, and I found myself looking down on the still brilliantly lighted stage.

Before me in a great chair that was almost a throne, an old man sat gazing tenderly down upon the stage below him. There was a calm, gentle wisdom upon his face and he moved his hands slowly this way and that.

I looked down and saw that although the curtain had fallen and the hall was empty, the performance was still going on in the same, aimless, inexplicable manner.

Perhaps the old man was practising his art, or perhaps he did not know that the curtain had fallen and the audience gone away—in any case he sat there with a sweet intent smile, passing his outspread hands slowly to and fro over the heads of those foolish, inept figures beneath.

And even then I could see no wires, no connection between those mesmeric hands and the tottering figures.

A strange diffidence had come over me. From where I stood it appeared an immensely difficult task to control and guide the movements of those dolls below.

My anxiety to instruct died out of me. I began to marvel at the dexterity with which the old man would sometimes raise a falling doll by the lift of his little finger. And from my new point of view I thought I could at least discern some purpose in the play. . . . .

For a time I stood motionless, watching, and then I looked again at the operator seated in his great chair. He was quite unconscious of my presence. He wore always the same serene, gentle smile. He was in no way perturbed when his dolls stumbled and fell. He sat serene, intent; and his hands moved ceaselessly to and fro over the great stage.

I crept away softly and found my way out.

When I reached the square again the moon had risen.

I looked up and saw the little railway station a few hundred yards away.

It was a stiff climb, but I reached home in ten minutes.

The town was, after all, quite a small place. . . . .

In the morning I wondered whether the old man still sat in the same place manipulating his dolls.

I wondered whether he was a charlatan or only very old, and very, very foolish.

ART, RELIGION AND SCIENCE

James Oppenheim

THERE is noticeable among many of our American artists, poets and religious-minded men a deep distrust of science, even, at times, an anti-scientific spirit. They look upon science the way the Romans looked upon the Huns: evil barbarians come to destroy the glories of civilization. And for the scientist they have even harsher names: he is a mechanistic intellectual, he is uncreative, he is a standpatter taking the world as he finds it and breaking it up into diagrams and laws; he lacks intuition, reverence, joy, humanity. In short, he is like his offspring, the machine. But such a picture of science and the scientist is inaccurate and ridiculous. There are, it is true, poor-brained thin-blooded futile scientists just as there are poor-brained thin-blooded futile poets. There are, moreover, those scientists who come under the heading "pure"—men of the mathematical bent, the high priests of knowledge who attempt to build up cults. But beyond most men the true scientist stands forth as the adventurer and rebel and prophet of the modern world. The glow of the human spirit in the laboratory is often not a whit less intense and marvellous than the glow in the poet's hall bedroom. Let us try to envisage this.

The first function of science is to understand. Its method leads to discovery; discovery is thrilling and revolutionary, and wakens emotions which lead inevitably to action. Hence, when Copernicus stood up and said that the Earth revolved about the sun, he was as great a revolutionist as the first rebel who stood up and said that kings have no divine rights. By a terrific inner compulsion the scientist is compelled to publish his discoveries and to stand by them in the face of ridicule and persecution. He is one who has beheld a vision a little deeper in one direction than anyone else, and he must return to his fellows and report it. So Harvey who discovered the circulation of the blood, so Darwin, Freud, so Langley who first invented the aeroplane, so Zeppelin, so a host of others—the moderns who have stood on peaks of vision, and fought and beat the hostile world down to a new belief.

The high tension of soul demanded of the real scientist is hardly appreciated. He is nothing more than a man, brought up in and congenitally inheriting instincts, creeds, moralities, taboos, attitudes of mind. He must be ready to sacrifice these things in his search. The god he adores may be destroyed by the fact that he uncovers: that which he fears he may bring upon himself. Yet he must keep on. Of him is demanded often that most difficult thing—suspense of judgment. He cannot leap to his conclusion, in the easy manner in which most of us do: he must tunnel toward it with cruel patience, ascetic concentration, lonely labor. And after years of seeking, he may find, only to discover later a new set of conditions which destroy his finding and compel him to work anew. So there is built up in him an attitude—a complex of receptivity, humbleness before life, courageous pioneering, the use of trial and error, the willingness to accept reality as it comes to him, not as he wishes it to be.

This attitude we call the scientific attitude, and the fruits of the scientific attitude have quite revolutionized our thinking, our beliefs, our physical and our mental world. The old poetry of existence is replaced by a new poetry—the static gives way to the dynamic. Where the pre-scientific world saw man a creature fallen from godlike estate, life a punishment, Earth a vale of tears, and the future a supernatural heaven or hell, with, over all, the tyranny of omnipotent destiny, the new world of science sees man as one who has risen from the primal flood and terror of the past, risen into consciousness and creativeness. Earth then becomes his home and workshop, his school and government, and in the twilight of the gods the dawn of human godlike beings slowly opens. Instead of lamenting the past, we turn to the future, our opportunity: we set ourselves to the task of making man, we change from creatures into creators. Such are the fruits of understanding—of really going down into the dust and the slime and searching and sorting out atoms, probing into disease and filth, looking at nature not in the day-dreams of phantasy but through the telescope and microscope, with hard thinking and resolute courage.

It is true that we have great losses to set against such gains. Out of science has come modern machinery, and out of modern machinery, industrialism. Actually the mass of men have gained in certain comforts only to lose joy in their labor, creativeness in their tasks. Uniformity has inevitably replaced the beautiful variety of ancient life, and speed and size threaten to make us shallow folk. But is this not because we have not enough science? What happened was that a handful of men turned over to an unscientific race the great new powers, and the race has used these powers on the old basis. The machine is a social tool requiring a collective handling; but it has been handled on the basis of individual ownership and self-seeking. What would seem necessary is the training of science on society and on the human soul, to bring man up to the level to which power has been brought; to do with man, in understanding, tapping of resources, utilization of himself, what has been done with nature. In short, to liberate his spirit. And such is the process we see actually beginning—such things as social hygiene, the survey of government and industry and education, the new individual psychology.

But the fear of the religious-minded man is that all such means lead to the desert: that they are outside of the realm of human emotions and human ideals: that we will cease to be quickened, to aspire, to set divine goals before ourselves, to transcend ourselves. These are foolish fears. They are on a par with the fears of theologians over the blasphemies of Darwin. What is religion essentially? Is it not the feeling of inner harmony, the sense of the miraculousness of life, the contact with the sources of one's own existence, out of which springs a belief in the value of striving and of greatness? Surely religion is not dependent for existence on its phantasies and pictures—its heavens, gods, supernatural miracles, its rituals. If this is so, then where shall we have greater religion than in the man who deeply understands—knows himself down to his buried instincts and motives, his deepest needs, his unorganized forces, and learns the technic of how to transform animal energy into human power—the procreative and destructive into the creative—the ego-instinct into self-surpassing, and the herd-instinct into social will: who knows a reality about him whose tiniest atom is an ineluctable mystery, and who goes, without fear, forward, as part of a vast process which his own body sums up, re-lives and advances? Is it more to be a son of God than a son of the starry heavens, the Earth and all of the past? Is self-surpassing to be less sought after because it leads, not to being an angel, but to bringing about a glorious human race? If renunciation was once the mark of a religious man, then today the greatest renunciation is the mark of the scientific man: for he is willing to live to the uttermost, to serve and create at his highest, not purely for a personal, but also for an impersonal end. Instead of the crown and reward of immortality he waives life itself in favor of the future: he gives himself to his living contemporaries and to his unborn descendents. And he gives himself not for a goal which is phantastic, but for a goal which is projected after a study of human tendencies, human possibilities, human impulses—a goal not too far ahead to be humanly unattainable.

To build a great bridge, the engineers must know steel, mechanics, labor-power, tides, climate, a host of things: to create a greater human being we must understand biology, psychology, environment, the individual differences; to create a greater society we must know history, sociology, and all the other sciences. It is true that in former times the intuition of prophet or poet outstripped the racial advance, and flashed a future that was latent in his contemporaries. But such intuitions were uncorrected by precise and deep knowledge, and hence worked as much harm as good. The past is strewn with the tragic wreckage of the creeds, with the broken lives of men who attempted what was not for human nature. The monastery, the religious massacre, the persecution, the superstitious bloody rites, the fanaticism, bigotry, idolatry, the oppression and enslavement of ignorant people by fakers who spoke in the name of a terrible God, the vileness cast upon human nature by loathing of the flesh, the diseases and plagues that were allowed untrammeled ravage because they were visitations of the Lord, the manacling and torture of the insane because they were possessed of devils—these are some of the fruits of uncorrected intuition. We cannot think of such things in connection with true science.

The future for the artist then lies not in rejecting science, but in absorbing it, and above all, in gaining the scientific attitude. It is said truly of science that it destroys nothing that exists: it merely discovers what exists, and destroys our misinterpretations. Hence, if the religious impulse and intuition are actual faculties of human nature, no uncovering of them, no attempt to understand them, can destroy them. Rather, we may expect that here too understanding will lead to greater expression and power: that here too the mist of superstition and vague generality will be blown off, and the clear and lovely fact disclosed. But if it should be other—if the religious, the artistic impulse is destroyed, all we can say is that it is unreal, and that the march of man is toward reality, whatever the losses may be. No true man would care to be a child again because a child believes in fairy-tales: no true modern would give up the gains of our new sun-strong world for the dark beauty-haunted miasma of the pre-scientific era. A question one might put to artists and religious men is this: Is your faith in art, or in religion, strong enough to meet the clear unflinching gaze of Science?

But doubtless what is happening and what will happen is a temporary confusion and breakdown of art and the religious life. A revolutionary change seems at first to destroy the good as well as the bad. In this change, however, a new human spirit, a new mind and soul, are being wrought, and when this is achieved, we may well look for art that has never been before. The trouble is that our artists are conservative, if not reactionary. They are looking to the past, they are seeing what once produced art, and they fear that art will die in any other sort of world. What they must do now is to look to the present, face reality as it is, know the new dynamic energies released, and bring to the vast great human world disclosed to them, those emotions and talents which recreate reality, converting knowledge into vision, and the intangible and abstract into concrete forms.

THREE IMPROBABLES

Benjamin DeCasseres

I. *The Ruling Passion*

PIERRE CHARDON, professor of philosophy in the University of Paris and sharpshooter to Her Majesty, La Belle France, sat concealed in the branches of an old oak slightly beyond the first line of trenches in the Champagne.

A warm winter night of unusual clarity, although there was no moon. The hidden Lapidary of the Stars had put some magic substance into their gleam on this night, for their rays fell on the German trenches with mystifying potency.

Pierre was comfortable, crouched against a giant limb about five feet from the ground. He had slept all that day. His brain was clear and his eyes sparkled like two polished and aureate stones.

Now by one of those singular chances that many have noted in their lives there crawled toward that tree slowly and belly-wise Karl Kleine, professor of philosophy in the University of Heidelberg and scout to His Imperial Majesty, the King of Prussia.

About twenty yards from Pierre Karl was discovered. Pierre fired a shot at the moving mass. It struck the helmet. The German, still flat on his stomach, raised his hands in token of surrender, his rifle having got, somehow or other, under his long coat.

Pierre jumped from the tree and advanced toward Karl with his rifle pointed at his heart. Karl stood there motionless, hands up.

And then the strange thing happened, and strange things happen in quite other places than the "movies" in the strangest of all known worlds.

When about three feet from Karl Kleine, Pierre dropped his rifle in petrified astonishment and Karl's hands came down.

"Karl!"

"Pierre!"

They embraced one another. A shell went screeching over their heads
and a star dropped from Lyra into the nowhere.

"The last time I saw you, Karl," said Pierre, leading the German back
to the oak, while the butt of his rifle trailed the ground, "you still stuck to
the dillettantism of Renan as the last thing in philosophy. You were going
straight toward the pragmatism of William James. I never heard such a
specious plea for that old utilitarian stuff, and—"

"Ah!" said Karl, who had unconsciously squatted under the tree,
in front of Pierre, "you still believe, then, in that old necromancer and
moonshine-maker, Hegel, and all that spiritistic stuff! The Absolute is—"

"I never contended for the Absolute as thing-in-itself, and you can
never quote me to that effect," shouted Pierre. "You had that crowd with
you in that Heidelberg café that night, Karl, and you were ten to one; but
I repeat now, as then, that—and—I quote Spinoza—"

"Mon Dieu! Spinoza! At this late day," screamed back Karl, bringing
down his fist on his helmet which he had put on the ground, "and you
are going to bounce his modalities at me again? I put Epicurus against all
that Spinoza rubbish, and you, Pierre, have got to come around sooner or
later to the solid fact of experience—"

"Experience! Experience! Gott im Himmel!" interrupted Pierre,
kicking his rifle viciously, "what is experience? It is the content of an arc
of the Unknowable Mind, the contact of Spirit with—"

"With what? With what?" asked Karl menacingly, as a German shell
ripped a tree from its roots not a hundred feet away. (Neither paid the
slightest attention to this incident.) "Contact of Spirit with what? Ten
years ago at the picnic in the Bois you could not answer that question
because, as Voltaire wittily said—"

"Not beyond that old bore yet, either, I see!" thundered back Pierre.
"You know what Goethe said about Voltaire and that crowd! He said—"

"Never mind what he said, anyhow. I'm your prisoner, Pierre. Give
me a cigarette and take me in."

"You always did change the subject to something wholly beside the question when you got stuck, Karl. Every time I'd pin you down to your Epicurean-pragmatic-dillettante sophisms you'd switch to something else. Oh, well, come along. But I'll finish this out with you on my first leave of absence."

Both rammed their helmets on their heads. Pierre forgot all about Karl's weapon and both disappeared in the forest dragging the butts of their rifles, while the star-swept darkness echoed with "Schlegel," "Schopenhauer," "Haeckel," "Bergson," "Nietzsche" and "Diderot."

II. *The Truce of the Champions*

Guynemer, the great French aviator, rose into the sparkling light over the battle front. The day was hallucinatingly real, so real that, by the subtle law of the merging of opposites at the extremes of phenomenal visualization, the earth beneath him seemed to the eyes of the aviator to be a phantom world soaked and awash to its scalp in light.

At two thousand feet directly over Arras he made a circle, and his soul stood petrified with wonder.

To the north, toward the Pole, glowing in the ether, three figures in three cars were posed. They were in battle dress, their whips raised as though to strike the backs of their winged steeds, whose distended nostrils were pointed to the zenith. They vibrated, but did not move, and the lashes in the hands of these figures quivered, but did not descend.

They were Alexander, Caesar and Napoleon.

To the south, over the Northern Coast of Africa, on a direct level with the luminous figures in the north, three figures were posed. One was swathed in white, another in black, and the third shimmered against the heavens in naked contemplative glory. They stood upon altars of porphyry, their arms crossed. They vibrated, but did not move, and their arms quivered, but did not unlock.

They were Buddha, Christ and Apollo.

Guynemer, his mind struck to a stare, mechanically rose two thousand feet higher.

And beneath the figures posed in the north he saw columns of skeletons, the vestiges of warrior beings. These columns held the cars of the conquerors in the azure and reached down to the roots of the universe.

And beneath the figures posed to the south he saw columns of skeletons, the vestiges of billions of believing beings. These columns held the pedestals of the saviors in the azure and reached to the dark of the nadir.

Now toward Guynemer there came flying the plane of the great German aviator, Bielstock. A white flag was hoisted in his helmet. Their four eyes, which overflowed their goggles, flew at one another.

"Do you see anything?" called Bielstock.

"Yes," replied Guynemer, "just what you see. I'm ill."

"So am I," replied Bielstock. "Let us descend. *Auf Wiedersehen!*"

"*Au revoir,*" replied Guynemer.

The champions did not battle that week.

III. *Whom the Gods Love*

The Boy sat on the huge bank of snow that the snow sweepers had piled up in the middle of the street and hurled snowballs at the sun, then very low in the clear western sky. He was a golden haired boy, with large, expressive brown eyes. He was about eight years old, and in the transfiguring power of the sun he seemed to me to be a plexus of beautiful rays, a mosaic of prisms.

"Why do you throw your snowballs at the sun?" I asked the Boy.

"Because I want to put that great fire out. Of course, I cannot hit the sun, but I am trying my best, and some day I shall make a snowball big enough and hurl it far enough to quench that light forever," replied the Boy as he threw a particularly big snowball at the orb.

"But why do you want to put out the sun?"

"Because I love the stars better, and cannot see the stars until the sun dies."

"What will you do in summer when there are no snowballs to hurl at the sun?"

"Papa takes me to the beach in summertime, and then I shall make huge balls of sand and throw them at the great red flame as it descends behind the ocean. Then, too, I shall see the beautiful stars—all of them, for there are no houses on the ocean to hide the view."

The Boy looked far away, and the poised snowball dropped from his hand, as if arrested by a memory.

"Do you like rainbows?" he asked, looking up at me, crossing his little legs in a mannish fashion.

"Certainly," I replied.

"Well," said he, "in summer days after the rain I go coasting down rainbows right into the sea with my sled. Can *you* coast down rainbows into the sea? It is such sport!

"And when it rains I capture the finest, biggest raindrops and blow them up to big sparkling bubbles—bubbles as big as a room, and I jump into them, where I see the strangest and prettiest fairies, with long golden wings and eyes like tiny painted stars.

"And I eat the winds—the south-wind in April is like honey, and the north-wind in winter is like melted apple sauce."

"And when you grow up to be a man what will you do?" I asked the Boy, finally.

"Collect clouds," he whispered, "instead of money, like papa does."

But the sun was gone and it was night, so I took the Boy to his house, the house, I recognized, of a very rich grocer.

THIS UNPOPULAR WAR

John Reed

I T was one of those moist, stifling summer nights they have in Washington. After a perfect dinner we adjourned to the library and peeled off our coats, for comfort's sake. The butler brought ice, siphons and tall glasses, and things to smoke.

There were four or five of us; myself the stranger, and the others, clever youngsters a year or so out of college, now doing volunteer work on the Munitions Board, Hoover's Food Administration, or one of the innumerable sub-committees of the Council of National Defense.

They were well enough off to be able to do war work in Washington. None of them had had any real experience of competition for existence. Their minds inclined more to psychology and literary criticism than to political expediency. They had accepted the war and conscription as steps in the working out of a political theory whereby brains would ultimately rule mankind. Let me add that each was prepared to "do his bit," even to the extent of dying for his country. One was going to enlist in the aviation corps; the others thought they would be more serviceable in advisory or organizing positions than in the trenches.

"No one of any intelligence," one boy was saying, "thinks the war is popular.

"The other night a bunch of us dined together—Joe and George and Newton, some of the War Department men, and a few of the big business men in the sub-committees of the Council of National Defense.

"We wanted to think up a 'talking point,' as drummers call it, to 'sell the war.' For three solid hours we sat there cudgelling our brains, but we couldn't think of a single reason not patently a lie which was important enough to excite the patriotism of the man on the street. Of course our own reasons were sufficient, but for an advertising campaign they are much too—well, 'highbrow.' "

The aviation enthusiast spoke up, lying on his back and blowing expensive cigar smoke at the ceiling.

"Do you know what is needed? Only one thing—the same that did the trick for England. Casualties. At first it was impossible to interest the English masses in the war; they could not be made to see that it was their affair. But when the lists of dead, wounded, mutilated, began to come back—and, by the way, England ought to be grateful for the German atrocities—then hatred of the Germans began to soak into the whole people from the families of the wounded and the dead. This social anger is patriotism—for war purposes.

"If I had the job of popularizing this war, I would begin by sending three or four thousand American soldiers to certain death. That would wake the country up."

Now if this young man could wake up America by the simple process of immolating himself, I think he would not hesitate to play Curtius—although he has no romantic illusions, and would only be playing upon public sentimentalism to accomplish a highly rational end. However, he knows well that nothing he could do—even if action were not foreign to his temperament—would stir the American people in the slightest degree. The only thing which *would* stir them is pain, grief, a sense of unutterable loss. So, for our own good, let's slaughter several thousand boys.

Life is cheap now, and if by destroying some thousands of young men—less than a day's toll on the world's battle-lines—one clear step could be taken toward the freedom of mankind, I know where to find men for the job—and not conscripts, either. But to be compelled or to be lured by cheap extravagances into furthering political theories too complicated or too subtle to fire the mass of the people, seems to me the same old undemocratic string-pulling which set Europe aflame.

I spent a year and a half in the various countries and on the various battle-fronts, visiting all the belligerent capitals and seeing action on five fronts. One of my best friends has accused me of not grasping the significance of the war, of not being impressed with the tremendous human contrasts of this universal cataclysm. He says I went over there with the fixed socialist idea that the capitalistic ruling classes had cynically and with malice prepense tricked their people into war; and that I refused to see anything else.

I admit I went abroad with an idea, and that my idea *was* substantially that. Everybody had at least one theory at the beginning of the war. But I was soon disillusioned; I found that the various peoples were not reasonable enough to make trickery necessary—even the socialists and anti-militarists shedding their beliefs like old skins when the colors and the drums swept down the street.

I'm afraid I never did properly understand the drama and the glory of this war. It seemed to me, those first few weeks coming up through France, as if I would never get out of my mind again those beflowered troop trains full of laughing, singing boys—the class of 1914—bound so gaily, unthinkingly to the front. And then Paris—not stern, stoical, heroic, as the reporters all described it; but sick with fear, full of civilian panic, its citizens trampling down women and children in their wild rush to get on the trains for the South.

I saw so many ugly things—rich people putting their handsome houses under the protection of the Red Cross, and later when the Germans had retreated to the Aisne, withdrawing them. Small tradesmen making money out of things needed by the soldiers. Little political fights between the military medical corps and the Red Cross, whereby thousands of beds in the city were vacant, and the wounded died lying out on the cobbles in the rain at Vitry.

Against that, what? A nation rising *en masse* to repel invasion, but without much stomach for a slaughter most people, I think, felt to be utterly stupid and useless. The flags, the emptiness, the spy-crazes, the wild-eyed women, the German aeroplanes dully dropping bombs from overhead into the streets. The shock, and then the slow inevitable dislocation of ordinary life, the growing tension. Later on, the one-armed, one-legged, the men gone mad from shellfire; in side streets the lengthening lines of wretched poor at the public kitchens.

The battle of the Marne was something to go wild with delight about—but by that time there was no one left in Paris to celebrate. Decked with thousands of flags, the city lay smiling vapidly in the bright sunlight, her streets empty, her nights black. There were no glorious tidings, no heroism, no tolling bells and public rejoicings. Those things cease to be when the whole of a nation's manhood is drained into the trenches. There is no such thing as heroism when millions of men face the most ghastly death in such a spirit as the armies of Europe have faced it these three years. Millions of heroes! It makes military courage the cheapest thing in the world.

Why is it I saw this kind of thing? I tried to see the picturesque, the dramatic, the human; but to me all was drab, and all those millions of men were become cogs in a senseless and uninteresting machine. It was the same on the field. I saw a good deal of the battle of the Marne, I was with the French north of Amiens during the beginning of trench warfare. Almost always it was the same mechanical business. At first we were curious to know what new ways of fighting had been evolved; but the novelty soon wore off, as it did to the soldiers in the trenches.

At the battle of the Marne I spent the evening with some British transport soldiers at the little village of Crécy, in sound of the great guns stabbing the dark away off to the north. These "Tommies"—why had they gone to war? Well, they didn't rightly know, except that Bill was going, and they wanted to get away from home for a spell, and the pay was good.

Along about October first, 1914, I had to stay the night in Calais, and out of sheer loneliness found my way finally to the town's one and only "joint," where there was liquor, song and girls. The place was packed with soldiers and sailors, some of them on leave from the front. I fell into conversation with one *poilu,* who told me with great pride that he was a socialist,—and an internationalist too. He had been guarding German prisoners, and waxed enthusiastic as he told me what splendid fellows they were,—all socialists too.

"Look here," I said. "If you belonged to the International why did you go to war?"

"Because," he said, turning his clear eyes upon me, "because France was invaded."

"But the Germans claim that you invaded Germany."

"Yes," he answered gravely, "I know they do say that. The prisoners tell me. Well, perhaps it is true. We were probably both invaded. ... "

London, plastered with enormous signs, "Your King and Country Need You! Enlist for the War Only!" In all open spaces, knots of young men drilling—bank-clerks, stockbrokers, university and public school men, the middle and upper middle classes; for at this time the workers and the East End were not interested in the war. The first Expeditionary Force had been wiped off the face of the earth coming down from Mons; England was getting mad, at the top, and "Kitchener's Mob" was forming.

The great masses of the people of England knew little about the war and cared less. Yet it was up to them to fight, volunteer or conscript. Business and manufacturing concerns began to discharge their employees of military age, and a patriotic black-list saw to it that they got no other work; it was "Enlist or starve." I remember seeing a line of huge trucks sweep through Trafalgar Square, full of youths and placarded "Harrods' Gift to the Empire." The men inside were clerks in Harrods' Stores, and they were being driven to the recruiting station.

There were other things in London which nauseated one. The great limousines going down to the City of a morning with recruiting appeals on their wind-shields, and overfed, overdressed men and women sitting comfortably inside. The articles for sale in the shops, with the "Made in Germany" signs torn off and new cards affixed, "Made in England"; the Rhine and Moselle wines they served in restaurants, their labels painted out, the immensely snobbish Red Cross benefit concerts and dances that made the fall of 1914 "London's gayest autumn."

All the talk of "German militarism," and "the rights of small nations," and "Kaiserism must go"—how sickening to know that the rulers of England really did not believe these pious epithets and platitudes! It was only the great masses of simple folk who were asked to give their lives because "Belgium was invaded," and the "scrap of paper" torn up. Just as in this our own country, where persons of intelligence cannot help smiling—or weeping—when President Wilson talks of American "democracy," and the "democracy" America champions in this war.

Berlin was less patently charged with hypocrisy, as one might expect; for Berlin had been getting ready for this for years. There was less need for advertising than there was in either London or Paris—the Germans had less differences of opinion about the war. And yet to see those hundreds of thousands of gray automatons caught inevitably and irreparably in that merciless machine, hurled down across Belgium in mile-wide, endless rivers, and poured against the scarps of death-rimmed fortresses in close-marching battalions, was more horrible than what I saw in other countries.

Will anyone now dare to claim that the German people were told the truth about the war, or even told anything to speak of? No. The whole nation was sent to the trenches, without opportunity to know, to object, a little more ruthlessly than other nations—except Russia.

I was at the German front, where men stood up to their hips in water, covered with lice, and fired at anything which moved behind a mud-bank eighty yards away. They were the color of mud, their teeth chattered incessantly, and every night some of them went mad. In the space between the trenches, forty yards away, was a heap of bodies left over from the last French charge; the wounded had died out there, without any effort being made to rescue them; and now they were slowly but surely sinking into the soft mud, burying themselves. At this place the soldiers spent three days in the trenches and six days resting back of the lines at Comines, where the government furnished beer, women and a circulating library.

I asked those mud-colored men, leaning against the wet mud-bank in the rain, behind their little steel shields, and firing at whatever moved,—who were their enemies? They stared at me uncomprehendingly. I explained that I wanted to know who lay opposite them, in those pits eighty yards away. They didn't know—whether English, French or Belgians, they had not the slightest idea. And they didn't care. It was Something that Moved—that was enough.

Along the thousand-mile Russian front I saw thousands of young giants, unarmed, unequipped, and often unfed, ordered to the front to stop the German advance with clubs, with their defenseless bodies. If anyone thinks the Russian masses wanted this war, he has only to put his ear to the ground these days when the Russian masses are breaking their age-long silence, and hear the approaching rumble of peace.

No one will ever describe the unimaginable brutality of the old-time Russian military system, through whose machinery went Russia's young men. I have seen an officer on the street of Petrograd knock in the teeth of a soldier who didn't salute with just the proper amount of servility. Soldiers were treated like animals, as a matter of course. To the Russian peasant, what harm was in the Japanese, the Persian, the Turk, the Austrian, or the Prussian—before whose cannon his body crumpled down in alien lands far from his pleasant home? What care he if Serbia were invaded by Austria—or Belgium by the Germans? Hear him now, in those simple tones so exasperating to the "democracies" of the west:

"No annexations, no indemnities."

"Every people has a right to dictate its own form of government."

In Serbia, I was struck first by the unbelievable damage wrought by war and pestilence among a race of "still unbroken men"; and secondly, by the evidences of the network of intrigue in which the great powers had enmeshed the rulers of Serbia, driving straight to war. One young Serbian told me how the plot to kill the Austrian archduke had been formed, and how the Serbian government tolerated the conspiracy, and all about the money paid by the Russian minister. It is no secret that the Serbian peasant, when called to arms to protect his beloved country against the Magyar hordes, was not enlightened about what had gone on between Premier Pashitch and Vienna, and Petrograd.

Happily, I was in Bulgaria when she was forced into the war by her king and German diplomacy; and I had an opportunity to study a modern nation in the act of tricking its people. For seven out of the thirteen political parties in Bulgaria, representing a majority of the people, were against going to war, and through their regularly appointed delegates conveyed their position to the king, demanding the calling of parliament. But the king, the ministers and the military authorities responded by suddenly decreeing mobilization,—with a stroke of the pen converting a nation into an army—and from that moment all communication between citizens, all protest, ceased—or was choked in blood.

I could go on telling of Italy, of Roumania, of Belgium under the Germans, how everywhere I saw the one main fact, repeated over and over again, that this was not a war of the peoples, that the masses in the different countries had, and have, no motive in continuing the struggle except defense, and revenge; and that even now the millions of men on all the fronts would stop fighting, lay down their arms and go home, at a word of command.

In the cities, especially in the capitals of the fighting countries, there is bitterness, hatred for the enemy, which has been slowly distilled from the grief of those who have lost their dear ones—or their property. The farther from the firing line, the stronger is the animosity. But in the trenches themselves there is almost none. Men are too busy fighting to hate. Hatred, after all, is an emotion only possible for the mass of people to sustain if they are idle, with nothing to occupy their minds but the sense of wrong. At the front there is grim cheerfulness, and potting the enemy is a sort of game. Almost everywhere there is some human communication between the trenches, sometimes—like the Christmas truce of the first winter, the hurling of newspapers and gibes from trench to trench, the morning armistice for breakfast. ... Watch a German soldier, or a British Tommy, when prisoners come by; the conqueror usually goes out of his way to be decent, to supply the enemy with food, or tobacco, or bandages. There is little personal feeling left toward the enemy, at the front. It is a job to do, that's all. ... God help the boys in the other trench who've got to do it.

Perhaps the most significant thing I noticed in Europe was the stubborn persistence of internationalism, in spite of the war. Especially in those neutral countries between belligerents was it so. There citizens of enemy countries met in natural friendly communion, bound a little closer, it seemed to me, by the blind grapple of their fatherlands. It was wonderful to perceive by a thousand signs the truth that internationalism is an instinct in mankind. In Holland I have seen even British and German interned soldiers, who could not speak each other's language, fraternizing; while in Switzerland, and in far Roumania, Germans and Frenchmen met to talk the business out, and pledge each other a deeper friendship.

Soon it will be hard for us in America to realize that we ever had German friends, or ever will have them. The casualty lists of the great conscript army will begin to come in, and what my scientific young friend in Washington described will begin to happen to us; we will begin to hate,—"the social anger that is patriotism." Already we've had a taste of what will come, a thousand times intensified, in the beating of "pacifists" by soldiers and sailors—and in arbitrary arrests and suppressions by the police everywhere. It is getting to be as much as a man's liberty is worth to say that this is not a popular war, and that we are not going democratically about "making the world safe for democracy."

Yet both those things are true. In all the nations of the world—even including Germany—this war was not a popular war; nor is there one place left on the face of the globe where the government has dared to put it up to the fighting men whether they would begin the war, and having begun it, whether they will fight on. In all these embattled nations, whose proud crests just now flaunt in chief the word *Democracy,* a small class of immensely wealthy people own the country, while an enormous mass of workers are poor. Belgium, the ravished innocent among nations, was in times of peace the cruellest industrial oligarchy in Europe, with the poorest, most exploited people. And it was this laboring proletariat which was thrown against the might of imperial Germany, to defend its masters.

Now comes our turn. Now millions of young American men are to go to Europe and kill Germans or be killed, in the name of "democracy." Most of these young men are workers, who may or may not know that their employers' patriotism never prevented them from squeezing the ultimate energy from "factory fodder." They may or may not realize that political power without economic power makes "democracy" a hollow sham. It may perhaps have occurred to them that the democratic way to make war is to ask the consent of those who are to do the fighting.

It will be said that it is easy to complain of the "undemocratic" methods of our government—but what was to be done? I think President Wilson could have stopped and asked almost any man he met on the street—he would have told him that.

Here is the way I diagnose the common man's attitude. At the outbreak of the war he felt pretty neutral as between the two belligerents. Later on his sympathies swung to the Entente cause—but never strongly enough to persuade him to bleed and die for it. Certainly, whether you like it or not, Wilson was elected because "he kept us out of war."

The common man's programme was this. His conscience hurt him a little at the shipping of arms and ammunition to Europe—or anyway, he felt that it was unfair. He would have cheerfully embargoed our munitions export trade. He thought Americans had no business travelling in the war-zone, any more than playing tag in a pest-house and he was all for warning them to keep out of there, or anyway, to keep off the vessels of belligerent nations. Compulsory military service he regarded as distinctly un-American, to say the least.

I don't say this frame of mind lasted three years, with the entire press, the churches, the universities, the banks and business agencies all screaming one endless chorus of fear and hatred, overwhelmingly unanimous. No, he couldn't stick it out; pretty soon he simply threw up his horny hands and began to believe that the Allies were right and all the autocracy was in Berlin. But nevertheless, the simple ideas I have outlined above were the common man's reactions to the war; and I think that if he'd been consulted about what to do, the course of American history would have been changed. Anyway, the common man's cerebrations seem to me a perfectly valid, sensible and wise comment on the war.

The thesis of our "intellectuals" is, of course, that common men are unfit for self-government. I'll admit there is justification for that belief. For without their active desire, and even against their dawning understanding, the so-called self-governing peoples of the world allowed themselves to be hurled into war upon each other; and in countries whose very reason for existence was detestation of tyranny, forcible military service and military coercion were accepted almost without protest. Still, it seems a little shameful that this more or less obedient, more or less dumb mass of creatures, whose feeling about the war was characteristic and self-evident, should have been made to betray its own will—and that by clever juggling—from above ; and even then not asked whether it would or no.

In the exclusive club to which I belong, a group of Platts-burghers were sitting at cocktail time, one day just before the President read his war message in Congress. The papers said that the Germans had torpedoed another American ship, and that American citizens had been drowned.

"It's true," one youth was drawling, "that they have been destroying our ships and killing our citizens—but I must confess that my ardor was somewhat dampened when I read that one of the victims was a negro...."

FRIDAY, JUNE 22, 1917

Hendrik Willem van Loon

FOR God's sake, will not someone give us an ideal? The world is waiting for the word that will set it free. The world is anxious to shed its blood and its dearest possessions. The world awaits a deed of leadership.

Meanwhile what does it get?

Words, words, words. Sentimental inanities and the revaluation of those worn-out doctrines which have sent women into sweatshops and have driven men to acts of utter despair.

Yet, we all know that this could be a right war. It could be damnably right. But the articulate expression of our hopes and our longing is drowned in the mushy banalities of official explanation. We ask for a prophecy. We get the recruiting poster.

In the field of material preparation our government has done its duty. Our army is drilling. Our navy is on the ocean. Our flying men are learning their craft by day and by night. We have given of our treasures and our hard-earned savings. Faithful Earth has been set to perform her miracles. Meanwhile we have neglected the most important part of all. We have not mobilized the spirit.

What of the mass of our people? We are groping and we talk to each other in hollow phrases. We pretend to feel certain emotions. We are lying to ourselves and we know it. The war is still a stranger to us. The aims of the war are a cause of indifference. And therefore, I, as one who shall have to take his share, I will try and state in positive terms for what alone I am willing to fight with more than the brute strength of my inexperienced hands.

I have heard much about national doctrines and the Free Ocean and Democracy and the rights of this and the rights of that. All this means little to me and I will not fight for any of these worn-out ideals. I will fight for only one cause which is good and holy. *To make the world safe for my children.* I have been told that one country was wicked—that one man was wicked—that one system of leadership was wicked. I do not believe it. Neither do I care. The agonizing recollection of my own country's failures does not allow me to sit in judgment on my neighbors. Yet, I am willing to sacrifice all. Because I want this world to be safe for my children.

I do not believe in the Millennium. I fully understand the inert slowness of all progress. I also know that this world can be a place of reasonable happiness, reasonable comfort, a garden in which to spend a short while and meditate upon those things which are eternal. And for such a world I am willing to fight.

I am anxious to go forth and meet death that the foul visitation of war may be made impossible. Not through paper Leagues of armed Peace and societies of enthusiasts. I do not believe in new fire-escapes for a decaying old building. My deepest intuitive thought tells me that no constructive future is possible without the complete demolition of our ignoble past. I do not want this war to be the vindication of one set of bad principles over another. I fail to see the superior virtues of one racial unit as compared to another. The idea of atonement for present crimes I am willing to leave to the judgment of posterity. I recognize but one purpose. That I shall bestow a better world upon those who are to follow me.

What sort and manner of world, then, do I imagine? I shall tell you. The basic structure of my world shall be the earth and the people thereon. Man shall acknowledge that he is of this world and by this world and for this world. He shall have no other gods but his own undying soul. He shall accomplish no miracles except through his own genius. He shall be ruled by knowledge—he shall be guided by facts—he shall follow the law which has been seen by the eyes of wise leaders. The dire inheritance of revealed authority he shall disclaim because it is cowardly to accept it. He shall forever struggle in the full understanding of his mysterious task—without despair—without resentment—patiently and triumphantly. He shall claim no reward but love and the consciousness of a firm duty, honorably and courageously performed.

Those who have eyes to read, let them read. Ask me to fight for this. I shall come. And I shall not be alone.

RUDD

Waldo Frank

RUDD'S wife had been sick for a long time; Rudd was not sure any more how long,—but the glad years when he had come back evenings from work with the kitchen gleaming and the boys eager and the dinner ready seemed altogether dim, and true only as things remembered are if one have faith in them. Of course, all that could not have been so very far in the past, for there was Andy, the oldest, only eight, and Jack but six. Helpless, smitten lads they had become when their mother took to her bed. And at once, the kitchen had begun to chant its grey refrain. And so real was the pall over the flat, so far-reaching the emptiness of life with the bed filled in the little room, that nothing happier seemed ever to have been. The happy part had faded—like the cheerful chapters of his religion.

Rudd had been forced to work harder and longer during those weeks when the time away from home was even so more unending and labor at all a strain. He had been forced to work at night—to help the boys to their supper, to give Mary her drink of medicine, and then to leave for the ragged-end jobs that he procured after hours. And through it, there stirred in his mind, vaguely removed from his consciousness, the thought that all this was a bitter joke life played on him. The thought was—it seemed to him—"next door"; like a sound that one hears from the real world when one is dreaming. The dream is bad; the sound calls from a reality where the dream will die. But still, one goes on dreaming, fascinated, foolish, helpless, merging the outer sound into the nightmare's texture. So, somehow, Rudd was aware of the joke that life was playing on him. And somewhere his fancy had woven a picture of what must be, when he grew fully conscious of it.

Rudd was a bricklayer.

His trade was little in his life beyond a capable and fairly steady means to what was everything. He took pride in the way he worked. But he had a greater pride.

The foremen knew his worth, but when they spoke of it always there was a smile of reserve on his lips that they failed to understand. The smile said: "If you knew my real masterpiece!" But to the foremen, to his mates, the smile had if anything a flavor of contempt. So that the men who most admired Rudd, expressing themselves, came to be the men who liked him least. There was an aloofness, an unconcern about him that they could not forgive. And the consequence must be that Rudd would always get what he deserved—and never any more.

He was a spare tall man, with grey eyes and heavy hands and a rhythm of muscle forever playing beneath the drab of his clothes. His smile was a thin curling of his lips above a jaw that was sheer, yet gentle rather than commanding. And the masterpiece of which the smile made boast was his home.

Here was his great work, as he understood it; and here, in truth, was where he dwelt. For a fault gnawed in Rudd; he was proud of his happiness and he was prone to bask in its sun.

He had not counted on Mary's failing in her part of his pride. He looked upon her illness in that light. She had been a slender, pretty woman, proud of her husband as he was of her. They had many acquaintances of whom none could resist envying and admiring their state. And if they had no real friends among these, the cause lay completely in themselves. They needed no friends. They had no desire to give of their real selves. They prized each other and their children and the relative glamor of their home. They were unwilling in any generous sense to share their happiness, since they were sure, instinctively, that to do so had been to lessen or at least to dim it. They had the isolation, then, of all truly happy people. For in those who would win contentment there must dwell a passionate singleness of purpose much like that which leads the artist to greatness or the prophet to revelation.

There was, however, no mere conceit in Rudd's pleasure of his wife. Mary had chosen him from a full field. She was clever and quick and clean, and miraculously able to scrub by day and shine by night. And now, all of a sudden, here she was failing of her great part in his pride! Here she was, drawn of face, languid of gesture, dull of charm:—and then, at length, moistly huddled in her bed, feverish and limp.

It was the first trick that fortune had played on Rudd. He took it stoutly at first. He did his share in meeting it. Not until Mary had sunk beyond the brink of knowing did his feeling of anger and resentment rise above his sorrow. But since this was the true reflex of his nature to misfortune, it was sure eventually to come. For Rudd in his own family of life was a spoiled child. And he had spirit—the same spirit that had won him his contentment—to fling now against its disappearance.

Rudd knew that the Lodge doctor was lying when he shook his head and looked down at his womanish hands and said:

"I wish I could encourage you, old man. I'll be back tomorrow."

It was such nonsense, innumerable little instances of it, with which he doubtless built up his practice, as bricks mount into a wall. Mary was not yet thirty! And last Christmas they had danced together at the ball till the sun came and made the other women look like painted pictures in a book. But the sun had made Mary glow like one of the flowers she cared for in the kitchen window. They had gone home singing—silently though it was. For all of the night they had been dancing together, though the men made faces—and the women too. Rudd was sure of that, because Mary had told him so. And such a wife did not deserve to be a mere brick in a doctor's wall of alarms.

Rudd discharged the Lodge physician and engaged another and began to work at night to pay his daily visit. But at last the visit became a twice daily happening. And then, there was the same long face, the same shake of the learned head, the same hateful, pious clasping of white hands.

But not yet did Rudd believe. What frightened him, however, was that he did not disbelieve so steadfastly—that to do so was a more strenuous summoning of will. He did not dare to discharge this doctor. He did not dare to face him, any more than the truth behind his coming. He kept on working at night and joking with the boys. And since to be with Mary much was to face the doctor's truth, he did not dare that either. Here his work helped him. But the fine edge of Mary's consciousness was blurred, so that perhaps this did not make her suffer.

And then like a burst of storm belief in what the doctor said did come to Rudd. And under it his spirit crumpled and collapsed.

Why work, now, at night? It was only a matter of time before the end? Would he care for funds after that?

Rudd spent his evenings at home in the big room where he could hear his wife's hard breathing and the easy slumber of the boys. At length, his wife's hard breathing came equally by day as by night. And something robbed the airy bloom from the boys' sleep—it was never more clear to him than that. And then, Rudd spent also his days at home.

He sat at the kitchen table, his shoulders tremorously drawn in, his hands forever clenching and distending, his eyes wilfully flashing and then bathed in their own hot repression—the picture of a man who had been insulted. And a true picture it was. For this was the theme of his growing mood. Without reason and without warning, he was being grossly, desperately insulted! And as if ropes bound his muscles, he must sit there and take the insult.

Andy came back from school, bringing Jack who had been playing in the street. The elder boy placed away his books, the other his ball, with a new quietness. They looked without nodding at their father and then, to his relief, went in to their mother.

Rudd was uncomfortable in their presence. What lowered over his home was a loss to them. Yet a loss in some lights can be an honorable thing. They who were little boys could not feel it as a slur. But since it was a slur to him, so full and clear, Rudd felt that his sons must know it. And this was unbearable—that his sons should see him humiliated and without respect. And this was why Rudd felt relief when the boys went in to their mother. And this was why it was impossible for him to follow.

The two boys felt the stressed reserve in their suddenly strange father and left him alone. Their voices had become low and their eyes vagrant, in their home.

They had been born close enough to life, they had sprung up through a layer of it vivid and vital enough to have a sentiment of what was death. But also, they retained the candid stoicism of their youth—the quality of acceptance that springs from want of space or time to conceive otherwise. Their world, since it partook of whatever happened, was merely going on. Their father's world, since it was builded on a past, was disappearing.

So Rudd sat quietly at the table and heard the door close, gently shutting out the boys and his sinking wife; and yearned for the grief he knew he felt, to overwhelm him as respite from this far more bitter sense of degradation. These things were the currency of life. He thought of his mother who had lost three children and her husband before the beginnings of his memory. He thought of a friend who had fallen from a scaffold and became a cripple with a crippled mind. He thought of the fire in the next block which had spared an old couple and killed both their children. He found, as he thought, that these thoughts meant little; that they were vague, unreal puffs of cloud in some atmosphere he had no need of. Every day he read the papers; and they were filled with these calamities and jests of fortune. And they, too, belonged to a plane of being that in no way impinged on his own. The mishaps of those he knew, the reports in the papers, the concise dramas of the motion-pictures—all of them dwelt alike outside, contactless with himself, brewing if anything a liquor of excitement that he paid pennies, nickels, to partake of. Yes: even the sorrows of his friends, in the last measure, had heightened the reality of his own peace—no more. Was his sorrow, now, doing the same thing for other calm spectators? Was his destruction, somewhere, a mere nickel's worth of fun?

Rudd jumped to his feet, his fists clenched. And then, limp, he sank down again. He could not find this "show," so he could not destroy it. He could only play his part. For he knew, dimly, that he had been paid for it in advance.

These were flashes in the thick cloud of his consciousness. They went, leaving the heaviness and the greyness and the encompassing bar to the sun.

His thoughts were compressed and tight and slow-moving. They drove into him like a blunt mallet in the hand of a dull giant. And their direction was downward. Rudd's hands slid out over the table and his head fell on his arms. His eyes were open. His eyes took in the steady, rough grain of the wood that was just below them and that so quickly ran beyond—a hard meaningless surface against his vision, which somehow, in the running of the grain, did have a meaning. This engrossed Rudd. He thought of nothing. He felt in the nearness of the table's surface shutting out his sight that he himself was hidden. He found a security in this opaqueness. He found a soothing note in the sheer rough rhythm of the grain. And then, he looked up, feeling the eyes of his two boys.

They stood slightly aloof, taking him in. With an angry emphasis, Rudd threw up his head.

"Well?"

He did not know what leaned him toward the yielding figures of his boys as a relief from the hard surface of the table—and then, what drew him savagely, revengefully. Perhaps, without his guessing, he envied and abhorred their isolating fitness for what must come.

Andy spoke: "Mother fell asleep—fell asleep."

His little wiry body—its life—was a burden of protest to such a sleep. His hand clasped his brother's. They stood side by side, as if they had been suppliants before a throne.

Rudd gripped himself more easily as he saw this. His weakness, then, had escaped them.

"It's good for Mother to sleep. Let her."

"It's not good!"

The words were from the younger child. But they were not his, consciously. He said what he felt rather than what he knew. His father caught the fatal austerity of this.

"Go for the doctor!"

The command was for the older boy. Rudd caught Jack in his two arms and lifted him on his knees, while Andy had flown out; and held him straight, vicing his shoulders, seeking his gaze. He found it. He held it. His child's spirit flowed to him.

They sat there, motionless, rigid, upright. And neither of them knew, while the child sat on his father's knee, with his frail body clamped in the strong hands, that it was he who was strong and who sustained the other. But both of them knew that the woman who slept was dead. . . .

There was no relief for Rudd ; and also there was no change. The little room was still full with its ironic emptiness. The jest of life stayed balanced, as if revelling in its climax. Rudd's nerves were more tautly drawn. His head was duller underneath its load. The silence about his breast was a more stifling one. Everything was the same. Merely, everything was keyed a little nearer to a shriek.

For Rudd had not been able to raise up his sorrow that it might cleanse his degradation. With all of his old self that his sorrow mourned, his sorrow lay submerged. ...

But at last, the gaunt, silent, eloquent vestige of Rudd's pride was laid away. He thought: when he saw home again, at least it would be really empty, even if it could never again be home. It would be altogether of the broken present. It would be too bare even to remind him of the happy past. Things must grow better then—the sing of his nerves told him—or they must break!

As he rode to her grave, he felt how wrong he was. The lads were close about him in the carriage, like thoughts, like memories, like pain. They throbbed and were mute and were ubiquitous in just this way. He was their father. That meant that he must master them. He felt his failing to. Had he been master, they would not have been so enduring, so cloying-close. In all ways, they were like his senses that clung with him, while he, acknowledging them bluntly, could neither understand nor cast away. They were the true remains of his life, the true point of the jest that was his life. That which rolled silently along before them, with its wreath of immortelles, was no longer anything at all. There was no sense in burying that. It was dead—that death! But there was another death—the death that his two boys, clinging close to him, were forever bringing back. That death was alive! Why could not they be buried?

But they could not be buried. They would go home with him. They would remain with him. They were like his thoughts. There was no escape from them. Even, he would have to nourish *them!* That which he had deemed the climax of the jest was the point of its starting. It would weave into the texture of his love for the living his horror over the love that was lost. It would continue laughing slowly through all his life. ...

The thinking of these things was a drone and a rhythm:—one, first, with the swing of the wheels, and one, at last, with the swing of his breath.

Swathed in the things he thought, Rudd stood over the broken earth and looked down into the grave. Beyond him waved the world. A fringe of trees rolled over the hill that was golden and purple in the sun. The sky glanced against it and its infinite steadfastness made a wave of the landside and a mood of the trees. The wind ran tremorously along. Rudd saw only the grave; but the wind sang in his ears and what it sang was the secret of all it had traversed to reach him. On the horizon, the brow of the hill touched a cloud. And the cloud's top touched the sun. And the wind had come from the horizon.

So a great need came over Rudd. He could escape his thoughts. He knew a way. But these living, growing forms of his thoughts, that clasped his hands? He must escape them first!

Rudd drew free his hands. He did not look at the faces of his boys. Simply, he walked away from their faces. And his harsh gait, as he strode out of earshot, was a measure of his disordered will.

Three days Rudd did not return. He wandered about. He drank enough to blunt the edge of insult cutting his nerves. He kept himself at that. He had a mist about him to dim the direction of his thoughts. But he still had a sense of their stirring, of their nearness, of the danger of their approach. He did not dare to lose this altogether. Something held him from taking liquor to that end. And this same thing it was that at last drew him home.

His living through these three days had been like a siege for him. Within, safe for the moment, was a self that did not see and did not hurt. Without, was the bitter and beating and intolerable mass of his emotions which he had managed to thrust away, but which drove stubbornly back toward their home. As the siege wore on, he knew that they would return. He was not surprised, as he opened the door of his flat. He had never reasonably figured out another course. And he had not drunk enough entirely to lose his reason.

A woman who lived below and whom he had seldom seen faced him, as he stood slightly hesitant in the threshold. Behind her, seated, doing nothing, were his two sons. The flat had a vast and vacant air to his veering senses. In it, the boys were petty and out of scale. The realities were the looming strange emptiness of the place where he had lived, and the sudden challenge of the woman. Rudd glanced beyond her to the table which was bare and to the stove which was cold. It was early evening. The shadows came up from the street and into the window. Another shadow lay against the room from the door of the little chamber, and made the room almost blindingly light by contrast. The door was open. Everything was larger than its wont, and new with a sudden oldness. Rudd saw the sewing-machine with its little stool. It was huge. He saw the painted china statue and the colored picture. They were flushed with a fever. From these abandoned marks of his past came a shrill tremor that caught in his brain and made him dizzy.

Rudd stood very still and bent his mind to steadiness. Why were his two sons so small and quiet? The woman's voice broke in and made him listen.

"Well, Mr. Rudd," she said, "So you've come home at last? And are you expecting me to feed you too, as I have your sons?"

Rudd swayed a bit. This was what the woman needed to unleash her.

"A fine father you are!"

He saw his sons, meekly quiet, their eyes lowered from their father, their bodies withdrawn.

"You'd 'a' let 'em starve, I suppose—you big brute!—abandoning your children when they've gone and lost their mother. God! you men—carousing for three days. Well, I ain't no millionaire. I got no more food to spare for 'em. I guess it's up to you to get 'em their dinner."

She marched directly upon him.

"Let me pass," she sneered. With a heavy arm, she thrust him aside. The door slammed.

The noise showered out and went through Rudd like steel, sobering him. He saw himself, alone with his two sons. A great shame possessed him, shrivelling up all his other senses. Barely, he made out his sons, still sitting there. They were eloquent in their withdrawal from this father who had shamed himself. . . .

Rudd clenched his fists. He could not bear this subtle proof of his disgrace. He must win over his sons, though the task sickened him. He must blot out their mute shy calm that branded him more clearly, even than the words of the woman. They had listened while this stranger flayed their father!

He had lost his love—his life. And now this living humiliation was heaped on the grave of his pride—on the remains of death? A woman had spoken in that way before his sons? Had struck at him so, with her service to his sons? Always—his sons! They were there, eternally then, to quicken his disgrace!

The impulse surged in Rudd to wipe them out. Another impulse came to fall on his knees before them—told him that this completion would be sweet. But Rudd threw up his head.

"Come, lads," he cried. "We're going out to supper."

They put on their hats and coats with the same cowed look of accusation. They said nothing. It was their silence which Rudd found insufferable. For through it came more clearly their contempt and their disgust, and the sharp contrast with what once had been.

As they walked down the street, he tried to alter this. He tried to joke, to ask them questions. But how could he joke when he had last seen them at their mother's grave? And how could he ask them questions without questioning how they had been since she had left them? And how could he hear them speak without looking in their faces from which he had walked away? They entered the restaurant in a cold stillness.

On one side of the narrow room was a counter fitted with stools revolving on iron rods. On the other was a squad of tables bare of cloth, cluttered with canisters and thick dishes and the sprawling elbows of the eaters. Above the counter was a glass pasted with cardboard notices of food and prices. Behind it worked an unshaved man in an apron of dirty white. Another, even a little greasier, worked the tables. The place was alive with men and women; silence swarmed over their drab movements like a slow rotting. It was as if the squalor of the place, rather than the food, were stifling their hunger.

Rudd and his sons sat down. Rudd took the bill of fare. Here was one topic of talk where he could venture. Into it he put all of himself, all of his starved capacity of father. From it, in some mad way, he seemed to seek redemption.

"Well, lads," he announced, "what will you have to eat? Anything you want. Now, make sure!"

He read down the list, stressing the delicacies, putting a tinge of rhapsody gleaned from another and true pathos into his voice as he pronounced them, slurring the common meats as if they were beneath the splendor of his rite. The boys listened with unaltered faces. Rudd grew lyric over the desserts. And then, he paused.

"I want some fried eggs," said Andy, with a cold decision that seemed to have been made before the reading of the bill of fare.

"Me too," said Jack. His tone was the same.

The father quavered over this abyss from his proud comedy. He feared for his balance.

"Aren't you hungrier than that?" he pleaded.

"Mrs. Wagner gave us a whole lot for lunch."

Rudd winced. The waiter was standing over him, supercilious and ready for the order.

"Very well," declared Rudd, beating down the still rising pain.

"Fried eggs, three times," he gave out. He avoided looking at the waiter. His presence was hostile to him. He had heard Rudd's prandial oration,—and its anti-climax. This may have been an initial cause. For the fellow had dared to smile. And the poison of that smile had seeped now through all Rudd's personality.

"And what with it—potatoes?" the waiter asked, his head also up.

Rudd turned to his boys in question. They nodded almost imperceptibly.

"How?" asked their father. It was as if he had been addressing some unreality. That was why he found it painful to control his voice.

"Boiled," was their low answer.

"Boiled potatoes on the side," ordered Rudd, and the other man lounged off.

Once more there was silence.

The one topic of talk was exhausted. It had helped not at all.

Rudd waited, tapping the floor with his foot. But even this he ceased to do. He became altogether still. His two sons gazed vacantly ahead, with their hands clasped and their eyes glistening and their spirit altogether pinched and broken.

And then, an infinite air came and held all three,—an air that was cloying and thick and unbreathable, and that they had to breathe—an air of Permanence. In its drawing chill, in its measured penetration, Rudd recognized it.

At last, the waiter returned and laid their food before them on the table.

YOUNG SPAIN

John R. Dos Passos

T HE *señores* were from Madrid? Indeed! The man's voice was full of an awe of great distances. He was the village baker of Almorox, where we had gone on a Sunday excursion from Madrid; and we were standing on the scrubbed tile floor of his house, ceremoniously receiving wine and figs from his wife. The father of the friend who accompanied me had once lived in the same village as the baker's father, and bought bread of him; hence the entertainment. This baker of Almorox was a tall man, with a soft moustache very black against his ash-pale face, who stood with his large head thrust far forward. He was smiling with pleasure at the presence of strangers in his house, while in a tone of shy deprecating courtesy he asked after my friend's family. Don Fernando and Doña Ana and the Señorita were well? And little Carlos? Carlos was no longer little, answered my friend, and Doña Ana was dead.

The baker's wife had stood in the shadow looking from one face to another with a sort of wondering pleasure as we talked, but at this she came forward suddenly into the pale greenish-gold light that streamed through the door, holding a dark wine-bottle before her. There were tears in her eyes. No; she had never known any of them, she explained hastily—she had never been away from Almorox—but she had heard so much of their kindness and was sorry. . . . It was terrible to lose a father or a mother. The tall baker shifted his feet uneasily, embarrassed by the sadness that seemed slipping over his guests, and suggested that we walk up the hill to the Hermitage; he would show the way.

"But your work?" we asked. Ah, it did not matter. Strangers did not come every day to Almorox. He strode out of the door, wrapping a woolen muffler about his bare strongly moulded throat, and we followed him up the devious street of whitewashed houses that gave us glimpses through wide doors of dark tiled rooms with great black rafters overhead and courtyards where chickens pecked at the manure lodged between smooth worn flagstones. Still between whitewashed walls we struck out of the village into the deep black mud of the high road, and at last burst suddenly into the open country, where patches of sprouting grass shone vivid green against the gray and russet of broad rolling lands. At the top of the first hill stood the Hermitage—a small whitewashed chapel with a square three-storied tower; over the door was a relief of the Virgin, crowned, in worn lichened stone. The interior was very plain with a single heavily gilt altar, over which was a painted statue, stiff but full of a certain erect disdainful grace—again of the Virgin. The figure was dressed in a long lace gown, full of frills and ruffles, grey with dust and age.

"*La Virgen de la Cima*," said the baker, pointing reverently with his thumb, after he had bent his knee before the altar. And as I glanced at the image a sudden resemblance struck me: the gown gave the Virgin a curiously conical look that somehow made me think of that conical black stone, the Bona Dea, that the Romans brought from Asia Minor. Here again was a good goddess, a bountiful one, more mother than virgin, despite her prudish frills. ... But the man was ushering us out.

"And there is no finer view than this in all Spain." With a broad sweep of his arm he took in the village below, with its waves of roofs that merged from green to maroon and deep crimson, broken suddenly by the open square in front of the church; and the gray towering church, scowling with strong lights and shadows on buttresses and pointed windows; and the brown fields faintly sheened with green, which gave place to the deep maroon of the turned earth of vineyards, and the shining silver where the wind ruffled the olive-orchards; and beyond, the rolling hills that grew gradually flatter until they sank into the yellowish plain of Castile. As he made the gesture his fingers were stretched wide as if to grasp all this land he was showing. His flaccid cheeks were flushed as he turned to us; but we should see it in May, he was saying, in May when the wheat was thick in the fields, and there were flowers on the hills. Then the lands were beautiful and rich, in May. And he went on to tell us of the local feast, and the great processions of the Virgin. This year there were to be four days of the *toros*. So many bullfights were unusual in such a small village, he assured us. But they were rich in Almorox; the wine was the best in Castile. Four days of *toros,* he said again; and all the people of the country around would come to the fiestas, and there would be a great pilgrimage to this Hermitage of the Virgin ... As he talked in his slow deferential way, a little conscious of his volubility before strangers, there began to grow in my mind a picture of his view of the world.

First came his family, the wife whose body lay beside his at night, who bore him children, the old withered parents who sat in the sun at his door, his memories of them when they had had strong rounded limbs like his, and of their parents sitting old and withered in the sun. Then his work, the heat of his ovens, the smell of bread cooking, the faces of neighbors who came to buy; and, outside, in the dim penumbra of things half real, of travellers' tales, lay Madrid, where the king lived and where politicians wrote in the newspapers,—and *Francia* and all that was not Almorox ... In him I seemed to see the generations wax and wane, like the years, strung on the thread of labor, of unending sweat and strain of muscles against the earth. It was all so mellow, so strangely aloof from the modern world of feverish change, this life of the peasants of Almorox. Everywhere roots striking into the infinite past. For before the Revolution, before the Moors, before the Romans, before the dark furtive traders, the Phœnicians, they were much the same, these Iberian village communities. Far away things changed, cities were founded, hard roads built, armies marched and fought and passed away; but in Almorox the foundations of life remained unchanged up to the present. New names and new languages had come. The Virgin had taken over the festivals and rituals of the old earth goddesses, and the deep mystical fervor of devotion. But always remained the love for the place, the strong anarchistic reliance on the individual man, the walking consciously or not, of the way beaten by generations of men who had tilled and loved and lain in the cherishing sun with no feeling of a reality outside of themselves, outside of the bare encompassing hills of their commune, except the God which was the synthesis of their souls and of their lives.

Here lies the strength and the weakness of Spain. This intense individualism, born of a history whose fundamentals lie in isolated village communities—*pueblos,* as the Spaniards call them—over the changeless face of which, like grass over a field, events spring and mature and die, is the basic fact of Spanish life. No revolution has been strong enough to shake it. Invasion after invasion, of Goths, of Moors, of Christian ideas, of the fads and convictions of the Renaissance, have swept over the country, changing surface customs and modes of thought and speech, only to be metamorphosed into keeping with the changeless Iberian mind.

And predominant in the Iberian mind is the thought *La vida es sueño:* "Life is a dream." Only the individual, or that part of life which is in the firm grasp of the individual, is real. The supreme expression of this lies in the two great figures that typify Spain for all time; Don Quixote and Sancho Panza. Don Quixote, the individualist who believed in the power of man's soul over all things, whose desire included the whole world in himself. Sancho, the individualist to whom all the world was food for his belly. On the one hand we have the ecstatic figures for whom the power of the individual soul has no limits, in whose minds the universe is but one man standing before his reflection, God. These are the Loyolas, the Philip Seconds, the fervid ascetics like Juan de la Cruz, the originals of the glowing tortured faces in the portraits of El Greco. On the other hand are the jovial materialists like the Archpriest of Hita, culminating in the frantic, almost mystical sensuality of such an epic figure as Don Juan Tenorio. Through all Spanish history and art the threads of these two complementary characters can be traced, changing, combining, branching out, but ever in substance the same. Of this warp and woof have all the strange patterns of Spanish life been woven.

II.

In trying to hammer some sort of unified impression out of the scattered pictures of Spain in my mind, one of the first things I realize is that there are many Spains. Indeed every village hidden in the folds of the great barren hills, or shadowed by its massive church in the middle of one of the upland plains, every fertile *huerta* of the seacoast is a Spain. Iberia exists, and the strong Iberian characteristics; but Spain as a modern centralized nation is an illusion—perhaps a delusion; for the present atrophy, the desolating result-lessness of a century of revolution, may very well be due in large measure to the artificial imposition of centralized government on a land essentially centrifugal.

In the first place there is the matter of language. Roughly four distinct languages are at present spoken in Spain: Castilian, the language of Madrid and the central uplands, the official language, spoken in the south in its Andalusian form; Gallego-Portuguese, spoken on the west coast; Basque, which does not even share the Latin descent of the others; and Catalan, a form of Provençal which, with its dialect, Valencian, is spoken on the upper Mediterranean coast and in the Balearic Isles. Of course, under the influence of rail communication and a conscious effort to spread Castilian, the other languages, with the exception of Portuguese and Catalan, have lost vitality and died out in the larger towns; but the problem remains far different from that of the Italian dialects, since the Spanish languages have all, except Basque, a strong literary tradition.

Added to the variety of language, there is an immense variety of topography in the different parts of Spain. The central plateaux, dominant in modern history (history being taken to mean the births and breedings of kings and queens and the doings of generals in armor), probably approximate the warmer Russian steppes in climate and vegetation. The west coast is in most respects a warmer and more fertile Wales. The southern *huertas* (arable river valleys) have rather the aspect of Egypt. The east coast from Valencia up is a continuation of the Mediterranean coast of France. It follows that, in this country where an hour's train ride will take you from Siberian snow into African desert, unity of population is hardly to be expected.

Here is probably the root of the tendency in Spanish art and thought to emphasize the differences between things. In painting, where the mind of a people is often more tangibly represented than anywhere else, we find one supreme example. El Greco, almost the caricature in his art of the Don Quixote type of mind, who, though a Greek by birth and a Venetian by training, became more Spanish than the Spaniards during his long life at Toledo, strove constantly to express the difference between the world of flesh and the world of spirit, between the body and the soul of man. More recently, the extreme characterization of Goya's sketches and portraits, the intensifying of national types found in Zuloaga and the other painters who have been exploiting with such success the peculiarities—the picturesqueness—of Spanish faces and landscapes, seem to spring from this powerful sense of the separateness of things.

In another way you can express this constant attempt to differentiate one individual from another as caricature. Spanish art is constantly on the edge of caricature. Given the ebullient fertility of the Spanish mind and its intense individualism, a constant slipping over into the grotesque is inevitable. And so it comes to be that the conscious or unconscious aim of their art is rather self-expression than beauty. Their image of reality is sharp and clear, but distorted. Burlesque and satire are never far away in their most serious moments. Not even the calmest and best ordered of Spanish minds can resist a tendency to excess of all sorts, to over-elaboration, to grotesquerie, to deadening mannerism. All that is greatest in their art, indeed, lies on the borderland of the extravagant, where sublime things skim the thin ice of absurdity. The great epic, Don Quixote; such plays as Calderon's *La Vida es Sueño,* such painting as El Greco's *Resurrection* and Velasquez's dwarfs, such buildings as the Escorial and the Alhambra—all among the universal masterpieces—are far indeed from the middle term of reasonable beauty. Hence their supreme strength. And for our generation, to which excess is a synonym for beauty, is added argumentative significance to the long tradition of Spanish art.

Another characteristic, springing from the same fervid abundante, that links the Spanish tradition to ours of the present day is way is the strangely impromptu character of much Spanish art production. The slightly ridiculous proverb that genius Consists of an infinite capacity for taking pains is well controverted. The creative flow of Spanish artists has always been so strong, so full of vitality that there has been no time for taking pains. Lope de Vega, with his two thousand odd plays—or was it twelve thousand?—is by no means an isolated instance. Perhaps the strong sense of individual validity, which makes Spain the most democratic country in Europe, sanctions the constant improvization, and accounts for the confident planlessness as common in Spanish architecture as in Spanish political thought.

Here we meet the old stock characteristic, Spanish pride. This is a very real thing, and is merely the external shell of the fundamental trust in the individual and in nothing outside of him. Again El Greco is an example. As his painting progressed, grew more and more personal, he drew away from tangible reality, and, with all the dogmatic conviction of one whose faith in his own reality can sweep away the mountains of the visible world, expressed his own restless, almost sensual, spirituality in forms that flickered like white flames toward God. For the Spaniard, moreover, God is always, in essence, the proudest sublimation of man's soul. The same spirit runs through the preachers of the early church and the works of Santa Teresa, a disguise of the frantic desire to express the self, the self, changeless and eternal, at all costs. From this comes the hard cruelty that flares forth luridly at times. A recent book by Miguel de Unamuno, *Del Sentimiento Trágico de la Vida,* expresses this fierce clinging to separateness from the universe by the phrase *el hambre de inmortalidad,* the hunger of immortality. This is the core of the individualism that lurks in all Spanish ideas, the conviction that only the individual soul is real.

III

In the Spain of today these things are seen as through a glass, darkly. Since the famous and much gloated-over entrance of Ferdinand and Isabella into Granada, the history of Spain has been that of an attempt to fit a square peg in a round hole. In the great flare of the golden age, the age of ingots of Peru and of men of even greater worth, the disease worked beneath the surface. Since then the conflict has corroded into futility all the buoyant energies of the country. I mean the persistent attempt to centralize in thought, in art, in government, in religion, a nation whose every energy lies in the other direction. The result has been a deadlock, and the ensuing rust and numbing of all life and thought, so that a century of revolution seems to have brought Spain no nearer a solution of its problems. At the present day, when all is ripe for a new attempt to throw off the atrophy, a sort of despairing inaction causes the Spaniards to remain under a government of unbelievably corrupt and inefficient politicians. There seems no solution to the problem of a nation in which the centralized power and the separate communities work only to nullify each other.

The attitude of Spain to the war is an outgrowth of this. The country is pretty evenly divided into Germanophiles and Frankophiles, as they are called, not from any broad convictions on world politics, but from the hope that the victory of one or the other will throw weight on the side of one of the contesting parties. The reactionaries, the clergy, and the ignorant priest-ridden classes—the high aristocracy and the lowest peasantry—are strongly pro-German, or rather, pro-Austrian. Perhaps the faint hope of a new Metternich sustains them. The liberals of all colors, the intelligentsia, and the munitions manufacturers, who have been growing very wealthy in the North, are fervidly pro-Ally. Then there is a further regional division: the Basque provinces, Portugal, Galicia and Catalonia, the portions of the peninsula that have most connection with the modern world, are pro-Ally; the central and southern parts pro-German.

But the most important influence of the war on Spain is this. The cost of living is constantly rising, and labor is wretchedly underpaid. Meanwhile the governing classes plunder, the intellectual classes talk and prophesy and despair, and a few towns in the North, like Corunna, grow suddenly rich on munitions. But under the surface the moment comes nearer and nearer when the tension will snap. Famine is the mother of revolutions. The trouble is that the revolutionary classes have so many different aims. In Catalonia they want a republic and virtual autonomy from the rest of Spain. In Andalusia they want, very simply, food and decent wages. In Galicia they want to be let alone and allowed to grow rich in peace. Fear of failure is everywhere, a fear that any move may make matters worse, may lift again into the saddle the incubus of the clergy and the reactionaries. So Spain, hot with discussion, holds aloof from the war.

On every side, however, in thought if not in fact, the ice of national stagnation is breaking. The war of '98, which to us was merely an occasion for a display of the school history-book style of patriotism, combined with an amazing skill in sanitation, was to the Spanish people a great spiritual crisis. It was the first thorough unmasking of the hopeless atrophy of their political life. From '98 indeed has sprung the present generation, a generation of men strangely sensitive and self-conscious, some despairing, some pressing on very boldly up the logical paths of Spanish thought—toward anarchism, toward a searing criticism of the modern world in general and Spain in particular. Gradually, laboriously, with unexampled devotion, these men are piecing together the tattered shreds of national consciousness. Not national consciousness wholly in the present capitalistic-patriotic sense, however, but something more fruitful, more local.

The two most important novelists in the younger generation, Pio Barroja and Blasco Ibañez well illustrate this mood. The first, who very probably is one of the foremost writers of our time, has spent his life in delineating Spain against the background of the world today, exposing her weakness with frank pessimism. Barroja's attitude has a certain affinity to the attitude toward America of the early Henry James, though as artists there is no comparison between them. The Spaniard has a sense of life, a buoyancy, a power to tell a story that make sickly beside them the pale artifices of the Anglo-American novelist. Far different, too, from James's quiet dissent from ideas American is Barroja's burning criticism of his country's inaction. Through him Nietzsche has reached the present generation, and a worship of things Anglo-Saxon, of the efficient Roosevelt virtues, which sounds strangely in the ears of Americans used to reacting in the opposite direction from their red-blooded national ethics. Blasco Ibañez, a belated Zolaist of slightly lurid tendencies, attacks Spanish life from the opposite point of view, from that of his socialist's vision of the world. He is less of an artist, but probably his ideas will be ultimately more fruitful than the old-fashioned cosmopolitanism and Anglo-mania of Barroja.

In the Spanish poetry of the day there is much the same sense of purpose. Rubén Darío, the Nicaraguan who dominated the Spanish-speaking world for the past decade, was full of his call to the Spanish peoples to unite, to build a new ideal of life that would defeat what he called the *Yanki* ideal of dollars and steel. In his bold metrical inventions, in his continual breaking of the conventional chains of Spanish thought, he was the prophet of an era of solidarity for the Spanish peoples of the world, with a humaner literature and a humaner religion. Antonio

Machado, writing his passionate love for the grey iron hills and the yellow plains of Castile, and for the dark reliant peasants who till their soil, has made some of his greatest poetry in attempts to stir his countrymen to realization and action. Throughout his strong repressed poems runs the plaint of the ancient glory of Castile, "fecund mother of captains in the old time, today bringing forth puny drill-sergeants." Another poet, Juan Ramón Jiménez, has introduced a prosody developed from the French vers librists which approximates in some measure the verse of Amy Lowell and Richard Aldington. He has substituted a vague, rather Celtic mood for the traditional clarity of Spanish verse, and a delicate irregular cadence for the heavy lilt of its ballad rhythms. He is the poet of Andalusia the gay, the center of the ruined dream of Moorish Spain, while Antonio Machado represents somber visionary Castile. And, in the same manner, each poet of modern Spain can be assigned to his province, to his *pueblo.* In literature the triumph of the commune over Madrid is near at hand.

The regional character of Spanish music of the present generation is even more obvious. This is probably largely due to the varied character of the rich store of still unexploited folk-music, roughly of Celtic origin in the North and West, and of African in the South and Levant, which up to the present has found no genius strong enough to fuse it into a truly personal work of art. Spain is saturated with this native music. Even the light opera of the cheaper theatres in Madrid has, when the source is not muddied by imitation Viennese tinsel and syrup, moments of great charm and true musical value. Often in a trivial and ill put-together *zarzuela* appear almost unconscious traces of old thrilling motives handed down from the Moors or the Celt-Iberian mountaineers. Perhaps Spanish music is in the condition of German music before Beethoven. No one has yet appeared to collect the scattered strands into a great racial art. Among recent composers, neither Granados nor Albéniz have to my mind thoroughly mastered their material. They and probably Fallo and the other composers of the moment, who are so busily engaged in collecting and interpreting what they can of the stream of musical richness that flows past them, will be the stepping-stones for the genius who must follow to make of Spanish music a great and original expression.

First, however, in Spanish music as in Spanish painting, one influence must be overcome: Paris. Paris has hitherto done one of two things to Spanish artists; it has subdued them entirely to the prevailing French mode, or it has turned them into mongers of the picturesque, of romantic Spain, for export purposes. There seem, in Spanish art as in American, few personalities strong enough to gain the technique of Paris without becoming as enslaved as Circe's swine.

The great vitality of Spanish painting in recent years is partly due to the fact that it has been an expression of local schools. Sorolla was a thoroughly Valencian painter before he went to Paris, and his best work is that which shows most the influence of the local tradition. In Zuloaga can be seen again and again the influence of his uncle Daniel, the Castilian ceramist. In the Basque painters represented by the brothers Zubiaurre, localism in style and technique becomes almost a mannerism. Indeed it is hard to realize how much good painting is being done in small isolated groups in Spain. Seville, Granada, Bilbao, Corunna, Barcelona, Valencia, have all their circles of extremely active painters; while Madrid is the palm of victory. There live all the thoroughly successful artists, and those the war has driven away from the lotus-trees of Paris. But even in the rather vulgar and cosmopolitan—in the worst sense—artistic circle of Madrid, the cult of the god Success and of the god Foreignness has nothing of the power and universality it enjoys in corresponding circles in America. Perhaps the reason is that a sincere inborn sense of art is part of the heritage of all classes of Spanish society.

IV

It was after a lecture at an exhibition of Basque painters in Madrid, where we had heard a wonderful old man, with eyes that burned out from under shaggy grizzled eyebrows, denounce in bitter stinging irony what he called the Europeanization of Spain. What they called progress, he had said, was merely an aping of the stupid commercialism of modern Europe. Better no education for the masses than education that would turn healthy peasants into crafty putty-skinned merchants; better a Spain swooning in her age-old apathy, than a Spain awakened to the brutal soulless trade-war of modern life... I was walking with a young student of philosophy I had met by chance across the noisy board of a Spanish *pension,* discussing the exhibition we had just seen as a strangely meek setting for the fiery reactionary speech. I had remarked on the very "primitive" look much of the work of these young Basque painters had, shown by some in the almost affectionate technique, in the dainty caress-ing brush-work, in others by that inadequacy of the means at the painter's disposal to express his idea, which made of so many of the pictures rather gloriously impressive failures. My friend was insisting, however, that the primitiveness, rather than the birth-pangs of a new view of the world, was nothing but the last affectation of an over-civilized tradition."

"Spain," he said, "is the most civilized country in Europe. The growth of our civilization has never been interrupted by outside influence. The Phoenicians, the Romans—Spain's influence on Rome was, I imagine, fully as great as Rome's on Spain; think of the five Spanish emperors;—the Goths, the Moors;—all incidents, absorbed by the changeless Iberian spirit ... Even Spanish Christianity," he continued, smiling, "is far more Spanish than it is Christian. Our life is one vast ritual. Our religion is part of it, that is all. And so are the bull-fights that so shock the English and Americans,—are they any more brutal, though, than fox-hunting and prize-fights? And how full of tradition are they, our *fiestas de toros;* their ceremony reaches back to the hecatombs of the Homeric heroes, to the bull-worship of the Cretans and of so many of the Mediterranean cults, to the Roman games. Can civilization go further than to ritualize death as we have done? But our culture is too perfect, too stable. Life is choked by it."

We stood still a moment in the shade of a yellowed lime-tree. My friend had stopped talking, and was looking with his usual bitter smile at a group of little boys with brown bare dusty legs who were intently playing bull-fight with sticks for swords and a piece of newspaper for the toreador's scarlet cape.

"It is you in America," he went on suddenly, "to whom the future belongs; you are so vigorous and vulgar and uncultured. Life has become once more the primal fight for bread. Of course the dollar is a complicated form of the food the cave man killed for and slunk after, and the means of combat are different, but it is as brutal. From that crude animal brutality comes all the vigor of life. We have none of it; we are too tired to have any thoughts; we have lived so much so long ago that now we are content with the very simple things,—the warmth of the sun and the colors of the hills and the flavor of bread and wine. All the rest is automatic, ritual."

"But what about the strike?" I asked, referring to the one day's general strike that had just been carried out with fair success throughout Spain, as a protest against the government's apathy regarding the dangerous rise in the prices of food and fuel.

He shrugged his shoulders.

"That, and more," he said, "is new Spain, a prophecy, rather than a fact. Old Spain is still all-powerful."

Later in the day I was walking through the main street of one of the clustered adobe villages that lie in the folds of the Castilian plain not far from Madrid. The lamps were just being lit in the little shops where the people lived and worked and sold their goods, and women with beautifully shaped pottery jars on their heads were coming home with water from the well. Suddenly I came out on an open *plaza* with trees from which the last leaves were falling through the greenish sunset light. The place was filled with the lilting music of a grind-organ and with a crunch of steps on the gravel as people danced. There were soldiers and servant-girls, and red-cheeked apprentice-boys with their sweethearts, and respectable shop-keepers, and their wives with mantillas over their gleaming black hair. All were dancing in and out among the slim tree-trunks, and the air was noisy with laughter and little cries of childlike unfeigned enjoyment. I thought of a cheap dancehall in America. How much healthier this seemed, in the open air, without restraint or hidden obscenities, this merrymaking of people who were so unaffectedly at ease in the world.

Here was the gospel of Sancho Panza, I thought, the easy acceptance of life, the unashamed joy in food and color and the softness of women's hair. But as I walked out of the village across the harsh plain of Castile, grey-green and violet under the deepening night, the memory came to me of the knight of the sorrowful countenance, Don Quixote, blunderingly trying to remould the world, pitifully sure of the power of his own ideal. And in these two Spain seemed to be manifest. Far indeed were they from the restless industrial world of joyless enforced labor and incessant goading war. And I wondered to what purpose it would be, should Don Quixote again saddle Rosinante.

BLACK MAGIC

Margaret Widdemer

O F course nothing in this world is absolutely one person's fault. Any amount of people and things and environments, most of them well-meaning, are to blame every time something breaks. Yet it does seem to me that if Catherine's own people had been just a little more fantastic in their point of view nothing need have happened. If they had not tried to make a conventional young lady out of a woman who could have been the leader of a great movement or the prophetess of a faith——

But there it is again. They saw things as most fathers and mothers in the world would have seen them, from the sensible, walled-in cell of middle age: as Catherine herself might have seen them if she had married and had daughters of her own.

No more could Mira help being what she was, I suppose. She always reminded me of some destructive natural force. She mayn't have been normal, but she was certainly amazingly dynamic, and people say now that the way your brain is built is responsible for whether you are kind-hearted or not. She was always a little afraid, herself, of going mad, I know. No, I suppose in a way it was nobody's fault. But I always wanted to have Mira punished for it. Such as she usually get poisoned in the end by some anonymous person, in their proper habitat, the Renaissance. Those good days are over, alas!

Catherine James was the stuff from which are made saints and martyrs and perfect mothers. She was strong and singlehearted and—there are very few people to whom the word really applies—noble-minded. I have never known her to believe even the most obvious evil of anyone. Yet—strong? I scarcely know. Perhaps I should have said strong to endure. It was never a strength of aggression.

She grew up clipped into conventional shape by a mother and governess who were even more afraid of "queerness" than they were of undesirable friends. If you have fine enough material you can twist it into almost any shape, and Catherine at twenty must have been as good a semblance of your sensible, narrow-interested, pleasure-loving girl as heart could wish—or break over. All the wild white dreams had been laughed down and scolded under and hushed out of sight. Catherine was the kind of girl your own people held up to you as an example.

If she had been the ordinary romantic, sentimental dreamer it would have made no difference. She would have enjoyed not being understood, and married somebody on the strength of it, and everything would have been all right. But she was great-minded, which means humble-minded, and when they told her that to be unusual was to be wrong she believed it. The little people around her said she was silly. They were older than she, so of course they knew, she thought; and she crowded under all the wild, innocent, noble wishes and desires and struggles and beliefs that go to the making of heroines, and hid her Shelley and Kant away, and dutifully read young-girl books that bored her piteously. One will do almost anything at twenty not to be different. Of course all the realities in her were burning hard, ready to break through at a touch.

Well, the touch came—through a perfectly proper, meritorious church-work errand. The Girls' Friendly, or some such thing, sent Catherine to visit among others a girl named Mira Doremus. Mira was sixteen then, and she and her aunt had just come to the city. She is a great actress now, Mira, married to a foreigner with a title, her second husband, I think: but then she was merely a thin, wistful-looking child with hungry black eyes and a mop of incongruous light-brown hair. Nine years afterward Catherine told me about their first meeting, dwelling on the little details as a mother dwells on the things a dead child has done.

"She was sitting quite alone in a high green chair in the very middle of the room, like a little princess," she said. "She rose and took both my hands, and said in that wonderful voice of hers, 'So you are the Catherine they said I would love! I think they were right.' "

I do not know what Catherine answered. I don't believe she knows. But Catherine had met Romance.

Of all Mira's gifts the most subtle and wonderful is her capability of making you feel that to you, and you alone, she is most attuned. And you know that Catherine had never found anyone like herself in all of her life before. Can you imagine the stifling loneliness of it? And can you think what Mira seemed to Catherine? All the things they had told her were foolish, the things that were everything to her, Mira divined and echoed and made great. All the questionings and breakings of conventional idea and belief that Catherine had dreamed and wondered over secretly, Mira played with unafraid. And Mira, wrapped in that subtle quality, magnetism, charm, personality—call it what you will—exerted every scrap of power in her to hold Catherine. She loved her genuinely for awhile. She is still fond of her in a way, I think. Catherine is a very lovable person. She was even more lovable then, according to Mira. "A Gabriel Max Madonna with a touch of Brunhild," is Mira's description of what Catherine was at twenty. Mira always speaks in hyperbole—she sees things that way. Life is all Turner sunsets and Ibsen dramas to her. But Catherine at twenty must have been very lovely, for she is sweet-faced now. She had the coloring of apple-blossoms, Mira told me, and her fair hair was so heavy that it massed naturally around her face, like a halo. The "touch of Brunhild," the height and straightness, and boyish, austere impatience of shams and sentimentalisms and pettinesses—she has them still.

Some people cannot give all of themselves to anyone, even if they want to. Catherine has never been able to give except entirely. Such people as she always do throw down everything at once. They would be glad if their love were returned, but if it isn't—why, that doesn't stop them from giving. Mira, with her wonderful gift of seeming likeness of soul, drew out of Catherine, or was freely given, everything. Then she began to hurt Catherine as much as she could, to see how much power she had, and just how far Catherine would bear. I suppose power was a new plaything for her in those days, and she wanted to see what she could make it do.

She did everything to Catherine's soul that an ingenious mind, interested in proving its own power, could suggest. You know how people can hurt you when they know everything about you, and your least, most noble (which can be made most ridiculous) inward feelings. They have what Holmes calls the "back-door key" to your soul, and they can enter at will. The better you are, the larger-minded, the more forgiving, the happier hunting-ground there is for people with a fondness for soul-vivi-section. Mira knew that whatever she did to Catherine's feelings, for very loyalty's sake Catherine would pretend not to be hurt.

It may have been good for Catherine, in a way. I know that she thinks it was. Mira boasted to me once that she had "developed and strength-ened the range of Catherine's emotions." Doubtless she told the truth. She did make out of her a most wonderful instrument for the registering of fine shades of feeling. Like her predecessors in the molding of Catherine, she had fine material to work in. She had Catherine's nerves trained at one time to the thrilling, fine responsiveness of violin-strings, and—Mira played the violin. No one took what went on with any particular amount of seriousness. They were both so young, you see. By the time anyone noticed, and it took some years, it was too late to do anything.

By the time I knew the girls Catherine was beyond the most acute suffering-point, or was trained to a very wonderful stoicism. I think myself that the vibrations were deadened, spoiled by over-use. You can't suffer, even at the hands you love best, beyond a certain point.

It was at Mira's I met Catherine. I scarcely noticed her at first, under the spell as I was of Mira's slow, thrilling voice and passionate personal-ity. Gradually she became a real figure to me, the smiling blonde girl who was always in the background, smoothing down the sharp things Mira said and showing off the flattering ones. Something, finally, in her atti-tude, a certain determined lightness of manner at variance with a natu-ral placidity and dignity, attracted my attention sharply. Anywhere else I would have seen nothing incongruous, but at Mira's one was in a state of heightened mental tension which took note of morbidly small things— a sort of clairvoyance. Mira's atmosphere—well, someone described her once as a "mental cocktail," and it wasn't bad. You would spend a tense evening talking to her, and go home with mind and body keyed to the height of their powers, as if you'd been taking a drug. Indeed, next day you would be quite as exhausted as if the drug had been a physical reality.

The first time I saw anything real of Catherine was a night when Mira kept me too long to be able to get a train home. Catherine volunteered to put me up for the night. All the way back to her house, and for hours afterwards, we talked of Mira, how wonderful she was, what a living force——

"But she's—cruel, isn't she?" I asked timidly. I was very young, and not quite sure, as yet, how much one might speak of emotions. But I had to—emotions were what Mira exhaled. She played on your nerves, and deliberately woke for her own interest all those elemental feelings you had supposed were only in book-people—not you.

"Cruel?" said Catherine with her little laugh. "Yes, I suppose so, but don't you think she's worth it? She can give you—thrills. Thrills are all that's worth having—don't you think so?"

That was what Mira had done to her in four years.

We went on talking—talked late into the night. Both our tongues were loosened by the strong stimulant of Mira's personality. Catherine showed me, little by little, all the soul of her: the amazing loyalty, the honesty and innocence of purpose, the thwarted instincts of protection and motherhood—and the cruel havoc, too, that Mira had wrought. Mira had made Catherine so that her chief desire was for emotional excitement—"thrills." She had taught her to analyze herself as she analyzed others, and to find her greatest interest in people's feelings. It sounds over-strained, I know, but it reminded me of the superstition that if a vampire sucks your blood something of the vampire-nature is left in you. Mira had laid Catherine's soul out and dissected it till the girl herself learned to take an interest in the process. Mira could not kill the gentleness, nor the instinct of motherhood, the guardianship of anything weak or hurt, but she had taught Catherine, nevertheless, something which was a passionate, selfless sympathy, but which still watched your soul hungrily for signs of its workings—even while she helped it through some black place.

She was trained, too, to a curious scorn of men. Mira had the Brunhild-austerity of her to work on in the beginning, of course. The love and protectiveness that goes with the type Mira diverted to herself; the mating instinct, of no use to her, she tried to crush out. Mira's own attitude to men, at that stage of her development, was inevitable. She did not attract them, then; she alarmed them by oddness; so she hated them, and trained her devotees to hate them too. It was a self-defensive, automatic thing. You couldn't like a man and Mira at the same time. So Catherine crystallized Mira's mood of the time, and despised men with her whole innocent, serious mind.

The more you knew of Catherine the lovelier she was. Long after I had seen all that was necessary to conviction of Mira's temperamentalisms, Catherine and I were very close to each other. Mira's schooling had made her the ideal friend; I suppose she knew what not to do to the last iota. But she never spoke of herself, only of yourself—and Mira—things you were interested in—and Mira—music and books and pictures—and Mira. She talked wonderfully, wisely, with a tolerant sympathy and interest for everything, but Mira was the continuous overtone of it all. I don't mean that she spoke of her so much. It was, as well as I can describe it, that Mira was in the air when you were with Catherine, affecting your senses as vividly as the faint wood-violet scent Catherine always had on. She was a part of Catherine's life in the literal sense of the word.

Once Catherine tried to break the spell. It was after a very cruel scene with Mira, who was angry at someone else. She wasn't sufficiently sure of the other girl to act to her as she felt. So she summoned Catherine, late at night, and spent four solid hours wilfully wounding and insulting and humiliating her by every means in her knowledge, all in that wonderful, cello-like voice that Catherine loved so dearly. Catherine sat under it all silently. In the end she rose, dazed, and—if you can believe it—not resentful in the least; only hurt, hurt, hurt so badly that it was worse, she told me, than any physical pain she had ever known.

"I don't think we had better see each other any more," she managed to say in a low voice, rising to go away. Mira darted after her and caught her wrist hard.

"You'll be the first to crawl back," she said. "I may take you if you are very abject! Now, go!"

Catherine went home physically ill. It was a week before she ate or slept normally. After that she held no communication with Mira for a month. She sent back all her letters, and her maid answered the telephone and refused her to Mira about once a day. Catherine used to lie on her couch, she said, gripping its sides with both hands to keep from rising and taking the receiver herself and replying. But finally she fought herself to a point where she could think of Mira quietly, and with no desire to see her. If her mother had been willing to have her go away for awhile just then I think she could have got free enough to hold firm, for Mira's spell is a personal one to a great degree, weaker the farther away she is. But for some reason it was not convenient, and Catherine's mother would not let her go. Fascination and the power of personality were as ridiculous to the mother as a belief in ghosts. If Catherine's loyalty had permitted her to tell her mother some of the things Mira had said to her Mira would never have been allowed in the house again, I know. Unfortunately, those were just what Catherine would not tell.

The end of it was that Mira slipped into the house unchallenged one day, gained Catherine's sitting-room, and fled across the room into her arms.

"Oh, comfort me, comfort me!" she sobbed. "I've been so wicked and cruel to you that I can never be happy any more!"

Catherine, worn and blanched as she was with the struggle Mira had caused, sat up and closed both weak, protecting arms around Mira and— comforted her. The fetters were locked on again.

All this was a long time before Catherine met her lover. She was thirty when he came, and I was married. Mira was away. It was at my house they met—he was my cousin, Hugh Allan.

Catherine is not the kind that has many lovers. Even if she wanted them, she demands a very great deal, and stoops to none of the little alluringnesses men desire. Any lover of Catherine's would have to go all the way alone without help from her. But Hugh was ready and glad to go every inch of the way. He loved her as soon as he saw her. He did not, or I think not, see all the high, brave soul of her, under the sweetness and straightforwardness that were her most visible charm. But what man ever does love a woman for the things in her that are most loveworthy? Hugh cared for her so entirely that whatever she did or was or said was perfect because she did it, and would have been—will be—to the end of time. He was a man any girl would have been glad to marry, aside from the worldly part of it, for his sheer sweetness and straightforward, unself-conscious strength and charm. Any girl, that is, not blinded and drowned in Mira's ruthless fascination.

Hugh laid siege to Catherine as steadily and swiftly as if he had been one of the knights she used to dream about. Soon it seemed that he had won. I was very, very glad, but a little frightened. It seemed too good to be true—too happy an ending for anyone as strong to bear suffering as Catherine. They were so youthfully, carelessly happy—I never remembered being as light-hearted as they were. It was the most beautiful thing to see them going about together, Catherine flushed and serious and girlish, and Hugh watching her in the unmistakable lover-fashion. It was so new to Catherine to be petted, and have her feelings considered and her wishes watched for, that she must have felt bewildered. She bought pretty, fluffy clothes and did her hair to please Hugh, and for one little month she was a real, normal woman with a lover, and all the little vanities and foolishnesses and merriments that go to lover-time. She had been living so long on heights of strained emotion that this descent into the valleys must have been very wonderful to her. If any two people ever were brave and kind and merry, and absolutely fitted to make each other's happiness for a lifetime, those two were.

We met them one night in the lobby of a theater, after a musical comedy, talking nonsense to each other like a couple of children.

"She looks like a Christmas-card angel, doesn't she?" Hugh said fondly, looking down at her mischievously. I looked too, and smiled. She did indeed, tall and straight, and pink-cheeked with excitement, with her pretty yellow hair all curled, and her blue eyes laughing and childlike above the swansdown of her long white cape.

"I'm not an angel at *all!*" she protested, laughing and glancing up at him challenge-fashion. He bent and whispered something that made her flush and drop her eyes.

It was all such a poignant contrast to my first memory of Catherine, smiling and enduring behind Mira's chair in that little room full of tense emotion, that something came over me—a wave of second-sight, I've thought since.

"Oh, Hugh dear!" I said, "I do wish you'd marry her soon—tonight—this week! Marry each other quick, before anything happens to stop either of you from being happy!"

"It would be an adventure, at least!" laughed Hugh. "What do you say, Kitty—shall we take her and Ralph for witnesses, and go off and do as she says?"

He loved her as much as a man can, but I don't think he knew what he had achieved in winning her through the crystallized distaste for men that Mira had taught her. He was just as sure of her, naturally, as he was of sunrise.

"Oh, no, no!" said Catherine gaily. "What would happen to our lovely wedding and all the blue bridesmaids? We have all the rest of our lives to stay happy in."

"If Mira lets you," I said involuntarily.

The girl-look faded for a moment, and the old expression of devoted endurance crossed her face, followed by her little old Mira-laugh—not the childish mirth of girls with lovers.

"You always think Mira is so dreadful," she said. "She'll like Hugh almost as much as I do."

But it was only three days afterwards that Mira came back and the thing I had feared happened. I never knew much more than the brutal fact that Catherine broke off short with Hugh. Mira needed her to sit behind her chair, with the old look of pleasant, patient watchfulness on her face, I suppose. At any rate, there were two evenings alone with Mira—and Catherine was back under the spell. Cocaine or opium would have been as easy a thing to fight.

It was a long while since I had been near Mira, but I went straight to her then.

"How could you *dare* do what you did to Catherine? Do you know that you've spoiled her life and maybe Hugh's?" I cried out as she ran into the room, childish and vibrant and seductive as ever.

"Dare?" laughed Mira, lighting on a corner of the table like a butterfly. She always seemed poised for the moment, rather than seated like other people. "Don't be melodramatic, you foolish child! I haven't done anything to Catherine—the thing's ridiculous. Catherine doesn't really care for the man at all. She doesn't like men any more than I do. She was just amusing herself with him, I suppose. He's ridiculous, too—forgive me, dearest! And Catherine's a free agent—you know that perfectly well. You always talk as if I had her in my power, like a melodrama!"

It does seem impossible and melodramatic, one woman's complete power over another by sheer personal influence, and Mira knew it and acted on it in all her dealings with her satellites. She laughed at me, and then grew angry, and denied and mocked and laughed again—went through her series of moods artistically, and enjoyed herself very much. She knew there was nothing I could do, and I knew it, too.

Hugh fought hard, of course, but what could any man do against Mira's powers of darkness? Mira had mocked a little and appealed a little and cajoled a little—and the thing was done. Moreover, Catherine denied in all sincerity that Mira had any connection with what she had done. She was mistaken, she said—it was not right for her to marry—there were other things to do in the world—that was all. It would have been the same, she said and believed, if Mira had never existed.

Hugh went away, at last, out of the country. He made me promise before he went that I would send him word if ever Catherine expressed the least desire to see him. He is away still. I wish it hadn't been Hugh, of all people. Most men would not have kept on caring.

Catherine sat behind Mira's chair for two years more, smiling and comforting the girls when Mira hurt them too much. Then suddenly the natural, inevitable thing—the thing that none of us had ever thought of—happened. Catherine called me hurriedly over the telephone one morning.

"Mira's going to be married," she said breathlessly without preface. "*Married.* And…She always said marriage was dreadful and degrading…I thought she didn't like men…Isn't it—queer?"

Mira had taken Catherine from her lover. She had taken her from most of her friends. She had taken her youth, and deadened her capacity for the enjoyment of normal people and normal things. She had even taken her away from her God—that kind, concrete God, half Keats, half clergyman, whom Catherine used to go to for comfort when Mira hurt her first. She had put herself, Queen Mira, instead of all these. And now she was taking herself away.

Catherine's voice was steady, and she told the story almost brightly. Oh, she had learned stoicism well! "Isn't it—queer?" That was all.

"But she doesn't love him at all," she went on. I could see that there was a happiness to her in that last, forlorn comfort. "She is only marrying him because he is rich and can put her on the stage—you know Mira will make a wonderful actress. He is mad about her—you should see him!"

She was always so proud when anyone was mad about Mira.

There isn't very much more to it. Catherine was maid of honor at the wedding. It was a very beautiful wedding, and the man was undoubtedly mad about Mira, and she, in spite of her assurances to Catherine, was undoubtedly mad about him for the time. When they went away there was on his face, it seemed to me, Catherine's very set, bright smile, the mark Mira lays on her chief worshipper.

Nobody wanted Catherine any more, but it was too late for her to swing to normal again. The last breath of her girlhood had died when she gave up Hugh. She is—what is it they say of steel that has been permanently warped by electricity? "Depolarised" is the word, I think. Anyway, it describes what has happened to Catherine. There is the same set brightness about her that there was in Mira's day. She devotes a great deal of time to her mother, who likes waiting on. For interests, she amuses herself with little passing adorations of first one woman and then another. She laughs at anything you say about loving men or children. But then she laughs a little at everything. So did Hugo's Gwynplaine, you remember.

I don't mind what women do to *men*. It's a fair game, as old as Eve, and the balance has always been on men's side. But to take a great white soul like Catherine's and set it to playing pitiful little games in the dust with little souls not worth tuppence——

If it was Catherine's mind she'd hurt—but that's a clear, strong, straightforward thing, as it always was, and I've always understood that in any life hereafter your mind doesn't count much. It was the straight-standing, sweet soul of her, that might have been so great, that is crippled.

She has one pitiful comfort left, I know. I don't often see her now, but one afternoon we met by accident, and fell to talking what Catherine calls "insanities" in the old way. The talk swung round to reincarnation, and she said breathlessly and strongly, "Oh, but it's so—it must be so!"

I smiled.

"One likes to play with the idea," I said, "but, dear, you don't mean that you really hold to the belief, as your mother does to predestination?"

"I have to," she said. Then she caught herself up, and laughed a little in the old way, to make her words seem light. "Mira and I have an appointment under the walls of Babylon in a thousand years, you know—just we two!"

She laughed again, but I didn't dare to. I was afraid I would cry.

FARMHANDS

Mabel Dodge

THE first thing that Jerry was conscious of in the raw early morning was the wind howling past the house. It had howled so for a week past—day and night—day and night. It had hustled him up the long road to the house, late the night before on his way from the saloon. He shuddered at the sound and turned to the cement wall without opening his eyes. He had stumbled into the cellar in the dark, and fumbled his way to the old sofa in the washroom. He never trusted himself to climb all the stairs to the third story when he came home drunk in the night.

His clothes were gathered into hard lumps on his body and pressed against his shaking nervous flesh.

He wished he need not open his eyes and see all around him the terrible same things.

He had been ten years on the farm—ten years—winter and summer.

For ten years he had opened his eyes every day on the same things; the white farmhouse turning grey from the smoke of the passing trains below at the river edge, the barnyard with its cowhouse, the stalls for the horses, the pig pen, the chicken houses ... always the same—always backed by the ruin of the great cement haybarn, gaunt and empty, with its walls roofless to the sky, since it had been burned out fifty years ago.

Each year, though, it had seeemd to Jerry to be different, each winter more dreary, each summer more heavy to carry. And this made him go oftener to the village for drink to change his view of it. Oftener and oftener he had to get the drink now, to change his view of the Farm—to make him forget the plots.

Everyone, he thought, was plotting. He did what he could, and he never bothered anyone. Why couldn't they, then, leave him alone? Last night when he had come in, he had stumbled against a cardboard box in the passage in front of the door, and as he fell he had heard the bottles in it crash together and break. Who had put it there to catch his stumbling feet and throw him? He wouldn't have done a mean trick like that to nobody. . . .

The wind came around the corner with a roar and he felt it reach his disgusted body—chilling him.

With a terrible sinking in his spirit he opened his eyes and faced the Farm, and with the remnant of his sickened courage he got off the sofa and went out into the early chill morning.

Already the animals were moving—claiming him—calling him. They always claimed him—the animals—morning and night. Morning and night he felt their heavy call on him——their incessant, cold clamor.

Long successions of animals had passed and gone, over the last ten years. They were always the same. All cows were the same—all pigs—all fowls. They never let him be. He hated their heavy, cold, impatient eyes, and he felt sick as he answered their look. Their eyes were distant and cold and yet urgent upon him. He was indispensable to the animals, and yet he was nothing to them, nor they to him. So soon as he portioned out their food to them they turned their gaze away, and he was forgotten by them. He hated them still more when he was utterly forgotten by them.

He moved over the uneven cobble-stones of the barnyard and passed into the hollow, roofless haybarn. It was more aloof than the village church in its empty bareness. It would never have a roof on it again. It stood there so empty. It made Jerry know his own empty feeling. He felt the wind race around in it and shake his clothes on him. He felt the wind was at him.

He went out again and stood chewing on a wisp of hay as he looked over the fields in front of the farmhouse.

He felt his old dizziness come over him as he looked out over the plowed-up land. Plowed for corn—plowed for potatoes—plowed for vegetables—days of plowing more acres than had ever been plowed up in all the ten years he had been on the place. Why?

"I can't never cover it all," he mumbled. "I just can't get over that land." He felt weak and faint as he looked. Then the thought came to him that it had been done to him on purpose. It was just their meanness. He knew, now, what McCarty had meant when he had told him about plowing up more land.

McCarty came over from his own place and ran the Farm for the Boss. He came over often. He gave the orders. Then he went away.

When he had told Jerry to plow up that land he had come straight from a talk with the Boss.

"*She* says," said McCarty, jerking his thumb in the direction of the farmhouse, "we got to get out'a this land all there is in it, and from the look of her she means to get *more* out of it than there is in it," and he spat on the ground between his high boots.

He seemed to transfer to Jerry some of the hard, unrelenting purpose of the Boss. Jerry had felt her drive ever since she had come on to the place two years back, when she rented it from the Carsons. She had worked him harder than they had—she had driven him at a faster pace through his rounds on the farm. He had felt her hand heavy on him through the repeated visits from McCarty, who brought him her orders, and saw them carried out. He had seldom seen her in the barnyard—most often he saw her as she rode down the road in her motor. He had rarely had any talk with her, but always he felt her eyes on him through the windows of the farmhouse. He felt her driving him faster on his everlasting circle. And this plowing for more corn—more potatoes—it was just meant to get more out of him, too, than there is in him.

He wondered why he was marked out for all this, and why everyone plotted against him.

While Jerry wondered, his eyes fell on the new brooder standing near the barn. He saw that its cover lay half on the ground—one end wrenched off its hinge.

He went up to it and stood looking. Someone had done that on purpose.

He had left the cover of the brooder open and someone had turned it back and half wrenched it off to show him he had forgotten to close it.

He felt again a wave of sickness and dizziness and a sinking hatred of everything.

He picked up the new water feeder of the ducklings, and hurled it with the slam of the weak man, against the cement barn.

McCarty suddenly appeared in the doorway.

"Here you blamed ass! What's that you're doing? What's wrong with you? Drink again, hey? You want to lose your job, I guess. You want to look out. *She's* getting sick of your drinking. Now look at that brooder cover! Did you leave it open for the wind to wrench it off?"

The wind. All right, then—the wind was against him like everything else was.

He seemed to have lost his identity and his sense of being human. He was worked like the land was worked, for more than was in him…and the wind worked wrong to him as it worked wrong to the young saplings.

If he made a move to get out of this deep, dreary fatality of nature, he would lose his job.

His "job."

What was his job? Was it something good for anything that he should be threatened with losing it?

What if he did lose it?

His slow eyes moved across the plowed fields to the village.

The village meant the saloon for him.

Without his job he couldn't go to the saloon. Without the saloon he couldn't keep his job, for he couldn't go on seeing things as they were and do his work, yet if he drank to forget how things were he would lose the job.

He saw no way out of this. He knew he couldn't work without drinking or drink without working.

McCarty went on talking. "Now what I want to know is what's the meaning of that pile of manure being out there by the chicken roost with that old dead cat under it? The dog just unearthed it. What kind of work is it for you to be leaving that kind of thing around the barnyard? Haven't you any *pride* in your work? Don't you *care*—man?"

Jerry didn't answer him, but he dragged himself over to where the cat lay in the manure half protruding its ugliness, and he took it up on a shovel and carried it out to the field and buried it in the field.

The field was the new plowed field where the corn was to go. Then Jerry went to the kitchen for his breakfast.

He avoided the eye of the cook, for he suspected her of leaving empty bottles in the passage for him to trip over. It made him feel ashamed for her that she had done this.

He drank some coffee and ate a hunk of bread and his thoughts wandered over the fields to the village—the saloon.

What if he did let go and lose the "job"? What lay beyond? The world. What was the world? More barnyards full of cold watching animals? More plots? More heaps of forgotten refuse covering over dead cats? And the wind? And fields to plow? Or if not this, then thirst again—thirst—and hunger?

In the front part of the house the Boss was reading the morning paper.

There seemed to be a deep strong glowing in her. A strong energy was filling her.

She read out loud to the others in the room the phrases that moved her:

"For it shall come to be our privilege as well as our duty to arrogate to ourselves at this crisis in the struggle for democracy, the task of feeding the world."

HOURS WITH A REVIVALIST

Theodore Schroeder

O N the outside of the church, a revival was advertised. That tempted me, as it was designed to do. Recently I had attended a negro church, there witnessing the only revival I had seen since my boyhood. Except for a few meetings of the colored folk, many years had passed since I had been inside of a church. Perhaps I could get a new sensation. It occurred to me also that it would be interesting to compare the black man's and the white man's "spirituality." I had read several accounts of that "great awakening," the New England revival which is credited to Jonathan Edwards, and I had seen those extravagant performances duplicated under the stimulation of one of the tribe known as "the colored Billy Sunday." Now, I thought, I might see at a white man's Methodist church a repetition of this extraordinary exhibition. The meetings and the subsequent events, however, were so different from my anticipations that I am impelled to record the facts.

The church had a seating capacity approaching six hundred and the seats were mostly occupied. In the pulpit was a young man of perhaps 35 years of age, well built and over six feet tall. He had a large square face, rather characterless, I thought, set upon a large neck supported upon large, broad, square shoulders. He must have weighed nearly two hundred and fifty pounds. Reared in Podunk he would have become the ideal village blacksmith. In Milwaukee his build would have qualified him for the job of Rausschmeiser. A mother's sentimentalism and an education had probably combined to make him a Methodist parson. Education, without the mother, might have made him a country lawyer or a village doctor. By unconscious processes the subjection to the maternal dreams, or something similar, had impelled him to stay on the pulpiteering job, though with an evident conflict between intellectual attainment and emotional compulsion.

When pleading with the audience to come to the mourners' bench, it almost seemed to me at times as if he expected us to express an emotional appreciation of divine love just because he considered this a perfectly logical thing to do. Then again it was as though we should come forward merely as a personal favor to God, or as a matter of living up to somebody's conception of good manners. Nothing was said or done to induce the conviction, or stimulate the feeling, that it was of any great consequence *to us* either that we or he should accept God. It was as if it were all for God's sake. Doubtless he was quite unconscious of all this, probably because his impulses were neither strongly religious nor coordinated with the needs of his audience. Of course, the thought came to me that his religion had never acquired real meaning to him in the sense in which religion had meaning to Jonathan Edwards or to "the colored Billy Sunday."

In sermon and prayer he told us what fine fellows were God and Jesus. In fact he recommended them both very highly. Yet, while he bestowed much rhetorical flattery on God, there was never a fervent appeal for his help to sinners. It was as if the parson didn't need help, or perhaps, never having received any from God, had no confidence in the efficacy of prayer. This was all so contrary to what I had heard in boyhood, or had recently seen at negro revivals, that I marveled and became interested in observing more closely its effect upon others.

One might have gathered the impression that the parson really desired others to identify him with God's work so that, as an added means to greater self-exaltation, it was expedient for him to extol the master. In trying desperately to persuade himself that the Methodists' God is really omniscient and omnipotent, he succeeded only in assuring his audience that God was "worth while."

There was none of the confident assumption of one who knows that he has God on his side, and that therefore he can point the way for others, compelling their assent to the need of salvation, and belief in his authority to offer it. It would not have been different if confessedly the exhibition had been that of a man defending himself against his own doubts, not claiming to be a confidence-inspiring leader of other doubters.

He told us that "we *really* ought to do" this, and that "we hope" that, and that "we cannot afford to take the position" of some persons. He told us how faith in the son of God was "reported" to have saved others but gave no assurance that he considered himself saved. He told us how the Bible "reports" what Christ is said to have done for the sinning woman 2,000 years ago, but expressed no confidence in any such service rendered in more recent times. He had many sorrows over the demons of lust, of drink, of covetousness, cards and dancing, but not a word of rebuke for the sin of unbelief, blasphemy, or hypocrisy.

In short, he spake not as one with authority, but rather as a hired man, too modest or too indifferent to use the personal pronoun, or to claim the authority of a true believer who has felt the "inspiration of the Holy Ghost." Once he half closed his eyes as he spoke in slow measure. I felt that he was more concerned to have us believe in *his* earnestness and his nearness to God than that we ourselves should become earnest, as seekers after God. Although occasionally he pulled the tremulo stop to his voice, and once or twice evinced great lung power on the basso profundo, yet it all seemed dead. The exhortation was drawing to a close and none had come to the mourners' bench.

On the first evening of my attendance he had especially requested the parents and teachers to see that the Sunday School pupils should come. For once he warmed up in good form. Manifestly he really and truly felt that religion was of great importance to children. Yet no children came to the mourners' bench. The revival season of a month was about to close, and out of the large audience in regular attendance during the whole month, only about a score had consecrated themselves to God. With pitiful humility he begged us to come forward, but no one moved. In deepest pleading tones he concluded with: "I need your prayers. Don't forget *me*." He mopped his massive brow, and the choir began its solemn function. This was Friday, the last night of the revival season. The next Sunday morning service would be the last of the present series of invitations to accept salvation. Then would come baptisms and receptions into the church.

I waited at the door for the pastor to emerge. Many detained him, as if to show their friendliness or even silently to express their apologies for disappointing him. At last he came out, seeming pleased that I wished to walk and talk with him. Evidently he had derived some comfort from what others had said to him on his way out. Wondering if I would prove a painful antidote, I proceeded directly to my object.

In reply to my first question he admitted his disappointment as to the fruits of his revival effort. When I asked him how he accounted for his failure, he spoke hesitatingly and half absent-mindedly of the power of evil and Satan, the stiffneckedness and pride of the people, and other such religious commonplaces. I expressed doubt as to this being the explanation of his failure, and then he turned my question back upon me. It was up to me, and I delivered myself about as follows:

It seemed to me that his audience was a fair average of religious audiences, just such an audience as Jonathan Edwards or the Rev. Charles G. Finney or Moody and Sankey would have got great results from. More than half were women over 45 years of age with sad and troubled faces. Roughly estimated, fifteen per cent were young women under 23 years of age; there were a few old men and some young men. Aside from the choir members and the ushers, there were scarcely ten vigorous, contented, healthy-appearing persons of middle age in the entire crowd. Manifestly these troubled souls were humble and distressed, and came there for help and consolation. They did not receive the spiritual uplift which they needed and desired. Manifestly also their craving for the "true spirit" and their conscious need of salvation, were as great as in any average gathering of Methodists. A few nights back, when all were waiting for some "hungry spirit" to go to the mourners' bench, an old man had arisen near the right front and in a few vehement sentences had appealed to sinners to repent and accept Jesus. Twenty-five *amens* had responded to his appealing voice. I said to the pastor: "Great possibilities were manifested in this little outburst of enthusiasm, which you never once elicited. Had your entire sermon been shaped and delivered with the fervid spirit of that old man, I believe you would have had abundant results for your effort. When you think upon this, don't you see that after all this was an average audience 'ripe for the harvest' "?

The parson hesitated a moment and then slowly said: "Well, I don't know but that you are right."

I persisted in my quest: "If the cause of failure in this revival is not in the special character of your audiences, then where are we to look for an explanation?" After a pause he said: "I don't know, I wish you would tell me what you think about it."

I reminded him that I was a stranger and therefore might not be pardoned for saying what an intimate friend might take a chance upon. He assured me, however, that he was much concerned and really would like some light upon the situation, and he thought he could stand anything I might be inclined to say. I accepted the invitation.

"The first evenings of my attendance I studied the audience and your effect upon them." So I began. "When I saw that the effects were negligible, I proceeded to study you. I began by listening to what you did not say. During my attendance upon your meetings you never made one statement about salvation on the faith of your own religious experiences. You quoted St. Paul or Jesus, just as one might quote Wilson or Roosevelt. You added nothing of your personal religious experience by way of reinforcement or to impress us with the value of your authorities. So impersonal was your discourse, even in form, that a mere agnostic could have delivered your sermon without doing much violence to his convictions. He too, could say 'the apostle Paul informs us' or, 'Jesus is reported to have said' and under his breath he might have added: 'What of it?' "

Then I commented upon his want of zeal and enthusiasm. I pointed out that his hymns were all like dirges, when they should have been of the rousing, thumping, rhythmic, "Onward Christian Soldier" sort, if they were meant to aid the revival spirit. The parson evidently was not selecting his music, any more than his sermon, with a conscious view to the emotional craving of his audience. All was too manifestly the unconscious choice of a morose temperament, probably made so by emotional conflicts within. If this conflict concerned doubt as to his efficiency or fitness for the preacher's task it might explain much of his conduct. Thus the character of his sermons might be determined by the unconscious urge to find rationalistic justification by a special plea for his presence in the pulpit. This same relative obsession with the internal conflict may have compelled him to ignore the emotional needs and "spiritual hunger" of his audience. I expatiated on these psychological aspects of his character and advised him to study his half-conscious and unexpressed moods, to discover if he might not be much happier outside the pulpit and church. He protested mildly against my conclusion and thanked me for my frankness. We had reached his home and now said "good night."

On Sunday morning, I went to the church to see if my talk had had any effect. After the service I again waited at the door and asked the parson if he would allow me to walk home with him.

He really seemed pleased that I had been there. Perhaps he thought that he had redeemed himself in my estimation. As soon as we had extricated ourselves from the crowd, he asked me with an air of confidence what I thought of the sermon. I told him that I concluded that I had irritated and stimulated him. He admitted that I had done him some good in making him more conscious of his privileges and duty.

"Yes," I said. "In the substance of your sermon you. were nearer right with God. Also you put a little more ginger into it than formerly. But"—I continued—"there were no newcomers to the mourners' bench, so evidently you were no nearer right with your audience than before. Perhaps you were preaching at me and again forgetting the needs of the great crowd. Perhaps you were making a new kind of defense for your own doubt, instead of focusing your attention upon the process of entrancing others. Where formerly you were defending yourself to yourself, today you seemed to be defending yourself to me. Intellectually and emotionally I am very unlike your audience and so once more your effort was inefficient in answering to *their* spiritual needs."

He demurred but could give no better explanation of his failure to induce anyone to "hit the trail." (This phrase of the Rev. Billy Sunday reminds me that my parson was one of a committee to invite the Rev. Billy to come to his city to revive the unregenerate. Incidentally the parson had expressed to me some disapproval of the Rev. Billy's methods, but thought that on the whole his large results were an ample justification.) I returned to my diagnosis of his troubles. I reminded him that in this sermon he had made two emphatic statements on his own responsibility. After the first he had paused a moment and then earnestly and deliberately said to the congregation: "And—this—is—not—mere—cant—but—is—said—out—of—the—fullness—of—my—own—heart." I asked him to focus his attention for a moment upon the probable effect of this statement upon his congregation, to estimate how many of them might have experienced a mild shock which, if it had become conscious and articulate, might have found expression in the question: "I wonder why the parson thought it necessary to defend his sincerity!"

He silently nodded his assent, showing me that he saw the point. Furthermore, he seemed more interested than offended, and this gave me courage to proceed with my efforts to help the man to a better understanding of his own psychology and the possible solving of a conflict which after all was largely far below the surface of consciousness. Had the parson been a conscious hypocrite he could not possibly have maintained a calm interest through the criticisms which I am reporting in condensed form. He was honestly interested in the self-revelation, just as he was honestly unconscious of the mental and emotional processes involved in his religious conflict. I believe he was quite unaware that he possessed a minimum of what I might call the differential essence of religion, which is a subjective experience. My parson had only an objectively derived conviction about certain theological formulas.

I proceeded thus: "When making the second statement on your own responsibility, your eyes unconsciously wandered over toward me, and when your gaze met mine you stuttered. I have been taught to believe that this signifies that upon seeing me your subconscious doubt about the statement you were then making was crowding toward the surface, for recognition and expression. In other words at that precise moment you were desperately near to a consciousness of your internal conflict. The stuttering was the product of an unconscious automatic effort to get time in which to solve your conflict, to dispel your doubt, and decide what was really true for you. In other words, that stutter, in the light of our prior conversation, convinced me that you are not fully at peace with yourself in the matter of your preaching."

I ignored another mild protest and continued my analysis by reminding him that in his opening prayer he had uttered a fervent appeal for the skeptics, telling God that perhaps during the past week some in that very congregation had been grieved and perplexed by their doubts and fears. I suggested that it seemed to me as though he had in mind his own doubts, perplexities and fears, and that he was really uttering that prayer for himself and not for the congregation.

Here came another protest, with the explanation that a minister always has poured into his ears the troubles of those who are sad and depressed, that he thought such experiences adequately accounted for the prayer, and that therefore my inference was unjust. I ignored the fact that even now he did not claim to have had any specific tale of doubt poured into his ears during the past week and that probably he was only attempting an intellectualized mode of suggesting to me an objective fact, the existence of which his conscience would not allow him to assert positively.

Instead I proceeded as follows: "Allow me to tell you another reason why your explanation does not explain. In your opening prayer you knelt on your left knee. Your right knee supported your right elbow, while your right hand covered your face from the eyes down. Your left forearm rested on the pulpit. Your left hand hung unsupported over the front of the Bible. In your prayer you implored the Almighty to restore peace in Europe. Here your voice was calm and your brow placid and the disengaged hand hung lifelessly. When you reached that part of your prayer where you implored God to aid doubters your brow was wrinkled, your voice grew more tense, and the left hand was raised almost to a straight line with your forearm and opened and closed several times, convulsively clutching at the atmosphere. These changes in face, voice, and hand evidenced an excitement within which did not exist when you prayed for peace in Europe, where perhaps more than a hundred thousand men had been killed or maimed during the week. If the inner excitement had been objectively conditioned, then it seems inevitable that it should have been more conspicuous over the war-slaughter of many who had not yet accepted salvation, than over two or three doubting Thomases who had told you of their troubles during the week. Only your personal afflictions are likely to outweigh the sorrows of the war. Therefore it seems to me that the excitement, unconsciously manifested, did not originate in other people's troubles but was occasioned by your own half-conscious conflicts and doubts."

I saw that this struck home. Then I tried to show him how to deal with such a conflict by allowing himself to become more conscious of its submerged elements and then to resolve the conflict by working toward a decision of it on the basis of its objective factors.

By this time we had reached the parson's residence. I had never been censorious in my manner, had never thought, felt, or implied any reproach. I had never discussed the truth or falsity of any tenet of his religion. I contented myself with trying to illuminate his understanding as to his own psychology, the behavior of the forces within himself. I was really trying to help the man, and he seemed equally willing to look squarely in the face his subconscious impulses and his conflicts. Hence there was never a moment of friction, never a particle of resentment on his part. Had he been a conscious hypocrite he would scarcely have been able to listen calmly. His conscious desires were really functioning on a pretty high evolutionary level and his desire to know the truth, even about his own emotions, was strong enough to eliminate the aversion which is often felt by less highly evolved persons. Quite in consonance with this estimate of him, he invited me to have Sunday dinner with him. I accepted.

After dinner the psychological study was resumed in his library. We covered a wide range but finally got back to his failure as a revivalist when he asked me what he could do to increase his efficiency in that part of his work. He insisted that he wanted to know the truth and that I might feel secure in speaking frankly. So I went on as follows:

"Those elderly women of your congregation showed in their sad faces the disappointments of a misspent life, disappointments produced by and in turn accentuating emotional conflicts. According to that school of psychologists whose theories are most convincing to me I quite believe that practically all of these emotional conflicts have their origin in disturbed sexual emotions. In short, we all have sexual desires, phantasies or experiences, which are more or less shameful secrets with us. Just as the feeling of shame is great, its conflict with desire is intense and our resulting anxiety keen. This anxiety about sexual sinning and suppressed desire, or unintelligent erotic expression, is the condition the revivalist must accept if he wishes to succeed. So then, your task is one of playing upon the guilty consciences of these disappointed older people, these adolescent victims of sex-suppression, who have not yet lost all the hope of realizing their desire. Preach an insinuating sermon on the sins of the flesh, until every suppressed desire, every shameful experience, has become a vivid, conscious phantasy. Then portray the penalty of these sins in terms of eternal torment amid the lurid gloom of hell. Above all things make the picture graphic and in swift, loud, excited speech suggest the agonizing shrieks of the damned, until the hearers' guilty imaginations are filled with pictures of themselves crying aloud in pain, and writhing amid loathsome fumes of fire and brimstone; until they can feel the very flames already consuming their clothes and scorching their limbs, until they actually cry aloud in agony over their own degradation. In this way you will induce 'the conviction of sin,' which the church recognizes as the first step toward salvation. After that will come the 'change of heart.'

"Then tell these love-sick sinners of the infinite love of God, who sent his only begotten son to redeem a sinning world. Picture him on the cross, his naked limbs exposed to the scoffers' gaze, with the bleeding side and sad, sweet, forgiving face of a near adolescent or early middle-aged divine man, in whom alone love is guiltless. When this portrait of the sweet agony of the divine lover has been so drawn as to create upon their already sensitized erotic imagination a correspondingly vivid phantasy almost as clear and insistent as would be the living presence, then woo them with mellow pleading and cooing voice and with outstretched hands ask them to embrace the gospel by coming to the loving arms of Jesus and accepting his gracious pardon and salvation without price, though purchased by his precious blood.—When you can do that efficiently, they will come to the mourners' bench even over the tops of the seats. Don't you think so?"

I had put considerable life into my narrative of the revival process. I now paused for a reply. Presently he said: "But I don't know that I am willing to do that." This sentence, in the light of what had preceded, tells the whole story of the decline in the influence of evangelical religion.

What, then, is the trouble with our revival preacher and with other preachers? They have been too well educated. Without knowing it they have more or less formed the habit of checking the intellectualization of their feelings by the use of at least a portion of the secular ideal. In other words our revivalist possessed theological opinions derived he knew not whence which he sought to justify by a more or less crude application of the scientific method. His audience had no appetite for his rationalistic processes, and he had outgrown the capacity for playing rag-time on their emotions. Therefore, he was inefficient and the audience largely disappointed. A Billy Sunday, black or white, is still in that backward state of development where he can successfully make the emotional appeal to those whose development is also arrested, mentally.

I feel quite certain that my revivalist had no conscious lack of faith in his creed, but manifestly it had relatively small positive value for him. His difficulty was not over credal formulas, because these are always subject to an interpretation that is quite consistent with the individual's other intellectual attainments. Instead of being concerned with the end product of his thinking, the difficulties had more to do with his feeling attitude toward those end products and toward the underlying intellectual methods by which these formulas are attained. By the unconscious effects of conscious educational effort this parson had been habituated to intellectual methods that incapacitated him for efficient work as a revivalist. His intellectual self-respect had come into conflict with his desire for efficiency, in a field where untrained or hysterical emotions are everything and calm intellectual processes, acting in conscious relations with objectives, are as nothing. The Rev. Billy Sunday and his negro imitators are more efficient because they are free from the handicap of a better intellectual development.

TWILIGHT OF IDOLS

Randolph Bourne

WHERE are the seeds of American promise? Man cannot live by politics alone, and it is small cheer that our best intellects are caught in the political current and see only the hope that America will find her soul in the remaking of the world. If William James were alive would he be accepting the war-situation so easily and complacently? Would he be chiding the over-stimulated intelligence of peace-loving idealists, and excommunicating from the ranks of liberal progress the pitiful remnant of those who struggle "above the battle?" I like to think that his gallant spirit would have called for a war to be gallantly played, with insistent care for democratic values at home, and unequivocal alliance with democratic elements abroad for a peace that should promise more than a mere union of benevolent imperialisms. I think of James now because the recent articles of John Dewey's on the war suggest a slackening in his thought for our guidance and stir, and the inadequacy of his pragmatism as a philosophy of life in this emergency. Whether James would have given us just that note of spiritual adventure which would make the national enterprise seem creative for an American future,—this we can never know. But surely that philosophy of Dewey's which we had been following so uncritically for so long, breaks down almost noisily when it is used to grind out interpretation for the present crisis. These articles on "Conscience and Compulsion," "The Future of Pacifism," "What America Will Fight For," "Conscription of Thought," which *The New Republic* has been printing, seem to me to be a little off-color. A philosopher who senses so little the sinister forces of war, who is so much more concerned over the excesses of the pacifists than over the excesses of military policy, who can feel only amusement at the idea that any one should try to conscript thought, who assumes that the war-technique can be used without trailing along with it the mob-fanaticisms, the injustices and hatreds, that are organically bound up with it, is speaking to another element of the younger intelligentsia than that to which I belong. Evidently the attitudes which war calls out are fiercer and more incalculable than Professor Dewey is accustomed to take into his hopeful and intelligent imagination, and the pragmatist mind, in trying to adjust itself to them, gives the air of grappling, like the pioneer who challenges the arid plains, with a power too big for it. It is not an arena of creative intelligence our country's mind is now, but of mob-psychology. The soldiers who tried to lynch Max Eastman showed that current patriotism is not a product of the will to remake the world. The luxuriant releases of explosive hatred for which peace apparently gives far too little scope cannot be wooed by sweet reasonableness, nor can they be the raw material for the creation of rare liberal political structures. All that can be done is to try to keep your country out of situations where such expressive releases occur. If you have willed the situation, however, or accepted it as inevitable, it is fatuous to protest against the gay debauch of hatred and fear and swagger that must mount and mount, until the heady and virulent poison of war shall have created its own anti-toxin of ruin and disillusionment. To talk as if war were anything else than such a poison is to show that your philosophy has never been confronted with the pathless and the inexorable, and that, only dimly feeling the change, it goes ahead acting as if it had not got out of its depth. Only a lack of practice with a world of human nature so raw-nerved, irrational, uncreative, as an America at war was bound to show itself to be, can account for the singular unsatisfactoriness of these later utterances of Dewey. He did have one moment of hesitation just before the war began, when the war and its external purposes and unifying power seemed the small thing beside that internal adventure which should find our American promise. But that perspective has now disappeared, and one finds Dewey now untainted by skepticism as to our being about a business to which all our idealism should rally. That failure to get guaranties that this country's efforts would obligate the Allies to a democratic world-order Dewey blames on the defection of the pacifists, and then somehow manages to get himself into a "we" who "romantically," as he says, forewent this crucial link of our strategy. Does this easy identification of himself with undemocratically-controlled foreign policy mean that a country is democratic when it accepts what its government does, or that war has a narcotic effect on the pragmatic mind? For Dewey somehow retains his sense of being in the controlling class, and ignores those anxious questions of democrats who have been his disciples but are now resenters of the war.

What I come to is a sense of suddenly being left in the lurch, of suddenly finding that a philosophy upon which I had relied to carry us through no longer works. I find the contrast between the idea that creative intelligence has free functioning in wartime, and the facts of the inexorable situation, too glaring. The contrast between what liberals ought to be doing and saying if democratic values are to be conserved, and what the real forces are imposing upon them, strikes too sternly on my intellectual senses. I should prefer some philosophy of War as the grim and terrible cleanser to this optimism-haunted mood that continues unweariedly to suggest that all can yet be made to work for good in a mad and half-destroyed world. I wonder if James, in the face of such disaster, would not have abandoned his "moral equivalent of war" for an "immoral equivalent" which, in swift and periodic saturnalia, would have acted as vaccination against the sure pestilence of war.

II

Dewey's philosophy is inspiring enough for a society at peace, prosperous and with a fund of progressive good-will. It is a philosophy of hope, of clear-sighted comprehension of materials and means. Where institutions are at all malleable, it is the only clue for improvement. It is scientific method applied to "uplift." But this careful adaptation of means to desired ends, this experimental working out of control over brute forces and dead matter in the interests of communal life, depends on a store of rationality, and is effective only where there is strong desire for progress. It is precisely the school, the institution to which Dewey's philosophy was first applied, that is of all our institutions the most malleable. And it is the will to educate that has seemed, in these days, among all our social attitudes the most rationally motivated. It was education, and almost education alone, that seemed susceptible to the steady pressure of an "instrumental" philosophy. Intelligence really seemed about to come into conscious control of an institution, and that one the most potent in moulding the attitudes needed for a civilized society and the aptitudes needed for the happiness of the individual.

For both our revolutionary conceptions of what education means, and for the intellectual strategy of its approach, this country is immeasurably indebted to the influence of Professor Dewey's philosophy. With these ideas sincerely felt, a rational nation would have chosen education as its national enterprise. Into this it would have thrown its energy though the heavens fell and the earth rocked around it. But the nation did not use its isolation from the conflict to educate itself. It fretted for three years and then let war, not education, be chosen, at the almost unanimous behest of our intellectual class, from motives alien to our cultural needs, and for political ends alien to the happiness of the individual. But nations, of course, are not rational entities, and they act within their most irrational rights when they accept war as the most important thing the nation can do in the face of metaphysical menaces of imperial prestige. What concerns us here is the relative ease with which the pragmatist intellectuals, with Professor Dewey at the head, have moved out their philosophy, bag and baggage, from education to war. So abrupt a change in the direction of the national enterprise, one would have expected to cause more emotion, to demand more apologetics. His optimism may have told Professor Dewey that war would not materially demoralize our growth—would, perhaps, after all, be but an incident in the nation's life—but it is not easy to see how, as we skate toward the bankruptcy of war-billions, there will be resources available for educational enterprise that does not contribute directly to the war-technique. Neither is any passion for growth, for creative mastery, going to flourish among the host of militaristic values and new tastes for power that are springing up like poisonous mushrooms on every hand.

How could the pragmatist mind accept war without more violent protest, without a greater wrench? Either Professor Dewey and his friends felt that the forces were too strong for them, that the war had to be, and it was better to take it up intelligently than to drift blindly in;

or else they really expected a gallant war, conducted with jealous regard for democratic values at home and a captivating vision of international democracy as the end of all the toil and pain. If their motive was the first, they would seem to have reduced the scope of possible control of events to the vanishing point. If the war is too strong for you to prevent, how is it going to be weak enough for you to control and mould to your liberal purposes? And if their motive was to shape the war firmly for good, they seem to have seriously miscalculated the fierce urgencies of it. Are they to be content, as the materialization of their hopes, with a doubtful League of Nations and the suppression of the I. W. W.? Yet the numbing power of the war-situation seems to have kept them from realizing what has happened to their philosophy. The betrayal of their first hopes has certainly not discouraged them. But neither has it roused them to a more energetic expression of the forces through which they intend to realize them. I search Professor Dewey's articles in vain for clues as to the specific working-out of our democratic desires, either nationally or internationally, either in the present or in the reconstruction after the war. No programme is suggested, nor is there feeling for present vague popular movements and revolts. Rather are the latter chided, for their own vagueness and impracticalities. Similarly, with the other prophets of instrumentalism who accompany Dewey into the war, democracy remains an unanalyzed term, useful as a call to battle, but not an intellectual tool, turning up fresh sod for the changing future. Is it the political democracy of a plutocratic America that we are fighting for, or is it the social democracy of the new Russia? Which do our rulers really fear more, the menace of Imperial Germany, or the liberating influence of a socialist Russia? In the application of their philosophy to politics, our pragmatists are sliding over this crucial question of ends. Dewey says our ends must be intelligently international rather than chauvinistic. But this gets us little distance along our way.

In this difficult time the light that has been in liberals and radicals has become darkness. If radicals spend their time holding conventions to attest their loyalty and stamp out the "enemies within," they do not spend it in breaking intellectual paths, or giving us shining ideas to which we can attach our faith and conscience. The spiritual apathy from which the more naive of us suffer, and which the others are so busy fighting, arises largely from sheer default of a clear vision that would melt it away. Let the motley crew of exsocialists, and labor radicals, and liberals, and pragmatist philosophers, who have united for the prosecution of the war, present a coherent and convincing democratic programme, and they will no longer be confronted with the skepticism of the conscientious and the impossibilist. But when the emphasis is on technical organization, rather than organization of ideas, on strategy rather than desires, one begins to suspect that no programme is presented because they have none to present. This burrowing into war-technique hides the void where a democratic philosophy should be. Our intellectuals consort with war-boards in order to keep their minds off the question what the slow masses of the people are really desiring, or toward what the best hope of the country really drives. Similarly the blaze of patriotism on the part of the radicals serves the purpose of concealing the feebleness of their intellectual light.

Is the answer that clear formulation of democratic ends must be postponed until victory in the war is attained? But to make this answer is to surrender the entire case. For the support of the war by radicals, realists, pragmatists, is due—or so they say—to the fact that the war is not only saving the cause of democracy, but is immensely accelerating its progress. Well, what are those gains? How are they to be conserved? What do they lead to? How can we further them? Into what large idea of society do they group? To ignore these questions, and think only of the war-technique and its accompanying devotions, is to undermine the foundations of these people's own faith.

A policy of "win the war first" must be, for the radical, a policy of intellectual suicide. Their support of the war throws upon them the responsibility of showing inch by inch the democratic gains, and of laying out a charter of specific hopes. Otherwise they confess that they are impotent and that the war is submerging their expectations, or that they are not genuinely imaginative and offer little promise for future leadership.

III

It may seem unfair to group Professor Dewey with Mr. Spargo and Mr. Gompers, Mr. A. M. Simons, and the Vigilantes. I do so only because in their acceptance of the war, they are all living out that popular American "instrumental" philosophy which Professor Dewey has formulated in such convincing and fascinating terms. On an infinitely more intelligent plane, he is yet one with them in his confidence that the war is motivated by democratic ends and is being made to serve them. A high mood of confidence and self-righteousness moves them all, a keen sense of control over events that makes them eligible to discipleship under Professor Dewey's philosophy. They are all hostile to impossibilism, to apathy, to any attitude that is not a cheerful and brisk setting to work to use the emergency to consolidate the gains of democracy. Not, Is it being used? but, Let us make a flutter about using it! This unanimity of mood puts the resenter of war out of the arena. But he can still seek to explain why this philosophy which has no place for the inexorable should have adjusted itself so easily to the inexorable of war, and why, although a philosophy of the creative intelligence in using means toward ends, it should show itself so singularly impoverished in its present supply of democratic values.

What is the matter with the philosophy? One has a sense of having come to a sudden, short stop at the end of an intellectual era. In the crisis, this philosophy of intelligent control just does not measure up to our needs. What is the root of this inadequacy that is felt so keenly by our restless minds? Van Wyck Brooks has pointed out searchingly the lack of poetic vision in our pragmatist "awakeners." Is there something in these realistic attitudes that works actually against poetic vision, against concern for the quality of life as above machinery of life? Apparently there is. The war has revealed a younger intelligentsia, trained up in the pragmatic dispensation, immensely ready for the executive ordering of events, pitifully unprepared for the intellectual interpretation or the idealistic focussing of ends. The young men in Belgium, the officers' training corps, the young men being sucked into the councils at Washington and into war-organization everywhere, have among them a definite element, upon whom Dewey, as veteran philosopher, might well bestow a papal blessing. They have absorbed the secret of scientific method as applied to political administration. They are liberal, enlightened, aware. They are touched with creative intelligence toward the solution of political and industrial problems. They are a wholly new force in American life, the product of the swing in the colleges from a training that emphasized classical studies to one that emphasized political and economic values. Practically all this element, one would say, is lined up in service of the war-technique. There seems to have been a peculiar congeniality between the war and these men. It is as if the war and they had been waiting for each other. One wonders what scope they would have had for their intelligence without it. Probably most of them would have gone into industry and devoted themselves to sane reorganization schemes. What is significant is that it is the technical side of the war that appeals to them, not the interpretative or political side. The formulation of values and ideals, the production of articulate and suggestive thinking, had not, in their education, kept pace, to any extent whatever, with their technical aptitude. The result is that the field of intellectual formulation is very poorly manned by this younger intelligentsia. While they organize the war, formulation of opinion is left largely in the hands of professional patriots, sensational editors, archaic radicals. The intellectual work of this younger intelligentsia is done by the sedition-hunting Vigilantes, and by the saving remnant of older liberals. It is true, Dewey calls for a more attentive formulation of war-purposes and ideas, but he calls largely to deaf ears. His disciples have learned all too literally the instrumental attitude toward life, and, being immensely intelligent and energetic, they are making themselves efficient instruments of the war-technique, accepting with little question the ends as announced from above. That those ends are largely negative does not concern them, because they have never learned not to subordinate idea to technique. Their education has not given them a coherent system of large ideas, or a feeling for democratic goals. They have, in short, no clear philosophy of life except that of intelligent service, the admirable adaptation of means to ends. They are vague as to what kind of a society they want, or what kind of society America needs, but they are equipped with all the administrative attitudes and talents necessary to attain it.

To those of us who have taken Dewey's philosophy almost as our American religion, it never occurred that values could be subordinated to technique. We were instrumentalists, but we had our private utopias so clearly before our minds that the means fell always into its place as contributory. And Dewey, of course, always meant his philosophy, when taken as a philosophy of life, to start with values. But there was always that unhappy ambiguity in his doctrine as to just how values were created, and it became easier and easier to assume that just any growth was justified and almost any activity valuable so long as it achieved ends. The American, in living out this philosophy, has habitually confused results with product, and been content with getting somewhere without asking too closely whether it was the desirable place to get. It is now becoming plain that unless you start with the vividest kind of poetic vision, your instrumentalism is likely to land you just where it has landed this younger intelligentsia which is so happily and busily engaged in the national enterprise of war. You must have your vision and you must have your technique. The practical effect of Dewey's philosophy has evidently been to develop the sense of the latter at the expense of the former. Though he himself would develop them together, even in him there seems to be a flagging of values, under the influence of war. *The New Republic* honorably clamors for the Allies to subordinate military strategy to political ends, technique to democratic values. But war always undermines values. It is the outstanding lesson of the whole war that statesmen cannot be trusted to get this perspective right, that their only motto is, first to win and then grab what they can. The struggle against this statesmanlike animus must be a losing one as long as we have not very clear and very determined and very revolutionary democratic ideas and programmes to challenge them with. The trouble with our situation is not only that values have been generally ignored in favor of technique, but that those who have struggled to keep values foremost, have been too bloodless and too near-sighted in their vision. The defect of any philosophy of "adaptation" or "adjustment," even when it means adjustment to changing, living experience, is that there is no provision for thought or experience getting beyond itself. If your ideal is to be adjustment to your situation, in radiant co-operation with reality, then your success is likely to be just that and no more. You never transcend anything. You grow, but your spirit never jumps out of your skin to go on wild adventures. If your policy as a publicist reformer is to take what you can get, you are likely to find that you get something less than you should be willing to take. Italy in the settlement is said to be demanding one hundred in order to get twenty, and this machiavellian principle might well be adopted by the radical. Vision must constantly outshoot technique, opportunist efforts usually achieve less even than what seemed obviously possible. An impossibilist élan that appeals to desire will often carry further. A philosophy of adjustment will not even make for adjustment. If you try merely to "meet" situations as they come, you will not even meet them. Instead you will only pile up behind you deficits and arrears that will some day bankrupt you.

We are in the war because an American Government practised a philosophy of adjustment, and an instrumentalism for minor ends, instead of creating new values and setting at once a large standard to which the nations might repair. An intellectual attitude of mere adjustment, of mere use of the creative intelligence to make your progress, must end in caution, regression, and a virtual failure to effect even that change which you so clear-sightedly and desirously see. This is the root of our dissatisfaction with much of the current political and social realism that is preached to us. It has everything good and wise except the obstreperous vision that would drive and draw all men into it.

IV

The working-out of this American philosophy in our intellectual life then has meant an exaggerated emphasis on the mechanics of life at the expense of the quality of living. We suffer from a real shortage of spiritual values. A philosophy that worked when we were trying to get that material foundation for American life in which more impassioned living could flourish no longer works when we are faced with inexorable disaster and the hysterias of the mob. The note of complacency which we detect in the current expressions of this philosophy has a bad taste. The congruous note for the situation would seem to be, on the contrary, that of robust desperation,—a desperation that shall rage and struggle until new values come out of the travail, and we see some glimmering of our democratic way. In the creation of these new values, we may expect the old philosophy, the old radicalism, to be helpless. It has found a perfectly definite level, and there is no reason to think that it will not remain there. Its flowering appears in the technical organization of the war by an earnest group of young liberals, who direct their course by an opportunist programme of State-socialism at home and a league of benevolently-imperialistic nations abroad. At their best they can give us a government by prudent, enlightened college men instead of by politicians. At their best, they can abolish war by making everybody a partner in the booty of exploitation. That is all, and it is technically admirable. Only there is nothing in the outlook that touches in any way the happiness of the individual, the vivifying of the personality, the comprehension of social forces, the flair of art,—in other words, the quality of life. Our intellectuals have failed us as value-creators, even as value-emphasizers. The allure of the martial in war has passed only to be succeeded by the allure of the technical. The allure of fresh and true ideas, of free speculation, of artistic vigor, of cultural styles, of intelligence suffused by feeling, and feeling given fibre and outline by intelligence, has not come, and can hardly come, we see now, while our reigning philosophy is an instrumental one.

Whence can come this allure? Only from those who are thorough malcontents. Irritation at things as they are, disgust at the continual frustrations and aridities of American life, deep dissatisfaction with self and with the groups that give themselves forth as hopeful,—out of such moods there might be hammered new values. The malcontents would be men and women who could not stomach the war, or the reactionary idealism that has followed in its train. They are quite through with the professional critics and classicists who have let cultural values die through their own personal ineptitude. Yet these malcontents have no intention of being cultural vandals, only to slay. They are not barbarians, but seek the vital and the sincere everywhere. All they want is a new orientation of the spirit that shall be modern, an orientation to accompany that technical orientation which is fast coming, and which the war accelerates. They will be harsh and often bad-tempered, and they will feel that the break-up of things is no time for mellowness. They will have a taste for spiritual adventure, and for sinister imaginative excursions. It will not be Puritanism so much as complacency that they will fight. A tang, a bitterness, an intellectual fibre, a verve, they will look for in literature, and their most virulent enemies will be those unaccountable radicals who are still morally servile, and are now trying to suppress all free speculation in the interests of nationalism. Something more mocking, more irreverent, they will constantly want. They will take institutions very lightly, indeed will never fail to be surprised at the seriousness with which good radicals take the stated offices and systems. Their own contempt will be scarcely veiled, and they will be glad if they can tease, provoke, irritate thought on any subject. These malcontents will be more or less of the American tribe of talent who used either to go immediately to Europe, or starved submissively at home. But these people will neither go to Europe, nor starve submissively. They are too much entangled emotionally in the possibilities of American life to leave it, and they have no desire whatever to starve. So they are likely to go ahead beating their heads at the wall until they are either bloody or light appears. They will give offense to their elders who cannot see what all the concern is about, and they will hurt the more middle-aged sense of adventure upon which the better integrated minds of the younger generation will have compromised. Optimism is often compensatory, and the optimistic mood in American thought may mean merely that American life is too terrible to face. A more skeptical, malicious, desperate, ironical mood may actually be the sign of more vivid and more stirring life fermenting in America today. It may be a sign of hope. That thirst for more of the intellectual "war and laughter" that we find Nietzsche calling us to may bring us satisfactions that optimism-haunted philosophies could never bring. Malcontentedness may be the beginning of promise. That is why I evoked the spirit of William James, with its gay passion for ideas, and its freedom of speculation, when I felt the slightly pedestrian gait into which the war had brought pragmatism. It is the creative desire more than the creative intelligence that we shall need if we are ever to fly.

IS NATIONALISM MORIBUND?

Bertrand Russell

I T may seem something of a paradox to ask such a question in the middle of a war inspired almost wholly by the spirit of nationalism, especially when this war is the greatest in extent and one of the fiercest in the contending passions which have ever been known to history. Nevertheless, analogies from the past make it not impossible that the conceptions embodied in the present war may have little influence upon the future. The Thirty Years War was the greatest of all the wars of religion, and it was also practically the last. Most of the ideas which have been potent in the world have started in the minds of a very few and have grown in extension while diminishing in intensity. At about the period when they began to dominate the beliefs of the great masses of the population, they ceased to be accepted by the makers of future opinion and lost the power of victorious vitality. It is in this way that wide-spread beliefs have begun to decay at the moment when they apparently achieved their greatest triumph. So perhaps it may be with nationalism.

People whose imaginations are not much affected by history are apt to suppose, at any rate in Europe, that nationalism is a fundamental and eternal fact of human nature, no more temporary than love or envy or ambition. This, however, is a delusion. In the ancient world, before the victory of Rome, civilized men were apt to feel a loyalty to their city, but this feeling died out during the centuries when the Roman State appeared coterminous with the world. The conception of the unity of civilization survived the downfall of Rome and remained dominant over men's thoughts through the Church and the law and the Latin language. The successive waves of barbarians, although at first they had some sense of tribal unity, soon took on instead a theological label, Catholic or Aryan, and merged their racial feelings in their new doctrinal allegiance. Throughout the Middle Ages the conception of nationality as we know it remained very dim, much more so than would appear from the reading of history as written in modern times English school-boys think of the battle of Crecy as a great victory of the English over the French, but this was not how the battle appeared to contemporaries. Edward III, like all the English kings of that period, was at least as much a Frenchman as an Englishman. He owned large territories in France, and did not appear to the French in the light of a foreign conqueror. The English and Scotch, owing to their insular position and their mutual hostility, were among the earliest disciples of nationalism. At the time of the Reformation Protestant England was stimulated by the resistance to Spain into the kind of belief in its own greatness and mission out of which true nationalism grows. Shakespeare's historical plays show the spirit in quite its modern form and have done much to foster it.

The essence of nationalism is the belief that some ideal of universal importance is in the special guardianship of the people inhabiting a certain area. So the ancient Jews, who were the only true nationalists of that time, were the chosen people and the custodians of the true religion. So the English believed themselves the champions of Protestantism in the time of Elizabeth, and of parliamentary institutions in the eighteenth century. So the French, since the Revolution, have believed themselves the champions of democratic liberty and intellectual enlightenment. So the Germans have made themselves the champions of Kultur (which is not to be translated "baby-killing"). And so Mazzini tried to make the Italian race the vehicle for the noble but rather mystical ideals by which he was himself inspired.

A nation's belief that it is the especial guardian of some important idea is as a rule a delusion, fostered by pride and self-interest. Pride makes the conception of the superior virtue of one's own group readily credible; self-interest makes it useful, since it justifies oppression and aggression in the name of humanity as a whole. Beneath the illusory beliefs of nationalism there is a substructure of instinct. The herd instinct, which in recent centuries has been most prominent in the shape of nationalism, is part of the fundamental structure of human nature, and may be regarded as permanent for all practical purposes. What is not permanent is the particular form to which the modern world is accustomed. Many other forms of herd instinct are equally natural to man. A man's herd may be his co-religionists, or the other members of his trade or profession or class, or the people with similar tastes and interests. There is no reason in human nature why a man's herd should be defined geographically as those inhabiting a certain area which he also inhabits, or racially, as those belonging to the same family or tribe. The conflict of herd instincts may be seen even in the midst of the war among English Roman Catholics, who are perplexed by the Pope's advocacy of peace, and hardly know whether they owe the more allegiance to Mr. Lloyd George or to Benedict XV. The essence of Marx's teaching was the endeavour to substitute a man's class for his nation as the object of herd instinct, an endeavor which so far has only proved successful among the very rich. There is, however, nothing contrary to human nature in the endeavor, and if it were supported by the newspapers and the elementary schools, there is little doubt that it would quickly achieve success. What is instinctive is the habit of feeling oneself one of a herd, bound together by mutual interests, which require to be vigorously defended against other herds, and demand for their defence a certain unanimity of opinion with a certain readiness to accept the mandates of recognized leaders. But the question what a man's herd shall be is one which is determined for him as a rule by the circumstances of his education—taking education in the widest possible sense.

There are various reasons for doubting whether nationalism will in effect be the dominant form of herd instinct during the next hundred years, and these reasons may perhaps be made especially clear by considering the case of America. I do not wish to dogmatise about America in the confident fashion to which Europeans are prone. I rely only upon certain broad and obvious facts, such as the enormous immigration of men of many different races. The America which made the Revolution was a genuine nation, bound together by love of liberty, by traditions and habits brought from England, by the principles of the Declaration of Independence, and by a generous hope of service to mankind which was accepted not only by the Americans themselves but by many notable sympathisers in Europe. This original America, broadly speaking, perished in the Civil War, but after the Civil War the North at least might still be regarded as a nation. Now, however, a very large proportion of the population of America consists of people whose nationalist feelings are still European—Slavs, Italians, Germans, and even, to a large extent, the Irish. Such people cannot have toward the United States that kind of intimate, passionate, narrow sentiment that they have toward the nations from which they have come. No doubt their children as a rule lose much of their European nationalism, but I gravely doubt whether they would be found to have acquired a new American nationalism at all comparable in force to that which they have lost.

No doubt war is one of the chief promoters of nationalist feeling, and perhaps some Americans may hope while some Germans may fear that participation in the present war is going to spread nationalism among classes of the population from whom it has hitherto been absent. But I do not myself believe that this effect will be produced. It can hardly be expected among German immigrants, and most of the others have already a sufficient stimulus in loyalty to the European countries from which they have come. Moreover war is not effective from the point of view of stimulating nationalism unless there is either some very obvious danger to be averted or some very obvious national gain to be obtained. The danger to America in the present case is not of a kind which would be obvious to the masses of the population. As for any national gain, the President has repeatedly stated that none is sought and that his purpose is an international one. In so far as this is accepted as a good reason for the war it would stimulate internationalism, and in so far as it is rejected it would certainly not form a ground for increased instinctive loyalty to the United States. For these reasons I do not believe that the participation of the United States in the present war will produce anything like that unity of national feeling in America which was produced, for instance, in England by resistance to the Armada and in Germany by the war of 1870.

If we were right in supposing that America is not going to develop a nationalism comparable to that of an old and homogeneous European country, is this result to be considered one for rejoicing or for regret? The question is very far from being an easy one. Indeed, if it is to be treated at all seriously, it must take us to the obscure roots of human nature. Nationalism, in a European country, is associated not only with race, not only with politics, but with all the somewhat old-fashioned sentiments associated with the word "home." I am aware that it was an American who wrote "Home, Sweet Home," but I do not think any American of the future is likely to repeat such conduct. Shall we be glad of this, or shall we regret it? The instinct for a home is one which man shares with many of the higher animals, but I think it is quite impossible for the instinct to be satisfied by any place very different from that in which childhood has been passed. Also it cannot be satisfied without a fair amount of privacy. Emigration and industrialism jointly are destroying all possibility of real gratification of this instinct. Wage-earners move from place to place and from country to country with rapidly increasing readiness. In great towns it does not occur to them to try to find any habitation sufficiently permanent or sufficiently their own to be capable of being regarded as home. In the ancient world there were only a few specially unfortunate men who were exiles. How passionately they felt this deprivation may be seen by a curious story in Herodotus concerning an Ionian Greek who became a trusted adviser of the Great King. He so thirsted for the sight of his native city that he sent emissaries to try to stir up a rebellion, with the sole purpose of being sent by the Great King to restore order and so get once more a glimpse of home. The passion which inspired him is as natural to men as it is to cats and pigeons. But in the modern world only a small percentage of the population are able to gratify it at all. The rest are always exiles throughout their lives. From this there results, as from all lack of instinctive satisfaction, a certain deep *malaise,* often hardly conscious, but producing a kind of cynicism and thinness of emotion, such as is fatal to all that side of human nature by which art is created and appreciated.

The best type of human being is only produced through at least a partial satisfaction of many instinctive needs, which have been recognised perhaps by some psychologists, but ignored almost universally by politicians, social reformers and ordinary men. The profound belief of the ordinary man is that if he has money he will be able to procure through its means everything else that is necessary to his welfare. This belief is most dominant in the economically most advanced societies, but through them it is penetrating to the peasants of Eastern Europe, and controlling (often without their consent) the lives of Central African negroes. There is consequently an uprooting of habit in the destruction of everything traditional. No doubt this process has gone furthest in America, but America in this respect probably represents the future. We may like or dislike what we see in America, but in many respects we must admit that what now distinguishes America from Europe is likely before long to prevail throughout the world.

Philosophical Conservatism, though it is not my own creed, is one for which there is much to be said. The arguments by which Samuel Butler's Erewhonians were led to the abolition of machinery may serve as a statement of the case. Indeed, all writers of Utopias, from Plato downwards, have been Conservatives of the deepest dye: not in the sense that they wished to preserve the society they saw about them, but in the sense that they wished to create a society which, once created, should never change. This applies even to Karl Marx; who never imagined further revolutions after the one which was to establish the social democracy. The political Conservative of our own day is not in effect, whatever he may be in intention, a representative of true philosophical Conservatism. When he is successful he does not prevent profound and intimate changes in the lives of ordinary men and women, since he does nothing to check the growth of industrialism, militarism, exploitation of inferior races, or war. The most that he can achieve is to prevent the changes which occur from having any rational direction or being inspired by any kind of ideal. Such ideals as he professes to believe in are dead. He is like a man who has embalmed his wife's corpse and set it up at the dinner table in order to persuade himself that he is not a widower; but in censuring such a man we need not deny that he has suffered a real loss.

It is not by an attempt to bolster up old ideals that we can prevent the harm which the philosophical Conservative deplores. The ideals which a society can genuinely accept are very largely determined by its political and economic conditions. In the Roman Empire it was useless to attempt to preserve the local cults which had belonged to the days of local independence. In a world-empire only a world-religion can in the long run prevail. The modern world is becoming more and more unified, and I doubt whether the present war will have done much to hinder this process. Local nationalisms of the old type will more and more cease to be acceptable to men with any experience of the world or power of thought, and it is difficult to see how they can be combined with that kind of internationalism which all who value civilization must desire as a safeguard against war. I do not deny that there is a kind of nationalism which might be a stimulus to civilization and not a cause of strife. Nations might take pride in what they had added to the common stock rather than in what they had robbed from others. Wherever this is still possible, it is to be desired. But I doubt whether it can be achieved very widely in a world where the economic forces are so hostile to local development, and where nationalism has fallen into the hands of rich exploiters who use it as a means of preventing the wage-earning classes from combining against them. Allegiance to a group which has a purely geographical definition is only possible in the long run when certain conditions are fulfilled which are increasingly impossible in the modern world. The bulk of the population must not travel much, and men of ideas must be conscious of very real and profound differences between the ideals prevalent in their own society and those prevalent elsewhere. Such conditions existed, for example, in the opposition between Christian and Mohammedan in the Middle Ages. The internationalism of that period was a purely Christian internationalism, which did not in any way embrace the infidels. Perhaps an opposition of this kind is still possible between the white and the yellow races, but as between different sections of the white race the really vital motives which now keep nationalism alive are merely pride and fear—the pride which desires to dominate, and the fear which dreads being dominated. Out of these passions nothing of real value to mankind is to be produced.

Nevertheless, the differentiation of mankind into groups, not necessarily hostile, but distinct one from another in culture and proximate purpose, is a thing of great importance for the diversity and progressiveness of human society. Without it life will have no richness of texture. It will become boring and uneventful. Conflict in the realm of ideas is as useful as conflict on the battlefield is harmful. It may be that a purely rational attitude would dictate a universal scepticism and prevent men from having those strong beliefs out of which vigorous action springs. Probably the preservation of such beliefs will require that men shall be divided into groups rather by their ideas and occupations than by the locality of their birth. Societies of artists or men of learning may serve to illustrate the kind of thing I have in mind. If you attend, for example, a meeting of Egyptologists, you will find a set of men assembled from the most diverse places, united by a belief that Egyptology contains the key to the universe, and that its more intense study is greatly needed in order to bring the millennium. You may smile at these men but nevertheless their opinion, though somewhat out of proportion, springs from the perception of a portion of truth which other people do not perceive. The pursuit of knowledge and a belief in its importance constitute one of the main impulses out of which human progress has grown; and, like all other impulses, in so far as it is genuine, it will not stop to consider at each separate moment how far the particular form which it happens to be taking has any utility outside itself. The welfare of the community as a whole is promoted by the existence of many groups with very diverse tastes and interests; the sheer diversity is necessary to the whole. Differentiation of function is absolutely necessary, and is best secured by preserving the natural differentiation of type which exists between different people.

In the modern world there goes along with industrialism and machine production a tendency to diminish the difference between one man and another through uniformities of education—a tendency which is perhaps carried further in America than anywhere else. Education at the hands of the public authorities corresponds to machine production; it turns out a more or less uniform product instead of the infinite diversity that resulted from older, more haphazard methods. It would be as useless and futile to attempt to return to the older method, or lack of method, in education as it would to urge a revival of handicrafts instead of machine industry. But in education, as in the industrial world, modern conditions have raised new problems which did not exist before. These problems will not be solved of themselves, but require deliberate thought and care to preserve the flavor of individuality in spite of the vast organizations by which our lives are controlled.

The spirit of nationalism, except in very small countries, does not tend to promote individuality. It tends, on the contrary, to give a common orientation to the efforts of all and a uniform stamp to all education. Those who believe, for example, that we should study science in order to be able to get the better of trade rivals are not likely to acquire the true scientific spirit, the interest in patient investigation of nature for its own sake out of which all great scientific work has sprung. The fundamental work, which is not immediately fruitful in a commercial sense, they will be willing to leave to others, and those others are not likely to be found among men in whom the nationalistic spirit is dominant. I think it is not nationalism as such that is fatal, but nationalism as embodied in organization, as the generator of mechanical systems which crush or distort the individual. These systems have the same kind of effect in cramping the human spirit that the Church used to have in the Middle Ages. When the group to which a man feels himself to belong is defined geographically this can hardly fail to be the case. It is an external accident, not something in a man's nature, that makes him a citizen of one State rather than another, and therefore in so far as States are in conflict one with another his citizenship is not a spontaneous expression of his individuality in the same way as membership of a learned society or a football club. The more readily people move from place to place and the more different States come to resemble one another, the more artificial becomes the opposition between them, and therefore the more violence has to be done to human nature in order to preserve the opposition. I am convinced that the future vehicle for group feeling will be found far more in such things as Churches or political parties than in nations. The dominance of the nation as the most important group is comparatively recent and is not, I hope and believe, a thing destined to last very much longer.

There is a certain danger in even the most lofty and sublimated national patriotism. Every nation tends to believe that it is in some important respect morally superior to other nations, that it has some contribution to make to the general stock of civilization which it will not be able to make unless it is great and powerful in a material sense. It is this belief in the importance of material power which is the source of harm. The nations which have done the most to influence the world's ideas have not been powerful in a military sense. Western civilization is a product almost wholly of the ideas of the Greeks and Jews; the Greeks in science and art, the Jews in religion. Yet neither the Greeks nor the Jews achieved any great degree of military power. The Romans, who had the power, had not the inventiveness, and became merely the vehicle for the mental victory of those whom they had conquered. The belief that material power is necessary in order to influence ideas is one of those delusions which are fostered by pride. Power is pleasant, and we therefore like to think that in pursuing power we are actuated by virtuous motives. The things that really can be spread by force of arms are very seldom the best things. Therefore a man's group feeling is apt to contain an element of brutality as soon as his group is one which is possessed of an army and a navy.

There seems little doubt that America is embarked upon a great military career. It seems reasonable to expect that America will become the greatest of all military powers. This does not mean that she will necessarily become militarist in spirit. It is quite possible that the military power of America may be used for the purpose of securing a universal diminution of armaments by international agreement, but this will certainly not happen if America acquires that kind of national pride which enjoys being able to force its will upon reluctant opponents, and this kind of pride is almost sure to be the outcome of a really vehement national spirit of the old type, if by any means such a spirit can be produced in America. America has led the world in the development of industrialism, and industrialism has probably destroyed for ever the possibility of many good things which existed in the past. If the human spirit is ever to learn to dominate the machine instead of being dominated by it, it is necessary to seek somewhat different goods from those which industrialism has destroyed. And as America has led the way in one respect, so we may hope that it will lead the way in the other. But it will do this through internationalism rather than through nationalism, through the attempt to realise a family of nations with a common, super-national government rather than through the attempt to become itself a dominant nation. The mixture of races and the comparative absence of a national tradition make America peculiarly suited to the fulfilment of this task.

There is, however, one respect in which the general attitude of America is likely to postpone for a long time the realization of any thorough internationalism. Internationalism will more and more be compelled to embrace not only the white races but also the races of Asia. Japan has already forced its way into the State system of the white races, and it is probable that China will be compelled to follow the same course. One can hardly suppose that India will remain for ever an appanage of the British Empire. India and China together are capable of becoming as important as the whole of the white nations put together, and any system which puts them in fundamental and irreconcilable opposition to the European nations is likely to lead at some future date to a war in comparison with which the present war will seem parochial and insignificant. The opposition on both sides is the outcome of our industrial system. We hate the Chinese because they work more industriously and more cheaply than we do. They hate us because we try to exploit their country and because we endeavour to force upon them our systems of trade and industry. It is difficult to see how this state of affairs can be remedied while the present economic system prevails. The world's production of goods by labor is in its essence co-operative. The person who produces consumable commodities is performing a service to mankind and not a disservice. But owing to the competitive system, the aspect of competition is much more prominent and visible than the aspect of co-operation. This is not an eternal necessity, but merely an incident of the existing system. Under a more socialized and more co-operative organization it would not be the case. Men ought to be paid for their willingness to work regardless of whether their work happens to be needed at the moment. This system already exists in many directions. Soldiers are paid in time of peace and not only while they are actually required to fight. Civil servants always enjoy a comparative permanence of occupation, and no one supposes that the work of government could be done if they were engaged by the day when there happened to be work for them to do. In any business office the men who have the more confidential part of the work to do remain year after year: it is only the underlings who are hired and dismissed as occasion requires. We are told that the competitive system makes for efficiency, and yet we find that it is not applied in just those cases where efficiency is most desired, for example, in national defence and in the higher grades of industry. In actual fact, a certain minimum of security and a certain continuity of work are powerful forces in developing a man's efficiency. If a man were paid for his willingness to work, he would not be so obsessed as he is at present by the thought of competition, and he would realise that anything which increases the efficiency of labor is a benefit to the community. This would go a very long way toward preventing that instinctive enmity which competition has fostered, and would make international co-operation possible as it never has been in the past. It is clear that modern war is not a good investment for a nation regarded simply as a business speculation, but nevertheless the enmity generated by the sense of competition is a powerful agent in promoting modern wars. Competition is not ineradicable or necessary, and whatever element of efficiency may really be connected with it is very dearly purchased by the evils of militarism and abject poverty.

I do not think that the relations of the white and yellow races are likely to be put upon a permanently sound footing until our present industrial system has been replaced by another. The present war has enormously accelerated the tendency to fundamental change in our economic system. In America, no doubt, it has not yet begun to produce the kind of effects which it is more and more producing in Europe. All parties in Europe seem to be agreed that vast and far-reaching economic changes are quite unavoidable; it is only as to their degrees that people differ. If the war lasts, as it well may do, for another two or three years, it can hardly be doubted that the changes will be at least as great as the wildest revolutionaries now imagine. Out of these changes it is possible that a new internationalism, no longer a mere sentiment but embodying itself in the economic and industrial system, will emerge triumphant. In such a world the old conception of nations may tend to disappear. Doubtless there will be rivalries, since rivalry is natural to man, but if the rival groups are constituted say by trades rather than by geographical areas, it is hardly conceivable that their conflicts will be carried on by force of arms. The old order is disappearing. If it is not to disappear into chaos, there will be need of active imagination and vigorous hope in constructing the new order. What it is to be, I do not know. It is not likely to be exactly what any one of us may hope; still less what we may fear. But I am sure that what it will need is energy in promoting new hopes rather than an attempt to preserve even the elements of real good which we value in the past. Mankind cannot afford to risk another great war. Every advance in technical civilization must make war more deadly, and a great war a hundred years hence might well leave the world in the exclusive possession of negroes. If we wish to avert this calamity we must be bold, constructive, and not afraid to be revolutionary.

YOUNG INDIA

Lajpat Rai

I N the long and extensive periods of the history of India going backward to thousands of years before the Christian era, never before had India looked so hopeless as in the early part of the last century. It seemed as if for the first time in its history its spiritual and intellectual background had given way. It had known foreign invasions before, but only in their military and political aspects. The Moslems were the first of its foreign invaders who professed to have a faith and culture which they considered superior to those of the country itself. Economically and intellectually India was never conquered; even much less spiritually and ethically. The influence of the British rule and of Christianity, however, in the nineteenth century, seemed at one time to involve the total collapse of Hinduism in all its bearings. The direct attack on religion was not so disastrous as the insidious influence of the whole system of European education and thought. The number of Indians who were converted to Christianity was small, very small, but the dissolving influences of European culture seemed to be far-reaching in their destructive and benumbing tendencies. When we say benumbing, we mean benumbing spiritually and morally. For a time, it looked as if India was dying for want of resisting power; that she had lost all vitality and with it her soul. The danger loomed large. It was as much cultural and fundamental, as political. The inauguration of British rule not only meant political subordination but a complete turnover of the native conditions of life and thought. The *loot,* following a military success, the people could understand, but the permanent and the steady decline of Indian art and industry which was foreshadowed by the inauguration of British rule, wherever it was introduced, was a thing unheard of in India before. The very things which the English call the blessings of their rule, viz, the school education they introduced, the religious freedom they guaranteed, the extensive foreign trade which they opened to the world, seemed to spell disaster and ruin. Under the Moslems the population followed their old pursuits and maintained their old standards of morality. The standards of social life were debased not under the influence of Moslem faith and culture, but in spite of them, and more as defensive measures than otherwise. The conviction that was actively fostered and encouraged by the priests that the changes in customs and social practises necessitated by foreign domination had the sanction of Hindu *Dharma* and *Dharma sastra* (Hindu religion and Hindu Scriptures), had in a way saved the situation. There was no change in the ideals; nor any in the spiritual or moral standards of the people. Even the social changes disclosed in actual practise retained their basic foundations. What the nineteenth century threatened, however, was a change in the ideals and basic foundations of life. The Christian dogma itself did not matter very much; it was the system of life and the standards underlying it which appeared to menace the foundations of Hindu culture and Hindu thought. The Brahmo Samaj, an indigenous religious reform organization founded by a Hindu, registered the first organized protest, but it did nothing to check the tide of the general influences that threatened the very foundations of life. In fact for a time its leaders were in the forefront of those who propagated a wholesale condemnation of Hindu religion and life.

The great Indian Mutiny of 1857 was in appearance a political upheaval only, but in reality it was much more than that. It was truly national. Behind the military and the political upheaval lurked the suspicion that *Dharma* and *Din* were at stake and that the destruction of *Dharma* and *Din* involved the loss of everything that made life worth living for. The quarter of a century immediately following the suppression of the mutiny was a period of great intellectual and spiritual stagnation. It seemed as if the race of Hindu divines, thinkers, philosophers and lawgivers was dead and the country, which had never been a borrower so far, in the spiritual, the ethical and the intellectual field was barren of all originality and genius. The condition of things brought into existence by English rule was without parallel in the whole range of Indian history.

The Moslems had conquered India and had imposed their political and military rule on her; but they never tried to make laws for the Hindus, much less to administer civil justice between them. All disputes of a civil character and all crime of ordinary nature were handled according to ancient methods by the people's tribunals known as the *Panchayets,* (Courts of five). Imperial revenues were levied and realized by the King's agents but all local taxation was left to the people, levied and managed by them by popular methods. In the matter of education, there were schools run by Hindus and Mohammedans but nothing was done to suppress the ancient learning or the spoken vernaculars. Art and industry was pure and indigenous.

Under the British, however, everything was changed. Every minute item of social and individual life came under foreign influence. No one could live by himself, however he would. The Government interfered in every detail of organized life. Native Courts were abolished. The Panchayets ceased to exist. The Industries were destroyed. Schools were established where English became the first language of instruction and foreign history, foreign poetry, foreign logic, foreign philosophy took the place of Indian thought and literature. True, all this was optional. There was no compulsion to attend the schools. But the organization of life ordered by the British was such as to leave no choice to the people. In their own interests they had to attend the schools established by the British and on the whole it was well that they did. So for a time it seemed that the edifice built and reared by centuries of thought and practise had crumbled into dust and the India of the nineteenth century had nothing to give to the world. The best among the Indians were only poor imitators. The ordinary and the mediocre among the foreigners were better placed and better situated. English manufactures, English language, English thought, English literature, English dress, English manners, English laws and English religion were approved. Everything native was held in contempt and occupied a back position. In imitation of their English masters the English-educated Indians looked upon the vast bulk of their countrymen as barbarians. Hindu religion, Hindu thought, Hindu literature, Hindu custom, and Hindu institutions were all disclaimed. The cry went forth for a complete anglicisation of life. The fine products of Indian handlooms, still dragging their miserable existence in villages and small towns, were not considered fit even to be looked at. I remember how as a boy I detested the idea of having any garment made of Indian hand-made cloth; how I longed for English shoes and how I hankered after clothes of English cut. How differently I think now. The best intellect of the country was in the service of the Government, engaged in popularizing foreign forms of administration, foreign thought and foreign products. The whole mentality of the English-educated people was employed in imitating their foreign masters, running down every indigenous idea and institution; and in making themselves useful to the authorities of the English Government. The only thing that did not change was climate; though in that respect also at times it looked as if, with the progress of English rule, the Gods that sent rain, had decided to keep off their bounty more frequently and more systematically than before. It looked as if all genius, talent, self-respect, self-confidence, self-reliance and manhood had left the country and with them the minor and resultant virtues also. The few that felt the degradation of the situation found themselves helpless. The great bulk of the people were passive, as if sleeping after a long day's work.

Then came the awakening. It expressed itself in religious life. The conversions to Christianity gave a shock and a reaction followed. People began to think and study; and then to discuss and plan. They concluded that Christianity was by no means a better religion, either spiritually or intellectually, much less ethically. The ordinary folk argued that a religion which did not ban liquor and meats could not be good religion. The intellectuals thought that a religion which laid emphasis upon Christ being born of a virgin; which denied the pre-existence of soul before birth; which condemned non-Christians to eternal damnation; which gave a clean record to every one who merely accepted the divinity of Christ, however black his previous career and life; which taught equality and brotherhood, yet sanctioned or encouraged distinctions of color and race, was not a good religion. The few who studied science began to look down upon it as opposed to the teachings of science. Bradlaugh and Ingersoll led them on to free thought and Herbert Spencer and Huxley to agnosticism.

It was at this juncture that men arose from the ranks of the Indians themselves, who directed the educated mind to the real spirit of Hindu religion, who pointed out with the authority of learning and logic, by chapter and verse, that the popular and superstitious forms of Hinduism were not the real Hindu religion and that all that was good, uplifting and elevating in the Christian religion or Christian thought was already there in the Hindu religion and Hindu thought. From a claim of equality, the next step was to one of superiority and that came soon after. A man arose, who did not know a word of English, who had received no schooling in the modern schools, who knew only his mother tongue and the sacred language of the Hindus, the Sanskrit, who had the audacious courage to say that the Hindu Scriptures were the fountain head of all religious thought in the world and that the Hindu religion as revealed in the Vedas was superior to all other religions. At first sight the statement appeared to be extravagant, revolutionary and incredible. But it did one good and that was to set people to examine and discuss. The man himself was a prodigy. He wrote, spoke, preached, discussed and challenged. Single-handed he carried the battle into the enemy's camp. He became aggressive and launched attack after attack on the citadel of Christian dogma. His speeches sent a thrill through the benumbed body of Hinduism. Nature, breeding, discipline, practise and meditation had endowed him with rare gifts. Learned, scholarly, logical, satirical, and witty, he was always ready. He spoke with a tongue of fire, with an eloquence all his own, so far unheard of in men of his class. What contributed to his success was his fearlessness and impartiality. He criticised the domestic pharisee as mercilessly as the foreign aggressor. He condemned the whole race of priests and ministers and missionaries, Brahmin and non-Brahmin. He denounced all superstition. He ran down evil customs and practices, advocated reform and appealed to reason and history. With a vigorous, piercing, clear intellect, he was possessed of a robust constitution. He had been a life-long hermit. If his logic was convincing, his personality and character were no less compelling. He did not convert all the English educated Hindus to his ways of thinking, but he instilled a spirit of national pride and self-respect in them. He appealed to them in the name of their past, describing it with an eloquence and enthusiasm which were contagious and soul stirring especially when, with unique pathos, he compared their glorious past with their miserable present.

Even those who did not accept his doctrine caught his spirit and lo! there was an awakening. That was the dawn of a new day for the defeated, discredited and suppressed Hindu. Once more he began to feel that he was alive. Christianity was not only not necessary; not only was it irrational and unscientific; not only was it as narrow and superstitious as popular Hinduism or perhaps even more, but above all, it was denationalizing and disintegrating. This man was Dayanand Saraswati, the founder of the Arya Samaj.

The Arya Samaj has, for the last thirty-five years, carried on a propaganda both nationalistic and rationalistic. The Society is the most influential of all the reform associations of the country. In the last census it counted over a quarter million adherents. It has wide-spread ramifications in all parts of India, with branches all the world over wherever Hindus are to be found in numbers. Its religious and social propaganda is characterized by the spirit of the founder. In its educational work (it has founded and manages numerous schools and colleges, scattered all over India), it combines the best of India with the "best" of Europe. In its philanthropic work, orphan relief, famine relief, etc., it has extorted admiration even from the British. The key-note to its activities is a virile and all-covering spirit of nationalism.

There were many kindred souls in the country who were thinking more or less on the same lines but who lacked the courage and the faith which characterized the challenge of Dayanand. The success of the latter encouraged them and they came out with their beliefs and opinions. Henceforth the pivot of the reform movement was shifted. So far people had looked outward whenever they wanted inspiration, guidance and light. Even those who could not accept Christian doctrine, took their cue from Christian literature. Others looked to rationalism and free thought for deliverance. Now they began to look inward. All superstitious beliefs and pernicious customs were tested in the light of the scripture. Reform was advocated not only on the ground that things were wrong in the light of reason but also because they were opposed to the spirit of the ancient law, the real Hindu Dharma—a Dharma that was based on truth and on the good of humanity—a Dharma that was for all the world and not for India and the Hindus alone—a Dharma that admitted of no distinctions of color, race and language. A vision of universal mission arose before the inner eyes of the reformer. He was no longer a petty reformer but an apostle—one who had a mission in life which was even higher than the good of the country. It was natural that a vision that spread over a multitude of people should place the awakened spirit of the nation on a level much higher than that of passive acquiescence in things as they were or as they might be by the grace of the ruling community. The awakening thus commenced in the sphere of religion and social reform was bound to extend to other spheres of life. The new spirit did not take long to cover the whole area of national life. It was soon discovered that in order to fit the nation to make its contribution to human welfare and to civilization it was necessary to organize and develop a system of education which should be national in its basic conception and world-wide in its area. It should secure the continuity of the nation, without narrowing its horizon. Taking its cue and inspiration from the past it should look forward and make a future worthy of the past. Such an educational system must have the merits of the past and the improvements of the present. It should be in accord with the genius of the nation, without ignoring what has been achieved by the world outside—fully taking advantage of the improvements effected by the genius of the rest of the world. The earnest minds of the nation at once set themselves to the task. They soon discovered that in an atmosphere of economic bondage and political restrictions, such as was the necessary outcome of the system of Government under which they lived, the evolution and development of such a system of education, which would prepare the nation for a life of freedom and equality with the other nations of the world, was impossible. The governing caste would not allow it. It was incompatible with their supremacy and authority. An India developing into a nation, claiming equality with the other nations of the world was not their ideal. What they wanted was a submissive, docile, divided India, which would look to them for leadership and guidance and would be contented and even grateful for the crumbs which they in their generosity might give them from their plentiful table. What they wanted was a dependent India not an independent India. Thus the reformer's ideal clashed with that of the Government and a conflict of ideals necessarily brought out a conflict of methods. The reformer wanted to do things in his own way, without consulting the Government. The latter could not tolerate it even if the action of the former was within the law. What they objected to was the underlying spirit and the potentialities involved. So new laws were made and the reformer was placed in the awkward position either of having to obey them or to close his activities. The reformer changed his methods. The Government replied by disseminating broadcast their suspicion and distrust of the reformer and his methods. All this confirmed the people that the present political conditions were incompatible with the growth of the nation on lines which would fit it for playing the spiritual role that it aspired to, among the free nations of the world. Thus they reached the conclusion that the first condition of life with honor and self-respect, with liberty to make progress on their own lines was political freedom and economic independence. The Indian nationalist does not believe in the economic or political exploitation of one nation by another. His nationalism is not aggressive in economic or political terms. He wants neither conquests nor markets. He is not so much a lover of *goods*. His ideal is simple living and high thinking—living in comfort, with plenty of leisure and opportunity to think and not a life of luxury, with plenty of things to be cared for. In his eyes, a life of such opulence as forces a man to devote the best in him to take care of his dollars and his property is as unnatural as a life of economic bondage. A slave of wealth, a slave of success, a slave of rank, position and title, is as much a slave as a slave who is bound to serve another at the latter's will and on his terms. The Hindu believes in service, in ungrudging service, provided it is free and the outcome of a sense of duty or of love. He has always considered *paid service* (dásta) to be the lowest of occupations. There is a saying in Hindustanee which places farming (growing things), at the top of economic occupations, trade and commerce next and service of others as the lowest of professions. In the eyes of a Hindu, a *Brahmin* and a *sannyasi* are the greatest of servants because they serve not for pay, but out of exalted motives and would receive no compensation for their service in any shape or form.

There is much in Hindu literature and Hindu life which gives a color to ideas current among foreigners about Hindu mysticism and Hindu asceticism. As a matter of fact neither mysticism nor asceticism is the best part of Hindu Dharma or Hindu philosophy of life. In proof you have the explicit rules of Hindu law which lay down that no one should adopt the life of an ascetic, without being a householder for twenty-five years of his life. Any one doing contrariwise acts contrary to both the letter and the spirit of Hindu law. Similarly strict Hindu law does not encourage mysticism. The *yoga* system lays down rules of sense control, of concentration of attention, of meditation such as are open to anyone who has the physical and mental fitness for their practise with the object of his improvement. It advances no claim to supernatural powers for those who practise them. It only promises them a good physique, a pure sense of perception, a keen insight into things which ordinary men cannot see, call it a psychical development if you please. As to *magic* and *clairvoyance,* there is more of it in America than in India. In India no one pays any attention to it. Not that we have no "magicians" and "clairvoyants" but that no one there will pay more than a cent to see a performance of "magic" or "clairvoyance." In ordinary estimation it ranks as a trick and hence the men indulging in it do not rank high. This is, however, only by the way. We were saying that the desire to lead our own life in our own way and follow our own national development led us to the conclusion that we needed political and economic independence.

Within the last twenty-five years India has witnessed a great revival of indigenous art and literature. In the field of poetry we can boast of a number of eminent poets and poetesses, only two of whom have so far found recognition in the West. Tagore is one of them. Mrs. Sarojini Naidu is the other. The first wrote and sang and composed in his own vernacular. The second uses the English garb. There was another Bengali poet, Torú Dutt, who wrote and composed in English and whose poetry has been highly appreciated in the British Isles.

But India is full of poets. Bengal alone can name half a dozen as great and noble as Tagore, if not more so. Similarly, the Maharashtra and Dravidian provinces (South), the Gujrat (West), the Madhya Desa (Central provinces), the Hindustan proper (Delhi, Lucknow, Agra, Benares) and last but not least, the Punjab, have all produced poets, whose theme, diction and transcendentalism is as high, pure, ennobling, nationalizing and uplifting as that of Tagore. In fact, in the region of patriotic songs and nationalist revival, other poets have achieved more remarkable results and more enduring fame than Tagore. This is as true of the Moslems as the Hindus. Tagore's writings are remarkable for poetry of a high order, exquisite imagery, great art, translating ancient mysticism into modern language. An English writer gives him credit for "synthetic mysticism." But modern India does not care so much for mysticism and transcendentalism as for literature which would rouse, electrify, and uplift the people. The need has been met by numerous writers in every province and in every vernacular, as India is a country of many vernaculars. The most famous and the most popular Nationalist song (Hail, Motherland!—*Bandemataram*) was composed by Bankim Chandar Chatterjea, the author of *Ananda Matha* (the temple of bliss), a work of fiction which has very considerably stimulated the revolutionary movement in Bengal. This work was written long before the idea of a revolt against the British rule in India had taken a definite form. Its scenes were laid during Mohammaden rule and its heroes and heroines picked from among those who made the love of country the basic foundation of spiritual progress. In this work the author gives a most rational and virile interpretation of popular Hindu beliefs and fills his volume with a fervid patriotism which is both suggestive and stimulating. Bankim has in this book raised the love of country to the dignity of a religion.

Another Bengali writer whose name deservedly stands high among the literary stars of Bengal is Dinesh Chandra Roy, whose patriotic songs are the most delicious and exalting pieces of poetry ever composed in any Hindu language. His *Amae desh* (Our Country) is the most touching and rousing national song ever composed in any language.

Bengal has also produced some remarkable women poets, among whom we might mention the names of Kamini Roy and Mankumari.

Among the writers of Hindustan proper the name that comes up first for recognition among the most noted writers in Hindu, is that of Harish Chandra of Benares, whose novels and plays and essays furnish an intellectual feast of a most agreeable kind.

Among the Moslem poets of note we will mention two names from the Punjab, those of Hálí and Iqbál. The former's "Rise and Fall of Islam" is a masterpiece which has played a remarkable part in the revival of

Islam. In this poem Maulâná Hálí gives a pen picture of the progress and decline of Mohammedanism with a force and pathos unique in the history of Urdu literature. Hálí is considered to be the founder of a new school of Urdu poetry in India. Among his other works the most noted are "The Lamentations of a Widow," a life of Sádi, the Persian poet, and life of Sir Syed Ahmed, the Indian leader, in prose, besides various other miscellaneous works in prose and poetry.

Iqbál, who is still in the prime of life, occupies a commanding position among living Moslem poets of India. His poems generally breathe a spirit of unity, love of country and a sense of exalted patriotism. His most touching poems (and most popular of course) are those in which he pleads for absolute unity between Hindus and Mohammedans. His language is exquisite and his similies and illustrations delicious. His poems inculcate an exalted love of country and a pride in which the great names of Indian history, Hindu and Mohammedan, play an equal part. His most popular poem is *Sárejáhán se achhá Hindustan hamárá* (the best in the world is our Hindustan). His "Song of an Indian Boy" is equally pathetic and great. In one of his poems he makes the present fallen condition of the Mohammedans the theme of his song, giving it the form of a complaint against God for having neglected them in spite of their iconoclastic theism. Then in another poem he embodies the reply of God and chastises the Mohammedans for their lethargy in the most scathing terms.

The other parts of India not specifically mentioned have produced equally admirable and high-minded writers, the burden of whose song and prose is unity, love of country, pride of the past and true religion.

What Young India loves is virile, masculine song that refers to the glories of the past, laments the weakness of the present and exhorts in compelling words to action for the upbuilding of the future. It delights their pride to be told with proofs that ancient India was great in peace as well as in war. Many young Hindus are devoting their time and attention to the translation and exposition of ancient Hindu works on government, law, medicine, hygiene, architecture, chemistry and other positive sciences. This fills them with self-respect and stimulates them to work for equally notable achievements in the present.

Some remarkable contributions have recently been made by Professor J. C. Bose to the world's knowledge of botany, biology, etc. Another eminent Bengali scholar, P. C. Roy, has written a highly interesting work on Hindu chemistry and has made original researches. It was only the other day that the United States Government gave a large reward to a Hindu student for his research. Several young men have won great laurels at Cambridge (England) in mathematics. Another has invented a new kind of printing machine which is being very favorably commented upon in scientific journals in this country. Hindu history is being gradually excavated out of the debris of forgotten literature and buried monuments.

Similarly we are witnessing a great revival of Hindu music. Thirty years ago the most vulgar forms of European music were all that was current in our theaters and places of entertainment. Indian instruments were being abandoned in favor of cheap European organs and harmoniums. Now, we notice a great revival of Hindu music. Music that had been discredited by Moslem puritanism and had been segregated to a position of isolation by being confined to professional singers, has once more been placed on a pedestal of respectability. Men and women of the highest respectability are cultivating it now and it is quite becoming a part of every young person's education, men and women alike, at least in Bengal and Maharashtra. Everywhere throughout India, girls are being encouraged to learn music, sing, and play on instruments. In religious schools and colleges, I mean schools and colleges maintained ostensibly for the propagation of religion, music is receiving great attention. What is, however, most significant is that a real taste for classic Hindu music, as distinguished from modern European music, is springing up. Master musicians are engaged in improving Hindu music on lines which will make its study and cultivation on modern scientific lines possible. One of them has invented a system of notation, which he is popularizing in great centers of culture and education like Bombay, Poona and Lahore, by opening special music academies. It is a sign of the times that Hindu music should have crossed the oceans to find hearers and admirers in far-off America. We have a fair representative of Hindu music right in our midst in New York in the person of Madame Ratan Devi. A Moslem master (Inayat Khan) is receiving attention in England.

Coming over to other fine arts like painting and sculpture, here again we notice a great revival and a change which promises to retain the best features of original Hindu art without ignoring what can be gained by a study of the modern technique. Twenty years ago the younger generation of the Indians looked down upon native pictures. The old pictures, their fine idealism, their exquisite spiritualism, their beautiful coloring and their rich and pregnant symbolism had ceased to appeal to them. The educated Hindu knew nothing about Hindu art and what he had been told about it had created a feeling of disgust and repulsion. When I was a young man I did not care to look at a Hindu picture. Then there arose an artist in the south who painted Hindu scenes, Hindu personalities and Hindu characters in European colors. His pictures became at once popular. His name was Ravivarma. With the rise of the Swadeshi movement (a kind of economic revival) the indigenous fine arts received a great push. Since then a purely Indian school of painting has arisen, whose productions have begun to receive recognition at the hands of the best art critics of Europe. Books on Hindu arts are now coming out in numbers and finding readers and purchasers in the best circles of the West. The best and most authoritative works on Indian art are those of Mr. E. B. Havell and Dr. Ananda Coomar Swamy.

In short we are in the midst of a renaissance which is at once remarkable and significant and through which we look forward to the regaining by India of her soul and thereby her place among the great nations of the world.

The Young Indian movement is thus a two-sided movement, political as well as cultural.

THE STORY OF THE *SEVEN ARTS*

JAMES OPPENHEIM

ALTHOUGH I was in my mid-thirties at the time, I was still shockingly idealistic. I believed that that lost soul among the nations, America, could be regenerated by art, and that the artist was always a Jean-Christophe with the power to do the job. I even had a definite idea as to how America was to become more human. It was the dream so many have had : a magazine, *the* magazine which should evoke and mobilize all our native talent, both creative and critical, give it freedom of expression and so scatter broadcast the new Americanism which would naturally have the response of America. I do not want to belittle my motives : I only want to expose them.

Nor were they "pure." I was inanely jealous of the gang of fellows who had shot the *New Republic* into existence, a "journal of opinion," mind you, when the real thing would be a journal of art. Perhaps, too, I wanted a job and a certain eminence. Motives do get mixed, however noble we try to be.

At any rate, there was my dream, and I was sick and tired of earning a living at popular fiction. I happened to be a poet, and fiction was an aside.

At the time I speak of I was more or less "popular" as a writer. In fact, a literary agent told me recently that if I had only stuck to my fiction I would today "be sitting pretty on top of the world."

It was not to be. One evening, at a small party, I was introduced to a young man who had been sitting in sullen silence and eyeing me with distrust. His name turned out to be Waldo Frank. He admitted later that, being an unknown, he expected that a known writer like myself would ignore him blatantly. By now he knows that most known writers at parties feel just as miserable as unknown ones. At any rate, we merged our misery in a talk and soon Waldo was coming down to see me in Washington Square.

One thing led to another, and one evening he and I had dinner with a voluptuous, but still unknown, lover of music, Paul Rosenfeld. We were in a deploring mood, as who shouldn't be in 1916? Europe was cutting her own throat with new mechanical devices, and this land was fat with loot, and down with fatty degeneracy of the heart and a sleazy spirit. All of us had lived through the cigar-store Indian period, wooden and dead, when nice people went in for "social work," when Howells was dean of American letters, and when stiff white collars held your chin up.

But we had also experienced a shock of joy in 1914, and after, when simultaneously, and from various unconnected quarters, rockets of poetry went up and burst in the sky over the heads of an amazed people. A renaissance! "The Spoon River Anthology," "Chicago Poems," "North of Boston," "Imagism," "Songs for the New Age," "Challenge" and "The Congo." Total strangers, say Amy of the Lowells and Scandinavian Carl Sandburg, looked at each other as if they were kin. Dreiser shuffled on the scene, the *Smart Set* was covertly selling bombs wrapped up in sweetmeats, and suddenly everything that was young, obstreperous, delightfully mad, colt-like and only partially twisted by American civilization became a local habitat and a name. It was situated south of Fourteenth street, took in Washington Square and then went west where the streets, so decorous and square to the north, rioted—where, indeed, Eleventh street collided with Fourth. Yes, of course, Greenwich Village.

The *Masses* used Karl Marx as an excuse for exploding in Greenwich avenue, the Provincetown Players were in MacDougall street, and Freud was in the air. Everyone was cooking up some sort of revolution, even Art Young. Socialism, sex, poetry, conversation, dawn-greeting—anything, so long as it was taboo in the Middle West. Just for a few years it looked as if the artist in America had at last got his chance.

Well, Waldo, Paul and I were wild enough to believe that the artists and critics could dominate America. But how? I shyly dragged out my dream of the magazine. Ecstasy! All we needed was money—something like $50,000. Since the three of us were unburdened, and since Crœsus and mad Ludwig of Bavaria were dead, it looked as if we had drawn a blank. You could get money in America for libraries but not for those who wrote their books.

Nevertheless, I went scouting, and finally was introduced to a lady who had a collection of Whistlers and was bored looking at them. Well, believe it or not, she sold them, signed a contract with me that the business department was to take orders from the editorial department, instead of *vice versa, (i.e.,* art dominating business), and she herself was to hold down a small clerical job just to cope with her boredom. So I signed up Waldo as Assistant Editor and we got to work.

We then proceeded to get seven prominent people to sit as an Advisory Board, which never sat, but made the magazine look authoritative. And then there was the call to arms; an impressive-looking circular. I quote from it :

> It is our faith and the faith of many that we are living in the first days of a renascent period, a time which means for America the coming of that national self-consciousness which is the beginning of greatness. In all such epochs the arts cease to be private matters; they become not only the expression of the national life but a means to its enhancement.
>
> Our arts show signs of this change. It is the aim of the *Seven Arts* to become a channel for the flow of these new tendencies: an expression of our American arts that shall be fundamentally an expression of our American life.
>
> We have no tradition to continue; we have no school of style to build up. What we ask of the writer is simply self-expression without regard to current magazine standards. We should prefer that portion of his work which is done through a joyous necessity of the writer himself.
>
> The *Seven Arts* will publish stories, short plays, poems, essays and brief editorials. Such arts as cannot be directly set forth in a magazine will receive expression through critical writing, which, it is hoped, will be no less creative than the fiction and poetry.
>
> In short, the *Seven Arts* is not a magazine for artists, but an expression of artists for the community.

II

If the reader has not skipped the above, he will notice that we were committed to something colossal enough to scare the two editors during an agonizing Summer and a worse Autumn, with some form of neurosis appearing when the first number was handed nakedly to the world for its vulgar scrutiny. No, we weren't aiming at any "little" magazine, anything in an ivory tower. The tower we had in mind was more like the Woolworth.

It began with a shower of manuscripts that stunned us. We conscripted Paul Rosenfeld, who soon held the field of music, Louis Untermeyer for the poetry, and anyone else handy, and it did not occur to us that we were, as it now appears in the camp of the Humanists, a bunch of "foreigners." I never felt less foreign in my life. Van Wyck Brooks was fond of quoting Emerson to the effect that Americans were "infinitely repellent particles," but Emerson felt it in the very sanctum of the Lowells, the Cabots, the Lodges and the Adamses, in pure unadulterated Colonial America.

All that I can say is that for a year our different national strains in the world of art and criticism somehow coalesced, came to a focal glow in the *Seven Arts,* though wise Van Wyck shook his head from the start and said it couldn't last. Actually, too, Brooks later became an associate editor, thus relieving us of the onus of being non-Anglo-Saxon. But, then, what could one expect if the magazine were to be really American? We stemmed from Walt Whitman, as the new poetry showed, as well as from Emerson, and we gave our blood a chance even if it had been imported, a few generations back, from Scandinavia, Germany, Russia, Italy, Ireland or France. The Dutch are honest folk, and their blood, through Whitman, gave us this chance for a start.

When I re-read our manifestoes, I am reminded of the *Sturm und Drang* period in Germany, when the young Germans threw out the French and went Teutonic; only this *Sturm und Drang* was soon silenced by a machine-war which took off the lid and showed us, naked and unashamed of itself, our machine-civilization. We had ousted Prof. Irving Babbitt only to be confronted with George F. Babbitt, realtor; we had exchanged Emerson and Longfellow for Ford and Hoover. But I anticipate.

The *Seven Arts* was duly installed in intimate unbusinesslike offices in Madison avenue, and Waldo guided a young interior decorator to decorate us. She did. I came in one day to find the artiest feeble and fragile furniture, all in gaudy colors, I have ever laid eyes on. All that was missing to make the place a tea-room was tea and cakes. *Sturm und Drang*—and this? I had a hot temper in those days and almost burst a blood-vessel. I went out and got some man-stuff to hide the originals as much as possible.

All was not well in those editorial offices. Here was I, a poet trying to rule the business department, write the ads, scare the printer, besieged by "native talent" until I almost refused to believe my eyes at some of the strange specimens that hissed, dared me, insulted me, or simply smelt to heaven so that I had to open the window after their departure and wash my hands; and here was Waldo (he was young then and has changed) telling me that in a hundred years from then people would make pilgrimages to his model-tenement apartment just to see the place where he had lived; and interlarding such audacities with an eloquence of persuasion over editorial policy, printing his stuff, and whatnot, so that I was left exhausted or cruel.

It just couldn't be. Waldo had steeped himself in France for some years and was so French himself that I was sorry I couldn't converse with him in that language. He needed to discover America, as later he re-discovered her; and I needed a balance wheel and a suit of armor. It was then that Van Wyck Brooks was invited in, and the fight was on.

Van Wyck was a temperate, shy little man, with eyes of an innocent blue only matched by those of Randolph Bourne. He was American in the old sense, as American, say, as George Edward Woodberry; with the difference that he had rebelled and gone over to Whitman. That was an issue in those days, however dim it seems now. It took no little courage for him to write what Lippmann called a "gallant" book, "America's Coming-of-Age"; and in the *Seven Arts* he proceeded to help put the Humanists on that dusty shelf where they lay until their corpses were exhumed just the other day.

Both he and Waldo were vicious workers. I mean they put in a day's work, and sometimes more. Waldo arose at 5 A.M., wrote a chapter on a novel, and then came commutation to the city, with a day ahead of him. Van Wyck was equally faithful. My temperament was more primitive. I loved to work furiously and then loaf miserably (you can't loaf happily in a land where everyone else is working). So I put off all the work I could on these faithful associates, and also on Rosenfeld and Untermeyer, the latter of whom read enough amateur poetry to cook a goose; and then I'd overwork, and get so hot under the collar that later on I discovered, to my amazement, that I was regarded as a tyrant; me, whom Lee Simonson called the kindest man in New York and whom Paul Rosenfeld dubbed fatherly. I hope to goodness the truth lay somewhere between.

At any rate, Van Wyck soon had us all shadowing America, not only to see what she was up to, but to find out if she came of noble lineage. I am referring to his attempt to find a "usable past," so that we might have a real tradition on which to nurture our new talent. Well, we had Walt Whitman, loud as a locomotive to overly sensitive ears; we couldn't string along much on Poe; Emerson was watery; Waldo found that Dreiser belonged to our pre-cultural period, hence making him a part of the usable past; but much further we didn't get, though "Moby Dick" was in the offing.

I should say roughly that between editors and contributors we had practically all the forces which were let loose on what the Humanists jeeringly call the 'twenties. There was the just-emerging Sherwood Anderson, there were Dreiser, Amy Lowell, Lee Simonson, Bourne, Bodenheim, Padraic Colum, Dos Passos, Jack Reed, Van Loon, DeCasseres, Dewey, Eugene O'Neill, Carl Van Vechten, and stacks of others, to say nothing of all the poets from Frost to Sandburg. Aye, and Professor Spingarn was with us, too, stirring up a hornet's nest.

III

Now for some red-letter days, some of them so red that I actually saw the color. If the reader has never been an editor, let him read the following, and have compassion on the tribe. I was innocently doing nothing at my window-desk one day, when there came, to use Poe's words, a tapping at my door. I called "Come in!" The door opened slightly, then shut again. Silence. Then another tapping. "Come in!" I shouted. The door opened wider and I had a glimpse of a tousled red head. It immediately disappeared and the door shut again. I felt helpless. Then came a rap. I shouted "Come in!" on a rise to my feet. A figure immediately appeared, hand clutching the door. I have met every variety of bum, including the kind I have at times represented; but this one was new; an on-purpose bum reeking of Art. In all faith, his shoes were broken enough, his attire shoddy enough; such things may be due to poverty; but not the rest of his get-up, which could be both seen and smelt.

He was scowling at me. "I don't see," he said venomously, "why in hell I should come here. You fellows pretend to encourage Art. You're a bunch of fakers. You don't know Real Art when you see it. You wouldn't even give a new man a chance."

I began to see the drift.

"You have a poem in your pocket," I said. "Well, fetch it out."

After roundly abusing the staff and myself, he sat down, and pulled out the poem. Then he had stage-fright and became timid. For as I glanced at the poem I thought I was looking at printer's pi.

"You see," he said, "it's a new kind of poetry. The poem describes the sensations one has when climbing a mountain; so you must begin reading it from the bottom, from left to right, then the line above it from right to left, and so on; so that as you read it you have the sensation of climbing yourself."

I tried the experiment, but words would unexpectedly pop out in sorry isolation, say, the word bush, or the word cave. I asked for help. He said of course when I came to the word bush it meant that a bush was in my way, and when I reached cave, I could stop to peer into its hollow depths.

Even with this guidance I was stupefied.

"What did you write this for," I asked, "an audience or just for yourself? If for an audience, you have us completely stopped; if for yourself alone, why didn't you go out into the wilderness and howl?"

He rose in wrath and departed; undoubtedly pigeon-holing me with all those benighted sots who don't get a kick out of Gertrude Stein and (gosh, I'm hopelessly aged) James Joyce. There is such a thing as defiling the English, and even the American language.

Speaking of which, there was a well-known woman writer who came in one day in a fury because of the grammar and style of our writers.

"You pretend to be leading cultural America," she said in effect. "You should be a model of English. And yet you allow faulty syntax, bad spelling and improper words. I have been a teacher of English and know the standard."

"What standard?" I asked.

"The standard of English by which every English writer is judged."

"But we don't write in English; we write in American," I said.

She turned pale.

"Do you mean to tell me that the English spoken by most people in this country is anything more than a corrupt dialect?"

"Well," I said, "I suppose if you had lived in Dante's time, you would have told him to stick to Latin and not write in Italian."

She was as infuriated at our being "improper" as the red-haired poet at our being "proper."

An editor is between the devil and the deep sea both as to policy and performance. But to get on:

There was the day when Amy Lowell breezed, burst or derricked herself in; a ton of woman, to misquote the Bard. Never shall I forget it. But I had been warned in advance and was primed. You see, first there was the name Lowell, second there was the bulk, and third the Manila cigars she smoked. Every editor in town had been terrorized by her. It was her custom to bark in, shrink the editor with her magnificent girth, her eyes and her powerful speech, and before he had recovered poise, she read a poem (and it might run to a dozen pages) out loud to him. Naturally, he bought it on the spot, and didn't come to until he saw it in print.

So the great Amy bore down on me. I lit a cigar myself. When the smoke cleared she had a bulky manuscript of verse spread in her hands and was beginning to read.

"Not much," I said sternly. "I won't listen."

She was apparently shocked.

"But, don't you see," she said, "if I read it to you, I will bring out all its values and you'll know what you're getting."

"No," I said firmly, though I trembled a little, "I am a poet myself, and I've made some pretty punk stuff sound beautiful. Any actor can do it. Besides that, our readers will have to read it in cold type, and I guess I had better read it that way myself, so I can get it the way they do. They won't have the advantage of your voice and your presence; so neither shall I."

She glowered a little, and later the staff put thumbs down on the poem. It wasn't a very good poem. She took it sportingly, and sent us some more, which we liked immensely.

Amy was one of the best of them. Her terrific energy, her will to experiment, her help to obscure poets, her fighting for poetry all over the United States, all these things helped make an era. Then she was so executive withal, with so much common sense. As she told me, she rose at noon, attended to business on her estate up Boston-way until evening, was sociable till midnight, and then locked herself in her study fronting the garden and composed till dawn. An heroic woman, surrounded by great dogs, I believe, mastiffs. Which was one reason why Randolph Bourne, a hunchback and physically weak, took a dislike to her. For he visited her, and the dogs set on him, and he was terrified until rescued.

She loathed Bourne in turn. After the *Seven Arts* days, and during the A.E.F. days, she came to see me down in Ninth street. She spoke of her loathing of Bourne. She said:

"His writing shows he is a cripple."

I answered, I am ashamed to say, in these noble words: "Aren't we all cripples?"

And instead of flaying me alive, she surveyed her monstrous girth and said simply : "Yes, I'm as much of a cripple as he. Look at this. I'm a disease."

Although she differed with me about our entrance into the war, she spoke of the *Seven Arts* as having something "warm" and "vivid" about it, and regretted its passing.

IV

Then there was the strange day when Edgar Lee Masters and I had our first and last talk. I was down in my room in Washington Square, and Masters telephoned that he was stopping at a hotel in the square, five minutes away: he'd be right over. I waited about forty minutes, and then happened to gaze down from my window. Leaning against the park rail opposite the house stood a stockish man, a little resembling William Jennings Bryan, with a broad felt hat, his gaze on me. I took a chance and nodded. He nodded back.

So I left the house and joined him. We took turns about the park, and I felt oddly up against a mixture of Thomas Paine, Ingersoll, Bryan, and the Middle West, with flashes of poetry stabbing the doughy substance. He was, on that very afternoon, out on a hunt for the meaning of life and we talked a balderdash of philosophy. Finally the evitable happened. 'Ware the approach of poets! They always have a pocketful.

I must say, though, as we sat down on a park bench, that Masters, if memory serves me right, handed me but one poem. Its title, I believe, was "Sloppy Sue"; but even if the title wasn't, the poem was—sloppy. I was in a tight corner. I greatly admired, and, for a time, a little imitated the work of Masters, and I wanted some of his best in the *Seven Arts*. But to tell a poet his work is sloppy isn't the best way to advance such a cause. So I said:

"We want your best work, Masters, and this isn't quite."

I haven't seen him since, and his opinion of me probably isn't fit to print.

No less astonishing was the first meeting with Sherwood Anderson. His "Winesburg, Ohio," stories had impressed me deeply. The *Seven Arts* made him. And after a bit he came down from Chicago and paid Waldo and Van Wyck a visit, ending with the trio coming into my room. I had built an Anderson out of the stories, a shy sort of fellow, a little mussed, slipping against the wall so as not to occupy too much space. Instead of that I looked straight at an up-and-coming ad man, with a stiff collar, and a bit of the super-salesman air. He had been, indeed, earning his living in the advertising game; and it was only later that I saw things in his face that don't go with advertising.

It so happened that we were paying him more than our other contributors, because his work was so good and because he needed it. But he came with an ultimatum that unless we raised the rate, he'd quit. I've been both an author and an editor, and I know very well that an author has a right to get what he can, just as an editor has a right to give as little as he must.

"But," I said, though my colleagues frowned a bit, "we're your only paying market. What magazine in this country will take your stuff—the somewhat Russian note, the somewhat frank sexuality? Will the *Post* take it? *Harper's?* The *Atlantic?*"

The idea was so preposterous—at that time—that we all laughed. Anderson in his day was as appalling to the respectable as Dreiser.

Seeing that we were spending money like drunken sailors, as Lippmann had advised us to do at the start, I had to be a meanie; a nice position for a poet to be placed in!

This narrative wouldn't be complete without a word or two about Louis Untermeyer. Louis, who used to look like a reduced replica of another Louis, the sixteenth Louis of France, had as much to do with setting up modern poetry in America as anyone else. He was witty and had almost a dapper mind. His home was a sort of *salon* for artists and intellectuals; although he was in the business of manufacturing jewelry in Newark. I used to visit his factory, and he showed me how he worked on his poems without arousing suspicion. He always kept the one he was working on in the center drawer of his desk, which drawer he pulled out when no one was present and snapped shut on the approach of footsteps.

Louis had a genius for spotting the young men and women who were about to take the limelight, but still were in the shadow of obscurity. He set up a correspondence with them, became to some extent their impresario, wrote criticism of them in the papers, and soon had turned the American trick of making oneself an authority on a subject, simply by hanging out a sign to that effect and refusing to take it down. O'Brien did that in the short story field; Louis in poetry.

The result was that all the poets, from Frost and Robinson down to the already forgotten, flocked to Louis just as down-and-outers used to make for the free-lunch counter. For poets can sing their greatness, but find it difficult to sell it. They sing; they don't speak.

One day Robinson, Frost, Jean Starr Untermeyer, Louis and myself had a poet's lunch at the Untermeyer apartment. Four of us were mute (Jean being a poet also). Socially at that time Robinson was a clam with haunted eyes. (I see the defect of that statement, but can't seem to change it.) Frost, though warmer than his name implies, was as silent as the snow on a New Hampshire hill. Jean was heavily morose. I was sunk.

I can imagine the frightful attempts we would have made if Louis had not been present. We would have attempted, first, to talk, failing that to eat, and failing that, even more dreadful, to go away. You just can't go away without saying something natural. But Louis simply sparkled with wit, with questions, with sallies, and whatnot. So soon all of us were comparing our methods of composing poetry. Jean's was the accretion method, Louis' the polishing method, and unless I am much mistaken the rest of us used the explosive method: that is, you bore into yourself until you disappear from view, there is an explosion and you find yourself in the world again, with a completed poem and a disordered stomach.

So much for touches of local color: I must be getting on.

V

Looking back on it, I believe I wasn't "culturally" there with my colleagues. Not that I was a low-brow, but I certainly wasn't a high-brow. I believe with Goethe, one look in a book and one in life. Living and fighting were as essential to me as art, so I could never make the grade with the *intelligentsia,* who must have looked on me as a bit of a savage. Unfortunately, this savage ruled the roost, wherefore they were, until near the last, polite about it. But hang it, a man isn't his occupation, though he may be tanned to his trade.

I remember a musicale at Paul Rosenfeld's, the room packed with soulful-looking people who listened to a rendition of some brand-new music with a sort of reverence that made my own feelings something like laughing aloud in church. Asked at the end whether I liked it, I said I didn't, and I remember the look of pain that spread about the room. But then Spitteler, the great Swiss poet, has said very aptly that one shouldn't spend time with a work of art unless one enjoys it, since art is not a duty, but a delight.

This notion of my being somewhat of a tyrant probably began to circulate in the middle of our year. For by that time I had learned something about editing. Good editing is a one-man job, just like good art. A board of editors creates an institution; an editor creates a living, changing, varied magazine. I took hold of the blessed thing and each month studied our available material carefully, composing the next number somewhat as if I were composing a symphony or painting a picture: there had to be balance, homogeneity, a something that united the whole, an ensemble effect that was pleasurable. Naturally, if Waldo had done the composing he would have done it differently; if Van Wyck, still differently. Since all three couldn't do it, and since I was the editor, I did it myself. There was no help for it. Of course I had expert aid.

At any rate, at just about this time the gallant figure of Randolph Bourne appeared, and I became the editor in good earnest. I shall never forget how I had first to overcome my repugnance when I saw that child's body, the humped back, the longish, almost medieval, face, with a sewed-up mouth, and an ear gone awry. But he wore a cape, carried himself with an air, and then you listened to marvelous speech, often brilliant, holding you spellbound, and looked into blue eyes as young as a Spring dawn. His coming was the greatest thing that happened to the *Seven Arts,* though in the end it was the main cause of our shutting down.

He was a pupil of Dewey's, but soon outpaced the master, especially when that master, pragmatically, went over to the war party in those terrible hectic days of 1917. The intellectuals, the reader may remember, claimed that they pulled our entrance to the war to make the world safe, etc. (The very words today are nauseating.)

Now, Randolph Bourne was the real leader, I take it, of what brains and creativeness we had at the time, and had he lived the 'twenties might have sparkled much more than they did. Mind you, this young man not only was a cripple, but wheezed in breathing, and was mortally physically afraid most of the time. More than that, he had one fear greater than any other. That was the fear of prison. He could hardly bear the thought of it.

Yet one day he came to me, possibly shortly after we entered the war. After a bit of talk, I asked him to write for us. He smiled.

"You wouldn't allow me to say what I want."

"Try us," I said.

And then he came back with an article which showed the supreme type of courage, and which quite possibly meant prison. It was called

"The War and the Intellectuals" and we published it in June, 1917. It opened up with this salvo:

> To those of us who still retain an irreconcilable animus against war, it has been a bitter experience to see the unanimity with which the American intellectuals have thrown their support to the use of war-technique in the crisis in which America found herself. Socialists, college professors, publicists, new-republicans, practitioners of literature, have vied with each other in conforming with their intellectual faith the collapse of neutrality and the riveting of the war-mind on a hundred million more of the world's people. And the intellectuals are not content with confirming our belligerent gesture. They are now complacently asserting that it was they who effectively willed it, against the hesitation and dim perceptions of the American democratic masses.... An intellectual class, gently guiding a nation through sheer force of ideas into what other nations entered only through predatory craft or popular hysteria or militarist madness! A war free from any taint of self-seeking, a war that will secure the triumph of democracy and internationalize the world....

Randolph Bourne had found himself. He told me that in his previous writings for the *New Republic* he had been "institutionalized" and that we had removed the gag from his mouth.

He wrote six articles on the war, all of which were published in the *Seven Arts*—that is, until we closed shop. He saw the war as the end of the period of art and criticism, the end of that renaissance which so briefly had its day. It threatened of course to doom the *Seven Arts,* which had brought American talent together, evoking it from hidden places and the varied racial strains; so it seemed incumbent to back Bourne to the last ditch.

But the air began to get hot, pro and con, mainly pro. Jack Reed, that romantic adventurer, who fought in Mexico and later went to Russia to join the Bolsheviks, flung us an article, "This Unpopular War," which almost sent us to jail. Later he had lunch with me and asked me to join an underground revolutionary movement to turn America upside-down. I didn't join, though by that time I was writing editorials in free verse (my colleagues told me I didn't know how to write prose, even if I was an editor) that were rather hot.

The illusion of a " free country" in which I had grown up simply exploded. It was something in those days to know one was shadowed, spied upon, trailed by snoopers, that one must whisper what one thought in a restaurant and even then be sure one's friend wasn't going to hand one over to the police. Prohibition is merely the *reductio ad absurdum* of the whole process. The lying propaganda had something foul and degrading in it. The exultation of the timorous stay-at-homes was rotten and debased.

"Enemies Within," shrieked the old New York *Tribune* and spat snake's venom at Bourne and the rest of us.

As the Fall loomed, with the ending of our first year, friends fell away right and left, though the circulation was climbing. Then the inevitable happened. The contract stipulated that there should be no interference from the business side. However, our backer, clerking still, was mortally terrified not only by the danger we found ourselves in, but by the word treason. She was of good old American stock, and besides, relatives of her's owned a great food industry. They pressed her hard. She came to me and said we would have to lay off the war, or there would be no more subsidy.

There was no more subsidy.

In a letter at the time, I wrote:

Our financial backer has withdrawn on account of our war-policy, and the dastardly attacks upon us. Besides this our business manager is getting out: our advertising man has resigned: my secretary is called away, and Waldo Frank is in the hospital recovering from an operation.

In short, we were sinking with our flag nailed to the mast. And then the staff—Van Wyck was against our policy, Bourne was misled—cleared out, after Waldo tried to raise money from his friends to take over control (he actually offered to make me his assistant editor!), and we waded on with the help of some East Side young men who worked gratis. Ben Huebsch, too, lent a hand. With our last number we sent out an appeal to readers and received an astonishing response; but it was too late.

One fine day, with our furniture and staff gone, I locked up the office and went home to start reading a history of the world in order to learn that man has always been in trouble. I managed to calm down, but Randolph Bourne remained a grieving lone wolf. He'd come and sit with me before my coal-fire on the dark Winter days, and we speculated much. But the blow which had been struck him was more than he could bear. He came down with pneumonia in December, and Huebsch called me up to say that Randolph Bourne was dead. I lifted the sheet from his face in a front room in Eighth street. He seemed to mean all that had been stopped.

After a silence of twelve and a half years, perhaps it is good to speak. That we should have thought that the arts and the criticisms could rule business appears so ludicrous now as to be beyond laughter; and that we should have tried to stop a war (and I don't think it was the intellectuals who started it) was a *beau geste* simply because of Randolph Bourne.

But I wouldn't have missed that year for kingdom come.

www.ingramcontent.com/pod-product-compliance
Lightning Source LLC
Chambersburg PA
CBHW021847010726
47493CB00005B/1589